Success
Secrets
OF THE
Motivational
Superstars

Success Secrets

OF THE

Motivational Superstars

AMERICA'S GREATEST SPEAKERS REVEAL THEIR SECRETS

MICHAEL JEFFREYS

ECHO POINT BOOKS & MEDIA, LLC

Published by Echo Point Books & Media
www.EchoPointBooks.com

ISBN: 978-1-62654-952-4

Cover photography by Agaton Strom and
courtesy of PopTech

Cover design by Adrienne Nunez,
Echo Point Books & Media

Printed in the U. S. A.

Contents

▼

Acknowledgments

▼

A GIGANTIC heartfelt thank you to all the men and women who agreed to be interviewed for this book. You are not only superstars in the world of professional speaking, but inspirational examples of what it means to pursue one's life vision with passion.

To all the assistants of the speakers, many of whom went above and beyond the call of duty to get me an interview with their "boss": Thank you for believing in me and my vision.

A Note to the Reader

▼

ONE of my goals in writing this book was to include many different kinds of speakers, so as to give you as many different viewpoints, philosophies, and ideas as possible. While some of the speakers' advice doesn't always agree with the others (thank goodness!), much of it does. And so, because of this, you'll find that many of their "Success Secrets" will be similar—after all, truth *is* truth. Rather than take out those key points that are repeated, I decided it would be of interest, and of value, to the reader if I left them in.

Introduction

▼

"The key to happiness is having dreams . . .

the key to success is making them come true."

THIS is a book about fifteen individuals who dared to dream big, and then had the audacity to go out and turn that dream into a reality. Their level of financial success and professional recognition is such that it places them at the very pinnacle of their profession. Indeed, these are the superstars of the speaking world.

Surprisingly, the tips and techniques they share about public speaking may be the least of what they have to teach us. For each one has had to overcome tremendous obstacles to get to where they are today.

For example, Les Brown was not only abandoned at birth by his natural parents, but was later labeled, "educably mentally retarded." Wayne Dyer grew up in an orphanage. And imagine coming here from another country and having to start completely from scratch to make your fame and fortune. Well, Art Linkletter and Brian Tracy are both from Canada and Roger Dawson and Patricia Fripp came over from England.

In fact, as you read each chapter, you'll find that each speaker has their own unique story to tell about perseverance, determination, courage and the power of believing in oneself that is nothing short of inspiring.

> *"The result of hearing a good professional speaker is that people learn how to change and improve their lives, their work, and their relationships.*
>
> *Great speakers raise one's aspirations, hopes, and ambitions."*
> —BRIAN TRACY

This is not to say that this book won't show you how to become a more effective public speaker and communicator in general—it will. In fact, it will give you insights into the speaking profession unlike those in any other book I have seen. How can I make such a claim? All I have to do is look at my bookshelf. On it are over thirty-five books on public speaking; some are good, one or two are excellent and most are poor. Why? Because they focus mostly on the mechanics of public speaking: speech organization, vocal quality, gestures, eye contact, memorable closes, etc. All of these are certainly important ingredients in putting together a successful presentation, but they're not enough!

What's missing? Why is it that with an estimated one hundred thousand speeches given each day in America, few are as dynamic, captivating and entertaining as they could be? Instead of walking out fired up and ready to take on the world, most audiences stagger out of these presentations exhausted and wondering where the coffee is.

As a public speaker myself, I had my own ideas as to why many presenters fail to hit the mark. But I wanted to find out from the experts, the men and women who sell out three-thousand-seat auditoriums around the country, not for their singing or their acting, but because of their ability to communicate a message. I wanted to find out from the very best in the world exactly what it was they were doing that made them such powerful and persuasive communicators. I interviewed fifteen of the biggest names in public speaking in America to find out what they were doing that made them so successful. In other words, I wanted to hear "from the horse's mouth" what, exactly, they were doing that made what came out of their mouths so effective.

My criteria for choosing these speakers was threefold: First, they had to be full-time professional speakers. (General Norman Schwarzkopf, Pat Riley, Oprah Winfrey and other "celebrities" make the rounds on the speaking circuit, but do not speak for a living and thus were not considered for this book). Second, they had to be nationally known (all the speakers I interviewed have at least one book published—most have several—and are consistently ranked as being the best in the business by Fortune 500 companies and major trade associations which use speakers). Third, they had to be successful financially (all the speakers I interviewed earn at least a million dollars a year and many earn tens of millions annually from the combined revenue of their speaking and product sales).

Two Myths about Public Speaking

When people ask me to cite the most important thing I learned from my interviews with these great orators, I tell them two things: First, that the commonly held belief that "great speakers are born, not made," is simply not true. The fact is that public speaking is a skill. Just like tennis, skiing, or any other skill, you can learn to do it well.

While the men and women I interviewed are all masters at connecting with and persuading audiences, and appear to do so with complete confidence in themselves and their message, I can assure you, it wasn't always like that. There was a time when they were just starting out, when they, like most people, were afraid of saying something foolish, and embarrassing themselves in front of a roomful of people. What changed? Were they suddenly struck by a lightning bolt of confidence? No. What gave these fifteen individuals the courage to overcome their fears and go on to become great speakers was their belief in their message. *These individuals had a vision of themselves making a difference in people's lives by sharing their message, one that was bigger than their fear of appearing foolish in front of an audience.* As a result, they were willing to go out and fall on their face in front of as many audiences as were necessary for them to "get it right." The attitude they took early in their careers (and that they still take) is that *you cannot fail at anything in life; you can only learn from your experiences and grow in the process.*

Everytime they made a mistake, put their foot in their mouth, or bombed in front of an audience, they simply picked themselves up, dusted themselves off and said, "Wow, I sure learned a lot from that experience . . . I'll have to remember not to do *that* anymore!" And they immediately applied what they had just learned to their next presentation, making each new speech that much better than the previous one. Eventually, they got to the point where they were doing so many things well, that they couldn't help but become good. However, they didn't stop there. They continued to hone and refine their speaking skills, constantly pushing themselves, trying new things, always learning, until they had achieved mastery.

All the speakers I interviewed became great because they became masters of their craft. They simply would not settle for "good enough." What is the difference between a good speaker and a great one? A good speaker leaves audiences thinking to themselves, "Boy, she sure was good," while a great speaker leaves them thinking, "Wow, I really can achieve my dreams!" See the difference?

I should also mention that the majority of the speakers I interviewed either said or implied that making a lot of money was never their primary goal. Rather, it was about helping other people live happier, more productive, more successful lives. The irony is that when they focused on helping others become more successful, the money, success and fame came their way as a natural by-product.

Great Speakers Are True to Themselves

The second point that became obvious after interviewing these fifteen communication experts was that each one prepared and delivered his or her talk in a way that was totally honest and consistent with who that person was as a human being. For example, Joel Weldon tends to be a somewhat serious, no-nonsense

type of person. As such, he routinely spends forty to fifty hours re-
searching his speaking client before every talk. This tremendous
amount of preparation gives him the confidence he needs to go out
and give a great presentation. Conversely, Dr. Wayne Dyer, who is
a very easygoing, spiritual type of person, prepares for each presentation by meditating for one hour. Obviously, what works for
Joel doesn't work for Wayne, and vice versa. Nor should it. This is
exactly why I interviewed so many different types of speakers—so
you, the reader, could be exposed to as many different styles and
approaches to public speaking as possible. The benefit to you is
that you can pick and choose those thoughts, qualities and success
traits that you feel are right for you, and discard the rest.

Wherever You Are Right Now Is the Perfect Place to Start

As you delve into each speaker's message, keep in mind that he or
she had to start somewhere; that they did not achieve their success
overnight. It took them years of effort and persistence before they
finally got to where they are today. So, don't get discouraged if
you fall down along the road to becoming an effective speaker.
Just pick yourself up and begin again. And as you do, keep in
mind George Bernard Shaw's powerful words:

> "This is the true joy in life: Being used for a purpose recog-
> nized by yourself as a mighty one, being a force of nature in-
> stead of a feverish, selfish little clod of ailments and
> grievances, complaining that the world will not devote itself
> to making you happy. I am of the opinion that my life be-
> longs to the whole community and as long as I live, it is my
> privilege to do for it what I can. It is a sort of splendid torch
> which I have got hold of for the moment and I want to make
> it burn as brightly as possible before handing it on to future
> generations."

CHAPTER ONE

BORN: February 29, 1960
BIRTHPLACE: Glendora, California

Anthony Robbins

*"For most of my life I've had a sense of destiny.
I can remember at seven years old having images
in my mind of reaching mass numbers of people
and making a huge difference."*

MANY people in the United States feel that Anthony Robbins is the most dynamic, most charismatic speaker on the platform today. His ability to electrify a crowd with his presence as well as his cutting-edge insights into human behavior have put Robbins in a class of his own. Simply put, Anthony Robbins is the Michael Jordan of the professional speaking world. How could this young man, who was only five feet and ten inches tall when he graduated from Glendora High School in 1978, go on to become a giant (literally—he stands a solid six feet, seven inches) in the human-potential field? How could someone who had been living in a four-hundred-square-foot bachelor apartment in Venice, California, and washing his dishes in his bathtub, go on to have two best-selling books, the most successful infomercial in the world, and form nine companies with annual revenues of fifty million dollars?

The answer, to use Robbins' own jargon, is that he made excellence a *must* instead of a *should*. He says that the single most important decision he made was to increase his own standards so that he *"demanded more from himself than anyone else could possibly expect."* By constantly pushing himself, taking new risks, and setting new and bigger goals, he soon reached a level of success that was as impressive as it was lucrative.

Infomercial King

Robbins' thirty-minute *Personal Power!* infomercial, which was produced by the Guthy-Renker corporation, airs somewhere in the United States every half-hour. Remarkably, the television program has sold a mind-blowing twenty-five million audio tapes (each course consists of twenty-four tapes and a journal, and retails for $179.95) and has brought in a whopping 180 million dollars in sales. No one else on the planet has come close to selling as many self-improvement tapes as this one-man conglomerate.

The earlier infomercials featured prominent actors, such as Martin Sheen and Levar Burton, as well as football great Fran Tarkenton. His latest—and fifth—infomercial came out in 1996 and features Quincy Jones, Ben Vereen, and many other successful business men and women. However, celebrities notwithstanding, it is Anthony Robbins' charisma and powerful ability to touch people emotionally, even across the airwaves, that accounts for his infomercials' phenomenal success.

Mr. Outrageous

Tony Robbins burst upon the self-improvement scene in the early 1980s and has never looked back. Right from the outset he quickly established a reputation for making outrageous claims, like the time he said on a radio show in Canada that he could cure a woman of a lifelong snake phobia *in less than an hour!* Remarkably, he was able to do just that, even getting the woman to hold the snake, much to his audience's amazement, as well as his own. The truth is that Robbins didn't know for sure if he could cure the woman; he had never tried it before. But he had such a high degree of confidence in himself that he figured he would find a way. This supreme self-confidence, combined with Robbins' resourcefulness, flexibility, and persistence, enabled him to succeed where many others would have failed or never taken the risk in the first place. This brash, oversized kid in suspenders wasn't afraid to take chances—and it was paying off.

For the remainder of the eighties and well into the nineties, Tony Robbins has spent an average of two-hundred days a year traveling around the United States and abroad, conducting various seminars. Always looking for ways to improve, he has taken his older programs—such as *Date with Destiny, Mastering Persuasion Techniques,* and his two-week *Certification Program*—and replaced them with more cutting-edge programs, such as his one-day business seminar, *The Competive Edge,* and his preeminent *Mastery University*. However, by far his most successful and popular seminar to date has been his *Unleash the Power Within* weekend (formally called *The Mind Revolution*).

Fear into Power: The FireWalk Experience

What makes this seminar so special? It undoubtedly has to do with the program's first night, which features possibly the most unique marketing concept ever created for promoting a seminar: *Fear into Power: The FireWalk Experience*. Not only do you get to spend five hours with Anthony Robbins, but at the end of the evening he takes you out for a stroll across a ten-foot pit of 1,200–2,000-degree red-hot coals . . . barefoot!

The fun begins on Friday evening in the largest ballroom of whatever major hotel the Robbins crew has taken over; usually a Marriott, Hilton or Hyatt. (In the beginning, Robbins drew 250–300 people per seminar; he now regularly packs in 1,500–2,500 per event, with occasional programs drawing 5,000–plus.) Although the doors don't open until 6:30 P.M., by 5:30 there is always a huge crowd of several thousand people swarming around the outside of the ballroom, like bees waiting to enter the hive. The buzz in the air is one of pure electricity. This is due to Robbins' enormous charisma and his ability to create a sense of excitement anytime he makes a live appearance.

When the doors open, salespeople, executives, teachers, students, actors, and other seminar attendees are greeted with loud, energizing music blaring from high-quality speakers brought in by the Robbins crew. The throng rushes to get seats up front so they can be close to "Tone;" however, they don't have a chance to sit for long as members of Robbins' staff quickly get them up and dancing enthusiastically to the music. After a brief welcoming by a staff member, the heart-pumping theme from the movie, *Rocky*, is cranked up and suddenly the energy in the room reaches thermal nuclear meltdown.

Then it happens: From the back of the room, like Zeus descending from Mount Olympus, Anthony Robbins—wearing a custom-made suit, suspenders, perfectly coifed hair, and looking larger than life—comes sprinting onstage. The audience roars, claps, and stomps its feet. He joins in the applause, flashes his one-thousand mega-watt smile, and nods his head as if to say, "That's right—you're here, I'm here, and we're going to have a great time!" Robbins exudes so much self-confidence, power, and raw energy that the already pumped-up crowd goes even wilder.

"My whole key is passion. I have so much passion about what I talk about that it just flows."
ANTHONY ROBBINS

The Robbins Charisma

The audience's response to Robbins' presence is more like that of adoring fans at a rock concert than of your typical self-improvement seminar crowd. However, since Robbins' raw charisma and sexual energy more closely resemble that of a rock star's than your typical seminar leader, their reaction is understandable. Call it charm, showmanship, or vibes, the fact is that there are certain people born into this world who exude so much energy, so much charisma, that you can't help but be captivated by them. Anthony Robbins is one of them.

(Without a doubt, Robbins' imposing size contributes greatly to his on-stage charisma. In the book, *Arnold: The Education of A Body Builder* (© 1977, Wallaby Books), Arnold Schwarzenegger, himself blessed with an abundance of charisma, points out the advantage of being big: "One thing is that people listen much more to bigger guys; the bigger you are and the more impressive you look physically, the more people listen and the better you can sell yourself or anything else. In business school I saw a study of how many big companies in America hire salesmen above a certain height and weight. Because it has been proven that big people are more impressive salespeople. They're more convincing. It's true. I found it out myself, that I can persuade people easier than a small person can.")

When the music stops, Robbins spreads his long arms out like wings and the audience follows suit. Then he and the audience let out a long "Wooooooooo" sound, starting in a low pitch and building to a crescendo. When the pitch is at its highest, Tony, followed by the audience, bring their hands together in a loud clap as they shout "Yessssssss!" Then Tony asks the crowd, "If you're happy to be here, say 'Aye!'" And immediately a chorus of 'Ayes!' comes right back at him. "Excellent. Now I want you to introduce yourself to four of five people sitting near you, go!"

This amusing and novel opening gets the audience participating in the seminar right from the start. In addition, because they are laughing and having a good time, it puts them in an upbeat state. And that's something Robbins is an acknowledged master at—making people feel good in his presence.

▶ **SECRET #1: Involve your audience in your presentation as quickly as possible.**

By getting people involved in your speech as quickly as possible, it helps them overcome any anxieties they may be feeling about attending a public gathering (E.g.: "Is my hair okay? Do I have a stain on my tie?" etc.). Remember, the sooner they are involved in your program, the sooner they will forget about themselves and the more they'll pay attention to *you!*

For the next five hours, Robbins takes command of the audience like a master conductor leading an orchestra. One minute he is making hilarious facial expressions that cause his audience to laugh hysterically, and the next he's lowering his naturally deep yet boyish voice to barely a whisper in order to touch them emotionally. A few moments later, the ever-passionate Robbins startles the entire group by slapping one of his immense hands against his chest, which results in a loud "popping" sound. He does this attention-grabbing gesture whenever he wants to dramatically emphasize a key point.

If you've never been to an Anthony Robbins seminar, it's a bit like being on a roller-coaster ride. It's fast paced, exhilarating, and, because of the sheer volume of information he gives you, often leaves your brain a bit scrambled. Tony acknowledges that he often overloads his seminar attendees with information, but he justifies it to them by saying: "I know I'm giving you a lot at once, but I really want you to get this!" And he means it.

Robbins' programs often go until 1:00 or 2:00 in the morning. Why? Because, as he likes to say, "I am committed to giving my audiences more than what they have any right to expect."

▶ **SECRET #2: Commit to giving your audience more than they have any right to expect.**

Maybe this is why so many people across the country view Anthony Robbins not just as a seminar leader, but as a friend and personal coach.

(Note how Tony's thinking is similar to that of Joel Weldon who, in his chapter, says: "Promise a lot, and then deliver even more." Both men do, and the result is that the two of them turn down considerably more speaking engagements than they can accept.)

Walking on Fire

Around midnight at Robbins's seminars, people begin to fidget nervously in their seats. "Is it time yet?" they wonder. A feeling of excitement, followed by waves of anxiety, sweep across the room. People's senses begin to play tricks on them. Is that smoke they smell? Flashbacks from Irwin Winkler's movie, *The Towering Inferno*, begin to flicker in their minds. Then the self-talk starts: "Maybe this isn't such a good idea. . . . What if I get burned? . . . What have I gotten myself into now?" They check out those sitting next to them to see if they, too, are experiencing feelings of hysteria. A nervous smile and widening of the pupils from their fellow seminar-goers gives them their answer—they, too, are quietly freaking out.

Sensing (anticipating?) the fear in the room, Robbins masterfully uses humor to change the audience's understandably nervous state: "Now, when we go out to walk, I don't want any of you to think of *charrrred, bloooody stumpppps!*" he says melodramatically, emphasizing the last three words with a little too much glee. After a few more humorous/morbid one-liners, which the audience responds to with spats of nervous laughter, Anthony delivers a few safety tips: "When walking, keep your eyes up; repeat the mantra, 'cool-moss! cool-moss!' wipe your feet on the wet grass at the end of the pit, and be careful not to step on any stray, hot embers." Finally, he shouts, "Okay, let's do it!" and like Patton leading his troops into battle, Robbins leads the pumped-up and incited mob out into the parking lot of the hotel to conquer their fears. The moment has finally arrived; it's time to walk on fire!

> **As they draw closer to the drums, the object of their fear lies before them like a fiery dragon in the night.**

As the frenzied throng exits the safe confines of the hotel ballroom and pour out into cool night air, they are greeted by the hypnotic sounds of African drums beating off into the distance. As they draw closer to the drums, the object of their fear lies before them like a fiery dragon in the night: four ten-foot rows of burning-hot embers. Their bright orange glow against the surrounding sea of blackness is at the same time both mesmerizing and perilous. The pyres are surrounded by sods of wet grass, which are constantly being hosed down by the Robbins' firewalk team.

After having the worked-up crowd remove their shoes and socks, Tony once again goes over the safety tips. Then, after taking a moment to get himself focused, Robbins, with pants rolled up to his knees, dramatically walks across the searing embers barefooted while shouting, "cool-moss! cool-moss!" His gait is brisk but steady, and it takes him less than four seconds to cross over the hellish terrain. Seeing him successfully traverse the fire pit without sustaining any injuries only makes the seminar-goers that much more eager to have a go at it.

Soon, housewives, doctors, school teachers, attorneys, salespeople, actors, students, and people, who never in their wildest dreams imagined they would do something like this, are now pushing their way to the front of the line so they, too, can "walk on fire." As each person makes it across, they are greeted with cheers and hugs from Robbins' staff volunteers, as well as their new "fire-walk friends." Clearly, this is a night that these people will never forget.

Neuro-Linguistic Programming

"The quality of your life is the quality of your communication, both with yourself and others."
ANTHONY ROBBINS

Throughout most of the eighties, Robbins' message centered around a technology developed by John Grinder and Richard Bandler called Neuro-Linguistic Programming, or NLP. Techniques such as matching and mirroring, modeling, anchoring, and reframing were taught by Robbins as tools to help people become more effective communicators.

Robbins belief was that a person could dramatically increase the quality of his or her life by learning how to manage their states, and by reframing their moment-to-moment experience so that it empowers rather than depresses. He said that if we lacked confidence, we should employ a technique called modeling, whereby we duplicate the mannerisms of confident people. The idea is that by standing up straight, smiling, and acting *as if* we are confident, soon we will acquire this most desirable of traits. In other words, we can literally "train ourselves" to behave in a whole new way.

Not only did Robbins feel that NLP was the most effective way to help people overcome phobias, as well as myriad other "challenges," but he also believed it was the quickest way to change. Robbins' passion and communication skills were so strong that he single-handedly took NLP, which at the time had a loyal but decidedly small following, to national consciousness.

Just as Wayne Dyer had built a grass roots following for himself and his book, *Erroneous Zones,* during the mid-seventies by traveling around the country doing TV and radio interviews, so too did Robbins, during the eighties, build a following for himself by conducting his "FireWalk" seminar in hundreds of major cities. By the time his first book, *Unlimited Power,* was released by Simon and Schuster in 1986, he already had an established market. The book quickly went on to become a bestseller and has been translated into eleven languages.

Ironically, around 1988, Robbins began to distance himself from the NLP movement that he had helped popularize. This came about as a direct result of all the new distinctions he had come up with while giving those hundreds and hundreds of seminars throughout the early and mid-eighties. Like Elvis Presley and his manager, Colonel Tom Parker, NLP and Anthony Robbins were a perfect match for each other when both were just starting out. NLP needed a charismatic spokesperson to bring its technology to the masses, and Robbins needed powerful seminar material to give his audiences. But unlike the king of rock 'n roll, who stayed with the Colonel until the end, Robbins had no qualms about severing the relationship with a partner he had outgrown. NLP had served as a launching pad for Robbins' career, but now it was time for him to venture out with his own techniques. His goal had always been to give his audiences the very best information on human behavior that was available. There was a time when NLP was it; now, having created a whole new body of material based on his own insights and research, he no longer felt NLP was cutting-edge technology.

The lesson is simple: If you want to stay at the top of your field, you must constantly upgrade your material to be sure that you are providing your audiences with the *very best* information available on your topic. If you don't, somebody else will surely come along who does, and *they* will be the one to reap the rewards.

▶ **SECRET #3: Constantly upgrade your material to be sure that you are providing your audience with the very best information available on your topic.**

The Speaking Career:
How It All Started

In an interview which appeared in the December 1992 /January 1993 issue of *Sharing Ideas* magazine, Robbins tells how he was first introduced to public speaking:

Mr. Cobb, my high school speech and history teacher, saw my potential. He came to me at the end of my speech class. I had never really spoken before. He said, "I want to see you after class." I thought he was upset because I was a real jokester trying to get a girl's attention.

He pulled me aside and said, "You are magical. You will be one of the best speakers who has ever spoken." I said, "Are you crazy?" He replied, "I'm telling you, you've got it. I don't want you to wait until next year. I want you to compete in a tournament this weekend. I found a speech I think is you. I want you to do persuasive oratory and interpretation. Memorize this speech; deliver it. You will win."

I took the speech home and was blown away. I didn't think I was a good speaker at all. The speech was called, 'The Will to Win.' I still don't know who it's by. I remember reading it and thinking, "This is my whole life! This is what I stand for; this is who I am." I memorized it and went beyond memorizing; I became it.

Robbins ended up taking first prize at that speech tournament and, although he didn't know it at the time, had just taken his first step down the road that was to one day make him one of the most successful motivational speakers in the country. The fact that Robbins didn't just give the speech by rote memorization but, as he put it, "became it," made all the difference to the audience and the judges that day. As a speaker, it's important that you don't just give your talk from your neck up, but that you give it with your whole mind, body, and soul. How do you do this? By embodying your talk! By going beyond simply learning the speech material to becoming absolutely *convinced* of its merits. By energetically delivering your material in such a way that the audience doesn't just hear you, but *feels* you. If you come across with this type of conviction and emotional energy, you will tap into your audience, and an audience who is touched emotionally can't help but be persuaded by what you have to say.

▶ **SECRET #4: Don't memorize your speech—become it!**

More than "Just a Speaker"

"What I've committed to in my life, continuously, is finding out what are the best strategies [for maximizing one's potential] and then sharing those strategies with people in a way that's entertaining."
ANTHONY ROBBINS

It's interesting to note that Robbins does not think of himself as "just a motivational speaker," but more as an educator who is extremely entertaining, as he revealed during our interview:

Speaking is a skill; communication is a power. I believe speakers are a dime a dozen but communicators are rare and unforgettable.

I don't look at myself just as a speaker, because I think I do a lot more than that. I have a core belief that says that most people would rather be entertained than educated. If you can entertain and educate simultaneously, then you have a chance to impact mass numbers of people. What I've committed to in my life, continuously, is finding out what are the best strategies [for maximizing one's potential] and then sharing those strategies with people in a way that's entertaining.

Connecting with the Audience

Robbins combines music, dancing, humor, dynamic body language, storytelling, audience interaction, small-group exercises, and even a massage train (where audience members give each other a 30-second back massage) throughout the course of his presentation. This allows him to reach his audience on many different levels. He is stimulating them not just with the words he's speaking (auditorily) and the tone of his voice (emotionally), but by the way he moves (visually), the music he plays (emotionally and auditorily), having people touch each other (kinesthetically), and the jokes he tells (laughing feels good both physically and mentally).

Robbins approaches speaking a lot like Steven Spielberg approaches moviemaking. Just as the famous director does in his movie, *E.T.*, Robbins brings his audience to tears one minute and then has them doubled over with laughter the next. In fact, Spielberg and Robbins both come at their audience at so many levels that they are able to take them through a full range of emotions. The reason they do this is because both men understand that what they are really selling are not words but *feelings* and *emotions*.

▶ **SECRET #5: The Spielberg Factor: Connect with your audience on as many different levels as possible.**

Think about it. A good movie or speaker moves you emotionally (like *E.T.*), and a movie or speaker that doesn't move you, is, well, boring.

▶ **SECRET #6: Remember that what you're really selling are not words but feelings and emotions.**

This is why when you get in front of an audience, in most cases, you want to avoid standing behind a lectern (because it presents a static picture to the audience). Instead, take a page out of Phil Donahue, Oprah Winfrey, and Anthony Robbins' books and move around! Point, gesture, allow yourself to get excited! "Get into it," as they say.

Go into the audience, touch people on the shoulder who are sitting on the aisles (they won't bite), and, if you can, go visit the people in the back once in a while. I understand that there are going to be times when you won't be able to leave the front of the room, like when you're on a stage, or you're being videotaped. But just keeping the thought in the back of your mind that *"I must do everything I can to connect with my audience"* will make your presentation more interesting. Even if you *are* on a stage, go stand next to the edge, as close to the audience as possible. That way, at the very least, you'll keep people's attention, because they'll be wondering whether or not you're going to fall off!

If you can incorporate music into your presentation, then do it. Anything you can use to break up your material, whether it be humor, stories, anecdotes, quotes, or audience participation, will only make your presentation that much more interesting.

Deliver Your Message with Passion!

One of the traits that's often used to describe Anthony Robbins is passion. And for good reason; he sounds extremely passionate when he speaks! How do you deliver material with passion? By being enthusiastic about your message and then transfering that feeling of enthusiasm to your audience.

We've all heard somebody say about a speaker, "He bored me; he was too wooden." What the person meant was that the individual didn't express enough of who they were in their presentation; they just spoke words as opposed to conveying emotions. As mentioned earlier, good speakers get their audience to not just hear something but *feel* something as well.

Keep in mind that you can't speak with passion if you're not passionate about your material. One of the reasons Robbins speaks with so much passion is that he's truly excited about sharing his message and his life-changing techniques with his audiences. All he has to do is open himself up and the audience can *feel* his passion; eventually, they can't help but get caught up in it themselves. In Robbins own words:

> Those speakers who work on being perfect rarely impact the heart of the human beings who they are trying to touch. They give a good presentation, people clap afterward, they get standing ovations, but it doesn't really change people. I don't care who you are, if you're passionate enough you're going to do well.

▶   **SECRET #7: If you want to speak with passion, then you have to be passionate about your topic!**

Three of Robbins' Presentational Strengths: Body Language, Tonal Variety, and Humor

Of the many exceptional skills that Anthony Robbins exhibits so well onstage, three that really stand out are: 1) His ability to use his body language to support and strengthen what he's saying verbally, 2) The way he dramatically raises and lowers his tone of voice to increase the impact of what he's saying, and 3) The timing and delivery of his humor.

Body Language

In a well-known study by Dr. Albert Mehrabian of U.C.L.A, the professor concluded that our understanding of another person's communication is determined seven percent by their words, thirty-eight percent by their tone of voice, and a whopping fifty-five percent by their body language. Clearly, the adage, "your actions speak so loudly, I can't hear what you're saying," isn't just food for thought—it's a fact! And one that's not lost on Anthony Robbins.

Words that describe Robbins' body language onstage are dynamic, powerful, playful, explosive, sexy, commanding, confident, and passionate. Sometimes his movements are quick and explosive like a tiger pouncing on its prey, and other times he is sexy and charismatic, like a Don Juan in a room full of women. Again, it all depends on what point he is trying to make at that moment. Much like a carpenter who uses a hammer to drive home a nail, Robbins uses body language to drive home his points. When he wants to make an explosive point, he'll often slap his hands together, slap his chest, or pound a fist into the palm of his other hand. It's as if he's putting a punctuation point at the end of his sentence with his body.

For example, he'll say, "And it's those individuals who know what they want in life (points at audience), and who are willing to go after it (slaps hands together) regardless of the circumstances around them (gestures in a circle), who go on to make a difference in the world (he levels his eyes at the audience, so there can be no doubt that he means what he says)."

Other ways Robbins uses body language (and this is one of the reasons he is so entertaining to watch) is his physiological adaptation of whomever he happens to be talking about. If he's talking about a woman client who came to see him about her depression, he'll stoop his massive shoulders, hang his head, and look down at the ground as he mimics her voice. (In fact, his mimicry skill was the source of some major entertainment for his fellow students when Robbins was in high school—much to his teachers' chagrin.)

If you want to maximize what you're saying, throw your body behind it. If you've ever watched ice skaters live or on TV, you'll notice how they put everything they've got into every move, gesture, and mannerism. Even a tilt of their head seems to emanate from their toes. They are completely committed to whatever action they are carrying out, and they make this happen by incorporating their entire being into the movement. Yet, if you look at many speakers, they tend to project only from the neck up. In doing so, they are only using a small part of their speaking arsenal.

If you're telling a story, actually "become" the character by adopting their mannerisms. When making a key point, be sure to add appropriate gestures that will support your points. It should be mentioned that a big part of Robbins' body language is in his face. If he's expressing amazement, he'll make his eyes really big. If he's pretending to be confused as to why a person acted a certain way, he'll furrow his eyebrows. If he's displeased, he'll make a frown. As you can see, Anthony Robbins, much like an actor, uses his body, along with his voice, to elicit different emotions from his audience, depending on the point he is trying to make.

Since there are entire books on the subject of body language (I recommend *The Secret Language of Success* by David Lewis [Carol & Graf, 1989]), I don't want to go into too much detail here. Just remember that your mouth doesn't have to do all the talking; allow your body and facial expressions to do their part, too!

▶ **SECRET #8: Use your body to punctuate and support what you are saying verbally.**

Tonal Variety

Anthony Robbins is truly a master at eliciting a range of emotions from his audience simply by changing the tone of his voice. When he wants to pull his audience's heart strings, he'll lower his already naturally deep and gravelly voice to almost a whisper and speak slowly. The result is that his words sound soft and emotional, and the audience leans forward so as not to miss what he is saying. Sometimes he'll speak in a playful, teasing voice that is fun and upbeat. Just as quickly, he will change his voice to sound commanding and motivating; he'll lower his pitch and let his words boom out like they were shot from a cannon. There's no mistaking his intensity when he does this. On more than one occasion he's barked to an audience, "Making a true decision means *committing* to achieving a *result,* and then cutting yourself off from any other possibility!"

Often, when he's making a key point like this, he'll slap his hand against his chest for emphasis. As I mentioned earlier, the result is a loud "popping sound" that serves to dramatically punctuate his point. As you can see, your body language should support your tone of voice, and vice versa. And of course both must support your words.

A good way to get a feel for how people use vocal variety is to turn your back to the TV while a soap opera is on. Just listen to the voices; you'll hear how the actors modulate their tone of voice to communicate their feelings. Drama, jealousy, rage, sexiness—it's all there.

A good exercise is to try delivering a line using a different tone of voice each time. First try it as if you've just seen an angel (awe and inspiration), then as if you just found out your lifelong puppy dog has run away (sadness), and then like you just won the lottery (exuberance). The ability to deliver the lines of your speech with just the right tone of voice is crucial to your success in becoming a great speaker. The last thing you want to do is sound like you're trying to be funny when you're really trying to inspire, or to come off as being sarcastic when you're really trying to be sincere. By developing a wide range of vocal varieties, and by knowing how and when to use them, you will have a powerful tool at your disposal through which to affect an audience.

▶ **SECRET #9: Use your tone of voice to convey a variety of emotions throughout your presentation.**

Humor

Robbins' ability to use humor so effectively is one of the main reasons audiences enjoy him so much. When he wants to make his audience laugh, he becomes a six-foot, seven-inch Robin Williams. Throughout his seminar, he's constantly telling funny stories, exaggerating, or playing with the audience. For example, when describing somebody who can't motivate himself to achieve his goals, he'll take on the physiology of a depressed person (shoulders slumped, eyes downcast, no energy, sourpuss expression on his face), and he'll drone in a whiny voice, "I don't know whyyyy nobody likes meeeee. . . . I'm so depresssssed." And everybody cracks up. Why? It's not because depressed people are particularly funny; it's just that Robbins gets us to see, in a humorous way, how powerless we are to change anything when we are in a state of depression.

In his own words, Robbins underscores the importance of humor in his presentations:

> I would say that humor is definitely a part of my personality, but it goes back to what I said before: I believe that people would rather be entertained than educated. So I realized that if you're playful and outrageous and you get people to have a good time, they're going to hear your message. Most of my humor isn't planned, it's just me being spontaneous. When I get a reaction, my brain remembers it, and the next time I get up to speak, I use it.
>
> I think that when people are in states of laughter, you have an opportunity in that moment to anchor the results that you've been sharing with them so they last long-term, because people remember what was humorous to them.

The bottom line is that watching Anthony Robbins onstage is entertaining, regardless of what he happens to be speaking about at the time. And while his natural charisma certainly plays a large part in this, it's also his sense of humor, playfulness, and willingness to be outrageous that all help to make him so enjoyable to watch. The lesson is clear: While you *can* deliver a presentation without any humor in it, you will greatly increase the odds of getting your message across and having it be remembered if you incorporate humor into your presentation.

▶ **SECRET #10: Humor is the lubricant that helps your message go down smoother.**

Strong Material: The Cornerstone of Your Presentation

Clearly, Robbins' presentation skills are some of the best in the business. But what really makes him so phenomenal, and why everyone from professional sports teams to presidents call on him, is because his material is so strong. After all, what good would it be if you had the greatest speaking skills in the world, but you used them to deliver tired, worn-out, dull material? Specifically, what makes Robbins so effective is that he has the ability to take complex information, simplify it, then break it down into doable steps, and then deliver that information in a passionate and enthusiastic way. The process of choosing strong material begins by making certain that what you are speaking about has relevance to your listeners. The more your audience can relate to the topic you are addressing, the more interested they are going to be in listening to what you have to say. Obviously, the converse is also true: The less the audience can relate to your topic, the less interested they are going to be in hearing what you have to say.

▶ **SECRET #11: Make sure you've done everything you can to make your subject as relevant to your audience as possible.**

Of course, it's up to you to *make* your topic have relevance to your audience. You do this by showing them how your topic specifically applies to them. For example, all of us ask ourselves hundreds of questions throughout our day. We say things to ourselves like, "Why did she say that? What did I do wrong? Why are things going so well? Why am I having trouble quitting smoking?" etc.

Yet, few of us have ever taken the time to consider the *quality* of the questions we ask ourselves. That is, until Anthony Robbins came along and explained the power of asking *high-quality* questions. In the following excerpt from one of his monthly *PowerTalk* tapes, notice how he clearly and logically explains the importance of asking ourselves a better *quality* of questions:

> If you want to be great, ask great questions. The quality of your life is nothing but the quality of the questions you ask yourself. If you ask questions like, "Why me? Why does this always happen to me?" then you'll be totally disempowered. But if you ask questions like, "How can I turn this around? How can I make it work? How can I utilize this? How can I use this to empower myself and others?" you're going to have some phenomenal answers, and answers give you power, the power to change your world.

Notice what Robbins does *not* do. He doesn't go into any complicated theories on the mind and the whole questioning process. Rather, by simply giving us a number of examples of disempowering questions, and then contrasting them with questions that empower, we have no problem understanding his point.

The Robbins Speaking Formula

Let's use the preceding example to take a look at "the formula" Robbins uses to deliver his message. By "formula," I mean the sequence of steps he goes through. If we can identify each step, then we can use them to improve the quality of our own presentations.

The first thing he does is state his main idea. In this case it's that, if we want to be great, we must ask ourselves great questions. This idea is as easy to follow as it is logical. Secondly, he tells us *why* questions are important: it's because they determine the quality of our lives. Thirdly, he gives us examples of some bad questions, immediately followed by examples of good questions. Again, the contrast of the two types of questions, one after the other, makes them much more powerful than if he had used only one type to make his point.

▶ **SECRET #12: Give your audience specific examples of the consequences that will happen if they don't immediately take action on your ideas. Follow this up by giving them the terrific benefits they'll receive if they do follow your ideas.**

Finally, he sums up his message by telling us the *benefits* we'll receive as a result of asking good-quality questions: that we'll get "phenomenal answers." This will give us the power we need to change our world!

See how logically everything flows together?

The Robbins Four-Step Speaking Formula

1. State your main idea.
2. Explain why it's important.
3. Give an example of what will happen if we (the audience) fail to act on your idea (the scarier the consequences, the better). Then give an example of what will happen if we do act on it (the more desirable, the better).
4. Restate your main idea and reinforce the benefits we'll receive by acting on it immediately.

The Power of Stories

Stories are, without a doubt, the most effective way to communicate your ideas to your audiences. Perhaps this is because they tend to bypass the critical left brain, and enter our consciousness via our more creative, intuitive right brain. One thing is for sure: People like hearing stories. And, like humor, your stories should always support or illustrate the point you are making.

For example, when Robbins wants to get his point across that "It's not what happens to you in life, but what you *do* about it that matters," he tells the harrowing true story about his friend and fellow motivational speaker, W. Mitchell. Mitchell was badly burned on over eighty-five percent of his body in a motorcycle accident. He was left horribly disfigured. While the facts of the story are disturbing enough, it's the way Robbins uses his voice to get his audience to feel certain emotions that makes the story a real heart-wrencher. For example, there's a part where he says, "And then the worst occurred—the gas cap popped off his motorcycle and the fuel ignited! Suddenly, Mitchell became a human torch," and you can hear the sense of danger and peril in his voice. In addition, the grave expression on his face helps convey the seriousness of the situation. Robbins goes on to tell how Mitchell courageously fought back from the motorcycle accident, only to become paralyzed in a plane crash a few years later! At this point, you can't help but be moved to tears. However, Robbins tells how Mitchell fought back from this tragedy, too. Believe it or not, Robbins has you laughing by the end of the story as he relates how, when Mitchell ran for Colorado State congress after the accidents, his campaign motto was: "He's not just another pretty face."

Robbins drives home his point by talking about how, despite all Mitchell has been through, he continues to live each day to its fullest and experiences real joy in his life. And if *he* can, then there's no reason why we can't too. It's a powerful story, and one that stays with you long after the seminar is over.

One final, gentle reminder: Be patient with yourself when you're first developing your stories. Good stories can take months, even years, to get down before they are at the level you would like them to be. But eventually, after enough honing and tweaking, if you don't give up, one day you'll tell the story, and it will feel terrific because it communicates everything you want it to and more!

▶ **SECRET #13: The most effective way to illustrate your ideas is through the power of stories.**

Good Speakers Both Motivate and Teach Skills

As good as Robbins is at motivating his audiences, he feels it's equally important that he provide them with the tools they need to make long-term changes:

> What I try to do is give people both philosophy and skills that can change their life. I think people need both. A lot of

people will teach things like positive thinking and that's invaluable, but I think along with that positive thinking we've really got to learn the specific how-to's: How to master our finances, how to change our physical body, how to really make our relationships work.

The key word here is *balance.* You want your program to be motivating and exciting enough so that people will be stimulated to go out and use your ideas; and you want your ideas to be strong enough so that, when people do implement them, they will achieve the results they are looking for.

Robbins' Advice for Someone Just Getting Started in the Speaking Business

When I asked Robbins for the advice he would give someone just getting started in speaking, he replied:

> I would say that the most important key to speaking is not to be perfect or to know exactly what you're going to say or how you're going to say it. But rather, that you have incredible passion about what you're speaking about. Your emotional intensity is what people will remember.

▶ **SECRET #14: You don't have to be perfect to speak; it's your passion and energy that your audience will remember.**

Next, Robbins recommends that you:

> Go out and speak to every single person you can. There's nothing that can replace the power of going out and trying to persuade someone. I believe that the most powerful speakers are persuaders—people who aren't just talking to inform, but talking to influence in a positive way. If every day you go out and you give your all with absolute passion, and you notice what works and you're flexible, you're going to succeed. The key is that you have to believe in what you're talking about.

You have to know what your goal is when you're speaking, and you've got to be incredibly flexible in your approach until you get the result that you're after.

And from Robbins' book, *Awaken the Giant Within*:

I became an excellent public speaker, because, rather than once a week, I booked myself to speak three times a day to anyone who would listen. While others in my organization had forty-eight speaking engagements a year, I would have a similar number within two weeks. Within a month, I'd have two years of experience. And within a year, I'd have a decade's worth of growth.

My associates talked about how "lucky" I was to have been born with such an "innate" talent. I tried to tell them what I'm telling you now: Mastery takes as long as you want it to take. By the way, were all of my speeches great? Far from it! But I did make sure that I learned from every experience and that I somehow improved until very soon I could enter a room of any size and be able to reach people from virtually all walks of life.

▶ **SECRET #15: Speak as often as possible!**

Speaking Allows You to Make a Difference in Other People's Lives

In the following, Tony talks about the tremendous opportunity speakers have to make a difference in other people's lives:

I can remember several times when I got up to speak that, when I was done, I knew that the people in that room would never forget what we had talked about that day . . . never! I've had people come back ten years later and share with me that even though a decade had passed, they still remember that talk and it affects them almost every day of their life.

If you can do that even with a couple of people during your lifetime—much less the millions I've had the privilege of reaching through my seminars, books, tapes, and infomercials—then I think your life is worth living.

Being an effective speaker takes a lot of work. Learning how to write, organize, and deliver a speech in a way that is both inspiring and entertaining can take years. If you are willing to put in the necessary time to develop these traits, you will be rewarded on many levels. Besides the obvious financial rewards that go to people who can powerfully present good ideas, you will also receive the satisfaction of knowing you made a difference in other people's lives. This is an extraordinary feeling that no amount of money can buy!

Regardless of Your Past, You *Can* Succeed

One of the goals of *Success Secrets of the Motivational Superstars* is to show how many of the speakers, who are now considered to be some of the very best and most successful in the business, began without any advantages. In fact, many started out with distinct disadvantages, such as Wayne Dyer and Les Brown, who were both abandoned by their real parents at birth. The point is that, regardless of your past or where you came from, if you work hard enough and want it badly enough, you can succeed.

Tony Robbins has mentioned during many of his seminars (and on the first page of chapter one in his book, *Unlimited Power*) that he once lived in a 400-square-foot bachelor apartment in Venice, California, and how he had to do his dishes in the bathtub because the place didn't even have a kitchen. In doing my research for this book, I was listening to one of Tony's *Power Talk* tapes, and he happened to mention the address of the apartment building. Being curious by nature, I decided to check it out for myself.

The 400-Square-Foot Bachelor Apartment

It was a sunny day in the beach community of Venice when I pulled up across the street from 2516 Pacific Avenue. As I got out of my car, I looked up and there before me stood a little, rundown, two-story apartment building.

Crossing Pacific Avenue, I pushed open a rickety, old, three-foot-high brown wooden gate. Seeing a set of stairs, I took them to the top and found myself staring at apartment 3A. After pausing for a moment, I knocked on the door. I was curious to see if the current tenant had any idea that Anthony Robbins had once resided in his home. No one answered and so I knocked a second time—but again, no answer.

After climbing back down the stairs, I stood in front of the drab edifice and just stared up at the second-story windows. I noticed there were old lime-colored sheets hanging in them instead of curtains, and that the entire place was in desperate need of a paint job.

Suddenly, and completely unexpectedly, a feeling of great inspiration came over me. And then a smile slowly crept across my face. Why? Because I pictured a twenty-two-year-old Tony Robbins, laying there inside this diminutive structure, listening to the cars pass by at night as he dreamed—dreamed of making a difference in the world and becoming financially successful in the process. And then my mind flashed on his magnificent 10,000-square-foot castle in Del Mar, California—and a chill went down my spine.

He had done it. The boy from Glendora, California, who had been kicked out of his home by his mother on Christmas Eve at age seventeen, who found himself having to sleep in his Volkswagon while he sold seminars for motivational speaker Jim Rohn, who after gaining thirty-eighty pounds and ending up in this run-down Venice dwelling, turned it all around through perseverance and a compelling vision. He had achieved fame and fortune beyond his wildest dreams. Where his neighbors had once consisted of surfers, winos, and the down-and-out, Anthony Robbins now rubs elbows with heads of states, presidents, sports team owners, famous actors, and the rich and powerful.

To truly appreciate how far Robbins has come, read what he wrote in his 1991 best seller, *Awaken the Giant Within*:

> In the beginning of 1980, I was a nineteen-year-old kid. I felt alone and frustrated. I had no financial resources. There were no success coaches available to me, no successful friends or mentors, no clear-cut goals. I was floundering and fat. Yet within a few short years I discovered a power that I used to transform virtually every area of my life.

The Power Robbins Used to
Turn His Life Around

What had Anthony Robbins discovered that had transformed his life? What was this miraculous power that, as he writes:

> . . . once I'd mastered it, I used it to dramatically increase my level of confidence and therefore my ability to take action and produce measurable results. I also used it to take back control of my physical well-being and permanently rid myself of thirty-eight pounds of fat.
>
> Through it, I attracted the woman of my dreams, married her, and created the family I desired. I used this power to change my income from subsistence level to over one-million dollars a year. It moved me from my tiny apartment (where I was washing my dishes in the bathtub because there was no kitchen) to my family's current home, the Del Mar Castle.

This awesome force that Robbins had tapped into was *the power of making a committed decision.* He figured out that if he was going to have an inspiring, compelling life, he was going to have to make the *decision* to create it.

"It's your decisions and not your conditions that shape your destiny."
ANTHONY ROBBINS

Sadly, many people in this world spend their lives hoping and wishing for an exciting, interesting life. Deep down inside they're secretly waiting for the day that their purpose in life will suddenly strike them like a bolt of lighting. And until that big day arrives, these individuals put off fully living . . . and all the while their lives are slowly passing them by. They're living their life settling for less than they are capable of. And the tragic part is that they know it.

What Anthony Robbins discovered is that if you want to have an exciting and rewarding life, with goals that truly inspire you, it's up to *you* to create that life for yourself. No one is going to do it for you. What's more, until you do, you are destined to drift aimlessly through life, being tossed about by the winds of change and other externals.

"A man without a purpose is like a ship without a rudder."
THOMAS CARLYLE

Make no mistake about it; people who have achieved great things during their lifetime didn't do it by accident. They made a conscious decision somewhere along the line that they were going to accomplish something great. This doesn't mean that those people who pass through life without achieving their dreams, goals, and desires are bad people; it just means they never made an unequivocal decision to make it happen.

Of course, if you decide not to go after your dreams, then you've also made a decision, as Robbins astutely points out:

> If you don't make decisions about how you're going to live, then you've already made a decision, haven't you? You're making a decision to be directed by the environment instead of shaping your own destiny. My whole life changed in just one day—the day I determined not just what I'd like to have in my life or what I wanted to become, but when I decided who and what I was committed to having and being in my life.

Robbins' whole life changed the day he *decided* to never again settle for being less than he was capable of becoming.

▶ **SECRET #16: Your whole life changes the day you make the decision that you will no longer settle for mediocrity.**

The Power of Raising Your Standards

Anthony Robbins' life changed forever the day he made the decision to raise his personal standards to an entirely new level. No longer was "just getting by" acceptable to Robbins. For the first time in his life, he got clear on not just what he wanted, but what he was *committed* to achieving during his lifetime. Then he identified those attributes and qualities he knew he absolutely *must* have to achieve those goals. These qualities included perseverance, flexibility, a positive attitude, and the belief that he could accomplish anything he set out to do. Likewise, he vowed to eliminate any behaviors, such as procrastination, negative thinking, laziness, et cetera, that would be detrimental to the accomplishment of his goals. The day that Robbins made this one powerful decision—to raise his standards—was the day that his career, in fact his whole life, took off.

Why did making a decision to raise his personal standards to a new level have such a profound impact on Robbins? Because he realized that if he allowed himself to continue to do just enough to get by, he would never perform up to his full potential (or even close to it), and his dreams would *never* become a reality. His new standards allowed him to create results in his life that in the past would have been unattainable. As Robbins says:

> If you don't set a baseline standard for what you'll accept in your life, you'll find it's easy to slip into behaviors and attitudes or a quality of life that's far below what you deserve. You need to set and live by these standards no matter what happens in your life. Even if it all goes wrong, even if it rains on your parade, even if the stock market crashes, even if your lover leaves you, even if no one gives you the support that you need, you still must stay committed to your decision that you will live your life at the highest level.

Is this idea of raising your personal standards and committing to a vision an easy thing to do? No. If it were, everyone would do it. The fact is, most people cave-in to short-term pleasures rather than delay them for long-term, big-time, major gains. Why? Because they never stop to think about the price they're paying for giving in to instant gratification and whether that price is too high.

In an interview with Robbins in the January/February 1994 issue of *Selling Magazine*, Robbins summed it by saying:

Any time you start making short-term decisions to avoid pain in the short term, you create pain in the long term. People who succeed are willing to do whatever is necessary in the short term, because they have a vision for the long term and are committed to that vision and will do whatever it takes. And I think that's the common denominator of success.

Put Your Dreams, Goals, and Desires in Writing

Once Robbins decided to raise his personal standards and design a new future for himself, he didn't stop there. He put his vision into a more concrete form—he committed it to writing:

> In 1983, I did an exercise that created a future so compelling that my whole life changed as a result. As part of the overall process of raising my standards, I established a whole new set of goals, writing down all the things I would no longer settle for, as well as what I was committed to having in my life. I set aside all my limiting beliefs and sat down on the beach with my journal.
>
> I wrote continuously for three hours, brainstorming every possibility of what I could ever imagine doing, being, having, creating, experiencing, or contributing. The time line I gave myself for achieving these goals was any time from tomorrow to the next twenty years. I never stopped to think whether I could actually achieve these goals or not. I simply captured any possibility that inspired me and wrote it down.

Robbins created a compelling vision for his life, and you can too. The key is that *you must put it down in writing*. Writing forces you to get *specific* about your goals. It helps your mind get clear on what it is you really want. There's something magical that happens when you take pen in hand and begin to write out your dreams. It's almost as if your mind says, "Oh, I guess he's (she's) serious about this!" And because your mind is a goal-seeking mechanism, its wheels begin to turn in the direction of how it can make your dreams into a reality.

> *"What the mind of man can conceive and believe,*
> *it can achieve."*
> NAPOLEON HILL

Just as Robbins did that day on the beach, get away by yourself and put every one of your goals, dreams, and desires down on paper. Don't stop to think, "Well, this isn't realistic," or "I don't know how I could possibly achieve this." Just let it flow. *The most important step during this whole process is that you don't put any limitations on yourself.* Have enough faith that if others have been able to achieve their goals, there's no reason why you can't as well.

▶ **SECRET #17: Put your dreams, goals, and desires in writing.**

Once you've completed writing out all your dreams, goals, and desires, you'll immediately experience a feeling of excitement. Why? Because by writing them out, you're now one step closer to actually making them a reality—and that *is* exciting!

The Power of Commitment

Writing down your goals and dreams is a crucial step—one which, according to studies, less than five percent of the population does. However, just writing your vision down is not enough. *It is absolutely critical that you become one hundred percent committed to achieving that vision.*

Robbins asks his audience the following rhetorical question:

Is there a difference between being interested in something and being committed to it? You bet there is! Many times people say things like, "Gosh, I really would like to make money," or "I'd like to be closer to my kids," or "You know, I'd really like to make a difference in the world." But that kind of statement is not a commitment at all. It's merely stating a preference, saying, "I'm interested in having this happen, if I don't have to do anything." That's not power! It's a weak prayer made without even the faith to launch it.

The message here is obvious. If you are serious about achieving your goals, dreams, and desires, you must commit to them one hundred percent, as if your very life depends upon it. Am I exaggerating? No. Not if you're serious about achieving them.

Another Year, Another Set of Broken Promises

The first week of January every year, the news media likes to do stories on how people have already broken their New Year's resolutions less than forty-eight hours into the new year (statistics show that the average person lasts only two weeks!). Overweight people are shown eating ice-cream, and smokers are shown smoking. And all they can do is look into the camera, smile weakly, and say, "Oh, well, maybe next year."

While these individuals may be shrugging off their lack of will power with a grin on the outside, the truth is, they feel saddened, dejected, and defeated on the inside. And why not? They either made the resolutions knowing full well they were never going to keep them in the first place, or they simply gave up after the very first few hunger pangs or nicotine cravings. Whichever it was, the message that was sent to their brain was the same: Lying and not following through on your promises is acceptable behavior.

The distinction that Tony Robbins made (as did all of the successful individuals I interviewed) is that lying and breaking promises to yourself is simply not acceptable. They understand that before you can achieve anything of consequence, you must develop the habit of following through on your commitments. This means that when you make a promise (to yourself or to others), you know beyond a shadow-of-a-doubt that you *will* keep it. That if you say you're going to do something, it's as good as done. Period.

Once you develop the habit of following through on your commitments, there's no telling how far you'll go in life. There's something very empowering about being able to look an obstacle to one of your goals right in the eyes and say, "You can't stop me!" and know that it really can't!

"I think the purpose of life is to do something that contributes and helps you to touch people beyond our lifetime. I think the purpose of life is to do something that will outlast it."
ANTHONY ROBBINS

How do you develop this kind of total commitment or "definiteness of purpose," as Napoleon Hill calls it? As I mentioned before, it is done by making the achievement of your dreams, goals, and desires a *must*. Not thinking that it would be nice to achieve them, or it would be great if you achieved them, but acting as though your life depended on your achieving them. And you know what? It does!

Each time we set a goal for ourselves and then give up in frustration, a little part of us dies in the process. And so we settle for being, doing, and having less than we are capable of. We rationalize to ourselves, "Well, I didn't want to write a book anyway," or "Owning a home is just a pain in the neck." We must resist the urge to sell ourselves short. We must develop the habit of successfully achieving our goals, and that the fact that we do is as it should be. In other words, instead of being surprised when we achieve our goals, we should be surprised when we don't!

Words cannot describe how good you'll feel the day you realize that you have it within you to accomplish a goal that you once thought impossible . . . and all because you made it a "must" instead of a "should"!

▶ **SECRET #18: The key to achieving your goals is that you must make them a "have to," a "gotta have it," and a "can't live without it."**

Anthony Robbins' meteoric rise to success was made possible because he did three things: He raised his standards, he created a vision for himself (which he put down in writing), and he made *succeeding* a must.

Like all great achievers, Robbins determined the price he would have to pay for success, and then he resolved to pay that price. *Succeeding on a massive level, giving his best,* and *helping others achieve success:* Robbins made these the single greatest source of pleasure in his life. Just as importantly, he made not *succeeding,* not *giving his best,* and not *helping others* a source of unbearable pain. With this type of leverage on himself, is it any wonder why he succeeded? In Robbins' mind, *not* succeeding was simply never an option!

"If one advances confidently in the direction of his dreams, and endeavors to live the life which he has imagined, he will meet with success unexpected in common hours."
HENRY DAVID THOREAU

Make the decision *today* to create a powerful and compelling vision for your life. Once you do, commit to achieving that vision regardless of the sacrifices you will have to make along the way. If you do, your reward will be, to paraphrase Thoreau, "A life unimagined in common hours."

How Anthony Robbins would like to be remembered:

"He loved deeply and he touched many."
ANTHONY ROBBINS

Anthony Robbins'
Success Secrets Summary

SECRET #1: Involve your audience in your presentation as quickly as possible.

SECRET #2: Commit to giving your audience more than they have any right to expect.

SECRET #3: Constantly upgrade your material to be sure that you are providing your audience with the very best information available on your topic.

SECRET #4: Don't memorize your speech—become it!

SECRET #5: The Speilberg factor: Connect with your audience on as many different levels as possible.

SECRET #6: Remember that what you're really selling is not words, but feelings and emotions.

SECRET #7: If you want to speak with passion, then you have to be passionate about your topic!

SECRET #8: Use your body to punctuate and support what you are saying verbally.

SECRET #9: Use your tone of voice to convey a variety of emotions throughout your presentation.

SECRET #10: Humor is the lubricant that helps your message go down smoother.

SECRET #11: Make sure you've done everything you can to make your subject as relevant to your audience as possible.

SECRET #12: Give your audience specific examples of the consequences that will happen if they don't immediately take action on your ideas. Follow this up by giving them the terrific benefits they'll receive if they do follow your ideas.

SECRET #13: The most effective way to illustrate your ideas is through the power of stories.

SECRET #14: You don't have to be perfect to speak; it's your passion and energy that your audience will remember.

SECRET #15: Speak as often as possible!

SECRET #16: Your whole life changes the day you make the decision that you will no longer settle for mediocrity.

SECRET #17: Put your dreams, goals, and desires in writing.

SECRET #18: The key to achieving your goals is that you must make them a "have to," a "gotta have it," and a "can't live without it."

CHAPTER TWO

BORN: May 10, 1940
BIRTHPLACE: Detroit, Michigan

D_{r.} W_{ayne} W_. D_{yer}

"I'm honored to be out there onstage. I'm honored that people are willing to show up to come hear me talk. When I go out there in front of thousands of people, I feel so humbled by that, that I feel at the very least I've got to be authentic and enthusiastic."

SHAKESPEARE said, "To thine own self be true, and it must follow as the night the day thou can'st not then be false to any man." One speaker who is truly a remarkable example of what one human being can achieve when they stay true to themselves and their vision is Dr. Wayne W. Dyer.

Dyer's book, *Your Erroneous Zones,* was the number-one selling book in the United States from 1977–78. In fact, it was the top-selling book for the entire 1970–80 decade; no other book on the planet sold more copies during that ten-year period. What's more, it has been translated into twenty-six languages. Since then, he has gone on to write many more best-sellers, including *Pulling Your Own Strings, The Sky's the Limit, Gifts from Eykis, You'll See It When You Believe It,* and *Real Magic.*

His Nightingale-Conant audio-tape albums, which include, *How to Be a No-Limit Person, Secrets of the Universe, Choosing Your Own Greatness, Transformation: You'll See It when You Believe, Real Magic,* and *Freedom Through Higher Awareness,* have sold millions of copies and helped people all around the world improve the quality of their lives.

In 1988, *Time* magazine selected Dyer as one of the "Prominent Figures in American Culture" and asked him to write a letter—which was published in the October 17 issue—stating his views and ideas to those who will inherit the earth in 2088.

His public appearances often draw several thousand people, and his radio and television interviews number over five-thousand. Clearly, Dyer is one of the most successful self-help speakers/writers this country has ever known. How has this psychotherapist, who now resides in Fort Lauderdale, Florida, been able to achieve such phenomenal success? Well, one thing's for certain—and this is what makes his achievements all the more impressive—he began life at the absolute bottom rung of the success ladder.

Developed Independence
at an Early Age

Wayne W. Dyer grew up in a series of foster homes and orphanages until he was ten years old. It was in this sink-or-swim environment that he was forced to develop the characteristics that he would one day write about, such as independence and personal responsibility, simply to survive.

On an issue of *Insight,* the Nightingale-Conant corporation's monthly audio-tape series, Dyer talked about his early experiences:

> I learned self-reliance where it was necessary to learn self-reliance. I learned that you had to rely on yourself, because no one else was going to do it for you. I learned about earning my own way at a very young age and not expecting anybody else to do it for me.

Interestingly, it seems that Dyer didn't have to go through years of pain and frustration before discovering these important success traits. Rather, he seemed to intuitively know that thinking for himself and "marching to the beat of his own drum" was simply the most effective way to live his life. Even when he was still quite young, he honestly couldn't understand the "head trips" that the people around him put themselves through. Feelings of guilt, anger, refusal to forgive others, and other limiting beliefs or "erroneous zones" (as he would come to call them) were simply foreign to his natural way of thinking.

The fact that much of Dyer's wisdom seems to have been innate is not lost on himself, as he revealed to Anthony Robbins during his interview on Robbins' monthly *PowerTalk* series:

> My purpose, whatever it is you want to call it, was about teaching other people that they didn't have to be depressed because of the circumstances of their life. And I seemed to always have known that.

Charisma: A By-Product of Self-Confidence

As a result of Dyer's deep insight at such an early age, he displayed a sense of confidence and maturity beyond his years. This supreme self-confidence made him a natural leader among his friends, and he feels it is what is responsible for much of his enormous charisma, as he revealed to me during our interview:

> I think that there is a quality in a person who really feels very peaceful, very harmonious, very comfortable, and very confident in themselves that gets displayed. I can remember having it when I was playing football on the fields in the east side of Detroit, as a little kid.
>
> When we went to the huddle, somebody had to talk, somebody had to tell people where to go and who to block-out. I was the person who did that and others would listen, because I had the confidence and the willingness to act on that confidence.
>
> I think that same quality of being in the huddle, being the person who was willing to say, 'You go down to the Plymouth and turn right, and you block out the guy over there by the Ford, and I'll throw the ball over the middle,' and doing it with a sense of confidence, a sense of love, is what I guess can define charisma.

Wayne's story about being the one who took charge during his boyhood football games gives us some insight into how we can become more charismatic as speakers. Obviously, when you are standing in front of a group, the more charisma you project, the more effective you will be in winning your audience over to your way of thinking.

As Dyer makes clear, being confident is part of the charisma equation; however, it's only half of it. The other half is love. It's the *combination* of presenting your thoughts, beliefs, and ideas in a confident *and* loving manner that will increase your personal charisma. This means speaking with boldness in your voice and love in your heart. It means looking into the eyes of your audience with both confidence *and* compassion. And it's something that can't be faked.

▶ **SECRET #1: You can greatly increase your charisma by presenting your ideas in both a confident and loving manner.**

Dyer believes that true charisma is not something to be turned on and off, but is actually a way of *being:*

> This isn't anything that just has to do with speaking. This has to do with your whole way of living. They would say about Christ that when he would come into a village, that his presence would change the whole consciousness of the village. And they said this of Buddha. They say this of Mother Teresa; this little four-foot, ten-inch, woman who weighs eighty or ninety pounds can walk into a room and suddenly her presence affects others around her.

By learning to believe in yourself and your ideas, and by communicating those ideas in a confident and loving manner, you can actually increase your personal presence (charisma) and, in so doing, become a more effective communicator not just on the platform, but in all areas of your life.

A Childhood Vision

Like Anthony Robbins, Dyer, at a very early age, envisioned himself sharing his ideas with large numbers of people. During the 1950s, while he was growing up, he would watch Steve Allen hosting *The Tonight Show,* and in his mind he would imagine himself being a guest on the show. Curiously, the pictures he had of himself being interviewed by Mr. Allen were not of a thirteen-year-old (the age he actually was), but were of an adult. He would see himself on television, all grown up, talking with Mr. Allen about his beliefs, the way he looked at the world and his other ideas, which he knew could help others. Of course, when he would tell his brothers and friends that someday he was going to be on *The Tonight Show*, they simply dismissed it as the overzealous imaginings of a kid who, in their eyes, was already "a bit out there" anyway. Wayne says that his internal pictures were never damaged by the attitudes of others. This is quite a feat; often children's dreams are unwittingly squashed by the people around them. Parents and teachers tend to foist their own limiting beliefs on the minds of the young and impressionable. And because children are raised to think that adults know more about life than they do, they come to believe that if mom or dad or a teacher says something can't be done, or that it's foolish, then that's the way it is. This results in their little dreams being chopped down before they even have a chance to take root.

Yet, Wayne W. Dyer was not like every other kid. He understood at a very early age that if he was going to be successful in life, he would have to trust in his own ideas and decisionmaking ability. By looking internally for support, rather than externally, this inquisitive young boy grew to believe in himself more and more with each passing day.

▶ **SECRET #2: Believing in your own ideas, abilities, and decision-making ability is the first step to achieving success in life.**

Enlists in U.S. Navy Right out of High School (and Quickly Discovers His Number One Core Value Is Personal Freedom!)

Like many teenagers during the late 1950s, Dyer enlisted in the military right out of high school. Unfortunately for him, it was during this time—while he was stationed on the South Pacific island of Guam as a cryptographer—that he discovered just how much he valued his own individual freedom. An example of how far he was willing to go to avoid having to answer to others is illustrated by his Houdini-like ability to vanish any time there was an inspection. It seems that the first time he had to go through one, it sickened him to the point of nausea. He just couldn't stomach the idea of a young officer scrutinizing everything from his shave to his boots, and everything in between.

After that first inspection, Dyer made sure that he was always assigned to a task, *any* task, so that he wouldn't be around whenever an inspection came up. And you know what? He succeeded; for the next four years he was never inspected again—not once! The ability to find ways to live his life on his own terms, even in a highly regimented institution like the military, shows just how creative Dyer can be when he feels his personal freedom is being restricted.

Later on, we will see how Dyer once again does things his way by circumventing the major publishing houses and bringing his first book, *Your Erroneous Zones,* directly to the public.

The First Member of His Family to Attend College

After he got out of the Navy, Dyer wanted very much to go to college. Unfortunately, one major hurdle stood in the way: lack of money. While many people would use this as an excuse to give up, not Dyer. To him obstacles were seen as minor detours, not stop signs. And so he made up his mind that he would simply save up the necessary funds for college, even if it meant living like a pauper for over a year. Says Dyer:

> I knew that I did not have the necessary funds [to attend college], so for eighteen months I managed to live on ten percent of my salary and to save the remaining ninety percent. That's right. I saved ninety percent of my salary for a year and a half, and I had it all put into a bank account for the purpose of paying my tuition for the full four years of school.

> No one in my family had ever attended college, but I focused on attending Wayne State University in Detroit. No one in my family had ever accumulated the money necessary for school, but I concentrated all of my thoughts on what I had, which was a bank account that was growing steadily every

two weeks. I expanded what I thought about, and what I thought about was what I had, rather that what I did not have, or what the history of my family had been.

By choosing to focus on a meaningful goal and practicing self-discipline, Dyer was able to make his dream of going to college a reality. The key was that he concentrated on what he had and what he wanted, not on what he lacked or didn't want. He demonstrated perfectly the power that Napolean Hill called "definiteness of purpose," that what the mind can conceive and believe, it *can* achieve!

▶ **SECRET #3: That which you think about expands. Therefore, develop the habit of always focusing on what you want, not on what you don't want.**

Two Life-Changing Events

It was years later, in 1974, while Dyer was a professor at St. John's University in New York, that two events took place that had a profound impact on him. The first had to do with his father, whom he had never met. Dyer had been searching for years for the man who had abandoned him, his two brothers, and his mother when he was just a baby. Through a series of what can only be described as bizarre and mystical events, he discovered where the man who had haunted him all his life was buried.

As he stood there that day in Biloxi, Mississippi, over the grave of Melvin Lyle Dyer, Wayne sobbed uncontrollably for over two hours. During that time, he was able to tell his father things he had been carrying around inside of him all his life. He was finally able to ask the questions that every little boy or girl who has been abandoned by his or her parents feels compelled to ask. Finally, at the end of this heart-wrenching ordeal, he did something he had not been able to do for thirty-four years: He forgave his father.

This emotional catharsis so freed him that it set the stage for the second major event in his life: the writing and subsequent publication of his first book, *Your Erroneous Zones* (1977, T. Y. Crowell Company). But first, Wayne had some tough decisions to make.

Getting His Life "on Purpose"

Though he loved teaching, something happened inside of Wayne that day at his father's grave. He knew it was time to shift gears and take his life in an entirely new direction. After struggling for almost a year with the idea of giving up the security of his bi-monthly paycheck from the university, he finally decided the time had come to get his life "on purpose." It was time to start speaking and writing full-time. While many of us dream of pursuing a new career or life path, far too often we quickly talk ourselves out of it. We say things to ourselves like, "I don't have what it takes," or "I'd just fail anyway," or "I'm not being realistic." We tell ourselves that we're too old, too young, too fat, too thin, too inexperienced, or too whatever to achieve our dreams.

Tragically and needlessly, these excuses, which are born out of fear, prevent many of us from finding the true happiness and inner peace that can only be found by pursuing our passion. There comes a time when we must resolutely make up our mind that nothing is going to detour us from going after our dreams. For Wayne Dyer, that time had come. While the decision to walk away from the security and comfort of a steady paycheck and a prestigious job was not an easy one, Dyer, like all people who are eventually successful, was willing to take *whatever* risks were necessary to pursue his life's purpose.

▶ **SECRET #4: True inner peace will always elude you until you get your life "on purpose.**

Clearly, the price we pay for not pursuing our passion is huge. We must turn "someday I'll" into "I'm doing it, I'm doing it!" Does this mean that going after that which is most meaningful to us is easy or without obstacles and setbacks? No. As the saying goes, "every rose has its thorns." But the feelings of satisfaction and aliveness, as well as the true sense of joy you experience, makes you realize that whatever the price, it's more than worth it for the privilege of staying true to your inner-most being.

Trusting the Vision

Once again, like when he was a teenager, Dyer visualized himself addressing large numbers of people. The only difference was, this time, he had the power to take action and turn his "mental pictures" into a reality. Here's how he did it (from his book, *You'll See It when You Believe It*):

> I had wonderful pictures in my mind's eye. I saw myself talking to everyone in America about the ideas I had just finished writing about in *Your Erroneous Zones*. I could see in my mind that the book was going to be very successful.

The fact that Dyer could *see in his mind* that the book was going to be successful, before he ever set out on the road, played a major role in his eventual success.

▶ **SECRET #5: When pursuing a goal, the most important thing is to continually hold in your mind the picture of yourself successfully achieving that goal.**

By actually seeing yourself succeeding in your mind's eye, you tell your mind exactly what you want. The idea is to play the whole thing out, just like you're watching a movie, with as much clarity and detail as possible. Repeated often enough, your brain will get the message that "this is the way it's *supposed* to be," and it will begin to move you in that direction. As Dyer discovered, this process can be both peaceful and exhilarating:

> The morning came when the picture was very clear in my mind. I saw myself all alone in my venture, without any guarantees, and yet as peaceful as I had ever been in my

lifetime. I knew that this was the day, that within a few hours I would officially be out on my own, no longer able to rely on a paycheck.

When I arrived on campus, I went immediately to the dean's office. [There I] announced to the dean that I was resigning, effective within a few weeks at the end of the current semester.

Our conversation was brief. I said I wanted to go out and do something that I genuinely believed in. She asked me to reconsider and discuss it with my family and some of my colleagues, but I told her that it was already accomplished in my mind—my thoughts—and that I was now simply going through the formality of making it real in the physical world as well.

She pointed out all of the risks, how unlikely it was that I would be able to make a living writing and speaking, and that jobs such as the one I held were exceedingly difficult to come by in the 1970s because of the glut of professors and very few openings in the academic world.

Resistance from Others—You Can Count On It

As Dyer discovered, when you make the decision to go after your dreams, you can count on getting resistance from certain people in your life. Why does your decision to go after your dreams make others around you uncomfortable? Because it reminds them that they have given up on their own dreams, and since they're a member of the "I've given up on my dreams" club, they want you to stay in the club, too (remember the old saying, "misery loves company"?). But, of course, you will have no part of this. You are going forward with your dreams, goals, and desires. And those people who *will* support you are those who are pursuing their own dreams and who have gone through the same feelings and emotions that you are now experiencing. Those are the types of people you should seek out as you begin the most exciting journey of your life: pursuing your purpose. While one assumes that Dyer's dean meant well, she, like so many people who come from fear and limitation and "are only being realistic," attempted to dissuade this eagle from taking off and soaring. Once again though, as has been the pattern throughout his life, Wayne listened to his own inner guide:

> I told her I was aware of the risk, and that was one of the big reasons why I was taking this turn in my life. I was headed down the path that Robert Frost called "The Road Less Traveled:"
>
> > Two roads diverged in a yellow wood, and . . .
> > I took the one less traveled by,
> > And that has made all the difference.
>
> When I left the dean's office, I walked to my own with an inner glow. I was free, free to advance confidently in the direction of my dreams.

Pursuing His Dream

When Dyer made the decision to go after his dreams, he experienced a profound sense of inner peace and tranquillity that comes whenever we follow our heart. Once Wayne became committed to his goal, he tapped into a power in the universe that's available to all of us when we fully commit to our dreams. The German philosopher, Goethe, wrote magnificently about this power:

> Until one is committed, there is hesitancy, the chance to draw back, always ineffective, concerning all acts of initiative (and creation). There is one elementary truth, the ignorance of which kills countless ideas and splendid plans: that the moment one definitely commits oneself, the providence moves, too.
>
> All sorts of things occur to help one that would never otherwise have occurred. A whole stream of events issues from the decision, raising in one's favor all manner of unforseen incidents and meetings and material assistance which no man could have dreamed would have come his way. Whatever you can do, or dream you can, begin it. Boldness has genius, power and magic in it. Begin it now.

What Goethe is saying is that, until you actually make the mental decision to *fully* commit to your dreams, there will always be hesitancy on your part. And this hesitancy could be the *very* thing that keeps you from achieving your goals! But once you say, "I don't care what it takes, I am committed to making my goal a reality, no matter what," doors open and events seem to go your way that simply cannot be explained. It's as if there's an energy that gets released by you when you are committed to something, an energy that let's the universe know you are serious.

Until this energy (commitment) is put forth, achieving your goals can often feel like a major struggle. It's ironic; the very thing you are most afraid to do—commit one hundred percent to your goal—is the very thing that has the power to take it from being a long shot and turn it into a virtual certainty. All it takes from you is total belief in yourself that you can do it, one hundred percent commitment, and a little faith.

With the vision of himself as a full-time speaker and writer still dancing in his head, Dyer begins the most exciting journey of his life: turning those pictures into a reality:

> I cleaned out my desk, made some announcements to my students and doctoral advisees, and drove home along the expressway knowing that I was taking the biggest step of my lifetime. Here I was, completely unknown to the media, leaving my secure position to go out and tell the world about the ideas in my new book. Yet, I was ecstatic, for I had seen all of it in my mind before experiencing it in the world of form.

▶ **SECRET #6: The clearer you see a goal in your mind, the easier it is to know what action you need to take to achieve that goal.**

You read earlier how Dyer, in need of enough money to go to college, used his mind to focus on what he wanted, rather than on what he didn't want. Again, this seems to be a skill that he has possessed his entire life:

> Even as a very young boy, I would use my mind to center on what I wanted, rather than on what other people had or what was missing in my life. It always worked for me and continues to do so today.

Let's get back to the story in which Dyer had made the decision to leave the university and pursue his powerful vision of promoting *Your Erroneous Zones* around the country:

> Every obstacle that came my way became an opportunity. I was told that there were a minimal number of copies of my book in print, and that even if I did go out and talk to people in the media, it would do no good because most bookstores would not have my book in stock. So I decided to buy up a large quantity of books and take them out to the people myself. I literally became my own distributor.

Instead of getting discouraged, Dyer simply took matters into his own hands. The idea of packing up his car with books and going on the road to do interviews in little towns across the country was not scary or risky to Dyer. Rather, it was simply what needed to be done to fulfill his vision.

▶ **SECRET #7: In order to achieve your vision you must be self-reliant; if you cannot find the circumstances that you need, then you must go out and create them.**

> I left my books on consignment with store owners across America in 1976, and I had the great fortune to have some wonderful people come into my life at just the right time. One such person, Donna Gould, became such an ardent believer after reading my book that she worked on her own to help me get bookings all across the country. Donna knew I was paying most of my own expenses, and she contributed many, many hours of her time and tons of her energy to help me. My publisher became more of a believer as he saw the results of my excitement about this project. Before long I was out in my own car, traveling from small city to smaller city appearing on talk shows and doing local newspaper interviews.
>
> First I went up and down the East Coast, then to the Midwest, and ultimately on a long cross-country tour with my wife and daughter, paying my own expenses, staying in cheap motels, and, most importantly, enjoying every single minute

of this new adventure. I seldom thought about making money. I had published three successful textbooks and many professional articles without financial profit; consequently, I was not motivated now by a desire to make a fortune. I was simply doing something that I loved to do and answering to no one along the way. Since I was using my own savings to finance this trip and to purchase the books, I had total control over every aspect of this promotion.

These last two sentences give us some more insight into Dyer's core values. First, as we have seen time and time again, it's vitally important to him that he do what he loves. Secondly, that he "answer to no one" (as his Navy inspection story has already made clear), and thirdly, that he "have total control." While these values aren't for everybody, they are mandatory for those individuals who are not afraid of risk, and who relish the challenge of turning their vision into a reality.

Obstacles: You Can Count On 'Em

When you have a vision that you are truly committed to, you can count on obstacles coming up. In fact, everybody who has ever achieved anything worthwhile has had to overcome obstacles. So, the question is not *will* you encounter obstacles along the path to creating your vision—you will. Rather, the question is *how* will you choose to deal with them when they come up?

The difference between those who achieve their goals versus those who don't is that the latter allows the obstacles to immobilize them while the former do not. Successful people face many of the same obstacles as do unsuccessful people; the only difference is that the successful ones don't give up. Remember, no one cares how many times Hank Aaron struck out; what we remember is that he hit more home runs than anyone else in the history of baseball. Similarly, how many times you "strike out" on the way to achieving your goals in life is not what counts. What's important is that you persevere *until* you successfully achieve your goal. Again, this may mean making adjustments to your game plan, but it *never* means abandoning your game plan.

Persistence

Dyer has shown us the way: If one door is closed to you, you simply try another door. And if that one is closed, you try another. And if that one is closed you try still another. The point is, you don't give up! This is critical. You simply keep on trying different approaches until you find one that works. Thus, obstacles are merely used for feedback: "Okay, this way isn't going to work. Fine, now that I know that, I'll try it another way." This is the kind of thinking that will get you to where you want to go in life.

▶ **SECRET #8: When it comes to pursuing your life's purpose, giving up is not an option.**

Consistent and Committed Action Pays Off

Not surprisingly, Wayne's consistent and committed action toward getting the word out about his book was beginning to pay off:

> As the months rolled by, my interview schedule increased to as many as fifteen a day. Bookstores in cities that I had visited began to reorder from the publisher. At the start, I had been able to get bookings only in the smaller cities, but now the media in larger cities were beginning to book me on their shows.
>
> I had been told by an "expert" in publicity and publishing that the only way to talk to everyone in America in the 1970s was on network television, but that this option was pretty much closed to me because I did not have a national reputation. He suggested I should be happy if I sold a few thousand books in the local New York area, had a couple of printings, and got a publication credit toward a promotion at the university. This was the view of many others who knew the publishing industry inside out. They seemed to me to be unaware of the great truth of Victor Hugo: "Nothing is more powerful than an idea whose time has come."

Again, notice Dyer's confidence in himself and his vision. While others might have been influenced by the so called "experts" and considered giving up, Dyer did not. True, he had no "hard evidence" to support his beliefs, but he did have one powerful element in his favor: a belief in himself and his vision that would not be denied.

▶ **SECRET #9: If you believe in your ideas even when there is no evidence to support them, soon there will be!**

This is the key. You must believe in your ideas even when there is no evidence to support your belief. If you do this, eventually the evidence will begin to manifest itself. As the title of one of Dyer's own books states: "You'll see it when you believe it." The bottom line (and this is what made all the difference) was that Wayne's vision of his book catching on was bigger than the "experts'" limited vision of the book having a "couple of printings." Says Dyer:

> What is an idea but a thought? The experts had their own ideas, and they acted on them. I, too, had my idea. I agreed that the easiest way to talk with everyone in America was through the network media, but I believed it was not the only way. I could reach everyone in America if I was willing to take the time, spend the energy, and absorb the risks that go with such an approach. I was willing and very eager as well. I would use every barrier as an opportunity to see if I could get past it. And it worked every single time. As much as I was making things happen through my thoughts, I was also letting things happen by not fighting anyone or anything, by doing it all with good cheer and love. It was great fun, every single day, every interview, every new city, every new friend. All very exciting.

Notice Dyer's excitement about his vision. Like all individuals who eventually achieve success in life, he went about the process of turning his dream into a reality with tremendous zeal and enthusiasm.

▶ **SECRET #10: Your upbeat and enthusiastic attitude toward your vision not only helps keep you motivated, it gets others excited about your dream as well.**

Dyer Accomplishes What the Critics Said Couldn't Be Done: *Erroneous Zones* Lands on the *New York Times* Bestseller List

Through persistence, hard work, flexibility, a steadfast commitment to his beliefs, and a sense of adventure and joyousness throughout the process, the day arrived when Dyer's vision became a reality:

> The months became a year, and my family and I were still on the road. Somehow the financial stuff took care of itself, and then one day, while I was appearing on radio station KMOX in St. Louis, I received a call from Arthur Pine, my friend and agent, who informed me that my book would appear on the *New York Times* national bestseller list the following week, debuting at position number eight. I had accomplished what almost everyone said was impossible. Without one national television or radio appearance, I had been able to go to the people of this country and have enough of those people buy my book to put it on the national best-seller list. I was in awe and in shock.

The *Tonight Show* Calls

Dyer's story could have ended here, with his book making it to the top of the bestseller list (where it would stay for nearly two years), and it would have been a great conclusion to his amazing adventure. However, the story does not end there. Incredibly, his boyhood vision of appearing on *The Tonight Show* with Steve Allen became a reality!

It all started when he began getting calls from talk shows that had originally turned him down. One of these calls came from *The Tonight Show*—a member of *The Tonight Show* staff had been handed a copy of *Your Erroneous Zones* at a party. They invited Dyer to NBC studios for a preshow interview.

A week later he found himself sitting in the office of Howard Papush, sharing with *The Tonight Show* executive his positive life philosophy, in which he believed so ardently.

Having done hundreds of interviews by now, Dyer had discovered that the very best thing for him to do was simply be himself. His own natural way of speaking and being had a warmth and intelligence to it that others found engaging. When you combine these two qualities with his charming sense of humor, and articulate, yet down-to-earth speaking style, Dyer made for a great interview.

The night of his first *Tonight Show* appearance, comedian Shecky Greene was the guest host. Before the start of the show, Wayne decided to call his wife. As he was telling her how elated he was, he looked up and saw a man using the phone next to him. Suddenly, his heart stopped. It was none other than the man he had seen in his mind interviewing him on *The Tonight Show* when he was a kid—Steve Allen! It turned out that Allen was the first guest scheduled for that night's show. An amazing coincidence?

By Dyer's own admission, the fifteen minutes he spent on national TV telling the country about his ideas were terrific. However, just before stepping on the plane to fly back to the east coast he got a phone call from Papush. He regretfully informed Wayne that the show he had just been on was being preempted by the Republican National Convention. Ironically, it was the first time in years that *The Tonight Show* had been bumped.

As he flew home that night, Dyer wondered if the show would ever air. However, the next day Papush called again and asked him back on the show, only this time it would be with the man himself, Johnny Carson. Excitedly, Dyer hopped on a plane the very next day and flew back to Los Angeles to tape that evening's show. Unfortunately, because all the previous segments had run long, he ended up getting only six minutes with Johnny.

Yet, once again the gods were smiling on Dyer, as Carson asked him on the air to come back for the Friday night show, just two nights away. Dyer stayed over the two days and taped his third tonight show appearance in less than a week!

What's more, a week from the following Monday night the preempted show aired. So, the guy who one year earlier couldn't get on a single major talk show to save his life, suddenly found himself making three appearances on the biggest talk show of them all.

Dyer felt that this just affirmed what Thoreau had meant when he said, "If one advances confidently in the direction of his dreams, and endeavors to live the life which he had imagined, he will meet with a success unexpected in common hours." Dyer writes in *You'll See It when You Believe It:*

> *Your Erroneous Zones* was eventually published in twenty-six languages around the world. Other books have followed, as have tapes, articles, international travel for professional speaking engagements, and an opportunity for me to make a difference in the lives of millions and millions of people. I received more money in the first year I was out on my own without the security of a regular paycheck than I had in the entire thirty-six years of my life before then.

Luck or Preparation?

Believe it or not, some people have called Dyer's phenomenal success *luck.* They said he just "happened" to come along with the right book at the right time. As you can see, luck had very little to do with Dyer's success—unless you use the following definition: Luck is when preparation meets opportunity. Then one could say that Dyer had been *preparing* all his life, starting with the very first time when he, as a teenager, visualized himself being interviewed by Steve Allen, to his writing of *Your Erroneous Zones.* Then, when the *opportunity* arose—i.e., when *The Tonight Show* called and when bookstores wanted his book—he was ready. It goes without saying that, if he hadn't put in the necessary preparation beforehand, *The Tonight Show* would have never called and the world would have never heard of *Your Erroneous Zones* or Wayne W. Dyer. Luck? No. Hard work, persistence, believing in one's dreams, willingness to take risks, caring about others, and having a genuine desire to make a difference in the world—*yes!*

▶ **SECRET #11: It's amazing how "lucky" you can get when you work hard, persist, believe in your dreams, are willing to take risks, care about others, and genuinely desire to make a difference in the world."**

Scared to Death of Public Speaking As a Teenager

If you happen to be one of the many people on this planet who rank public speaking over death as your greatest fear, take heart. Dyer confesses that when he was a teenager, having to get up in front of his classmates to give a book report nearly caused him to have a coronary thrombosis (heart attack):

> My greatest fears that I can remember as a young boy were having to get up in front of the class and do oral book reports. I can remember lying in bed at night and literally breaking out into a cold sweat. I would hope that my teacher, whom I liked very much, would have a mild case of something very severe so she wouldn't show up that day and call on me to get up there and give that talk in front of the class. So it was this enormous fear that I had about standing in front of audiences as a high school kid.
>
> And yet, I always realized afterward that it was such great joy to be up there doing it. I would be relieved that I no longer had to live with that anxiety until the next horrible report came along, yet, while I was doing it, it was really a great, wonderful, powerful feeling. I decided to take a speech course in high school because I've always been the kind of person who, if something was overwhelming to me, if I had difficulty with it, preferred to face it rather than run away from it.

Rather than let his fear of public speaking overwhelm him, Dyer went after it head-on by taking a speech course. Eventually, he overcame his fear of speaking by simply getting up and doing it over and over until the fear gradually went away and was replaced by confidence. In order to get where you want to go in life, you must face your fears head-on, and do whatever is necessary to overcome them. Allowing *anything* to keep you from making a difference in the world is simply unacceptable when you're truly committed to your vision.

▶   **SECRET #12: The way you conquer a fear is by facing it head on.**

As it turned out, Dyer's speech teacher was very supportive:

The teacher of this speech course told me that I was the best student she had ever had. My speeches were always extemporaneous; there were never a lot of notes; there was not a lot of organization, but they were always very authentic and filled with humor. It was at that point I realized that this was something that I was going to do.

When I got into the Navy after high school, I began to teach some courses in philosophy. I couldn't wait to get up in front of those classes, which kept getting larger and larger. I decided at that point that I wanted to go into teaching; a teacher is really a public speaker. I became a school teacher and taught at all levels. I taught from elementary to the university level for many years.

"If you say that someone is a good teacher, it's usually because they're a good speaker."
WAYNE W. DYER

I was teaching at St. John's University in New York during the 1970s, and my classes were always overly full. I was very popular as a professor because I was entertaining and a good speaker. If you say that someone is a good teacher it's usually because they're a good speaker. And people like to take classes from people who are good speakers, especially if you're going to be sitting there for two-and-a-half hours.

From University Professor to Public Speaker

I would have fifty people enrolled in my class, but sometimes two hundred people would show up. I would have a subject that I was teaching, a curriculum, but I would just go wild with it. I would involve the class with it and do all kinds of antics and dress in a funny way and get up on top of desks. I was taping all of my talks and people were saying, "These are so good. You should do this other than through the university."

So I put an ad in a little local newspaper on Long Island, *The Port Washington News*. It was advertised as a course in human development, a four-week course, and I was charging something like five dollars for it. About thirty-five people paid to take the course. When the four weeks were up I said to the students, "Wow, the four weeks are up and we've hardly even covered the topic. Would you like to continue for another four weeks?" And this time about 150 people showed up; that was in the spring.

When the fall came, they said, "Oh, you've got to do that course again." We decided to rent the high school auditorium this time and we had twelve hundred people show up! We did this every Monday night for eight weeks. I think we were charging twenty dollars a person by then. So, here I was, making more money speaking on a Monday night than I was making as a professor at a university the other six days of the week!

In fact, the first time I got paid one hundred dollars to give a speech, I thought the world was going crazy. . . . I mean, something was really wrong! I spoke for three hours; and I'm not talking about fifty years ago, I'm talking about in the seventies.

When *Erroneous Zones* came out and I began getting speaking engagements through my agent in New York, Artie Pine, I couldn't believe that somebody would pay me that amount of money for one speech! Then it just mushroomed from there. Now I get so many requests that I have to turn most of them down.

I hope reading about how Dyer got started in public speaking is as motivating to you as it is to me. The fact that he "thought the world was going crazy" the first time he was paid $100 for a speech is a funny thought when you consider that today he makes well over $10,000 per appearance!

Having Butterflies Before You Speak Is Normal

Many speakers are often overcome with feelings of fear before they go out to give a presentation. These are often referred to as butterflies, and, as the saying goes, the secret is to "get them to fly in formation." If this is something you experience before you speak, you're in good company. Dyer admits that he, too, puts himself through the wringer before getting up to speak:

> The worst thing is the stuff I put myself through before I give a speech. I always say to my wife the day I have to speak, "I don't know why I keep putting myself through this." I don't need any more fame, I don't need to sell any more books, I don't need any more money. Yet, I keep accepting the speaking engagements and I keep traveling. Then, after I've given the speech, and it's all over, I call my wife—I always call her before and after every speech—and I say to her, "Now I know why I do these things." And she says, "Okay, go ahead, tell me."
>
> There's this paradoxical thing to speaking. As Katharine Hepburn said about this internal turmoil we call *butterflies:* "When you lose it, you might as well never go onstage again." When I receive a standing ovation after a speech, then go on to sign books and talk to people for an hour and a half afterward, I go back to my hotel and know exactly why I did it.

As Wayne discusses in both his live presentations and his book, *Real Magic,* meditation plays a major role in his life. Before each speech he meditates for an hour about his purpose. This is his way of centering himself, quieting the turmoil, and getting clear on his purpose for speaking.

► **SECRET #13: Meditating on your purpose before you speak helps calm and focus your mind, thereby causing any butterflies you may be feeling to "fly in formation."**

The next time you feel the butterflies flying around in your stomach before you're about to give a presentation, close your eyes, quiet your mind, and gently ask yourself: "What's my purpose?" It's amazing how calm you can become when you "get off of yourself" and focus on your purpose. (Since your mind cannot focus on two things at once, start it thinking about your purpose so it can no longer focus on being nervous!)

Lack of Enthusiasm and Authenticity Makes for a Boring Speaker

While Dyer was a college student, he says that he was subjected to one dry and boring lecture after another. However, he knew that whether the subject was math, English, or geology, it didn't need to be this way. As he was sitting in his classes, he found himself analyzing what the professors where doing, or more accurately, what they were not doing. It didn't take him long to realize that they simply had no enthusiasm for their subject matter and they weren't being authentic. They were delivering their material as if they were reading from a script. As a result, Dyer made the decision to never use notes when he speaks, and to always speak from his heart and with enthusiasm.

"I speak to an audience the same way I would speak to somebody in the living room of my home. From my heart, with integrity, and with enthusiasm!"
WAYNE W. DYER

Dyer's Two Rules for
Public Speaking

Not surprisingly, Dyer's experience in college helped shape his feelings about what it takes to be an effective speaker:

> My first rule for speaking is to be authentic. I have to walk the talk. What I'm talking about onstage, I am working on and living in my own life. And if I'm not doing it at the level I would like to, I'm willing to share that. If I make a mistake in my life, I'm willing to share that and I'm willing to poke fun at myself. And I'm willing to come from my heart. There have been times when I've cried onstage. There are times when I make myself laugh onstage. It's being authentic.

► **SECRET #14: Being real and authentic in front of an audience requires that you speak from your heart and not your head.**

> I'm able to do this because I create the speech in my mind before I go onstage. In other words, I meditate on it. I see the whole thing working. I see every little detail, from my arriving, to where I go in, what the room looks like, how the people are going to react to my speech, what I'm going to say when I walk out there, how I'm going to dress, how the lights are going to be. I play the whole thing out in my mind, in the meditation, hours before I speak. I get very, very peaceful with that. It's a very comfortable, joyful, kind of blissful experience.

► **SECRET #15: The more vividly and repeatedly you see yourself successfully giving your presentation in your mind, the easier and smoother it will go when you actually give it.**

> I don't use a lectern and I don't get wired; I just use a hand mike. onstage I have a stool, a piece of chalk, and a blackboard. And when I want to sit, sometimes I sit for forty-five minutes while I'm talking. I've created all this in my mind beforehand, so I always walk out onstage in a blissful state, because meditation gives you that.

Watches Self Give Speech

[While I'm onstage] I watch myself give my speech. It's like leaving your body. My body is out there and it's giving a talk, but who I am, the invisible part of me, is in back of my body watching me give the speech, watching the audience react to my speech.

Uses Mental "Post-It" Notes

My whole way of delivering is to tell little anecdotes and stories and so on. I also have little flags that go up . . . these mental flags. And when I get to talking, people think, "Oh boy, he's gotten off the point, he's lost," but it never happens. I will circle all around it and eventually I will get back to my point.

Puts Together "Pieces of Puzzle" Right Before the Audience's Eyes

A publisher down in Australia, Margaret Gee, who heard me speak last year, said, "The best way I can describe your speech is: Somebody walking out onstage with five thousand pieces of a puzzle and throwing them out on the stage. Then you spend the next three hours building the perfect picture out of those pieces."

The other thing that I do, in addition to being authentic and meditating my way through it in advance, is to be enthusiastic! The word "enthusiasm" translates to "the God within." If you have that . . . if you are truly enthusiastic about what you are thinking about, and not acting out a role, not playing "rent-a-[speaker]," not being an actor, not delivering a script . . . If you are enthusiastically, excitedly delivering your talk, it will come across.

▶ **SECRET #16: You must be enthusiastic about your topic if you hope to get others excited about it.**

You see, I'm honored to be out there onstage, I'm honored that people are willing to show up to come hear me talk. When I go out there in front of thousands of people, I feel so humbled by that, that I feel at the very least I've got to be authentic and enthusiastic!

In addition to speaking with authenticity and enthusiasm, Dyer's advice to neophyte speakers is to not give somebody else's speech, but to give your own. Remember, audiences want to hear what *you* have to say about the topic, not what somebody else said.

▶ **SECRET #17: Always give your own speech; never give somebody else's.**

The Importance of Speaking for Yourself

While Dyer's purpose is to help make a difference in other people's lives, he is clear that the only person he needs to please when speaking is himself:

I never speak for my audiences; I really do it for myself. I don't focus on whether I'm doing the right thing for them and are they going to like me. I play it all out in terms of "What am I here for?" "What is my life about?" "What am I to teach?" And I do the same thing when I write. I don't worry about whether people buy my books or whether they go on best-seller lists or things like that.

▶ **SECRET #18: While it is important to focus on meeting your audience's needs, ultimately, you must stay true to yourself.**

No Role Models

One might assume that because Dyer grew up in an orphanage, he would have a lot of role models or heroes. Surprisingly, he did not.

While he was in college, he greatly admired Clarence Darrow and his courtroom summaries, and thought that Abraham Maslow was a great man, but he never really saw them as heroes. Likewise, when he got into public speaking, he found Ram-Dass to have a great speaking style, but he didn't view him as a role model. No, for Wayne Dyer, believing in himself and his vision is all the inspiration he needs:

> I haven't modeled myself after anyone. People will write me an analysis of my speaking and all of the things that you're supposed to do when you speak, and I never heard any of that. But I seem to do it all. I didn't learn it from anyone. It's just part of my purpose, it's what I showed up here to do. No, there really isn't anybody out there that I think of as a role model.

It is human nature to admire others who have achieved a great deal of success in a particular field. Using them as a role model can serve as a great source of inspiration and information. However, ultimately, our success comes down to one thing: how much we believe in ourselves.

Dyer's Philosophy on Wealth

Hoping to gain further insight into the mind of this millionaire philosopher, I asked Dyer to explain his philosophy for achieving success in life:

> Living "on purpose" is what my philosophy is; I have gotten my life "on purpose." And once you discover your purpose, then you get off of outcomes, you get off of "what's in it for me," and "how much am I going to accumulate?" You get off of all of that. And every day and every action that you do in your life is on that purpose.
>
> Life is about making a difference in the world. We show up, we have this parenthesis in eternity that we call "our life," and the measure of that is not what we accumulate or what

we get for ourselves, it's in what we give. I think everybody in the world wants to make a difference. They want to know that their presence on this planet made a difference.

For me, it's about giving, and it's about loving, and it's about serving, and it's what we're here for, to learn that lesson. I know that. And when you get there the irony is that all the stuff that you chased before, when you were on outcome, starts showing up in your life in amounts so big you can't even comprehend it. And the funny thing is, you don't even want it anymore.

Dyer's thoughts on wealth, which are gleaned from personal experience, are as wise as they are inescapable:

▶ **SECRET #19: When you stop focusing on money, and you get your life "on purpose," the money will come.**

Dyer's Message Has Evolved As He Has

It was when he was in his mid-thirties that Dyer began making major changes in his eating and exercising habits. One of these changes included running eight miles a day; and it's something he continues to do to this day. (Amazingly, he has run eight miles a day, without missing a single day, for over twenty years!) In addition, he gave up cigarettes, alcohol, caffeine, and fatty foods—cleaning out his entire system. The results were dramatic; he immediately began to experience a sense of vitality and well-being that he had never experienced before. His whole body and mind felt revitalized and rejuvenated, and were now operating at a whole new level.

His thoughts took on a tremendous sense of clarity and focus. For the first time in his life he began to experience his spirituality at a deep and profound level. This spiritual transformation that Dyer was going through began to express itself in both his speaking and writing. How could it not? After all, his speaking and writing had always been a reflection of wherever he was at in life:

My message has really evolved over the years. My speaking is nothing more than a reflection of where I am in my life at any given time. I speak without notes. Before I speak I always meditate and I visualize the whole thing in my mind. I don't think of myself as a person who gives speeches. I think of myself as a person who gets up in front of a public audience who wants to hear me. I share from my heart where I am, what I'm doing and what I've learned, and how you can apply these principles.

Fifteen years ago if you would have asked me [what my message is] I would have said it's about managing your emotions and knowing that you are the product of whatever thoughts that you have. That you can choose to be the kind of person you want to be.

If you would have asked me twelve years ago, I would have probably said my message is about not being a victim and not letting other people manipulate you. And if you'd have asked me eight years ago, I would have said it was about self-actualization and living at the highest level that a human being can live at. And that there's something much grander then just being "normal" and coping in life. That there's a level of living called "self-actualization" that's much, much higher.

If you'd have asked me four years ago I probably would have talked about the process of enlightenment. And today my message is about transformation, about the power of the spiritual side of you, the divine side of who you are as a human being.

"We are not human beings who are having spiritual experiences, but . . . spiritual beings having human experiences."
WAYNE W. DYER

And that's sort of a picture, in a few moments, of my evolution. From a person who focused on managing your emotions and not being victimized and living a self-actualized life, to understanding that we're not human beings who are having spiritual experiences, but that we are spiritual beings having human experiences.

A great many of the speeches that I accept are given in churches and in seminars. The people sell tickets and pay me a certain percentage and a percentage of it goes to their charities or whatever. That's where most of my speaking is, although I still do some speaking for other organizations.

So the message that I have today, for the 1990s, is really the title of one of my books, *You'll See It when You Believe It.* You are the product of the beliefs that you have and there is a part of you that is divine and special.

If you ask me this question three years from now, I'll be talking about how to manifest miracles in your life. That there's something called real magic, other than just illusions. That you can create this magic in your life by learning to go within and discovering the power of meditation and so on. Fifteen years ago I didn't even know what meditation was. And now I do it everyday. My speech or talks evolve as I do.

▶ **SECRET #20: Your message will always reflect exactly where you're at in life in terms of your own personal development.**

Like Dyer, your speaking will evolve as you do. This is as it should be. As a speaker, you are constantly growing as you seek to better understand yourself, your audience, and the world you live in. Dyer found that the calmer and more centered he felt within, the happier, more productive, more in tune with his purpose he became:

> The clearer I became, the less negative and judgmental [I was], [and] the more I began to treat my physical self in healthier ways. As I allowed my purpose to find me, I began to feel happier and more in harmony with myself. Ultimately, it was as if I forgot about myself and tuned in automatically to my strong sense of mission and purpose.

This is how the enlightenment process seems to work. One proceeds through a series of phases of first focusing on oneself and consciously working at improving oneself until the inner tumult disappears. As that inner turmoil fades, you find yourself feeling much more purposeful in sharing yourself with others. When you have an inner authentic sense of love and harmony, that is precisely what you have to give away.

As many of the great philosophers have said, the purpose of life is not to get but to give. It is only when we've taken care of ourselves, and feel good about who we are, that we are then in a spot where we can be of service to others.

The reason it is so important to take care of ourselves as speakers, and to truly like who we are, is that *who we are* dramatically impacts *what we say*. How could it not? After all, we can only give what we have inside. This is best illustrated by one of Dyer's most famous analogies, where he states:

When you squeeze an orange, the only thing you can get is orange juice, because that's what's inside of it. When people "squeeze you" (put pressure on you), if you get angry, it's because that's what's inside you!

This is another way of saying that "as within, so without." That our speaking is nothing more than a reflection of our thinking. When I asked Dyer how he came up with his "When you squeeze an orange . . ." analogy, he replied:

I don't even remember! Every story that I use, and all of the anecdotes and all of the things that I've been talking about and that are in my tapes, are things that came to me spontaneously while I was speaking. They would work, so I would hone and fix them and use them in a little different way.

Dyer has learned to trust in himself and in the whole speaking process, to the point that if he needs a particular story or example while onstage, he can find it by tapping into universal consciousness (or whatever you want to call that magical place where we know things we didn't know we knew). This is the same sort of state that a jazz musician is in when he goes off on a rift and plays "free-form," or when an athlete is in "the zone." When this happens, the result is usually awe-inspiring.

Why We Speak: One Person Can Make a Difference

At times, even the best of speakers can forget the impact that they can have on their audience. The following true story reminds us that we never know when something we say will have a profound, and yes, even life-changing effect on a person.

In 1988, after giving a forty-five-minute radio interview in Monterey, California, Dyer decided, on a whim, to stop by the church bookstore where the woman who had helped set up the interview worked as a cashier. She was thrilled to see Wayne, and asked him if he wouldn't mind autographing copies of his books while he was there. While he was doing this, a man standing six feet, ten inches tall burst into the bookstore with tears streaming down his face. He said, "I've got to have Eykis! I've got to have Eykis!" referring to Dyer's novel, *Gifts from Eykis,* which he had talked about during his radio interview. The cashier said to the huge man, "The author is right over there. Why don't you go over and say hello?" He walked over to Dyer, put his arms around him, picked him up, and gave him a big hug. Then he said, "I was going to kill myself today! This was the day I was going to do it. . . . There was no doubt in my mind . . . and so I went to this park to think about how I was going to kill myself. I had brought with me a radio and I happened to tune into this A.M. radio station, where I heard you speaking."

One of the things that Dyer had said during the interview was "to always choose life." Miraculously, not an hour later, this man, who Dyer had never met before, was standing before him, sobbing, and saying that he was going to choose life. As speakers, we often have no idea the enormous impact our message will have on somebody. Clearly, our job is to just "put it out there," and let the universe, as this story with Dyer so powerfully illustrates, take care of the rest.

▶ **SECRET #21: As a speaker, you never know when your message will be just what someone in your audience needed to hear at that exact moment.**

How Wayne Dyer would like to be remembered:

---

*"I don't care what they say about me after I'm gone.
It just doesn't matter. That's not what I'm about,
worrying about what other people say or write about me.
They can call me an asshole or they can call me a saint,
it doesn't make any difference to me. What they say or
write about isn't who I am anyway."*
WAYNE W. DYER

Dr. Wayne W. Dyer's
Success Secrets Summary

SECRET #1: You can greatly increase your charisma by presenting your ideas in both a confident and loving manner.

SECRET #2: Believing in your own ideas, abilities, and decision-making capabilities is the first step to achieving success in life.

SECRET #3: That which you think about expands. Therefore, develop the habit of always focusing on what you want, not on what you don't want.

SECRET #4: True inner peace will always elude you until you get your life "on purpose."

SECRET #5: When pursuing a goal, the most important thing is to continually hold in your mind the picture of yourself successfully achieving that goal.

SECRET #6: The clearer you see a goal in your mind, the easier it is to know what action you need to take to achieve that goal.

SECRET #7: In order to achieve your vision you must be self-reliant; if you cannot find the circumstances that you need, then you must go out and create them.

SECRET #8: When it comes to pursuing your life's purpose, giving up is not an option.

SECRET #9: If you believe in your ideas even when there is no evidence to support them, soon there will be!

SECRET #10: Your upbeat and enthusiastic attitude toward your vision not only helps keep you motivated, it gets others excited about your dream as well.

SECRET #11: It's amazing how "lucky" you can get when you work hard, persist, believe in your dreams, are willing to take risks, care about others, and genuinely desire to make a difference in the world.

SECRET #12: The way you conquer a fear is by facing it head on.

SECRET #13: Meditating on your purpose before you speak helps calm and focus your mind, thereby causing any butterflies you may be feeling to "fly in formation."

SECRET #14: Being real and authentic in front of an audience requires that you speak from your heart and not your head.

SECRET #15: The more vividly and repeatedly you see yourself successfully giving your presentation in your mind, the easier and smoother it will go when you actually give it.

SECRET #16: You must be enthusiastic about your topic if you hope to get others excited about it.

SECRET #17: Always give your own speech; never give somebody else's.

SECRET #18: While it is important to focus on meeting your audience's needs, ultimately, you must stay true to yourself.

SECRET #19: When you stop focusing on money, and you get your life "on purpose," the money will come.

SECRET #20: Your message will always reflect exactly where you're at in life in terms of your own personal development.

SECRET #21: As a speaker, you never know when your message will be just what someone in your audience needed to hear at that exact moment.

CHAPTER THREE

BORN: March 4, 1951
BIRTHPLACE: Philadelphia, Pennsylvania

Barbara De Angelis, Ph.D.

"If you're talking to one person or five people,
you have to do it with as much love and everything
else as you would for 10,000 people.
Because if you don't, when you get to 10,000,
you won't know what to say."

▼

CONNECTING. That's the name of the game. Great speakers are adept at connecting quickly, efficiently, and naturally with their audiences. One speaker who is a master at connecting with her audiences is Dr. Barbara De Angelis. Her ability to walk onstage and instantly develop rapport with people is truly awesome. How is she able to do this? Is it because Barbara is attractive? Dresses smartly? Has a beautiful smile? Is intelligent? While all these factors certainly play a role, what makes her so powerful on stage is the energy, passion, and genuineness she exudes. It's the combination of confidence and vulnerability, the ability to have people laughing one minute and teary-eyed the next as she discloses a personally painful life lesson that makes audiences feel so close to her. In a word, she is "real."

In an era when many leaders in our society strive at all cost to maintain a carefully crafted image—as unrealistic as it may be—thank God that we have speakers like Barbara who are willing to share themselves, "blemishes and all." By opening up her own heart first and speaking from a place of authentic emotional honesty, DeAngelis sends out a powerful vibration that resonates deep inside the hearts of everyone in her audience. You can almost hear the plaster cracking as the audience, sensing her realness, can't help but begin to lower their own guarded and heavily armored walls.

When Two Come Together As One

The outcome is that Barbara is no longer "giving a speech." Rather, because the walls have been lowered, De Angelis is able to tune in to the audience at a deep level; much deeper than your average presenter. The powerful result is that the two separate entities, speaker and audience, come together as one. The energy that now exists in the room is not unlike that of two good friends who haven't seen each other in a long time and have some eagerly awaited catching up to do. The connection is there, everything flows, and Barbara's words have a ring of truth to them that rocket directly to the heart of each audience member. You can actually look around the room during one of her seminars and see people sitting in their seats, nodding their heads, and saying to themselves (even out loud), "Yes, that's so true!" "That's exactly how I feel!" "Oh my God, that is exactly what I do!"

Barbara's uncanny ability to "hit the nail on the head," to speak to the truth of whatever she is talking about at that moment, combined with her powerful rapport skills, are two of the major reasons she is so successful. And because she has connected emotionally with her audience, she not only affects their minds, but their hearts as well.

People leave her seminars feeling uplifted, empowered, and, most importantly, glad they came. They realize they were part of an experience that went far beyond your typical speaker-listener relationship. They were part of an event where, for a few hours, a room full of human beings were willing to risk "being real" in front of each other. In a love-starved society like ours, this can have a very healing and rejuvenating effect on even the most hardened of hearts.

Bestselling Author, Infomercial Queen, and Talk Show Host

De Angelis's willingness to share her pain, wisdom, and insights into men, women, and their relationships, have made her one of the wealthiest and most successful speakers and authors in the country. Her first four books, *How to Make Love All the Time, Secrets About Men Every Woman Should Know, Are You the One for Me?,* and *Real Moments* are all best-sellers. And her *Making Love Work* infomercial, which was named best infomercial of the year by the National Infomercial Marketing Association, has sold over 300,000 audio-video tape programs. Besides being a frequent guest on *Oprah, Donahue, Geraldo, Hour Magazine,* and *The Sally Jesse Raphael Show,* she hosted her own daily television show for CBS. In addition, she appeared weekly for two years on CNN as their Newsnight Therapist, as well as hosting her own popular radio talk show in Los Angeles, for two years, on KFI Radio. As if that hasn't kept her busy enough, when she's not writing books, appearing on talk shows, or leading seminars, she's busy writing magazine articles for such publications as *Cosmopolitan, Ladies Home Journal, McCall's, Reader's Digest, Redbook,* and *Family Circle.*

She Has Her Life "On Purpose"

Clearly, De Angelis is committed to making a difference in the world while she's here. She has gotten her life "on purpose," and has made it her personal mission to help her fellow brother and sister earthmates have happier, healthier, and more fulfilling relationships (including the relationship with one's own self!).

> *"People don't care how much you know*
> *until they know how much you care."*

In everything she does, one thing comes through loud and clear: Barbara truly cares about people. As the saying goes, "People don't care how much you know until they know how much you care." The only way that you, as a speaker, can deliver the kind of on-the-money, bulls-eye advice that truly changes people's lives is if you *genuinely* care about them. Barbara truly wants people's lives and relationships to be better, *believes with all her heart that they can get better,* and knows that what she has to share with them *can* and *will* make a difference in their lives.

▶   **SECRET #1: You must believe with all your heart that what you have to say to your audience can and will make a difference in their lives.**

Don't Just Say It, *Feel* It!

Part of what makes De Angelis such an effective communicator is that audiences don't just hear her, they *feel* her, too. Her loving and rejuvenating energy comes through with every word she speaks. And when she smiles at her audience, she doesn't just raise the corners of her mouth; she smiles from deep within her soul so that her eyes twinkle and her whole being lights up. You could say that she smiles with her entire body! Even the stodgiest of audience members can't help but smile back.

Emotional Energy

Unfortunately, we've all seen speakers who gave a half-hearted smile or laugh, with the result being that they didn't come across as being sincere. Why did we perceive them this way? Because their words and body language were hollow; they lacked *emotional energy.* Or worse yet, their emotional energy didn't match what they were saying. A classic example of this is when a wife puts on a new dress she has just bought and asks her husband, who is watching a ball game on TV, what he thinks of it. Without much more than a glance in her direction, he mumbles, "It looks great, honey." And when she explodes, he comes back with, "What's the matter, I said it looked great. Why are you upset?" She's upset because he said the right words, but he didn't put the right feelings, the emotional energy, behind the words.

▶ **SECRET #2: Your emotional energy behind the words you speak is even more important than the words themselves.**

By the way, this is the reason it is very hard to ignore someone who is really angry. Their explosion of emotional energy forces us to deal with them. When you are speaking in front of an audience, the more emotional energy you are able to put behind the words you are speaking, the more the audience will be compelled to watch, listen to and, most importantly, *feel* you— feel your power! While this might call for saying less, what you *do* say will carry much more weight. Besides, your audience isn't going to remember every word you say after your presentation is over with anyway. But they *will* remember your energy and the overall feelings and pictures your words created in their minds. The more effective you are in leaving your audience with powerful and meaningful word-pictures, the more effective you will have been in persuading them to your way of thinking, which should be your goal as a speaker.

Monitor Yourself As You Are Speaking

The next time you're giving a presentation, monitor yourself. If you catch yourself focusing too much on what you're saying and not taking the time to actually *feel* the energy behind your words, pause for a moment to re-group. Then, let yourself vividly and emotionally experience your words as you are saying them. If you say, "Boy, was he surprised!" then act surprised yourself. If you are speaking about something sad, let yourself become sad, too.

▶ **SECRET #3: The way you get your audience to feel your words is by first letting your words emotionally impact you.**

I can't emphasize this enough. To be at your most effective as a speaker, you want to get in the habit of *feeling* your words as you say them. This is how De Angelis, Robbins, Dyer, and all the other speakers I interviewed are able to sound so passionate when they speak. It's because they genuinely *feel* passionate inside themselves about their ideas and their message. When they get up to speak, all they are really doing is articulating how they genuinely feel.

The Importance of Video- and Audiotaping Yourself

Often we are unaware of how we look and sound to an audience. I want to encourage you to both audio- and videotape your presentations whenever possible. By listening to the audiotape, you won't have the picture to distract you, and you can focus on your voice to see if you sound as sincere, enthusiastic, or as persuasive as you think you do. You'd be surprised how you can think you sound one way, and in reality come off sounding completely different. Or, perhaps with one little change you can dramatically increase your effectiveness.

For example, what if, after making a really powerful point, you paused for a moment to let the point sink in to your audience's mind. Would that make a difference in your effectiveness? You bet! Remember, it's not just by reading valuable tips like these, but by *implementing* them that will have you well on your way to becoming a dynamic and effective public speaker!

The obvious advantage of seeing yourself on videotape is that the camera will reveal things about you that audio can't. For example, is your body language supporting or detracting from what you are saying? Remember, *everything* you do, your words, facial expressions, mannerisms, vocal tone, and body language must all work together, in concert, to support the point you are endeavoring to get across. If one element is off, it can greatly distract from your overall effectiveness.

A Hair-Raising Experience

I once saw a man who was running late for his presentation, rush into a room and immediately begin addressing the audience. Apparently, all his rushing got him to work up a pretty good sweat because, two minutes into his speech, he decided to take off the pullover sweater he was wearing. Unfortunately, as he pulled it over his head, static electricity caused a clump of his hair to stand straight up in the air! The poor man looked like a porcupine. After setting the sweater aside, he nonchalantly tried to pat down the unruly strands as he went about addressing the group. Not surprisingly, the audience's attention was focused on the top of his head and whether or not he'd be able to quash the rebellion going on up there. Thankfully he was finally able to quell the uprising, and we were once again able to focus on his presentation.

Learning from Your Mistakes

*"Those who do not learn from the past
are condemned to repeat it."*
GEORGE SANTAYANA

Like this gentleman, you are going to make mistakes, have mishaps, do something embarrassing, or feel that you could have said or done something better during your presentations. That's okay. Life is about learning and one of the most memorable ways you can learn something is by messing up! Beating yourself up over it won't do you or anybody else any good. The most important thing you can do is learn from your mistake and then move on. As a great philosopher once said, "Some days you're the bug and some days you're the windshield!"

▶ SECRET #4: Learn quickly from your mistakes and then move on. Beating yourself up over them doesn't help you or anybody else.

Overcoming the Illusion of Separateness

One of my favorite questions to ask people who are experts in their particular field is, "What is the biggest obstacle you had to overcome to get where you are today?" When I asked Barbara this question, her answer surprised me:

> Overcoming the temptation to believe that my audience and I are separate and different from one another. That I have to figure out some kind of trick or process to be able to connect with them. Remembering that we are all taking the same journey and that we are all absolutely related. That there's no difference between us. Not speaking to them as strangers, but talking to them as if I'm back with old friends.

That's my particular style; that's what I think has made me successful. I create an intimate experience, even if it's with five thousand people. I don't come in to impress them, or get their approval, or teach them, or be smarter than they are. I come in to be with them and to share our process together. To create intimacy within the first two minutes, which I tend to do, I have to overcome the illusion that we're separate. That we're strangers and that I'm giving a speech to a group. I have to remember who they really are and who I really am.

Now, I wouldn't have said this five years ago. I've gone through a tremendous transformation as I continue to grow spiritually in terms of who I'm talking to and what my real purpose is in talking to them. When I stopped "giving speeches" and started being with people, I became a lot better!

▶ **SECRET #5: You will connect with your audience the moment you understand that you're already connected; that separation is just an illusion.**

Connecting

Connecting with your audience is your first job as a speaker. Just as a toaster doesn't work until you plug it in, neither will your audience truly hear what you have to say until you "plug in" to them. Ironically, the idea of connecting with others is really an illusion, since you are never actually separate from them in the first place. It's only our ego that has us believing that we're somehow separate from others. When we connect, what we're really doing is removing the obstacles that blocked the connection—not reconnecting.

Taking Your Foot off the Hose

Imagine trying to water a bed of roses with one foot on the hose. How much water is going to come out of the hose? Not much. The solution is not to connect the hose to another spigot, it's to lift your foot off the hose and let the water flow! The connection is there; it's just blocked. It's the same thing with connecting to other people. You're *already* connected (since the day you came into this world!); you just need to allow the energy to flow. By being open, authentic, vulnerable, and coming from love, you remove the blockages of separation and differences that your ego would have you believe are real. And you know what? When you do this, a funny thing happens: People tend to respond in kind. The truth is that people really do want to connect; they are just afraid of being rejected. Your job as a speaker is to make it as easy as possible for your audience to feel connected. Once you let them know that you really care about them and that you are just like they are, the energy between you and your audience will flow freely, unencumbered, just like it's supposed to.

Keep in mind that the first few times you go before an audience totally open and vulnerable, it might feel a little scary. That's okay. To quote the title of a book by Susan Jeffers, "Feel the fear and do it anyway." Let the child in you—the one with no hidden agendas, the one who says, "Hey, world, this is who I am!"—come out and play. The good news is that even if you mess up, if the audience gets that you are being "real" with them, they can be extremely understanding, even supportive, as the following story illustrates.

A Little Boy's Terror in Front of 16,000 People

Imagine getting up in front of 16,000 people and singing the National Anthem. Sound a bit scary? Well, one evening on my local TV news sports segment, they showed some tape of a little boy singing the National Anthem at an NBA basketball game. The boy couldn't have been more than four or five years old. After getting out "Ohhhh, say can you seeeeeeee, by the . . . ," the boy suddenly had a panic attack. The first seven words sounded great, and then, all of a sudden, it was as if he realized for the first time that 16,000 people were staring at him. He just freaked out! Then he did what any of us would have done if we were in his size three Reeboks: He started to cry. Then he grabbed on to the person standing nearest to him for dear life, which mercifully was his father, and screamed at the top of his lungs, "I can't! I can't! I can't!" As I watched the scene unfold, I wondered what the audience's reaction was going to be. As you know, sports fans have been known to boo singers who have sung off-key, or who have, in some other way, desecrated the National Anthem (such as Rosanne Barr). However, the little boy's heartfelt and totally honest admission that he was scared to death struck a cord in the hearts of everyone in the arena.

The people could feel for the little boy, because they understood how scary it must have been for him. What did they do? The entire crowd let out a huge roar and began to clap and cheer him on. You could feel the energy and inspiration they were sending the boy via their cheers; they wanted him to succeed! After getting a few words of encouragement from his father, the little boy picked up the microphone and tried again. You could see on his face that he was thinking about bailing out. However, the audience would have none of that. They began cheering even louder. The boy, realizing that everyone was on his side, began to relax and get into it. As he did, you could see (and hear) his confidence growing by the second. By the time he belted out, ". . . and the hommmme of the braaaaaaave," the little boy suddenly looked seven feet tall and was wearing the biggest smile you ever saw. The crowd went nuts! They gave him a standing ovation. He had done it.

If something should go awry during your presentation, as it did with this little boy, don't let it stop you. Just keep things moving—that's the mark of a pro. Remember, your audience will be looking to you to see how they should react. If you don't make a big deal out of it, neither will they.

The Time My Magic Fire Pan Didn't Light

I say this from personal experience. I remember one time I was performing a magic trick in front of six hundred people, and I was supposed to make a small computer appear in a pan full of fire. Well, the pan had a lighting mechanism inside of it (which, of course, worked perfectly in rehearsal), but wouldn't you know it, during the actual show the darn thing decided not to light. I didn't miss a beat; I simply covered up the "flame-less" pan, lifted up the lid, and voila, there was the "palmtop" computer.

The audience loved it. Not only did they not suspect a thing, but I got a huge kick out of the fact that a professional magician who was sitting in the audience came up to me afterward and said that he enjoyed my performance. When I explained what had happened, he said that he had no idea! (Don't think that didn't bring a smile to my lips!) The secret to my success was that I never let on to the audience that anything had gone wrong.

▶ **SECRET #6: Whenever something goes wrong during a presentation, your audience will look to you to see how they should react. If you don't make a big deal out of it, neither will they.**

A Life-Changing Experience

Being open, authentic, and vulnerable in front of an audience can be a lot of fun when things are going well in your life. But what about when the universe is throwing a lot of lessons your way; what then? As De Angelis told Anthony Robbins during an interview he conducted with her in his *PowerTalk* series, sometimes it takes going through a painful event for us to have a much needed breakthrough:

> [In 1990], I was in the process of getting a divorce. The marriage had ended in a messy way; I was not proud of how it ended. I had fallen in love with somebody else; there were all kinds of complications. I was in a tremendous amount of pain, because I had wanted this marriage to work so badly, and it had not.

> I felt that I had failed because I had not rescued my partner and fixed him. Two days after we decided to separate and I was in bed just hysterical, I had a seminar to give. There were people coming from all over the country, hundreds of them coming to the "love doctor" to fix their relationships and I didn't even know how I could go on.

My staff—I had to tell them about it; they were shocked. "Oh my God, how could you get a divorce, how could this happen?" and all this scandal. I realized there was only one way for me to do it; with total honesty—and to not walk in and pretend everything was fine. I was scared to death because of my picture that if I'm perfect I'll be loved, but if I'm not, I won't be.

So I walked in, eyes completely red, looking like a wreck, and they're all clapping and here we all are from all over the country, and I said, "I'm in a lot of pain. I'm going through the same thing you are. I'm going to take the seminar with you. I'm going to do all the processes. I need this, thank God it's here! I trust this seminar, for you and for me and, hopefully, it will work for both of us." I was scared to death because usually I am the ultimate cheerleader-visionary; and they just kind of all surrender to my belief that they can do it. I poured my heart out all weekend. I cried hysterically, I shared, I called on myself, I did every process. I was really baring my soul.

Saturday night, a man came up and said, "Are you ready to take another leap?" He said, "Close your eyes," and he put on our taperecording of the Bette Midler song, *Wind Beneath My Wings*. He had the lights turned down, and the whole room sang the song to me; and they all came up on stage, two hundred people, and just held me. I wept from such a deep place. I was experiencing unconditional love, which I let in, for the first time in my life.

They did not love me because I was perfect or because I was the teacher. They loved me because I was Barbara. I felt so cleansed and healed in that experience. I just sat there and wept and wept for fifteen minutes, and they kept playing the song over and over again. And they just swayed around me, and I really felt they had been sent from God to heal something very deep in me. My life really changed after that. It changed the way I deal with people, the way I teach, how much I let people in. It really cured me of feeling I have to be perfect to be loved.

▶ **SECRET #7: You are worthwhile and lovable simply because you exist. It's an illusion to think you need anyone else's approval.**

This experience allowed De Angelis to see that she was truly lovable simply because she existed; that she didn't have do or say anything spectacular or earthshaking in order to earn her audience's love and respect. Once she "got this," her speaking dramatically improved because she no longer had the pressure of trying to be "perfect" weighing down on her shoulders. She was free to just be herself, imperfections and all! And, as you have just read, once she was able to do this, it changed her whole life—not just her speaking career.

Many achievers tend to have a perfectionistic side to them. While we think that being incredibly hard on ourselves is going to get us where we want to go, the truth is that when we stop trying so hard to do it "just right," and we have faith in ourselves and in the process of life itself, things tend to work out just fine. Whoever put us here in the first place seems to have done all right without our stressing out about it. . . . I wonder why we so often forget this?

We Were Put Here to Learn How to Love Ourselves—Imperfections and All

Because so much of De Angelis' message has a spiritual quality to it, I felt it appropriate to include some of her thoughts on love, perfectionism, and our purpose for being here:

> Loving ourselves for not being perfect is essential to surviving the journey on this plane—without constantly feeling something's wrong with us. That is the whole purpose of manifestation, from all my spiritual experiences, and it's the hardest lesson to learn.

> That I can be imperfect and still deserve to be loved, and be happy, and be here, and God still loves me. In fact, I'm not supposed to be perfect. This is not a perfect place that we've

been sent to. That's the whole game of Earth; it's not perfection. Where we came from was perfection.

The hardest thing for me, as a spiritual person, to experience, to achieve, to accept, is this balance between striving for perfection and loving yourself in spite of it. It's a very fine line which I'm still learning how to balance all the time. Every lesson I've ever learned about life has always been about letting go of judgment, letting go of a picture, letting go of perfection—being with whatever is there and loving it *as it is*. That's a hard lesson to learn, especially for high achievers.

Learning to accept the fact that we are less than perfect, and being able to honor those imperfections and love ourselves regardless of them rather than beating ourselves up because of them—when we can do this, we will have made a giant step forward in our evolution to becoming the best speaker we are capable of being.

Didn't Set Out to Be Famous

While most people have heard of De Angelis via seeing her on TV, reading one of her books, or attending one of her seminars, her goal was never to become famous. Rather, it was to help teach people how to open up their hearts and love more freely:

I never wanted to be famous, but I did want to be influential. I know I've been sent here for a reason. I'm not the most brilliant thinker in the world or the most original, but I really understand communication. I think I know how to take important concepts and ideas, and reach people and touch them. I want to touch as many people as I can and open their hearts to love so that, hopefully, at the end of my life there will be millions of people who are living much more loving lives because of whatever I did.

While pursuing her life's purpose made her famous, being famous was not her goal. This is a theme we see again and again throughout this book. Wayne Dyer never set out to be famous, yet he has become world famous (remember, his books have been translated into twenty-six different languages!) because of the profound impact his message has had on people's lives. Joel Weldon simply wanted to increase his cassette tape sales, so he offered to give free talks to companies. Before he knew it, he was in demand and quickly realized he could make more money giving seminars than he could selling tapes.

The lesson here seems to be that if you specifically set out in life with the express goal to make a lot of money, you're most likely in for a long, uphill struggle. However, if your purpose is to provide an excellent service, to help increase the quality of other people's lives, and you stay committed to this outcome, the money and success seem to come naturally, of their own accord. And when this happens, to quote one of Wayne Dyer's book titles, "the sky's the limit!"

A Major Success Trap: Allowing the Audience to Put You on a Pedestal

---

"Be aware that a halo only has to fall a few inches to become a noose."

DAN MCKINNON

One of the traps that some very good public speakers have fallen into is allowing their audience to put them on a pedestal. While they may be saying, "Oh no, I'm just like everybody else," their actions speak differently. As the saying goes, "They have begun to believe their own press." The reason for their contradictory behavior is easy to understand when you take into account that many people in the limelight once came from a poor upbringing (like many of the speakers in this book) and an even poorer self-image (indeed, this is often what gives them the impetus to succeed in the first place—their quest to feel worthy). Thus, when they do achieve success, it can be very intoxicating.

What makes this trap so insidious is that no matter how much praise and adulation the speaker gets, it's never enough. Ironically, the fact that "it's never enough" is the *very thing* that drives them to do and achieve more—so they can get more recognition and positive strokes! The problem with being addicted to getting positive feedback is that you're doing all the right things, but for the wrong reasons. Going out and giving your best is what it's all about; however, your reasons for doing this should be because this is the standard you have set for yourself, and not to earn the praise of others. It should be the act of giving one hundred percent effort that makes you high, and not the feedback. Besides, what if the feedback you get is negative! What then? The solution is balance. You want to keep both the positive and negative feedback in check.

You must be clear that, as an effective communicator, you do what you do because you know you are making a difference in the world, not because you need the audience's approval. When you get past needing their praise, that's when your speaking career will really take off.

De Angelis Avoids Falling into the "Guru" Trap

De Angelis understands that there are people in her audience who look up to her as a role model. However, she takes her job as a teacher and communicator very seriously, and doesn't want to be placed on a pedestal. Furthermore, she feels very strongly that it is incumbent upon all speakers to do everything in their power to dissuade others from perceiving them as a "guru":

> People are anxious to put others on a pedestal. We all want gurus, we all want teachers, we all want somebody who has the answers and can give them to us and create instant enlightenment. I used to want that, but that's a whole other story. We are very anxious to make other people into heroes, who aren't. It's a whole psychological thing; we're all looking for Father-God. It's part of human nature.
>
> The problem is, many teachers, speakers, healers—I have to say particularly men—enjoy being placed above. I have seen

a lot of people use it to feed their own ego and perpetuate the myth that there's some separation between them [and their audience]. They get into the mini-guru complex, which I think does a tremendous disservice to your audience—your students—because it disempowers them. These people may think it empowers their students, but it doesn't. It totally takes away their power.

If anybody walks out of a speech saying, "She's great," I have failed. If they walk out saying, "I feel great," I have succeeded. And that's the difference. There's a fine line between appearing to give out information and really just pumping yourself up. It's nothing you say, it's an energy. It's creating a lot of energy around yourself versus truly stepping out of the picture and letting the information come through you.

It's about being a vehicle enough so that people truly remember the message and enjoy and appreciate the vehicle, but don't aggrandize the vehicle. That is a fine art form and a great temptation and challenge for every speaker—any person in the public eye—that many people do not rise to meet.

▶ **SECRET #8: By making sure others don't put you up on a pedestal, you never have to worry about falling off.**

Sharing Your Own Mistakes Is a Powerful Way to Connect with Your Audience

De Angelis found that there were specific things she could do (and that other speakers could, too, if they really wanted to) to keep from coming off as perfect and totally flawless in the minds of her audience. One way she found to be more down-to-earth was to simply and honestly share the mistakes that she had made in past relationships, and the lessons that she had learned from those mistakes. While on the surface this kind of self-disclosure might seem like the last thing you'd want to do in front of an audience, the truth is that it's this willingness to open up and share *all* of yourself, not just the good things, that will bring you closer to people. Says Barbara:

There are very clear ways you can make sure people don't [put you on a pedestal]. One way is to talk about yourself in a totally self-disclosing manner.

For instance, I could stand up and talk about "the challenge of love as a journey," and I could be very eloquent about it for fifteen minutes and everyone can be going, "God, she is so together!" Then I can add, "Let me tell you how hard this is for me. Last night my husband and I . . . ," and I could tell them a really honest story like I would tell my girlfriend.

Suddenly, I have made *me* very human. Now, I have also lost something, I have lost some of my shine. But I have given them something more than just inspirational eloquence, and that takes a lot of courage. I do not know a lot of people who do that. I didn't used to do it. I used to be afraid to show people my vulnerability; if I wasn't perfect, they wouldn't respect me or come to my seminars. I got into a lot of personal trouble for it because I wasn't living in complete integrity with myself.

I was forced, through all kinds of interesting events in my life, to publicly deal with my real failings. When I did, I knew I could truly trust my success because I knew people really saw me. They didn't see an image, or a few chosen stories that I thought made me look good.

It's about sharing with people when you're confused or going through a hard time—and not always sharing it after the fact. A lot of people like to tell stories about themselves, but they're always stories with happy endings.

I'm not saying I'm great for doing it my way—it's that I don't know any other way to do it and feel good. It would be nice if more speakers did it. I know everybody in this business, and they're going through all kinds of stuff! They don't share it, and so people start to feel inferior.

▶ **SECRET #9: When you're willing to share all of yourself with your audience—not just the good stuff—you will connect with them at a much deeper level.**

What Can Happen When a Speaker Presents a "Superman" Image to His Audience

While you want to be as polished and professional as possible in front of your audience, as we've discussed, it is a mistake to try to present an image that is flawless. What we haven't discussed is the problem this can cause for your audience. If you are perceived as having no problems, and thus you never discuss how to deal with life's challenges, then how are the members of your audience supposed to deal with their own fears and problems when they come up? They look at you and think, "Wow, she (or he) has it all together, why can't I?" And the result is that they either become confused and frustrated, because they don't have all the answers like you do, their "blemishless hero," or they will avoid the issue altogether and live in denial. The gentleman in the following story told by De Angelis did both:

> I met a man in the audience at a talk I gave in Portland, and I could tell by the way he was dressed, the way he stood, and the way he was looking at me, that he was trying to clone himself after a well-known male teacher, speaker, and writer. It was obvious; I got the vibe from fifty feet away.

> When he went up to the microphone, I could tell by his questions who his "guru" was. He was going through a struggle, having some very human feelings and reactions, and the person whom he modeled himself after had not created any way for him of holding what he was going through. It didn't fit into the mind-set. And this guy was going into a lot of denial about the problems in his life, because he kept thinking he wasn't doing something right.

> ***"In that moment, I felt a feeling of frustration with his particular teacher for not creating an avenue for people to be where they are and be okay."***

> He was just going through a hard time in his life, and I was trying to give him permission to just be where he was. In that moment, I felt a feeling of frustration with his particular teacher for not creating an avenue for people to be where they

are and be okay. I see this a lot and I'm always trying to encourage people in my field to be more disclosing—because the world needs it. We need people who are being very human to give other people permission to accept their humanness.

▶ **SECRET #10: Trying to project a flawless image to your audience creates confusion in their minds because it doesn't allow them any place to hold their own mistakes and fears.**

Gained Wisdom by Learning from Past

One of the reasons De Angelis is so successful is because of her amazing ability to provide her audience with insight into some of life's most fundamental and key issues; areas regarding love, life and relationships. Areas near and dear to the hearts of all human beings. Often her answers are so "right on target" that it's not unusual to see De Angelis' entire audience nodding their heads in collective agreement. The question is, *how does she do it?* How is De Angelis able to bypass the ancillary issues and speak right to the heart of the issue? (And like Wayne Dyer, she seems to do this intuitively.)

The answer is twofold. The first part can be summed up by the saying:

> *"Good judgment comes from experience, and experience comes from bad judgment."*

As De Angelis shared with Anthony Robbins during an interview she conducted with him in his *PowerTalk* series, she's made practically every mistake in the book when it comes to relationships:

> I have made every mistake I write about in *Secrets About Men Every Woman Should Know*. I have done everything that I tell women not to do. I've given up my power to men, I've mothered them, I've sacrificed who I was in relationships with them, I've acted like a little girl and not really shown my strength, I've done everything!

I didn't do it because I was being anything but what I thought was very loving. I was trying to be the most loving woman I could be. Unfortunately, what many of us are taught about being loving is how to be powerless.

"My personal life and my professional life were so far apart it wasn't funny."

People are always surprised when they hear this because they see me on TV or they hear me on the radio and they say, "You've done these things?!" They're kind of shocked, but they're also relieved because they figure if somebody as "powerful" as I am, at least as they see that I am, could make these mistakes, then there's hope for them. My personal life and my professional life were so far apart it wasn't funny. I was absolutely a wimp in my relationships. I let myself be mistreated, I let myself not be loved enough. All in the name of being accepting and patient and understanding his point-of-view to the point where I lost myself.

What I was doing a lot of times was not loving them. I was, at the expense of loving myself, giving myself over to them. And it wasn't really loving them, it was sacrificing, it was trying to buy their love by being the perfect little girl, or perfect lover. And that was a very hard lesson for me to learn. It's just been in the last few years that I really faced it and looked at my own codependency, which I did not want to see. The result has been that I am in the healthiest, most fulfilling, balanced relationship I've ever been in.

▶ **SECRET #11: The wisdom, insights, and ideas you share with your audience are the most powerful when they come from your own personal experience.**

Removing the Emotional Blocks Led to a Connection with a Higher Power

The second part of the answer as to how Barbara is able to speak to the heart of whatever issue she is discussing has to do with opening herself up. De Angelis discovered that when she removed the emotional blocks inside of her, the calming sense of clarity that resulted allowed her to tap into a higher power (again, notice the parallels between she and Dyer). This higher power has been called everything from universal consciousness, to "the source," to God.

> *"It got to the point where if I allowed myself to tune into a certain place where I needed to know something . . . all I had to do was basically open my mouth and it would start to come through."*

The idea is that when we quiet the mind and become still, we will connect with a silence inside us that is the gateway to our source, the creator. It is here where De Angelis taps into that creative wisdom that she so powerfully shares with her audiences:

> As I became clearer and clearer in my own being, and continually removed the obstacles in my own heart and mind, I started to experience—and this began about fifteen years ago—a lot of moments where I felt rushes of information and knowledge just starting to pour through me. It got to the point where, if I allowed myself to tune in to a certain place where I needed to know something, or somebody wanted to know something, that all I had to do was basically open my mouth and it would start to come through. And it's pretty much been that way ever since. Yet there's obviously specific information that I give out regularly that I use as cornerstones or foundations for all the principles that I've developed.

> When I write or speak now, most of the stuff that ends up coming out isn't anything I've decided to say; it's stuff that needs to be said. It's really a wonderful feeling to participate in that process. It's very different from what a lot of speakers do. I really rely on another source for a lot of what happens when I interact with audiences. It's a collection of a lot of things that I don't completely understand; it's just always there for me. It's because I've worked so hard at clearing myself.

> I can't ever tell anybody when they ask, "Well, tell me some tips for being a good speaker." . . . I mean, I can give them tips for being a good speaker, but the real thing that happens

that's magical when I interact with audiences has nothing to do with "good-speaker" tips.

"When people hear truth they light up."

It has to do with truth. When people hear truth, they light up. You can't decide that you're going to do that. That has to be something where you're a clear enough receptacle, and that takes a lot of work.

The other day my assistant was driving me to the airport; I had had an incredibly busy week, not even a second to do anything. And she said, "You haven't even prepared for this," and I said, "I have, I just haven't prepared the way most people would have." I had prepared myself spiritually, mentally, and emotionally. Then, when I walked onstage, I was clear enough to be prepared for whatever needed to happen. It's a very different approach from what a lot of people do, which is reading joke books and going to speakers' bureaus and this and that. I really have a kind of invisible speakers' bureau that I belong to!

▶   **SECRET #12: Getting quiet and tuning in to the silence within you will put you in touch with your highest self—the knower within you—the essence of who you really are.**

The Voices in Our Head

When asked what, specifically, keeps most people from tapping into this higher power within them, De Angelis explained that it's all the many little voices in our head that are causing interference and preventing us from "hearing the silence":

". . . and there's so much noise inside [your head], that you can't hear in the silence what needs to be said."

The only reason that all of us aren't totally tuned in to [this higher power]—and it's not like I have a monopoly on it; it's available to everybody—is that we all have a lot of other voices that are creating interference. Voices from our past, voices of negative patterns, voices of negative self-talk, voices of emotional stuff that hasn't been handled, voices of fear, voices of ego . . . and there's so much noise inside that you can't hear in the silence what really needs to be said. You can't tune in to people's hearts and what they need to hear.

So, it becomes a process more of imposing a speech on them that you have come prepared to give, that you have given a hundred times this month. This versus *being* with an audience and truly creating a space together in which you tune in to what that particular audience needs. With help from above, you deliver it. That's the shift I've made in terms of speaking, over the last ten years.

The first step is starting to listen to those voices inside. The problem for a lot of people in speaking is that they decide, "I want to be a speaker"—they think it looks glamorous and all that—and they create a whole process of what they want to say. Or, they go to Toastmasters, or they do whatever they do, and what they forget is that they already have so many speeches going on in their head—not healthy speeches—that there's not room for another speaker.

You have to first figure out what your inner cast of characters is doing. Truly take a look inside and know yourself, and know all the little personalities—your inner family, so to speak. Put somebody in charge of them so that they can all sit down and be quiet when that speaker part of you wants to talk.

For instance, somebody could be getting up and giving a speech for the first time—they know what they're going to say, they have their notes and they've practiced it—and within two minutes another voice inside of them, maybe its their critical voice or their mother, starts criticizing them.

It says, "I'm not doing well, I know it, I know it! Look at that man in the second row, he doesn't like what I'm saying." And suddenly, you're hearing that person, you're not hearing the source of what you want to tell everybody and you get confused and you get lost. And that's just one voice! There's another voice in there thinking about something else. Unless you have those inner voices under control, you're going to sound disjointed or maybe not real effective to people.

No one is going to say, "Gee, that person looks like they have ten subpersonalities on stage," but they're not going to get into a flow and a rhythm with you. So that's the first step, taking a look at what's already going on inside of you, what speeches you already give to yourself day in and day out— because we all give speeches to ourselves all the time.

Overcoming Nervousness and the Critical Voice

De Angelis brings up a good point that, quite honestly, I hadn't heard any of the other speakers I interviewed talk about. And the more I thought about it, the more I realized that it was true; we do all have lots of little voices in our head (whether it's many little voices, or one voice with lots of different personalities, is something I'll leave for the psychologists to decide).

The point is that we must get a firm grip on who is running the show. If we allow the critic to run amok, then we're going to be filled with anxiety and stress and our performance will suffer. Instead, we must say to ourselves, "The audience is looking forward to me giving a great presentation and a great presentation is what I shall give. I will be fully present and focused on them, their needs, and how what I have to say can and will make a difference in their lives. I know this like I know the back of my hand." If we truly believe it, then we will have few problems. When you hear that kind of self-talk in your head, you know you're in great shape and that you're going to give a fine presentation. But what about when you're feeling nervous and unsure of yourself? What then?

What We Resist Persists

The saying, "What we resist persists," definitely applies here. The more you try to push away the nervousness or get mad at yourself for feeling anxious, the worse it tends to make matters. What you must understand is that the nervousness and anxiety are things you're really feeling, and to deny them is to deny reality. So, the first step is that you want to acknowledge to yourself that that is how you're truly feeling. For example, you might say, "Wow, I feel really disconnected and unsure of myself right at this moment." You want to be sure and put in, ". . . at this moment," because, while you're acknowledging to yourself that that's how you're feeling now, it isn't necessarily how you could feel two minutes from now.

The second step, and the one that goes against our first impulse, is to not try to change how we are feeling. If we do, the "what we resist persists" law takes over and we end up saying, "I wish I could stop feeling so nervous, etc.," and before we know it all our energy goes into resisting how we're feeling. Instead, what we want to do is *fully experience* the *feelings*. Rather than resisting it, you ride it out, like a surfer riding out a wave. And you'll find that, like a wave, it will go as quickly as it came.

Now you may be saying to yourself, "But what do I do if I am about to give a big presentation and I'm feeling really nervous and I don't have time to ride it out? Is there anything I can do to speed up the process?" The answer is *yes*. You can dramatically reduce the time that it takes to get centered again by doing one thing: *unconditionally loving the feelings of nervousness*.

Now, this may sound strange to you, but it really works. All the nervous energy is your body's reaction to feeling stressed, and by loving it you're working *with* your body and making it okay for it to feel this way. As soon as it gets the message from you that you are willing to accept these feelings unconditionally, it immediately begins to relax and feel less stressed. And of course, the more you are able to accept yourself and your feelings unconditionally, without judging and labeling them, the better your presentation will go. This is because you are now better able to unconditionally love and support your audience because you are now unconditionally loving and supporting yourself!

▶ **SECRET #13: When speaking, any critical thoughts (old tapes) that come up are never resisted (because what we resist persists!), but are unconditionally loved and acknowledged. Rather than deny the feeling, you transcend it.**

De Angelis' Speech Preparation

It's interesting to note that while some speakers do massive amounts of research and preparation on their clients before speaking to them, De Angelis does very little. Why? The answer is twofold. First, since her topic is universal (love, relationships, communicating), it isn't necessary for her to find out tons of background information on her audience. What she has to say will apply to them whether they're Avon ladies or truck drivers or CEOs.

Secondly, because her goal is always to be real, authentic, and in the moment with her audience, she wants to speak from her heart and not her head (something that is required when remembering a lot of statistics, names and stories about other people). While her style isn't for everybody, it works quite well for De Angelis:

> I talk to the person doing the booking and find out a little about them, but I find [research] to be a mistake. Research reveals the history of the group or organization, and maybe you can say a few clever things and they think you like them and all that, but the bottom line is that they are human beings. They take off their coats and ties and they take off their badges and they go home, and they are dealing with the same issues.
>
> If I were speaking about profit sharing or management, yes, I would have to do some research. But what I'm talking about is very universal. I'm talking about life, I'm talking about living, I'm talking about relating. So, I talk to them like people. I do not sit there and say, "Now, I'm playing the role of the expert, and you're playing the role of the managers." I take off my role; I invite them to take off theirs and be together as human beings in the time that we have.
>
> I am invited to the corporate world, but not to speak about corporate things—I dislike that and it's not me. I leave it to other people who enjoy that. I like to deal with people who are dealing with things that I consider important and who are being real.

▶ **SECRET #14: All your research on your audience won't mean anything if you fail to connect with them.**

Her Speech Has Evolved As She Has

While De Angelis has built her career on talking about how men and women can learn to relate to each other more effectively, she is now shifting her message to focus on how men and woman can learn how to relate more effectively with themselves and the process of living:

> I started out very heavily in relationships and how to "make love work," and I've stayed in that realm for a long time. But what I talked about within that changed a lot as I deepened my understanding of it. It used to be just motivational-inspirational, then it moved to looking at the differences between men and women. Then it moved to understanding our emotional patterns and programming and freeing yourself from the past.
>
> And it wasn't like I kept shifting (topics), I just kept adding. Then it moved to relationships as a spiritual path; path of growth and challenges as a metaphor for everything else in life. Now what I'm talking about has nothing to do with "relationships," but it has to do with our relationship to life itself, which is what my book *Real Moments,* is about. As I've broadened my vision, what I talk about has stayed the same; but the way I've talked about it has changed tremendously.

► **SECRET #15: As you grow and your vision expands, what you talk about may stay the same, but the way you talk about it will change.**

The longer you speak on a topic, the more distinctions and insights you will have made, and the deeper your understanding of that subject will become. When this happens, your audiences will be in for a real treat. This is because you will be able to take them on an exciting journey, a journey where they will learn and discover new things that they may never even have thought of before; and all because of you!

For example, De Angelis began her career by talking about "relationships with the opposite sex," but eventually she realized that a person's relationship with themselves was the most important thing. So, her topic, as she has delved deeper and deeper into it over the years, has led her to discover all kinds of new and wonderful insights about just what relationships are really all about. And the neat part is that it's a never-ending process. As she evolves and gives more seminars and writes more books, her ideas will continue to grow and evolve, too. Of course, we, her audience, will be the beneficiary of all her new distinctions via her books, tapes and seminars.

How Does Your Audience Percieve You?

Good speakers are aware of how they are perceived by their audience. *Knowing your "image"* is not being egotistical or narcissistic. On the contrary, if you are to be effective in persuading a group of people to your way of thinking, you must know how they view you, that is, how you "come off." When I asked De Angelis how she thinks her audience views her when they look at her on stage, she replied:

> I think it depends on where *they're* coming from! People tell me that when they look at me they see somebody extremely human, which always surprises them. They see someone who is very disclosing. They see someone who is very vulnerable, but very tuned-in to the bigger picture—and able to share that vision. The combination is what has created success for me.

▶ **SECRET #16: Know the image that you project as a speaker, the strengths *and* the weaknesses.**

The words, "know thyself," are extremely important to strong speakers. You must know both your strengths and your weaknesses. For example, I love to sing, and I know that deep down inside my heart I was supposed to be the next Elvis Presley. Unfortunately for me, nobody told my vocal cords. As a result, I know not to sing in public. That's not being negative, just compassionate toward my audience. Instead, I focus on my strengths: my magic, sense of humor, my enthusiasm, and my ability to connect with an audience quickly.

What are your strengths? What are your weaknesses? The more you know about yourself, the more effective you will be at crafting a stage persona that works *for* you and not *against* you. When I say crafting, I don't mean being something you're not. On the contrary, I mean putting together all your strengths so as to show you off, just like you would any product, in the best possible light. Does this conflict with what I said earlier about showing your vulnerability on stage? Not at all. There's a difference between that which shows you as being real and authentic, and that which is distracting and takes away from your presentation.

Anything that would take away from your presentational impact, such as speaking too quickly (or too slowly), not dressing appropriately, not smiling or being too serious, saying "ah" or "um," wearing too much makeup (or not enough), or wearing too short of a skirt if you are a woman, should be immediately rectified (as prosecutor Marcia Clark had to do during the O. J. Simpson trial). Remember, everything about you and your presentation makes a statement to the audience about who you are. Make sure that statement is saying what you want it to say!

De Angelis' Greatest High Is Knowing That She Is Making a Real Difference in People's Lives

When asked what truly makes her happy these days, De Angelis told me the following story:

> I was in a restaurant the other day—this was the highlight of my day—and a waiter came up to me and said, "I heard you speak a year and a half ago, and I didn't have the guts to follow your advice. But I thought about it and thought about it, and I finally got up the courage and left the relationship I was in, and I've been happier than ever, and I wanted to thank you. You planted the seed that day and it was so strong that it blossomed eventually, when the time was right."

> I was completely thrilled. That was more fulfilling than the night I got up and gave the speech! And that happens to me all the time. There is a certain amount of love and adoration

that you get from a big crowd of people, but nothing compares to the connection you make with one person.

The Starfish Story

De Angelis' incident reminds me of a story I once heard Jack Canfield tell an audience. It was about a man who was walking down a beach. This man came across another man, who was picking up starfish and throwing them back into the ocean. When he asked the gentleman what he was doing, the starfish-thrower replied, "It's low tide and all of these starfish have washed up on shore. If I don't throw them back into the ocean, they'll die."

The first gentleman, after quickly surveying the starfish-covered shoreline, said, "But there must be thousands of starfish on this beach. You can't possibly make a difference." The second man smiled, picked up another starfish, tossed it into the ocean and said, "I made a difference to that one!"

I love this story because, like De Angelis' tale, it reminds us that, as speakers, we *always* make a difference. And even if it's only to one person, that's one more person's life who has been enriched, sometimes more than we even know, by our message.

The Young Mother and Hope

Recently, I gave a presentation at a meeting of mall merchants at a large shopping mall in Whittier, California. Afterward, a pretty, young woman came up to me and said, "I really needed to hear your message today, thank you." When I asked her why, she said, "Things have been kinda tough lately. I'm twenty years old, and I just gave birth to my third child . . . and it's from a different father than the first two." When I inquired if either father was around to help out, she slowly shook her head no. Then she added, "But my mother helps watch them while I'm at work." After a pause, she continued, "Also, my father is very ill, and with all the pressure here at work, I didn't know if I could go on . . . but you made me feel better; you gave me hope again."

Like DeAngelis, when people come up to me or send me a letter telling how my message personally impacted them, it never fails to touch my heart and remind me why I'm in the greatest profession in the world, the profession of public speaking.

Two Easy Things You Can Do to Make Your Audience Feel Special

Making each person in your audience feel special, as if you're talking directly to them, is an objective for which you should always strive. One powerful way you can accomplish this is by maintaining strong eye contact with individual audience members. Simply establish eye contact with someone, hold their gaze for three to five seconds as you are speaking, and then move on to someone else. No big deal; you simply move effortlessly and naturally from person to person (and section to section), just like you were speaking to them in your own living room.

You can even make a game of it: See how many people in the audience you can connect with "one on one" before your speaking time is up. Also, don't forget the people in the back. Just because you can't see them clearly doesn't mean they can't see you. Take the time to make them feel special, too.

Another powerful way to draw your audience in is by smiling at them. And if you really want to "grab" a person's attention, first make eye contact with them; once you have them locked-in, drop a "big ol' smile on 'em." Unless they're made of stone, you'll see them first physically soften and then, nine times out of ten, shoot a smile right back at you. Of course, during the whole time you are taking people in with your eye contact and smiling at them when appropriate, you are keeping up a comfortable yet lively delivery of your material.

▶ **SECRET #17: Two powerful ways to connect with your audience are through strong, caring eye contact and a genuine smile.**

If you ever get an opportunity to see De Angelis live, watch her as she glides around the stage, almost like she's on ice skates. First, she'll glide over to one side of the audience and take them in with her strong eye contact and beautiful full-mouthed smile, and then she'll confidently, yet gracefully, make her way over to the other side of the room and touch them with her energy, body language and charisma. While today Barbara is a master presenter, it's good to keep in mind that she, too, had to start somewhere.

Started Out Renting Rooms at the Public Library at Age Nineteen

A lot of speakers look at De Angelis today and all they see is the media star; they forget (or have no idea) that it wasn't always like this. She, like everybody else who achieves success, didn't start at the top. As the following story illustrates, De Angelis, too, had to pay her dues:

> I remember when I first started out, before I was doing relationships, I was a TM teacher and I was giving talks on Transcendental Meditation. That was my first public speaking; I was nineteen years old.
>
> I would rent these rooms at libraries and I would put a little ad in the paper calling the event for 8:00 p.m. At five minutes to eight, I would be standing there waiting, hoping that one person would come. Maybe there would be one or two people finally sitting in the room, and it would break my heart every time. Here I was feeling so vulnerable, offering my wisdom, and one or two people would show up. I would have to fight off feeling like a failure, but once I started talking to those one or two people . . . I didn't do anything different from what I do now in front of five thousand people. I gave them everything I had.
>
> Now flash to a year and a half ago. I was speaking at Peggy Bassett's Church of Religious Science in Huntington Beach, California. There were lines and lines of people, something like eight hundred or one thousand people. Next to this was a shopping center where there was a room that you rent out for talks. I was passing this when I saw a man standing outside with a little poster board that said something like, *Dentistry for the '90s*—he was obviously going to give a talk, and he was looking at his watch and waiting.

I was looking at him and I was thinking about myself and how now I have all these people there waiting. But I'm still the same person; I mean, I still wondered if anybody was going to be at Peggy's church waiting to come see me! The difference was, they were there now, but once I got onstage I was still talking to them in the same way I always have.

"You only really talk to one person at a time, anyway."

For anyone just starting out, if you're talking to one person or five people, you have to do it with as much love and everything else as you would for ten thousand people. Because if you don't, when you get to ten thousand, you won't know what to say.

You only really talk to one person at a time, anyway. That's what I'm really trying to say. If you are good, everybody thinks you are talking to them.

I just saw a girl at a party last night. She had seen me at some event recently, and she said, "You were completely talking to me! Everything you said, it was like you read my mind!" I hear that a lot of the time. When enough people say it, [that means] you were tuned in to something greater than *you,* [something] that was somehow giving everybody what they needed at the same time, which is kind of a miraculous process. That's the truth. And you can do that with one person or one thousand people.

If you just help one person, and they walk away from your little talk feeling great, who cares if you didn't have five thousand people! There are people who talk to five thousand people and don't help anybody!

So, don't underplay the importance of your little talk to five people in a living room. Those five people are five human beings! And if you have the privilege of changing them, that's fantastic. That's just as important as if there are five thousand people there. I'm not more important than someone talking to those five people. There's no difference, it's just quantity. And I think that's what people need to remember— to not diminish themselves because they're not making a difference in a bigger way. We all make a difference in a bigger way; we all make a difference everyday with everyone.

Some of us look like we're making a bigger difference, but we're really not. It's just an illusion. Inspiring one person is a fantastic gift.

▶ **SECRET #18: When you are tuned in and connected to your audience, each person will feel as if you are talking directly to them.**

How De Angelis Deals with (Ouch!) Criticism

One thing is certain in life: The more successful you get, the more people are going to find things to criticize about you. When I asked De Angelis how she deals with criticism, she jokingly replied:

I rip the person apart in my mind!

After we both laughed, she gave me her real answer:

Public proof, acknowledgment, and validation over the years that you are doing well give your ego a little ammunition and a little buffer, so when you do hear criticism you can say, "Well, four million people don't think that way!"

I always try to look to the source of any kind of feedback before I judge the feedback. Is it coming from somebody being reactive? Is it coming from someone who is going through something? Is it coming from someone who is envious of me? Is it coming from somebody who truly has a good point? Not just what they're saying, but who is saying it is always important to me.

▶ **SECRET #19: Before judging feedback, always look at the source.**

I probably have been my own most vicious critic. When I was doing my show on CNN every Wednesday night for two years, I would do it live and it would air by satellite all over the world. Then I would come home and they would replay it in Los Angeles at 12:30 a.m. I would get undressed, take off all of my makeup and sit in bed with a pad and pen and watch my show. And I would rip myself apart. I would think,

"How could you give that answer, you moved your head this way, etc." I did this for two years. I've done this with everything, in every speech.

So, the first appearance on CNN compared to the last was night and day, because I learned from my own process. A lot of people don't listen to their own tapes, they don't really evaluate their own delivery. I don't know why they don't. To me, it's the best way to learn.

▶ **SECRET #20: An objective evaluation of your own audio- and videotapes can often provide you with your very best source of feedback.**

I try to be one step ahead of any criticism by delivering it to myself, and constantly improving. To be honest with you, I very rarely get any kind of feedback about *how* I say what I do. It's more *what* I'm saying that might get some kind of criticism.

In the past, it was things like talking too fast or making insensitive comments about certain groups of people. When I get letters that say, "You were here, and you mentioned this, and it really offended me," I really pay attention to those, because I consider those messages from the universe . . . unless it's coming from somebody who has their own issue.

De Angelis' Goal in Life

My goal in life is not to be approved of, it's to grow. I think if your agenda is to be approved of, you're going to be miserable all the time. If it's to grow, every experience, even the painful ones, are blessings.

▶ **SECRET #21: Our purpose as speakers is not to be approved of by our audiences; it's to make a difference and to grow.**

How Barbara De Angelis would like to be remembered:

"As someone who reminded people of the importance of love."
BARBARA DE ANGELIS

Barbara De Angelis', Ph.D.
Success Secrets Summary

SECRET #1: You must believe with all your heart that what you have to say to your audience can and will make a difference in their lives.

SECRET #2: Your emotional energy behind the words you speak is even more important than the words themselves.

SECRET #3: The way you get your audience to feel your words is by first letting your words emotionally impact you.

SECRET #4: Learn quickly from your mistakes and then move on. Beating yourself up over them doesn't help you or anybody else.

SECRET #5: You will connect with your audience the moment you understand that you're already connected; that separation is just an illusion.

SECRET #6: Whenever something goes wrong during a presentation, your audience will look to you to see how they should react. If you don't make a big deal out it, neither will they.

SECRET #7: You are worthwhile and lovable simply because you exist. It's an illusion to think you need anyone else's approval.

SECRET #8: By making sure others don't put you up on a pedestal, you never have to worry about falling off.

SECRET #9: When you're willing to share all of yourself with your audience—not just the good stuff—you will connect with them at a much deeper level.

SECRET #10: Trying to project a flawless image to your audience creates confusion in their minds because it doesn't allow them any place to hold their own mistakes and fears.

SECRET #11: The wisdom, insights and ideas you share with your audience are the most powerful when they come from your own personal experience.

SECRET #12: Getting quiet and tuning in to the silence within you will put you in touch with your highest self—the knower within you—the essence of who you really are.

SECRET #13: When speaking, any critical thoughts (old tapes) that come up are never resisted (because what we resist persists!), but are unconditionally loved and acknowledged. Rather than deny the feelings, you transcend them.

SECRET #14: All your research on your audience won't mean anything if you fail to connect with them.

SECRET #15: As you grow and your vision expands, what you talk about may stay the same; but the way you talk about it will change.

SECRET #16: Know the image that you project as a speaker, the strengths *and* the weaknesses.

SECRET #17: Two powerful ways to connect with your audience are through strong, caring eye contact and a genuine smile.

SECRET #18: When you are tuned in and connected to your audience, each person will feel as if you are talking directly to them.

SECRET #19: Before judging feedback, always look at the source.

SECRET #20: An objective evaluation of your own audio- and video-tapes can often provide you with your very best source of feedback.

SECRET #21: Our purpose as speakers is not to be approved of by our audiences; it's to make a difference and to grow.

CHAPTER FOUR

BORN: January 5, 1944
BIRTHPLACE: Charlotte Town, Canada

Brian Tracy

"I look upon my way of speaking as the windshield-wiper method: left brain/right brain, left brain/right brain. First I tell you what to do, then I tell you why it works. People enjoy learning when you teach them not only that this is a good thing to do, but why this is a good thing to do."

▼

GEORGE Bernard Shaw said, "People are always blaming their circumstances for where they are. I don't believe in circumstances. The people who get on in this world are the people who get up and look for the circumstances they want, and if they can't find them, make them." Shaw's powerful words encapsulate the philosophy that has driven Brian Tracy and helped him become one of the wealthiest and most successful professional speakers in the world. What makes Tracy's story so inspiring is that he went from having literally nothing, to having everything a person could want. What was responsible for his remarkable turnaround? How could a man go from sleeping in his car to having stayed in the finest hotels all over the world, and from having no money to never having less than one thousand dollars cash in his pocket? From flunking out of high school to being hired for huge sums of money by such companies as Ford, Federal Express, Domino's Pizza, IBM, and Hewlett-Packard to teach *them* how to be more successful?!

The Magnificent Obsession

"When you reach the point where you think of nothing else but your goals, you will stop having them and your goals will have you. From that point forward, you will accomplish more than you ever have before."
BRIAN TRACY

The answer to how Tracy was able to so dramatically turn his life around lies in the fact that he had a magnificent obsession. What is a magnificent obsession? It's when you dedicate your life to a powerful and compelling cause. It's Edison working in his laboratory nonstop, often for two and three days straight, without sleep, because he was obsessed with inventing the light bulb. It's Eddie Murphy pretending he was Elvis and recreating the King's concerts in his basement for hours as a youngster because he so badly wanted to be an entertainer. It's two college students, Steve Jobs and Steve Wozniak, who sold their only two possessions, a van and a calculator, because they were obsessed with inventing a user-friendly personal computer for the masses. (And because they succeeded, I'm able to write these words on my Apple Macintosh!)

An obsession goes far beyond just wanting or desiring something. It's a one-hundred-percent commitment that you will do whatever it takes, by whatever means are necessary, to achieve your goal. For example, imagine somebody holding your head underwater. In a flash you realize that if you don't get this person's hand off your head you are going to die. Suddenly, you begin to kick and bite and claw and do whatever you have to to get the hand off so you can come up for a breath of air. This is the level of intensity that having a magnificent obsession evokes. Like the "Terminator" that Schwarzenegger played in the movies, nothing short of death is going to keep you from reaching your objective.

As a speaker, when you have this type of commitment to your message, your audience will sense this. Your passion and belief will rub off on them and you will go from merely giving a speech to impacting people's belief systems and changing lives.

▶ **SECRET #1: The day your message becomes a magnificient obsession instead of simply a speech, will be the day you go from merely informing people to changing their lives.**

So what was Tracy's magnificent obsession? It was his burning desire and intense commitment to find out the answer to one question: "Why are some people more successful in life than others?" In his book, *Maximum Achievement* (Simon and Schuster, 1993), Tracy says:

> From a young age, I wanted to know why it was that some people were more successful than others. I was mystified by the disparities of wealth, happiness and influence I saw all around me. Something deep inside me said that there must be reasons for this apparent inequality, and I was determined to find out what they were.

It's not difficult to understand why Tracy sought success and happiness, when you consider his upbringing.

Came from a Poor Childhood

As with many of the speakers I interviewed, Tracy did not have a happy childhood. His family was poor and, for the first decade of his life, most of his clothes came from the Goodwill and other charities. Tracy recalls:

> I came from a poor family and I didn't like it. My father was not always regularly employed and we never seemed to have enough money for anything but the bare necessities.

Adding to his problems was the fact that Tracy was an extremely angry young man. Constantly in trouble, he was always rebelling and being disruptive in class. He was suspended numerous times and kicked out of two high schools. In fact, he holds the dubious distinction of receiving more detentions than any other kid in any school he attended from junior high through his senior year in high school. Ironically, the man who today is considered by many to have one of the sharpest business minds in the speaking profession failed six out of seven courses during his senior year and ended up flunking out of high school! Not surprisingly, his lack of success in the academic world had a negative effect on his self-esteem:

> I held myself back and sold myself short for years, as many people do, because I didn't graduate from high school. I looked on university graduates with awe and respect. I unconsciously assumed that my future was limited. Because of this belief, I set only limited goals for myself, and I wasn't surprised if I didn't achieve them. After all, I did poorly in school—what could you expect?

After leaving high school, Tracy's first job was as a hotel dishwasher. From there he went through a series of labor-intensive jobs, including stacking lumber, digging wells, working on an assembly line, and in construction. Often, he slept in boardinghouses or rundown motels or even, occasionally, in his car.

When he was twenty-one, he got a job working on a Norwegian freighter as a galley boy, and for the next few years he got to see much of the world. This was an eye-opening experience for the young Canadian. However, he eventually ran out of money and was forced to seek employment on a farm as a day laborer. The days were long and hard, and the nights, which were spent sleeping on hay in the farmer's barn, were cold and uncomfortable. Clearly, a change was in order.

Gets Job in Sales

---

*"The reason why most people miss opportunity
when it comes along is because it comes
dressed in work clothes."*
BRIAN TRACY

When the labor jobs dried up, Tracy got a job selling office supply products. Of course, he had no experience whatsoever in sales, so, not surprisingly, things were tough from the get-go. In *Advanced Selling Skills* (Simon and Schuster, 1995) Tracy says:

> At the age of twenty-four, I was still walking the streets, making calls in a wash-and-wear shirt I rinsed out in the sink of my rooming house each night, and wearing the same clip-on tie I wore every day. I had one pair of used shoes, which were too large for me and which flopped a little as I walked. I was making a living, but just barely.

Despite the rough start, Tracy did have two things going for him. First, he wasn't afraid of hard work. He was willing to get up early and go knock on doors until late at night in an effort to find new customers. Secondly, he was eager to learn and grow from his experiences. It was this second quality that prompted him to seek out the top salesman in his company. The gentleman's name was Pete and he was very successful. He wore first-rate clothes, lived in a luxurious apartment, drove an expensive car, ate at the nicest restaurants, and always had plenty of cash on him. Hoping that Pete would share some of his "sales secrets," Tracy asked him for advice.

The veteran was happy to help, and he asked the young neophyte to show him his sales presentation. Sheepishly, Tracy admitted he didn't have one. His method, he told Pete, was to stand in front of the prospect and rattle off all of the product's features as they were listed in the brochure. Pete just nodded and then sat Brian down. Pretending that Tracy was a prospect, Pete took him step-by-step through his own presentation. Tracy was floored. He had never seen anything like it. Everything about Pete's presentation was logical and systematic. He went from asking general questions to more specific ones, until it became obvious that the product would do everything that he, "the customer," needed. The whole thing flowed naturally, right into the close.

From that moment on, Tracy changed his whole approach to selling. He learned to be a good listener and to take notes. Instead of dominating the conversation, he would ask questions and encourage the customer to talk. Only after he had a clear understanding of exactly what the customer's needs were—as well as any objections they might have—did he begin to highlight the features and benefits his product offered, and how they could help solve the prospect's problem.

Tracy realized that he wasn't selling a product per se, but rather a solution to a problem. Perhaps Charles Revson, the founder of Revlon Cosmetics, said it best when he stated, "In the factory we make cosmetics, but in my stores we sell hope." Once Tracy grasped this concept, his sales began to go up.

Learning to Ask for the Order

"All things are difficult before they are easy."
JOHN NORLEY

Tracy still had one more major lesson to learn, something that all salespeople must become proficient at: *Asking for the order.* Because of his low self-image, he simply couldn't get up the nerve to come right out and ask the customer to buy his product. At the time he was selling discount club memberships, and at the end of his presentation, he would hand the prospect a booklet which listed the club's benefits and then encourage them to "think about it." The problem was, that's all they did.

Being introspective by nature, Tracy thought about his situation. It suddenly dawned on him that the problem wasn't with the customers, it was with him. He realized he needed to change his self-image, thereby changing his behavior and thus his results. At his very next sales presentation, when the customer said, "Let me think about it," Tracy was ready. He smiled and politely informed the gentleman that he did not make callbacks because he was too busy making sales to customers. Then he said, "You know everything you need to know to make a decision right now. Why don't you just take it?" Tracy was stunned when the man responded, "Okay. I'll take it. How would you like to be paid?" That day turned out to be a key turning point in Tracy's career. From *Advanced Selling Strategies*:

> I walked out of that office on a cloud. That very day I tripled my sales. That week, I sold more than anyone else in the company. By the end of the month, I had been promoted to the position of sales manager with forty-two people under me. I went from making one or two sales a week to making ten to fifteen. I went from worrying about money constantly to earning a large salary with an override on the activities of all my salespeople. My sales life took off and, with few exceptions, it never stopped.

▶ **SECRET #2: High achievers never make a sales presentation without asking for the order. If you ask with confidence, you'll be suprised how often the customer will say yes!**

Learning to ask for what you want in life is one of the most important skills you can acquire, and it's something that all successful individuals have mastered. As Mark Victor Hansen says, "You can't G-E-T unless you A-S-K!" (A terrific book, which contains hundreds of true stories of how people got what they wanted in life simply by asking for it, is *The Aladdin Factor* by Jack Canfield and Mark Victor Hansen [Berkley, 1995].)

Turns to Books for Answers

"An investment in knowledge always pays the best interest."
BENJAMIN FRANKLIN

As Tracy continued his journey along the road to becoming a top achiever in sales, one question continued to gnaw at him: "Why are some people more successful than others?" Something inside of him knew there had to be a logical reason for the disparity he saw all around him, and he was determined to find out what it was. Although he had been a poor student, Tracy loved to read. Turning to books for the answer, he made a startling discovery. He found that he could learn how to be successful at virtually anything he wanted, simply by reading what the very best minds on the subject had written about it and then going out and applying his newfound knowledge. From *Maximum Achievement*:

> I had always been fascinated with the subject of happiness, and why it was that some people were obviously happier and more fulfilled than others. To find the answers, I studied psychology, philosophy, religion, metaphysics, motivation and personal achievement.

> To deal with my personality problems, I studied relationships, interpersonal psychology, communications and personality styles. I studied history, economics and politics to understand more about the past and present, and to learn why it is that some countries, and parts of countries, are more affluent than others.

Clearly, Tracy's thirst for knowledge played a significant role in his ability to turn his life around. Like myself, you too may have an extensive book and audiotape library. I must admit, however, that while I have always enjoyed and valued my library, I never fully appreciated just what a priceless resource it was until I attended a presentation by my friend and colleague, W. Mitchell. He is the author of the compelling book, *The Man Who Would Not Be Defeated* (1993, WRS Publishing), and one of the most inspirational speakers I have ever heard.

Mitchell was addressing the Los Angeles chapter of the National Speakers Association when he pointed to our chapter library at the back of the room and said, "Those audiotapes and books are literally a gold mine of millions of dollars' worth of ideas, just sitting there, waiting for you to put them into action." "Wow!" I thought, "he's absolutely right." By implementing many of the "golden nuggets" that can be found throughout this book, you can achieve virtually anything you want in life, *if* you are willing to work hard enough. The fact is that many people will read these speakers' great ideas and never put any of them into action. However, if you're one of the few who takes the time to really try them out and to expand your thinking and your belief as to what's possible, and you're committed to doing whatever it takes to get the results you're looking for, I promise you you will be successful. It's only a matter of time.

Learning from Those Who Have Come Before Us

"Success leaves clues."
ANTHONY ROBBINS

One of the reasons that reading a book like this one can help you become successful is because it can cut literally years off your learning curve. What has taken top achievers sometimes decades to discover, you can learn in a few hours simply by reading one of their books, attending a seminar or listening to one of their cassettes. In fact, Tracy credits much of his success to this very fact:

. . . In a few hours I could get the benefit of what had taken the best sales trainer many years to learn. I could save myself hundreds and even thousands of hours of work trying to learn the same things on my own.

▶ **SECRET #3: By reading books, listening to audiotapes, and attending seminars, you can learn in a few hours the knowledge that has taken successful men and women years to acquire.**

Without a doubt, Tracy's drive to study successful people kicked into high gear the day he made a most profound discovery that eludes fully ninety-nine percent of the people on the planet. What he had figured out was that you can achieve virtually *any* goal you desire by simply finding out what others have done who have achieved that goal, and then duplicating their actions. Says Tracy:

> The key to success is to learn from the experts. Study and copy the very best people in your field. Do what they do, day after day, until it becomes second nature. And then—Surprise! Surprise! You begin to get the same results.

This is fantastic advice, and again, it's exactly the premise this book is based on: By finding out what the very best speakers in the field do and how they think, you can begin to do the same things and think the same ways and, as Tracy says, "Surprise! Surprise!" eventually, if you don't give up, you *will* get the same results.

▶ **SECRET #4: By duplicating the actions of successful people, if you don't give up, you will eventually achieve the same results they did.**

The Sweet Smell of Success

"I will prepare and someday my chance will come."
ABRAHAM LINCOLN

Here, in his own words, is how Tracy's hard work paid off and how he went from "rags to riches" in just twelve short months:

Within a year, after buying every book, listening to every audiotape, and attending every sales training seminar or course I could find, I literally went from rags to riches. I went from living in a boardinghouse to having a large, beautifully furnished apartment with a maid.

I went from worrying about every dollar to never carrying less than one thousand dollars in my pocket. I flew on jets and dined in the best restaurants in the biggest cities in my market area. Eventually, they made me a sales manager and then a sales executive. They gave me six countries and a development budget, plus overrides on the sales of all my people.

By the time I was twenty-five, I had recruited and built a ninety-five-person sales force, covering six countries and generating millions of dollars per month in sales. I had apartments in three cities and I was living a life I had never dreamed possible. And it was all because I learned what the very best people were doing and did it over and over again myself, until I got the same results.

I hope reading the above inspires you as much as it does me. Every time I read another person's "success story," it always makes me think, "if he (or she) can do it, then so can I!" This is because, as Tracy points out below, if you or I follow the same exact steps as somebody else, we will get the same results. The analogy that Brian uses is that of a combination lock. It doesn't matter who turns the dial, as long as the right numbers are reached in the proper order, the lock will fall open for anyone. Here's Tracy on how this is done:

Life Is a Series of Combination Locks

"All the things that a person wants in life are available to him, if he will just simply do the things that other people who started with little or nothing have done to get the things they wanted!"
BRIAN TRACY

An analogy that I sometimes use with my audiences is that of a combination lock. A combination lock is neutral. It doesn't care who turns the dial, as long as the dial is turned to the right numbers in the right sequence, the lock will fall open. And it doesn't matter if you are young or old, smart or stupid, black or white, male or female. All that matters is that if you do the right things in the right sequence, you'll get the same results.

Life, in its simplest form, is a series of combination locks. All the things that a person wants in life are available to them, if they will simply do the things that other people who started with little or nothing have done to get the things they wanted. There's nothing miraculous about it; find out what other successful people have done, do the same things, and you will get the same results.

▶ **SECRET #5: Life is like a series of combination locks. What's more, the locks are neutral; they'll open for anyone as long as the dial is turned to the right numbers (i.e. the right steps are taken) in the right order.**

Puts Together First Seminar

"If you don't love what you do, you will never be successful at it."
BRIAN TRACY

In 1981, Tracy created a two-day seminar based on the "success techniques" that he had spent years uncovering and putting to profitable use. The program was called *The Inner Game of Success,* and Brian was quite excited about it:

I was on fire with the ideas in the seminar. The materials and ideas were profound and life-changing from the very beginning, and I had an intense desire to share them with others. I knew these ideas worked and I was convinced that anyone who would apply even a small part of this system could bring about rapid, positive changes in his or her life.

Note Brian's enthusiasm for the ideas and principles he was presenting. He didn't think or hope they could change people's lives— he *knew* they could—because they had changed his!

By 1984, the name of the program had been changed to *The Phoenix Seminar* (after the mythical bird that rises up from its ashes). It became so popular that the Nightingale-Conant corporation recorded it live, titled it *The Psychology of Achievement,* and put it out as a six-cassette album. It instantly became a best-seller and has gone on to sell over half a million copies!

Positive Knowing Versus *Positive Thinking*

> *"The average person has four ideas a year which, if any one is acted on, would make them a millionaire."*
> BRIAN TRACY

The essence of Brian's teaching is that once you develop an inner sense of knowing—which is much deeper than just hoping or thinking—you can be, do, or have virtually anything you desire. This is because you will be willing to take whatever action is necessary to achieve your goals. Tracy explained it to me this way:

It's more a matter of "positive knowing," rather than "positive thinking." In the final analysis, the person has to have the confidence to take action. All successful people are intensely action-oriented. It is the taking of action that generates the feedback, the motivation, the enthusiasm, and the self-confidence that leads to subsequent actions.

Sometimes a person has to learn to trust themselves and believe in themselves so they will take the necessary actions. But it is the actions themselves that lead to a person developing a deep-down sense of confidence that he or she knows that they are capable of doing things. This deep inner-knowing is a critical factor for success.

So, the message here is *act!* When in doubt, take action. If you do nothing, then nothing is all you'll get. However, if you take action, something positive is bound to happen.

▶ **SECRET #6: Successful people are intensely action-oriented.**

When the Student Is Ready . . .

I asked Tracy why he thought some people leave his seminar and immediately put his ideas into action and quickly begin to reap the rewards, both financial as well as personal, while others go home and do nothing:

> The best way to explain it is to take the person's way of looking at the world, which is formed starting in early infancy. If a person's way of looking at the world is benevolent, in that they see that the world is a good place, and that it contains opportunities for them to be and have and do more, then they will see ideas and information and insights everywhere. Not only that, they will look for them. They will be on an eternal quest for self-knowledge and personal growth.
>
> If, on the other hand, an individual has a negative worldview and, as a result of previous experiences, feels that he or she is not very good, not very capable, that the cards are stacked against them, then no matter what you present to them that will help them, they will find ways to justify not doing anything. The easiest way to justify not doing anything is to discount the messenger. It's to say, "The messenger is no good, so the message is invalid, so therefore I don't have to do anything."

▶ **SECRET #7: How you view the world plays a key role in how successful you will be.**

Tracy's answer is most illuminating. If we sincerely desire to improve ourselves, then we will take the information that is presented to us, whether it's from a book, tape, or seminar, and we will enthusiastically try it out so that we, too, can achieve the same results. However, if we believe that the deck is stacked against us and therefore "what's the use of even trying," then we will discount the information presented to us, even if it could help us! Tracy explains why:

> In psychology there's a principle called "cognitive dissonance," which says that a person cannot hold two contradictory ideas in the mind at the same time. When a person hears an idea that contradicts what they are doing and thinking, a conflict is set up. The mind of the individual attempts to resolve the conflict by one of two ways: The first is to accept the new idea and allow it to replace the old idea, which is what we do through repetition, affirmations, and visualization. The other way is to use the old existing idea—which is often called "the comfort zone"—to reject the new idea.
>
> We find that superior men and women have very open minds. It doesn't mean that they quickly adopt or abandon an idea. It means that their minds are open to the possibility that there are better ways of doing things. That there are better ways of acting and thinking that will enable them to be more effective, happy, and positive. Their minds are very much like a radar scanner; they're constantly looking for new ideas that can help them improve the things they are doing. They attend seminars, read books, listen to tapes in their cars and subscribe to different magazines and publications.
>
> The negative person is like a person with their blinds drawn. They want things to be better, but they fail to understand that, in order for things to change, *they* must change! And the prospect of change is very scary for a person who has a low self-concept or low self-esteem. Rather than change, the person will reject either the idea or the source of the idea and, therefore, will end up not having to change and, as a result, they will not be happy. They will become more frustrated, resist change even more so, and then will only associate with people who are like them—negative and going nowhere.

So you have some people on an upward spiral, where life gets continually better, and some people on a downward spiral, where life is quite stagnant and becomes increasingly worse.

It's true. Ask any successful person and they will tell you that life just keeps getting better and better, that this year is better than last year, and next year will be even better than this year. However, what should you do if you currently find yourself in a downward spiral and you want to break out of it? Tracy recommends that you keep in mind that:

> . . . men and women who have accomplished wonderful things, things that a person admires, whether they're financial, physical, or in their relationships, are not extraordinary or unusual. Everybody starts off with the same number of difficulties. We all start off with parents who don't know how to parent and teachers who in many cases don't know how to teach. We start off in environments that are predominantly not supportive and encouraging. So everyone starts off behind some form of "eight ball."

> The people who succeed are not unusual; they just have gone to work on themselves and their lives. It's a long process. It takes maybe ten or twenty years for a person to evolve as a fully mature, fully functioning, self-actualizing adult.

> One thing you can do to accomplish this is live your life by what is called "The Reality Principle," which says: "It is important that you face life as it is, not as you wish it could be."

▶ **SECRET #8: It's important that you face life as it is, not as you wish it could be.**

Learning to see life as it is, and not as you wish it to be, is one of the biggest steps you can take to becoming a fully functioning adult. I must admit that for a long time I thought that only "seeing the good" was the best way to live one's life. However, this was not a realistic attitude and would often lead to problems. The fact is, there are good people and bad people in this world, and not everybody thinks like you or I do. Once we come to accept this, only then are we free to deal with life "as it is and not as we wish it to be." To help accomplish this, Tracy recommends that you become:

> Be continuously aware of the thoughts and ideas you are taking into your mind, of the people you are associating with, and of your attitudes toward your work and your relationships. You must realize that in the simplest of terms, life is a cause-and-effect process. Whatever causes you initiate, you will reap the effects.

> It's important that you realize that everything that you say, or do, or think, has a consequence. If you think positive thoughts about yourself and your world, you will experience positive effects. If you think negative thoughts or say negative things or do nothing at all, then you will experience negative or disappointing effects.

> So we say, "Think and talk about what you want, not about what you fear." Do the things that are moving you in the direction of where you want to go, rather than the things that are not. Also, remember that everything counts. Everything that you do and everything that you neglect to do or avoid doing or procrastinate in doing, has an effect. That even not doing something is a cause that has an effect, the consequences of which are inescapable. It's not called the "theory" of cause and effect, or the "theory" of sowing and reaping.

> Throughout all of human history, in every religion and in every philosophy, the wisest men and women who have ever lived have come to the conclusion that all of life is a putting in and a getting out. You get out of life what you put into it. You get out of a relationship what you put into it. You get out of your work what you put into it.

> If you want a wonderful, happy, prosperous, healthy, exciting, abundant life, than you have to consistently and continuously put that sort of thought, word, and action into your life.

▶ **SECRET #9: Life is a cause-and-effect process; whatever causes you initiate, you will reap the effects.**

The question to ask yourself is this: "Is what I'm doing on a daily basis getting me closer to my goals?" If you find that you're no closer to achieving your goals today than you were a year ago, it's simply because you're not doing the things on a daily basis that are necessary to achieve them. Once you start changing your daily actions, your "cause," then, just as night follows day, your results, or the "effect" you're getting, will change.

This is one of the most important fundamental concepts on which our entire universe is based—yet ninety-nine percent of the people in this world have yet to figure this out. The good news is that once you do, your whole life changes because you realize that your destiny is completely in your hands. While this thought scares many people, it's simply the way it is. So, rather than see it as a negative, the best thing to do is say to yourself, "Okay, if I really do reap what I sow, than what actions do I need to take to get the results I want?" Let me assure you that once you become accustomed to this way of thinking, you'll wonder how you ever went through life believing otherwise. By the way, it should come as no surprise by now that Tracy's favorite quote is from psychologist William James:

"The greatest revelation of my generation is the discovery that by changing the inner attitudes of your mind, you can change the outer aspects of your life."

The Importance of Knowing Your Topic Inside Out

"A person only really understands something to the degree to which they can turn and explain it to another person, and have them understand it too."
BRIAN TRACY

One of the major differences between great speakers and average ones is the depth with which they understand their subject matter. The reality is that you simply aren't going to be able to communicate all the nuances of your topic to your audience if you, yourself, have only a surface understanding of it. This is why top speakers like Tracy are constantly devouring new information on their subject areas like a sponge. As Tracy points out, in order to teach a concept to others, it's not enough to simply know that it works, but you must also understand *why* it works:

> In order to change behavior and attitudes, you have to have new knowledge. You have to understand, mentally, why these ideas work, why they are good, and how they can be applied to one's life. In other words, a person only really understands something to the degree to which they can turn and explain it to another person, and have them understand it, too. The starting point to becoming successful in any field is to become absolutely excellent in one area.

▶ **SECRET #10: The starting point to becoming successful in any field is to become absolutely excellent in one area.**

It's true—the more you know about your field, the greater your chances of success become. This is the reason golfer Jack Nicklaus and cellist Yo-Yo Ma are the best in the world at what they do—because they know more about their respective fields than anybody else. Nobody understands software and how to market it better than Bill Gates, and so it's no surprise that Microsoft is the leader in the computer software industry. Once you make the commitment to become excellent in your line of work, it's only a matter of time before you will become a success at it.

Passing the Credibility Test

"I sometimes joke that success speakers often come to the seminar on the bus because they can't afford a car!"
BRIAN TRACY

Like all industries, the speaking field has become increasingly competitive over the past two decades. Yet, many of the people who go into professional speaking really have not earned the right to get up before an audience and speak. While it's true that you do not have to take a written test or apply for a license to become a professional speaker, there is one test that every speaker must pass: the credibility test. Ralph Didonato, a speaking colleague of mine, once told me about the time he saw a speaker get booed off the stage when an angry audience of salesmen discovered that the gentleman had never actually sold anything! Obviously, he failed the test. Here's more on having "walked your talk" from Tracy:

> The biggest mistake I see people make is that they want to talk about success and motivation, while being unsuccessful and unmotivated themselves. They want desperately to be successful and to be motivated, so they go out and talk about it before they have actually applied their concepts.

> I sometimes joke that success speakers often come to the seminar on the bus because they can't afford a car! Then they stand up in front of an audience and try to tell them how to be successful. However, the average person in the audience is very smart. He or she can see the truth of what a person is saying by looking at the person who is saying it. In other words, the medium is the message.

> You cannot teach others to do something that you cannot do vastly better. You cannot hold your life up as a sample to others unless your life is worthy of emulation.

> If a successful person stands up and speaks, he does not have to be an accomplished speaker. If he or she speaks from the heart and says, "This was my situation, this is what I did, and these are the results I got. If you are in a similar situation, you may find them helpful as well." That kind of a person has much more credibility than a person who has never had the experience of success, but has read all the books.

> The starting point of speaking on any subject is to care passionately about the subject, because you absolutely believe that the subject is important because you absolutely know that it works. And you can only know that it works if you've done it yourself.

▶ **SECRET #11: Great speakers can speak with confidence about their ideas because they know they work. And the reason they know they work is because they themselves have successfully used them.**

Fake It Until You Make It?

I asked Tracy how Anthony Robbins' concept of "fake it until you make it" fits in with what he just said about not speaking on a subject that you have not personally had success in:

> You cannot fake an accomplishment. I cannot fake an Olympic record. I cannot fake a graduate degree from Harvard. Those things must be earned. I think that, in the great cosmos, there is an absolute insistence upon impeccable integrity. And the people who are most successful over the longest term are those who are the most honest.
>
> However, when someone says, "fake it until you make it," that does not mean that you should not act courageously, or positively, or enthusiastically, or cheerfully, if you feel a little bit crummy. There's nothing wrong with that. In fact, we can actually control our emotions by controlling our behaviors.
>
> For example, we've all had the experience where we've been in the middle of an argument at home and the phone rings, and it's a friend. And our voice instantly changes from one of being angry to being very positive and pleasant. However, as soon as we hang up the phone we go right back to being angry again. So, we do control our behaviors, thoughts, and actions.

We Are Creatures of Habit

The wonderful thing is that we are creatures of habit. If we will control our actions, behaviors, thoughts, and words on a continuous basis, eventually those become habits. And so positive people are simply those people who have behaved and spoken in a positive way over and over again until it locks in and becomes a permanent part of their character and personality.

▶ **SECRET #12: Positive people have simply made thinking in a positive way a habit.**

Negative people are simply those who have spoken and acted in a negative way over and over again, so that's become an automatic part of their personality.

As the saying goes, "First we make our habits, and then our habits make us." I can tell you from personal experience that you can learn to become a positive thinker if you truly want to. Whereas I once let the outside world (which is often negative) affect my thinking, today this is no longer the case. I have trained myself to always look for the good in any situation. I did this through constant daily practice. You, too, can learn to see the world in terms of "How can I make this work for me?" rather than "Oh no, not another problem. Why is life so difficult?" which is negative thinking that will get you nowhere.

Whenever an event happens that appears to be negative, immediately think to yourself, "What new opportunities are now available to me?" and "No problem! Piece of cake! I can easily handle this!" At first this type of thinking might feel artificial to you, but I assure you that after you try it for a while you will come to believe it and soon your whole world will change. Try it for the next thirty days and see for yourself!

What's in a Style?

"People who like to know . . . why . . . they are being asked to do . . . something better or different, are attracted to my style."
BRIAN TRACY

One of the wonderful things about writing this book was that I got to interview so many different *kinds* of speakers. For example, whereas Wayne Dyer's style of speaking tends to appeal to more right-brained, metaphysical, "first you must believe it, then you'll see it" type of people, Tracy's speaking style tends to appeal to the more left-brained, analytical types who not only want to know how something works, but why.

The good news is that we can learn a lot from both approaches. For myself, I like to give my audiences a little of both; some metaphysical concepts and some straightforward "how-to's." I do this in order to reach as many people as possible.

Whatever style you choose, the most important thing is that you are comfortable with it. Here's Tracy on his speaking style:

> My approach is to deal with the emotions which control behavior and through the intellect, which controls thought and therefore decisionmaking. People who like to know and understand why it is that they are being asked to do or be something better or different, are attracted to my style.

The Windshield-Wiper Method

I look upon my way of speaking as the windshield-wiper method: left brain/right brain, left brain/right brain. What I mean by that is: Left brain is what to do, right brain is why it works. It's the practical plus the intuitive or understanding; the pragmatic plus the holistic and imaginative.

People you teach like to know not only that this is a good thing to do, but *why* this is a good thing to do. Explaining that allows them to say to themselves in the final analysis, "This makes sense to me. I think I'll do it and see if I get the results that Brian says I will."

The wonderful thing is that everything I teach is very simple. Anybody can make a subject complex, but the mark of understanding a subject—and I've spent thousands of hours on my subjects—is to make it very simple. Simple enough so that a person can take the idea and walk out of the meeting or the seminar, apply it, and get results.

▶ **SECRET #13: Great speakers make their ideas simple enough so that people can walk out of the meeting or seminar, apply them, and get immediate results.**

The Best Way to Market Yourself

"Most millionaires make their money after the age of 40."
BRIAN TRACY

Like many of the other speakers I interviewed, Tracy said that the very best way to market yourself is to do a great job every time you step up on to the platform:

> I think the very best way to market oneself is to do what you do as well as you possibly can. To be very well prepared. To be very well rested and to put your whole heart into every single talk, in front of every single audience, no matter what the size.
>
> If you do that really, really well, the marketing will take care of itself. If you don't do that really, really well, you can market all day and all night and it won't be sufficient.
>
> The audiences of today are more demanding of substantial content than they ever have been in history. The successful speakers of today and tomorrow, more and more, will be those whom the audience feels really gave them a lot of value in terms of content—that which is called "take-home value."

▶ **SECRET #14: The successful speakers of today will be those whom the audience feels really gave them a lot of value in terms of content, i.e. "take home value."**

Mr. Content

"The result of hearing a good professional speaker is that people learn how to change and improve their lives, their work, and their relationships. Great speakers raise one's aspirations, hopes, and ambitions."
BRIAN TRACY

If Tracy were to have a speaking nickname, it would have to be "Mr. Content." This is because not just in his speeches, but in his audio programs and books as well, Tracy packs in more meat— more practical and usable material—than just about any other speaker in the business. For example, he makes sure that the purchaser of one of his eighteen audio albums gets a minimum of one hundred or more "valuable, practical, usable, and uncomplicated ideas" from each program. Keep this *high content, more-bang-for-the-buck* philosophy in mind while you are developing your own products, and your customers will indeed be well served. In fact, when asked to give one piece of advice to speakers, Tracy says:

> Concentrate on high-quality, high content, honest, valuable information. Present it in an interesting, informative manner that really helps people to be more effective. This is the key to my success.

Tracy and Ziglar's $50,000-Day in Product Sales

One of the major reasons you should strive to pack as much good, usable material as you can into your programs is because people rightly assume that if your presentation contains a tremendous amount of good ideas, then so will your products.

I'll never forget the day I attended a one-day rally featuring Brian Tracy in the morning, and Zig Ziglar in the afternoon. As I entered the hotel ballroom—which was filled with some three thousand people—I was confronted with an unforgettable sight. There, sitting on top of nine tables set up in a horseshoe shape, was so much of Tracy and Zigler's products that you could barely see the people who were back there selling it! I'm talking about literally mounds of product, much of which was packaged together ("Buy three cassette albums and get a fourth one free!"). Some of these bundles of products sold for $395.00 and up.

By the end of the day, all the product was gone! In fact, the helpers behind the tables were now taking addresses so they could mail out more product when they got back to their offices. I roughly calculated that between the two of them, Tracy and Ziglar sold approximately $50,000 worth of product in just one afternoon! Not too shabby for a day's work, and something that all serious speakers should strive for—because if they can do it, so can you. Again, the key is to be so good that they want to take "a piece of you" home.

The Goal Is Not Fame, but Helping Others

"The idea of helping others to be better and to feel better about themselves is really the big turn-on for speakers such as myself."
BRIAN TRACY

When I asked Tracy what it felt like to be one of the most well-known professional speakers in the world, he said:

> I don't even think in terms of whether or not I'm famous. I think more in terms of being able to help people. I find that the other speakers that I know get most excited when they discover ideas, mostly through research, discussion and reading, or new synthesis of ideas that they have put together to give to people in order to help them improve their lives.

> The idea of helping others to be better, and to feel better about themselves, is really the big turn-on for speakers such as myself. I know Wayne Dyer, Tony Robbins, and most of the other speakers in this book. And my experience with them is that way down deep inside, their primary motivation is to help others be more happy and more effective. That's what they think about more than anything else. How well they're known is an offshoot of that. It makes them very happy to be successful at what they're doing, but it is not their major concern. Just as a doctor is concerned with healing, we are concerned with enhancing the lives of the people in the audience.

▶ **SECRET #15: It's never about fame or money for top achievers, but rather figuring out ways to help people live better and happier lives.**

Tuning In to a Higher Power

Almost all the speakers I interviewed, from Tony Robbins to Barbara De Angelis to Wayne Dyer, told me that their relationship with a higher power was very important to them. Tracy, too, felt that his ability to tune in to our creator was a necessary and positive source of inspiration in his life:

> My philosophy for life is that there is a greater power in the universe which I refer to as God, and believe in as God. And that if you attune yourself to this higher power and you live your life consistent with universal principles and follow your inner light, then you'll never go wrong.

How Brian Tracy would like to be remembered:

"Brian Tracy had a profound and positive influence on improving the lives of millions of people."
BRIAN TRACY

Brian Tracy's
Success Secrets Summary

SECRET #1: The day your message becomes a magnificent obsession instead of simply a speech, will be the day you go from merely informing people to changing their lives.

SECRET #2: High achievers never make a sales presentation without asking for the order. If you ask with confidence, you'll be surprised how often the customer will say yes!

SECRET #3: By reading books, listening to audiotapes, and attending seminars, you can learn in a few hours the knowledge that has taken successful men and women years to acquire.

SECRET #4: By duplicating the actions of successful people, if you don't give up, you will eventually achieve the same results they did.

SECRET #5: Life is like a series of combination locks. What's more, the locks are neutral; they'll open for anyone as long as the dial is turned to the right numbers (the right steps are taken) in the right order.

SECRET #6: Successful people are intensely action-oriented.

SECRET #7: How you view the world plays a key role in how successful you will be.

SECRET #8: It's important that you face life as it is, not as you wish it could be.

SECRET #9: Life is a cause-and-effect process; whatever causes you initiate, you will reap the effects.

SECRET #10: The starting point to becoming successful in any field is to become absolutely excellent in one area.

SECRET #11: Great speakers can speak with confidence about their ideas because they know they work. And the reason they know they work is because they themselves have successfully used them.

SECRET #12: Positive people have simply made thinking in a positive way a habit.

SECRET #13: Great speakers make their ideas simple enough so that people can walk out of the meeting or seminar, apply them, and get immediate results.

SECRET #14: The successful speakers of today will be those whom the audience feels really gave them a lot of value in terms of content, i.e. "take-home value."

SECRET #15: It's never about fame or money for top achievers, but rather figuring out ways to help people live better and happier lives.

CHAPTER FIVE

BORN: February 17, 1945
BIRTHPLACE: Miami, Florida

Les Brown

"It's an honor to be able to speak to people, to touch people's lives. You have the opportunity to change lives and to influence people and their decisions about themselves, their future, and their environment. Take that seriously and accept it as a blessing and commit yourself to giving them the best that you have."

▼

THE *American Heritage Dictionary* defines the word *dynamic* as: *marked by energy and vigor; forceful.* Perhaps more than any other quality, it's the ability to deliver information in an energetic and dynamic way that separates great speakers from the merely good ones. Of significance is the fact that being a dynamic speaker brings much more to a presentation than simply flashy showmanship. Studies show that the more dynamic a speaker is perceived to be by an audience, the more likely they are to remember his or her message. In their book *Argumentation and the Decision Making Process* (1975, John Wiley & Sons, Inc.), authors Richard Rieke and Malcolm Sillars write: "We know that dynamism in a speaker increases retention. One can easily see how greater physical and vocal activity would cause a person to retain more information simply because he would pay more attention to what was being said."

One speaker who not only understands the power of a dynamic delivery, but has made it his trademark, is Les Brown. To see him take charge of an audience is to see a master at work. With his booming voice, joyous smile, contagious laugh, heartfelt stories, and keen sense of timing, Brown doesn't just move audiences, he electrifies them! Brown's success story is all the more remarkable when you consider the enormous odds that he had to overcome to get where he is today.

> *"Wanting something is not enough. You must hunger for it. Your motivation must be absolutely compelling in order to overcome the obstacles that will invariably come your way."*
> LES BROWN

Abandoned at Birth

Life did not start off on an upbeat note for Leslie Calvin Brown. He and his fraternal twin, Wes, were born into this world on the floor of an abandoned building. Three weeks later their mother gave them away and they would never see her or their natural father again. (Years later, when Brown was told that he was adopted, he, like most adopted children, went through a period of many years where he hated his natural parents for abandoning him. And who could blame him? Yet, eventually, he realized that the anger he felt inside was only hurting him. Brown read philosopher Kahlil Gibran's writings, which explained that, although our parents bring us into the world, in the end, *we* are responsible for what we become. This helped Brown to finally let go of the pain and resentment he had been harboring for so long.)

A Silver Lining Named Mamie Brown

As the saying goes, *every cloud has a silver lining.* For Les and his brother, that "silver lining" came in the form of Mamie Brown, who at age thirty-eight, adopted them when they were only a few weeks old. Les' relationship with Mamie Brown could not have been closer had she been his biological mother. Like Elvis Presley and his mother, Les and Mamie had an affection and a love for each other that went much deeper than your typical mother-son relationship. Mamie Brown was a woman of tremendous determination and courage, and her strong will made an indelible impression on Les.

The two brothers, along with a little sister that was adopted five years later, grew up in Overtown and Liberty City, two of the poorest neighborhoods in Miami, Florida. Ms. Brown would leave the three youngsters with a neighbor who had kids of her own, while she went off to work as a cook in the M & M Cafeteria, and later as a nursing home cook, maid, and housekeeper. While they didn't have a lot, Mamie Brown never let her family go without food on the table and clean clothes on their backs—even if they were hand-me-downs from families she had worked for. Her hard work ethic along with her belief that "you must walk by faith and not by sight," helped her overcome many of the struggles that every single parent must face.

School + Young Les = Trouble

Once Les started school, he quickly showed that he had everything it took to be a poor student. That is, when he showed up. Often he'd simply ditch school altogether and find some trouble to get into which, due to his choice of friends, wasn't too difficult. When he wasn't cutting school, his quick tongue and short temper made him a frequent visitor to the principal's office. And when he was in class, his teachers had a hard time keeping Brown's attention due to his hyperactive and disruptive nature. To make matters worse, by the time he stumbled into the fifth grade, this self-acknowledged "class clown" had been tagged with a not-so-funny label—that of being "educable mentally retarded."

This, of course, only served to further exacerbate the boy's already low self-image. Now, since his teachers didn't expect much of him, he no longer had a reason to try very hard. He had been told over and over that he was a "slow learner," and once his brain accepted this label, he did not disappoint and quickly got the Ds and Fs to prove it.

Fortunately for Brown, his spiraling descent came to a halt when one of his high school teachers not only refused to buy into his label, but encouraged Brown to begin to question it himself.

Les Meets Mr. Leroy Washington

When asked, Brown will tell you that there are three people who have played a major role in shaping and influencing him as a human being and as a speaker. His mother (who, among everything else, passed on her love for telling stories to Les), Mike Williams (his advisor and best friend for over twenty-five years), and his eleventh-grade high school speech and drama teacher, Mr. Leroy Washington.

While Mamie Brown obviously loved and believed in her son, young Les lacked the support of a positive male role model in his life. That is, until Mr. Washington came along and told Les in no uncertain terms that he *could* succeed, that he could be somebody! Says Les:

> [Mr. Washington] changed the course of my life by opening my mind to possibilities that I had not dared to dream of. I was drawn to Mr. Washington for the same reason I had been drawn to our neighborhood minister. I had always fancied myself an orator of some sort, even though I may not have known exactly what an orator was.
>
> From the moment I first saw Mr. Washington and heard him speak, I wanted to be one of his star pupils. His students were the cream of the crop. I was not the cream of the crop, of course, but my attraction to Mr. Washington sparked something in me that had been stunted by the label of mental retardation. I began to feel a purpose churning in my mind.
>
> Thanks to my mother and, later, Mr. Washington, I grew up with the subconscious conviction that I was going to be somebody. And because of that, there was not going to be room in my life for drugs, alcohol, or criminal behavior.

While the saying, "One person can make a difference," has almost become a cliché, it is absolutely true. If Brown had not come in contact with Mr. Washington, there's no way to know where he might have ended up today. However, because of Mr. Washington's dynamic and motivational speaking style, Brown made up his mind to better himself. One of the things that Mr. Washington told Brown that made an impression on him was: "When you open your mouth, you tell the whole world who you are."

▶ **SECRET #1: "When you open your mouth, you tell the whole world who you are."—Mr. Leroy Washington**

Whether we like it or not, people *do* judge us by the way we speak. If we mispronounce words or in some other way demonstrate a poor command of the English language, it *will* negatively impact the way people view us. The good news is that there is an easy way for you and I to immediately begin improving our speaking skills and it doesn't cost a cent.

Enlist Your Family and Friends
to Help You Improve Your
Speaking Skills

One thing I've noticed about human beings is that if they sense that you are serious about achieving a worthy goal, they will almost always lend a helping hand if you ask them. Thus, one good way to quickly improve your speaking skills is to ask your family and friends to let you know any time you use a word incorrectly or speak in a way that's grammatically incorrect.

A friend of mine and I, whenever one of us makes a verbal miscue in the other's presence, make a point of calling the other on it. For instance: "Michael, you just ended a sentence with a preposition. Never say, 'Where should I but the bag down *at?*' You should instead say, 'Where should I put the bag down?'" When you have a friend who really enjoys correcting you, you tend not to forget it!

▶ **SECRET #2: One good way to quickly improve your speaking skills is to ask your friends and family to let you know any time you mispronounce a word or speak in a way that's grammatically incorrect.**

Of course, this little game only works if you and your friend know a little something about the English language. (A good book for brushing up on your grammar is *Essentials of English, 4th ed.,* Barron's, 1990).

Warning

I should warn you that not everyone is interested in improving themselves. I was once having a conversation with a woman over the phone who kept using a word that I had never heard. Being a writer, I love to learn new words. So, just as I was about to ask her what the word meant, she used it again. I then realized that the reason I had never heard of the word was because she was mispronouncing it. Now for the kicker: When I politely pointed this out to her, she got offended! Sadly, this kind of person is more interested in "being right" than they are in learning. The result is that they only end up hurting themselves, since this type of attitude is sure to keep growth at bay.

The fact is that Les Brown, as well as all the other great speakers I interviewed, did not get to where they are today because they were too proud to accept constructive criticism. On the contrary, they went out of their way to bring to light their weaknesses so they could then vigorously set about correcting them. This is true of all successful people.

Schwarzenegger's Calves

I remember reading one time about Arnold Schwarzenegger and how when he first began entering bodybuilding contests as a teenager the critics said, "Yes, he's got a good physique, but his calves are not as developed as the rest of his body." What did Arnold do upon hearing this? Did he squash his critics like a tomato? No. What he did was to immediately cut off the bottom of his sweat pants from the knees down. That way, every time he passed by a mirror in the gym he was forced to look at his "puny" calves. This gave him all the motivation he needed to do extra sets of calf raises at the end of every workout until he could barely walk. The result? Six months later he had some of the biggest and best calves in all of bodybuilding.

Turning Around a Weakness: Brown Works on His Vocabulary

Just as Schwarzenegger set about working on his calves to bring them up to speed, Brown decided at an early age to improve his speaking skills by strengthening his vocabulary. He knew in his heart that Mr. Washington's words—"When you open your mouth, you tell the whole world who you are"—were true. And while he possessed a naturally deep voice, he knew his command of the English language was poor. So, he got ahold of a dictionary and began memorizing large, impressive-sounding words. Though he didn't always use the words correctly, he developed a knack for linking them together in a sort of rap (long before *rap* was even invented!) that his classmates thought sounded very cool. Here is a sample of one of Brown's early displays of oratory prowess:

> "Hey, they call me Mister Vocabulary. Linguistically or oratorially, I'm emphatic that I possess an ad infinitum etymology which is simply unconquerable. However, I believe in simplicity of life so without further ado, I want to be like Columbus and discover you!"

Even if his classmates didn't understand the meaning of every word, suffice it to say that they, especially the ladies, were dutifully impressed. The point is that Brown identified an area that he was weak in, and then set about to correct it in a way that was both fun and productive.

Assessing Yourself

> *"Life is too short to go through it looking homely,*
> *tired, and ugly!"*
> LES BROWN

While the prospect of assessing ourselves can often be painful, it really is the only way to grow. And as a speaker, we can hardly ask our audience to take a look at their own lives, if we ourselves are not willing to do so. Here's Brown on the importance of honest, objective self-assessment:

> You have to assess yourself. Ask yourself the question, "What do I bring to the table?" Some people have a great voice, some a good presence. Or, you might be a person who

is very knowledgeable, but you might want to improve your skills on how you convey that knowledge. You've met people who were very intelligent but when they talked they put you to sleep. You can learn some techniques that will help you give that information you have with some special pizzazz, some spice.

There are some people who need to work on their voice. Your voice is a projection of your personality, of your feelings, of your experiences. How you use your voice has a lot to do with how people receive what you're saying.

What are your strengths? What are your weaknesses? Once you start looking at your strengths and weaknesses, you know what you need to work on. You might have to get some tutoring in one of those particular areas that you know is not quite where you want it to be.

Through some training, through some coaching, through some special instructions you can begin to strengthen yourself in that particular area. You want to really begin to assess yourself as a speaker and get all the information you can that will help you become a master communicator.

When you begin to assess yourself, it's very difficult to see all of your blind spots. You need to have some caring critics, some people to let you know some things about yourself that you don't know right now.

▶ **SECRET #3: Like Les did with his vocabulary and Arnold did with his calves, if you want to be successful you must be willing to objectively identify your weaknesses and then vigorously set about correcting them.**

Les' Dream

"When life knocks you down, try to land on your back, because if you can look up, you can get up!"
LES BROWN

After making it through high school, Brown got a job in Miami Beach as a city sanitation worker. However, he knew this job would never allow him to fulfill his dream, which at the time was to buy his mother a house. He loved her very much and felt that she deserved it for all the hard times he had put her through while he was growing up. So one day, he decided to go down to the local radio station with the intention of getting a job as a disc jockey, figuring it would not only pay more, but expose him to greater opportunity. The story, as Brown enthusiastically tells it on his PBS TV special, *You Deserve . . . !* , is a powerful reminder of what one person can accomplish when they have a dream in their heart and, as Les puts it, they are "hungrrrrry!"

Mr. Butterball, the Radio Station, and a Whole Lotta Perseverance!

It all began when Brown walked into the radio station and asked the gentleman in charge, Mr. Butterball, for a job. "Do you have any radio experience?" Butterball wanted to know. "No sir," replied Brown. "Do you have a background in journalism?" "No sir, but I can never get experience if you don't give me the opportunity," Brown answered optimistically. "I'm sorry," Mr. Butterball told him flatly, "we don't have any jobs for you." Brown nodded politely, thanked him, and left.

Mr. Butterball probably thought that would be the last time he would ever see the precocious youngster. But Les Brown had a compelling dream in his heart. As the saying goes, "When you have a big enough why, you can endure almost any how."

▶ **SECRET #4: When you have a big enough dream in your heart, you can overcome almost any obstacle.**

The next day, Brown went back to the radio station, found Mr. Butterball and said, "How ya' doing, Mr. Butterball? My name is Les Brown . . ." Butterball cut him off. "I know your name. Didn't I just see you here yesterday?" Brown calmly answered, "Yes, sir. Do you have any jobs here?" Butterball replied sternly, "Didn't I tell you yesterday we didn't have any jobs!?" "Yes sir," said Brown, "but I thought maybe somebody got fired or resigned. . . . I didn't know." And with that he politely said good-bye and left.

The next day—you guessed it—Brown again went back. "How ya' doing, Mr. Butterball?" *"Yes?"* replied the exasperated Mr. Butterball, looking up from his desk. And once again the persistent one matter-of-factly asked, "Y'all have any jobs here?" Incredulous, Mr. Butterball said, "Didn't I just tell you yesterday and the day before we didn't have any work!!?" "Yes sir," replied Brown, "but I thought maybe somebody died, sir . . . I didn't know. . . ." And again he thanked Mr. Butterball and left. Notice that Brown was never rude or pushy—just persistent. And as you're about to see, "polite persistence" can often make things happen where all other methods would fail.

▶ **SECRET #5: One of the best ways to win people over to your way of thinking is to be incredibly persistent, yet at the same time extremely polite. The two qualities are very hard to resist.**

Success!

The next day, Brown once again showed up as if he was seeing Mr. Butterball for the first time. "How ya' doing, Mr. Butterball? Do you have any . . ." But he never even got through the sentence. Butterball, knowing he had been licked, interrupted Brown and barked, "Boy, make yourself useful, go get me some food!"

Brown's commitment and perseverance had paid off. He started off working as an errand boy. He would get the disc jockeys their lunches and dinners and bring it to them in the control room. Once inside, he would stay there studying how they operated the control panel and try to memorize their hand movements. Eventually, they would look up, see him still standing there and kick him out. However, as each day went by, like a sponge, Brown was learning more and more.

Become a Student of Your Profession

This brings out an important point. Whatever it is you do for a living (whether it's speaking or anything else), you always want to do it to the best of your ability. This means becoming (like Brown did at the radio station, and later on as a professional speaker) a student of your profession. Ask questions and try to learn as much as you possibly can about everything that's involved in your line of work. Why? Because the more you know, the more people will be willing to pay you for your time and expertise.

I want to mention here that one of the things that really struck me about Les not only during our interview, but also during the two and a half days I spent with him at his *Speaking for a Living* seminar in Los Angeles in 1994, was just how seriously he takes his craft. Like a doctor, he considers it his duty to provide his patients (the audience) with the very best information delivered in the very best way possible. With this type of professional attitude, it's no wonder why he's one of the very best speakers in the business.

▶ **SECRET #6: Become a student of your profession and try to learn everything you can about it. The more you know, the more valuable you become and the more money you can charge for your time.**

Ego Check

By the way, it was at this seminar that I asked Brown to rate himself as a speaker from one to ten. When he said, "If I had to rate myself as a speaker I would give myself a five-and-a-half," I about fell out of my chair. After all, if the person who many consider to be one of the top five speakers in the country is only willing to give himself a five-and-a-half, then I don't know about you, but I have my work cut out!

Okay, let's get back to Les' story:

Chauffeur to the Stars

Pretty soon the disc jockeys at the radio station trusted Brown enough to send him out in their cars to pick up the celebrity singers who would come into town. So there he would be, driving superstars like Sam Cook, Diana Ross and the Supremes, the Four Tops, and the Temptations, all over Miami Beach in the DJs' cars—and he didn't even own a driver's license!

Throughout this period, Brown was planting seeds, making contacts, and continuing to expand his responsibilities at the station. It was only a matter of time before his hard work would pay off.

Seizing Opportunity

It's been said that luck is what happens when opportunity meets preparation. Meaning that if you're not prepared, even when the right opportunity comes your way, you won't be in a position to take advantage of it. Brown had been hard at work learning as much as he could about the radio station, so when an unexpected opportunity arose, he was in a position to pounce on it.

Drink, Rock, Drink!

One Saturday afternoon while Brown was at the radio station, he saw through the control room window that the DJ, a guy named Rock, was drinking alcohol while on the air. Brown thought to himself, "What if Rock can't make it through his show? None of the other jocks are available. Hmmm, this could be my opportunity." As he watched Rock continue to get sauced, a smile crept across his face as he thought, "Yes, that's right . . . drink, Rock, drink!" Heck, Brown admitted that he would have gone out and gotten him some more had Rock asked him to!

Within a few minutes, the phone rang. Brown picked it up and on the other end was the radio station manager. "Les, this is Mr. Kline." "I know," said Les. "Rock can't finish his program." "I knooooow!" answered Les, trying to contain himself. Kline asked, "Would you call one of the other disc jockeys to come in?"

to which Brown dutifully replied, "Yes sir." Then he hung up the phone and thought to himself, "Now he must think I'm crazy!" Brown then called his mother and his girlfriend and said, "Ya' all come out on the front porch and turn up the radio, I'm 'bout to come on the air!"

Look Out, "LB Triple P" Is on the Air!

After waiting for about fifteen or twenty minutes, Brown called the frantic station manager back and said, "Mr. Kline, I can't find nobody." Kline, by this time desperate, said, "Young boy, do you know how to work the controls?" "Yes sir." "Then go in there and don't say anything, hear me?" Brown's grin was so big he could have eaten a banana sideways. "Yes sirrrrr!" came the response. Brown made a mad dash for the control room. Putting on the headphones and his deepest disc jockey rapp'n voice, he sat down in front of the microphone and announced to the world:

> Look out, this is me, LB Triple P, Les Brown, your platter playing poppa! There were none before me and there will be none after me—therefore that makes me the one and only! Young and single, love to mingle, certified, bona fide, indubitably qualified to bring you satisfaction, whole lot of action, look out baby I'm your love man!

Yes, Les Brown finally made it on the air. He was willing to pay his dues, and his patience and persistence had paid off. This taught him a very valuable lesson: that if he worked hard and applied himself, he could achieve virtually anything he set his mind to.

A Dream Come True: Les Buys His Mother a House

Years later, Brown was indeed able to fulfill his dream:

> I'll never forget what it was like buying my mother that home. I drove up to the house, we got out, I gave Mama the

key and said, "Mama, this is for you." I'll never forget the look on her face. She said, "Oh my God no one could have convinced me when I adopted ya' all that this would happen, thank you." And then she said (lovingly), "And you—you caused me so many damn problems!"

Yes, even his own mother couldn't get over the fact that the little boy she had raised, who had caused her more than a few sleepless nights, had made a success of himself. Big time.

The irony is that, at $20,000 for a one-hour keynote (Brown's current fee), the boy who was once labeled "educable mentally retarded" makes more in a single day than his former educators who gave him that label earned in a year! And his company, Les Brown Unlimited, brings in a tidy four million dollars a year.

Remarkably, the troubled youngster who practically had his own chair in the principal's office while growing up, has received numerous awards for his outstanding achievements. In 1989, the National Speakers Association presented him with their most coveted award—*The Council of Peers Award for Excellence*. In 1992, Toastmasters International selected him as one of America's top five speakers, and in 1994 they awarded him *The Golden Gavel*, their highest and most prestigious award. What's more, Brown has had five enormously successful PBS specials, as well as his own nationally syndicated television program, *The Les Brown Show*. Not too shabby for an "average cornbread dude," as he likes to refer to himself.

Brown's Whole Life Changed When He Changed His Self-Image

How was Brown able to turn his life around so dramatically? The answer is that he let go of his old self-image and began to adopt a new, bigger, more capable vision of himself, the one that Mr. Washington saw in him:

No one knew what I was going to become. Goethe said, "Look at a man the way he is, he only becomes worse. But look at him as what he could be, then he becomes what he should be." What Mr. Washington did was that he looked beyond my faults and saw my needs. He said to me, "I see something in you." And I was thinking, "Oh God, I hope he's right." And I wanted to live up to his expectations.

One of the first things Mr. Washington told Brown upon hearing he had been labeled "educable mentally retarded" was that "someone's opinion of you does not have to become your reality." "Wow," thought Brown, "he's right. Someone's opinion of me *doesn't* have to be my reality." And for the very first time in his life, he began to question the label that he had grown up with for so long.

▶ **SECRET #7: "Someone's opinion of you does not have to become your reality."—Mr. Leroy Washington**

The truth is that many of us carry around self-defeating labels and beliefs that serve only to hold us back. And the worst part is that many of these beliefs are held at a subconscious level—we don't even know we have them! All we know is that we're not living up to our potential. Luckily for Brown, he had a mentor in Mr. Washington who believed in him and encouraged him to let go of some of the negative beliefs that were holding him back.

You Must Do the Work Yourself

It's important to note that while the seeds to Brown's transformation were initially planted by Mr. Washington, it was up to Les to take those seeds and make them grow. Lot's of kids may have heard Mr. Washington's message, "You have greatness within you." But how many actually believed it and made a decision to turn their lives around?

You see, Brown, like Anthony Robbins, knew inside his heart that he could be much more than he was currently demonstrating. The way Brown turned his life around was to replace the childhood image he had of himself as a *nobody* for the image of a *somebody*. He began to listen to motivational records (there were no audiotapes back then), as well as read motivational books, such as Dr. Norman Vincent Peale's *The Power of Positive*

Thinking. He came to believe within his heart that "God don't make junk," and that he, too, had greatness within him. This quote by Kingsley really embodies the essence of what we're talking about here:

"You have powers you never dreamed of. You can do things you never thought you could do. There are no limitations in what you can do except the limitations of your own mind."
DARWIN P. KINGSLEY

There's No Sin in Having a Poor Self-Image—The Only Sin Is Hanging on to It

As you've read through each speaker's chapter, you've no doubt noticed how many of them had to overcome a poor self-image. The truth is that it's no sin to have low self-esteem. The only sin occurs when, with all the information, tapes, seminars, books, and counseling available today, one doesn't take any corrective action to turn that low self-esteem around.

Letting Go of the Past

The biggest problem with having low self-esteem is that, as we seek to achieve a new goal for ourselves in life, old, negative thought patterns, like ghosts from the past, may come back to haunt us. When this happens we find ourselves having to struggle with our own self-worth, when that time and energy could better be spent on achieving the goal itself. When self-doubt does rear it's ugly head, we must remind ourselves that this is simply old programming talking and it's not who we are today. Who we are today is capable of achieving virtually anything we set our mind to. Unfortunately, this old self-defeating programming can be so ingrained in us from childhood that it often takes years for many of us to turn it around. In the meantime, the price that we pay can be enormous.

For example, the first time Brown ever thought about becoming a public speaker was when he was sitting in an audience watching Zig Ziglar. As Ziglar was getting the crowd going with his patented blend of motivation and stories, Brown thought to himself, "I could do that." However, it wasn't until *nine* years later that he actually took action on that original thought and went into public speaking.

What happened? Why did he wait nine years before going after his dream? The answer is *fear*. He let old, negative thought patterns talk himself out of "going for it." When he finally realized that his fear was not based in reality, that he did indeed have what it took to be a public speaker, he gave himself permission to go for it. And look what happened! If you have a dream in your heart, the time to start working on it is right now! Don't let fear keep you from doing what you know deep down inside you were put here to do.

Your Speech Can Only Be As Good As the Material in It

One reason Brown is such a good speaker is because he chooses good speech material. Where is the best place to find good speech material? Well, it's not in joke books or books called *1001 Speaker Stories*. As a professional speaker, you need your stories to be original. And the best place to look for compelling, original stories is in your own life. I don't mean they all have to have happened to you personally, but that you at least heard the story firsthand.

For example, when I heard on the news that the 1995 Miss America, Heather Whitestone, was completely deaf and that another contestant had to tell her that she had won, I knew it was a powerful story about overcoming obstacles. How did I know this would be a good story to tell? Because it moved me! That's the secret. The odds are good that if you are moved and inspired by a story, it will move your audience. That's why telling a story that doesn't touch you emotionally in some way is almost always a bad idea. Because if you don't feel anything for the material, neither will your audience.

In the following, Brown shares how when he heard an audience's reaction to a story a woman told, he made a point of remembering it. He knew that if it moved him and the audience he was sitting in, it would make for strong speech material:

> A woman who was being interviewed about her two children, [both of whom] faced physical handicaps, was asked, "How do you keep yourself together?" And she said something that was very profound: "Ask for help. Not because you're weak, but because you want to stay strong." Everybody in the audience responded in the same way. I said, "Hmmmm. I'm going to remember that." I never forgot it. I internalized it.

▶ **SECRET #8: The best stories to tell are those that move you. If you were inspired by the story, and you convey that to your audience, they will be inspired, too.**

Another good reason for telling your own stories, as Brown points out below, is that you don't have to worry about your audience having heard the material before:

> A lot of speakers go to books to find stories or jokes. I think that if you learn to become a good listener you'll find a lot of things around you everyday that will be very valuable, that will be fresh, that will be different, that will be unique. And you don't have to worry about anybody in the audience anticipating you.

> I heard a guy telling a story that everybody in the audience had heard. When he got to the end, several people in the audience said the punch line! It took all the power out of his message. If you want to become an original thinker and speaker, it's important that you learn how to become a good listener.

Since the last thing you want is somebody knowing how your stories and anecdotes end, you want to always keep your ears open for fresh material that everybody else isn't doing. Does this require more effort on your part? Absolutely. Is the feeling of confidence you will get knowing that your material is original worth it? You bet.

Avoid Giving a "Canned" Presentation

Just like we want to avoid telling generic stories, we also want to avoid giving a generic or "canned" talk. The best way to do this is by customizing or tailoring our presentation to fit the particular needs of the group we are addressing. A friend of mine once said to me, "Some speakers' idea of customizing their talk is a lot like the rock band who, when playing the Windy City, screams, "All right Chicago!" and feels as if they've overprepared.

While he's obviously exaggerating, his point is well taken. If your desire as a speaker is to stand out from the crowd, you're going to want to get away from giving "canned" talks. Instead, you'll want to find out as much information as you possibly can about your audience and then use it in your talk. The reason for doing this is obvious. The more specific and relevant your material is to your audience, the more meaning your presentation will have to them.

After all, if you worked for an advertising agency, which speaker would you find more helpful/appealing? The one who says, "It's important that you remain friendly with your suppliers," or the one who says, "As Julie and her staff in your media buying department know, the people at XYZ TV station can be tough to negotiate with. However, if you take the time to develop rapport with them and establish a friendly relationship up front, you'll find that things will go a lot smoother when it comes time to negotiate a late-night spot with them." You get the idea. The point is that the second message is much more specific and addresses their unique situation. Believe me, your audience *will* notice and appreciate that you did your homework.

Brown's Secret Weapon: Customization

Brown credits his decision to never give a canned presentation as one of the key factors that helped separate himself from the rest of the pack early on in his career. From almost the very beginning, he made it his business to find out as much as he could about the company he was going to be addressing. Eventually, he got so adept at doing his homework that he now uses the fact that he customizes every talk as a powerful selling tool. I asked him to explain how this all came about:

> I remember observing many other speakers and noticing how limited their repertoire was. I said, "I found my niche. I'm going to train myself to custom design a presentation to meet the needs of the audience." Now, sometimes you use some of the same stories; people request stories like they do a hit record off an album. But when I found my niche, that if I could train myself to be able to speak to any type of group and be the expert for that hour, I felt the possibilities were unlimited for me. I'd be able to break into the industry and make some noise and develop a reputation. And that's what I've done.
>
> I know some speakers who have given the same speech for thirty years and never changed and have no intention of changing. They have gone back to the same audiences and given that same speech several times and people still enjoy that.
>
> But I'm talking about the growing speaker; I'm talking about the person who's interested in mastering the art of communication. You want to always be saying to yourself, "What new things can I incorporate into my presentation that can take it to another level, that will have greater impact on the audience?" When you approach it from a growing perspective, as opposed to doing the same thing over and over, the possibilities are unlimited.
>
> You want to be a well-read person, you want to know the audience before you get there, you do a needs assessment to discover as much about that audience as possible. And you

create a speech that will meet that audience's needs. Each member of that audience has a sign on their head that says, *What's in this for me?* So you want to make sure that you create a message that has something in it for them.

Assessing Your Audience

The best way to customize your presentation is by asking a lot of questions and finding out what's really going on at that company. Many speakers, including Brown not only interview key people within the organization by phone, but also have the client fill out an extensive preprogram questionnaire. They do this so they can accurately identify both the organization's strengths and weaknesses. By taking the time to gather this information, you are able to both praise the group for what they are doing right, as well as give them some fresh insights as to how they can effectively turn around problem areas. Here's Brown on the importance of knowing your audience:

> Who are you going to be speaking to? See, in order to speak to these people, you've got to know who they are. You want to do your homework. You want to become the expert for that hour. I've had opportunities to speak for real estate organizations and I've heard people say afterward, "Oh, he had to be a broker there's no way he could know that!"

> I've spoken to the automobile industry and have heard salespeople say, "Yes, he used to be a dealer. In fact, I'll bet you he has an automobile dealership right now." No, I do not! I just did my homework. And you want to do that, too. You want to do the research, read all the publications of that particular industry or organization.

> Find out some unique things that they're doing. What are they involved in on a day-to-day basis? Find out things about the audience. Is it a high energy group? When you speak to sales organizations, they come in with a lot of energy. Many times when you're speaking to that type of group you have to start off at an energy level that might have ended your talk with another group.

What is the makeup, the body, the personality of the people who you're talking to? Once you know that, that will put you in a position to better prepare for them. You will use the stories and examples to bring it home to them, to make an impact on them unlike they've ever had before. [Doing this] will enable that audience to remember you because of the fact that you have done your homework.

▶ **SECRET #9: Successful speakers know their audience! Do your homework and find out as much as you can about the group you will be addressing.**

Warning: Be Sure You Know Where Your Audience's "Head" Really Is

As a speaker, you want to be sure that you really understand where your audience is it at when you get up to speak to them. In the following story, Brown was told that the audience needed to hear one thing by management. However, it became clear to him after talking with some of the employees that they needed to hear something else entirely if he was going to reach them:

I went to speak to a corporation and all they told me on the assessment that I sent to them was, "We want to be motivated." I asked them what the other issues were that they were facing on a day-to-day basis. All the managers said that there were none they could think of, that they just need to [be motivated to] sell.

While I was there, I started talking to some of the people that I was going to be addressing the next day. What I found out from them was that there were rumors that they were going to have a layoff, so moral was low. There was a lot of fear and uncertainty that existed there. Management did not want to acknowledge that. I don't care how fired-up and motivated I might have been and how strong the speech might have been, they would not have responded.

Addressing the Unspoken Conversation

Brown brings out an important point. If there is another issue that concerns your audience, an issue about which you aren't aware at the time you get up to speak, then you're going to have a difficult time making any kind of an impact. This is why talking to the actual employees, and not just management, can make a big difference. As an outsider, you're in a position to address topics and see things that those who work in management are often unable to see. Back to Brown:

> It was important that I give them what they needed to hear rather than speaking on top of that, and not addressing the unspoken conversation. When you're going to give a speech, you want to talk to the people who are bringing you in, as well as the people you will be addressing.
>
> Let the people in the organization give you some feedback. They can give you some input about their organization that only they would know. They can give you some pointers that will work extremely well with that audience that will take your presentation to another level. And then you'll mash this all together with the message that you've brought for them to hear and it will be a memorable experience for them.

▶ SECRET #10: Because the two groups may be coming from different places, make sure you get input from management *as well as* the people you will be actually addressing.

Organizing Your Presentation and Developing Your Outline

Developing your thoughts, ideas, stories, anecdotes, and examples into a flowing, logical, and cohesive presentation does not happen all by itself. And if you think about it, a speech can only be as good as its construction. If stories tend to ramble or the speaker jumps around from point to point, the audience is going to get confused and disinterested fast. This is why it is important that you take the time to organize your presentation into three main parts. Brown explains:

> Your speech has a beginning, a middle, and an end. These are the three areas where you decide to place the stories, the humor, your anecdotes, quotes, and statistics. The things you know that will make the speech entertaining, that will inspire people, that will empower people.

Use Your Opening to Develop Rapport

When you first come out, you want to have a smile on your face. They're watching your facial expression. Your posture must be straight, strong, and confident.

When I start off, I use this as an opportunity to develop rapport with the audience. I suggest that you do this as well. Sometimes I do it by stroking them. For example, I found out that an organization I was speaking to had done some charitable work, and so I said, "I'd like to first of all recognize you for the contribution that you're making to the young people in this country. Young people are sixty percent of our population, but they're one hundred percent of our future. And because of your contribution, in a historical context, this country will never be the same again. Give yourselves a round of applause!"

And they gave themselves a round of applause as they sat back with their chests out and thought, "Yes, this guy's right, we are great for what we've been doing!"

Use Your Opening to Show That You Are in Charge

Sometimes, I do it by giving them directions. I will have them repeat things after me because I want them to know that I'm in charge here. I might say to them, "Shake somebody's hand on your right and left and say, "You've got the right stuff, baby!"

I know that's from a commercial and everybody's heard it, so therefore when I give them that to do they are affirming each other—there's a nice buzz in the room. And so I'm checking them out as they do this, I'm listening to the energy of the room, the laughter. I'm reading them to see where they are in relationship to where I want them to go.

Important: Notice where Brown's attention is: on the audience! An error many beginning speakers make is that they focus on themselves when they first come out. This is a *big* mistake. You want to do as Brown is doing here and have your attention on your audience. You want to:

Listen to the Listening

As you're talking, you want to listen to how people are listening to you. There's such a thing as committed listening and not committed listening. If you're talking and there's a buzz going on, if you can hear people's forks and spoons moving on their plate, then hey, maybe what you're saying isn't interesting enough to hold them. Or, maybe you're speaking in a monotone voice. Now you've got to make some adjustments.

We've all been in an audience where people were talking and not listening to the speaker, and the speaker kept right on talking, completely oblivious to what was happening! I've seen this on many occasions. Those speakers were not listening to the listening.

If they're not with you, you've got to start experimenting and testing and pull them in. You've got to get them back to where you want them to be, to sitting on the edge of their chairs listening to the information that you have brought them. You want to be checking them out and seeing how they are reacting to your opening remarks.

Like a scientist, you want to evaluate the audience's mood and energy level and then decide on a course of action. For example, you might say to yourself, "Okay, that opening story usually gets a bigger laugh. Maybe they're still feeling a little full from lunch. Fine. What I need to do now is get them to relax and loosen up by telling some funny anecdotes about their company. Once I've won them over I can transition into the meat of my message." Get the idea? The more you do it, the better and quicker you get at assessing your audience's mood and then getting them to where you want them to be.

Okay, back to Brown on achieving your opening objectives:

> You want to have a beginning that can allow you to develop a level of identification and rapport, a kindred spirit with the audience. Come from your heart; don't just get up and say the words without allowing them to mean something for you. Feel what you're going to say. Know that people are with you. Smile, use your humor, use your voice. And pace yourself; sometimes you'll want to speak very fast and other times you might whisper.

Use Your Opening to State the Problem

> I also use the beginning to state the problem, to let them know I've done my homework. If I'm dealing with an organization where the sales are down, I will recognize that. I will say, "When the economy is bad, when money is tight and people aren't buying, how do you go out and sell today in this kind of market? How do you succeed when the competition is stiffer than it's ever been before? How do you continue to be a dominant force in the industry?"

The value of clearly stating the problem in the beginning of your talk cannot be overemphasized. Unless you paint a clear picture to the audience of what the problem is and how it's negatively affecting their lives (or how it could), they really don't have a good reason to listen to you. This is simply human nature. So, your first job as a speaker is to make what you're talking about relevant to your listeners. The more relevant you can make it, the more meaning it will have to them. Allow me to give you an example.

Suddenly the Flight Attendant's Presentation Had Meaning

Now too long ago, there were a string of stories on the news about how the smaller jet-stream airplanes were unsafe, and how occasionally they had this nasty little habit of dropping out of the sky like a lead balloon. As life would have it, I happened to catch a particularly scary story on just how unsafe these planes allegedly were . . . the night before I was scheduled to fly on one! The next day, moments before the rest of the passengers and I were about to board the small aircraft, we were told that they had discovered a mechanical problem and they would be putting us on their "back-up" plane. This information was met with nervous glances all around.

After I boarded plane number two, when it came time for the flight attendant to go over the emergency safety procedures, you better believe I wasn't day dreaming or reading the in-flight magazine. No way! I not only paid attention to every word she said, but I made a mental note of exactly where each emergency door was located, how many steps the nearest one was to me, and who I'd have to step on to get there (just kidding).

Needless to say, if I had not been exposed to the media coverage about the problem, I would not have been nearly as motivated to pay attention to the flight attendant's presentation. So, remember to take the time in the beginning of your presentation to clearly explain the problem to your audience, and how it affects them personally. That way, when you give them the solution, it will mean something.

▶ **SECRET #11: Use your opening to develop rapport with your audience, let them know you're in charge, and clearly state the problem (so they'll have a compelling reason to listen when you give them the solution).**

Use the Middle of Your Speech to Give Your Stories, Examples, Quotes, and Statistics

The next logical step, as Brown explains, is to build your case:

> After I've stated what the problem is, I go to the middle. And in the middle I use some examples, some stories, some quotes, some statistics, to begin to bring my point home. For example, I might say, "One of the things that you've got to do today is be creative and relentless."
>
> [As I say this] I will have a very serious, intense tone. I know they're on the edge of their seats; they're very quiet. I need to put some humor in at this point. Then I will use an example that will give me some humor, but also drive my point home. Or, I'll use a quote like, "Insanity is doing the same thing, in the same way, and expecting a different outcome." And I might engage them by saying, "Repeat after me. If you want to keep on getting what you're getting, keep on doing what you're doing."
>
> Now you've got them involved, you've got them listening. You're using some humor, some quotes, some stories to drive your point home. And you do this all in the middle. You begin to create a shift in their consciousness, to change their attitudes. You give them a larger vision of themselves to enable them to see that they can in fact reach the goals that they want to reach.

▶ **SECRET #12: Use the middle of your presentation for your stories, examples, quotes, and anecdotes.**

Your Personal Stories Help You Bond with Your Audience

One of the reasons you want to use lots of stories in your presentation is because they help bring you closer to your audience. This happens because, as you're telling your story, people are picturing similar incidents in their mind from their own lives. Thus, the two of you are forming a bond. Here's Brown on the power of stories:

> You can tap into the emotions and feelings of the audience by drawing on things that you have gone through that have touched you in a certain kind of way. In the process of doing that, you're developing a level of identification and rapport with your audience.
>
> In many cases you can create some breakthroughs and create an opening in somebody's mind. They might think, "If this person can go through that and handle it and be here to talk about it, then I can handle the events and the storms that I'm going through as well."

I think the above is an excellent point, and if you're interested in learning more about the power of stories, pick up Thelma L. Wells' book, *Capture Your Audience Through Storytelling*. I had the pleasure of introducing Thelma to the Los Angeles chapter of the National Speakers Association, and let me tell you this sweet woman knows how to tell a story like nobody's business! Another good resource is Grady Jim Robinson's audio tape, *Mastery of the Tranceforming Art: The Story*, which he recorded at the 1993 National Speakers Association Nashville Workshop. [Both Wells and Robinson are members of the National Speakers Association and can be contacted by calling the NSA headquarters in Tempe, Arizona, at (602) 968-2552.]

So far we've covered how, in your opening, you want to develop rapport, let the audience know that you are in charge and have everything under control, and state the problem. Then, in the middle of your speech, you want to cover your main points and tell your stories. Now it's time to transition into the last third of your speech: the ending.

The Ending Is Where You Give Your Solutions, Review Your Points, and Leave 'Em Feeling Good

As you begin to wrap up your presentation, you want to tie together all your main points, and then "bring it on home":

The end comes after you've set up the points that you want to make about the problem. Now you focus on solutions and you review the points and the things that you've said. You're bringing it home; you're summarizing and [reminding them of] the things they could do that will make a difference in their lives.

You want to give the audience a charge, take them to another level; to motivate and inspire them to transcend themselves and reach higher! You use your voice and your body language to do this: "As we now begin to look at where we want to go from here, to look toward the future, I challenge you now to leave here knowing that it's possible that you can live your dreams, that you can increase yourselves and your commission check. That you take personal responsibility to make it happen."

Now you want to bring your energy level up. You want to speak with such authority and conviction that they can feel it and they can internalize it. When you start summarizing like that and you get excited, they're going to get excited. And you leave them charged up.

▶ **SECRET #13: In your ending you want to focus on solutions, review your main points, and leave them on a high.**

The Close

The close is the end of your ending. It's the final thing you say to your audience before you walk offstage. Because it is the last thing you leave the audience with, it has to be well thought-out and strong. Here's Brown on the very end of your ending:

You want to take it on out with a quote or a powerful story or a poem that drives it home. Where they want to jump up, give you a standing ovation, and run out of the place and start selling or start improving their customer service, productivity, or moral.

Brown ends all his presentations with a powerful poem by Burton Brailey, which has become his signature close. As he is delivering it, he leans forward toward the audience, throwing his whole body into each word like a linebacker lunging to make a tackle. And all the while he's using his voice in a very powerful and dramatic way. Here's the poem:

> If you want a thing bad enough to go out and fight for it, to work day and night for it, to give up your time, your peace and your sleep for it. If all that you dream and scheme is about it, and life seems useless and worthless without it. And if you'd gladly sweat for it and fret for it and plan for it, and lose all your terror of the opposition for it.
>
> And if you simply go after this thing that you want with all of your capacity, strength and sagacity; faith, hope, confidence and stern pertinacity. If neither cold, poverty, famine or gall, sickness and pain of body can keep you away from a thing that you want. If dogged and grim you besiege and beset it, with the help of God you'll get it!"

Then Brown always signs off with:

> Ladies and Gentleman, this is Mrs. Mamie Brown's baby boy, Leslie Calvin Brown, saying it's been a plum-pleasing-pleasure as well as a privilege. Thank ya' all!

Brown's ending is so well crafted that the audience never fails to give him a prolonged standing ovation. Of course, this is in large part due to everything else he has done up until that point. However, being the pro that he is, he makes sure to leave 'em with a knockout punch, and so he brings home his already super-strong presentation with an electrifying ending.

▶ **SECRET #14: Take the time to craft a strong close. Remember, it's the very last experience your audience has of you—make it a memorable one!**

You Want to Leave Each Person in Your Audience Feeling As If You Were Speaking Directly to Him or Her

When your speech is over, Brown reminds us that:

> You want your audience saying to each other as they leave, "You know what, he was talking to me! I understood everything that he was saying."

This is a good point, and if you keep it in mind while you're speaking, it will help you deliver your material in a more personal manner.

▶ **SECRET #15: Great speakers make each person in the audience feel as if they're taking directly to them.**

There are people who are going through tremendous challenges and experiencing a great deal of fear and uncertainty, and because of what you say and how you say it they will never be the same again.
LES BROWN

How to Speak with Confidence: Owning the Room

A very powerful concept that Brown uses, which can make a big difference in your presentation, is the idea of "owning your room." You do this by acknowledging to yourself that indeed *you are the one!* that no one else is supposed to be up there but you:

> When you get up to speak, you must have the mind-set that "this is my room." You own this audience. This is your group. Feel the spirit in the room and claim the room. Talk to yourself and say, "Yes, this is my room."

> People are watching every move you make, even when you go to the rest room. So, watch your facial expressions, watch your posture. Carry yourself with a certain kind of poise and class and authority. You want to have the feeling and the expression and the attitude that "I'm the one. Yes, you came to see me and I've got something for you!" People like that.

> When they introduce you and you go to the podium, let your expression and body language indicate this. Before you speak, pause for a moment. Look around and smile confidently.

> And then you might want to say something like, "Good morning. How honored I am to be here with you. To be able

to share a few moments with you to remind you of some ideas that you already know. And as you practice with them, I believe, based upon my own experience, that you're going to produce some incredible results that you can be proud of." And now the audience is sitting there waiting to hear what it is that you're going to say.

The whole time you're saying to yourself, "Yes, I'm the one who's supposed to do this." You don't just throw the words out there, but you talk from your heart and you experience and feel your message. When you make that type of connection with an audience, you can literally change lives. There are people who are going through tremendous challenges and experiencing a great deal of fear and uncertainty, and because of what you say and how you say it, they will never be the same again.

Then you will experience a moment where someone comes to you and says, "I heard you speak and I was at a very low point in my life and because of what you said it changed my life and I just wanted to say thank you." When that happens to you, you can only feel very humble and sometimes it will give you chills. And you realize what a great responsibility you have to work on and develop yourself. And the more you do it, the better you'll become. And pretty soon the speech becomes you and people will know it.

Just reading these last several paragraphs before you get up to make a presentation can make a big difference in the impact you have on your audience. Remember:

▶ **SECRET #16: Claim the room as your own as soon as you get there. Say to yourself, "This is my room! I'm the one! No one else is supposed to be up here giving this presentation but me!" Everything about you should indicate this to your audience.**

A Word about Standing Ovations

While receiving a standing ovation certainly feels good, I don't believe it should ever be a speaker's goal. Rather, our purpose for speaking should always be to make a difference in other people's lives. And so, we want to end on a powerful note not for the applause, but because it's the best way to end. Therefore, you should never try to *trick* your audience into giving you a standing ovation. I recently attended a presentation where the speaker had everybody stand and do a silly little exercise just as he was concluding his speech. Well yes, technically, he did get a standing ovation, but did many of us in the audience feel manipulated? Do dogs bark? The point is, if you earned the standing "O," the audience will only be too happy to give you one; but if you didn't, tricking them into giving you one is extremely tacky.

Rehearsing Your Material

Okay, so how do you get good enough so the audience will *want* to give you a standing ovation? The answer can be summed up in one word: *practice.* This is how Brown became so successful. He kept practicing his material and honing it until eventually, through trial and error, he discovered what worked and what didn't. I heard a funny story about how hard Brown works on improving his public speaking from his best friend and marketing director, Mike Williams. One day Mike had gone over to Les' house where, upon entering, he heard voices coming from a back bedroom. As he got a little closer, he could hear Les talking to someone. Not wanting to interrupt, Mike quietly tiptoed to the bedroom door, only to discover Les standing in front of a mirror, practicing his speech out loud, complete with voice inflections and gestures. He was talking to himself!

Here are Brown's thoughts on the importance of rehearsing your speech:

> Once you organize your presentation, complete with quotes, stories, statistics, and anecdotes, what's the next step? The next step is to practice. You want to rehearse it, go through it, walk through it, time the stories, see how long it takes you to do it. Visualize the people out there. See yourself walking back and forth and standing up there doing what you've got to do to make the kind of impact that you want to make.

> If you can get your children or your friends to listen to you as you are rehearsing, that will help get some of the nervousness out of your system.

Practicing your speech allows you to work with the material, to live with it, to experience it. A lot of people memorize their speech and are so busy thinking about what they memorized and trying not to forget anything, that they don't experience the material as they are delivering it.

Experience Your Message As You Deliver It

Other speakers have said it elsewhere in this book, but it bears repeating—if you and I don't experience our message as we're delivering it, neither will our audience. And an unstimulated audience is a bored audience. Thus, we want to re-live what we're saying as if it's the very first time we've ever said it—with all the emotions and feelings right there:

> You want to experience [your speech], you want to really get into it. As you walk through it, it helps you get your rhythm together so you can flow through it, so you can communicate well and really connect with the audience. There are some speakers who will impress and there are others who will connect. If you're the one who will impress *and* connect, the likelihood is that they'll tell their family members and friends, "Hey, I heard this speaker, she was incredible . . . he was dynamite; you've got to bring 'em in!"

> You want to begin to find methods and techniques that will allow you to penetrate the heart, to touch and impact the emotions in a special kind of way. The more you practice before that presentation, the better you're going to be and the more confident you're going to be.

Brown Approaches Speaking Like an Actor Preparing for a Part

As you can see, Brown approaches speaking like an actor preparing for a part. He carefully goes over every word, vocal shift, and gesture. Nothing is left to chance. He knows exactly when he wants to lower his voice to draw the audience in, and when he wants to deepen it and "pump up the volume," so as to motivate and inspire them.

You can do the same by telling your stories to a friend or video camera. First do it very dramatically, then go back and tell the same story in a humorous fashion. By practicing different styles of delivery, like an actor, you will soon hit upon the one that "feels and sounds just right." However, if you only try one approach, then you won't know if the one that you're using is really the best for that particular story.

Sure, working on your material like this does take a lot of time and energy, but think about how great you'll feel when you're able to get up in front of an audience and deliver it with confidence. You won't have to wonder if the story will move the audience—you'll know! And that *is* a great feeling.

▶ SECRET #17: Great speakers prepare for a presentation like an actor prepares for a part; they work with the material until they've made it their own. This allows them to deliver it with confidence!

The Importance of Timing Your Talk

Brown explains the importance of knowing how long each segment of your presentation is:

> If a group tells you you've got thirty minutes, you want to make sure [your speech] will fit within the thirty minutes. You don't want to go over the time they give you; you want to be as close to the time as possible.

Professional speakers know the importance of "keeping to time." For example, suppose you are scheduled to give a talk from 1:00–2:00 p.m., but the program runs long and you aren't introduced until 1:15 p.m. Unless you're told otherwise, the correct thing to do is cut your presentation down to forty-five minutes and end promptly at 2:00 p.m. The audience and the organizers will both appreciate that you made sure that the program ended when it was supposed to. To insist on going overtime so that you can get in all your material is simply not being respectful of people's time.

See Yourself Giving a Great Speech at Night, As You Are Going to Sleep

Another powerful way Brown recommends practicing your speech is to see yourself giving it successfully in your mind's eye, at night, as you're going to sleep:

> When you go to sleep at night, just lie there and visualize yourself giving that speech; see yourself saying the things you want to say with authority, with power, with emotion, and with conviction! See the audience responding and applauding and interrupting you with applause. At the end, see yourself closing dynamically and the audience giving you a rousing standing ovation as you graciously bow and say, "Thank you, thank you."

No Bad Audiences, Only Bad Speakers

While Brown acknowledges that audiences can occasionally be reserved or somewhat stiff, he doesn't believe there is such thing as a "bad" audience:

> I don't believe that there are any bad audiences, only bad speakers. You become a bad speaker if you don't do your homework, if you don't research, if you don't learn how to become an expert for that audience on that particular day.

> When I decided I wanted to speak for corporations, I had some things going for me. I had a gift of gab, I love people, I have good energy, and I have pretty good communication

skills. But, I had never worked for a major corporation, so I had to do my homework.

I talked to people who worked for corporations. I read every book that I could find dealing with corporate training. I listened to tapes by the people who were speaking to corporations to find out what they were saying to them and how they were saying it. I wanted to learn from them. Every opportunity I got I would go to a corporation to watch someone give a presentation to see what they were doing; I would follow people around. You want to do the same thing.

Brown's right. If we do our homework, speak from our heart, and tell our stories and information in an entertaining way, there's no reason for us not to deliver a winning presentation.

Brown On His Famous Name

What do you do if you happen to have the name of a famous person? Well, Les handles it by acknowledging it in a playful way so as to build rapport with his audience:

I've got a very famous name so people come into the room and start talking, "Who is this guy? Where is he from? Is it Les Brown and his Band of Renowns?" "No, I think it's a motivational speaker."

So, I'll come and out and say, "No, it's not Les Brown and his Band of Renowns. Surprise!" And they're kind of shocked and it's an opportunity to laugh and to put myself in a vulnerable position and to gain rapport.

Notice how Les has a knack for being playful with his audiences, even when it comes to his own name. Audiences crave humor in a presentation and if you go too long without it, you risk losing people.

Recently I was on a program with another speaker when, as I was waiting for her to finish so I could go on, someone in the audience came up to me and said, "We need humor." I knew what he meant. Although the speaker's message was good, she was losing her audience because she was giving them too much content. After fifteen minutes of "you need to do this, this, and this," people's eyes begin to glaze over. That's why we must strive to inject some form of humor into our presentation every five to seven minutes. If we don't, we risk losing people, as this speaker did.

When *Not* to Use Humor

Is there ever a time when using humor is *not* appropriate? Yes. Brown recommends that you not open with humor when addressing young people or where alcohol is being served. Here's why:

> If I'm speaking to young people, I don't start off with laughter. Why? Because young people are not emotionally mature, and if you get them laughing in the beginning, you lose control of them. So I start off on a very serious note with them. At the end I will leave them laughing, but I won't start out that way—because a first impression is a lasting impression.
>
> If I'm speaking to a group and they're serving alcohol at dinner or lunchtime, I will not use any humor. People who are under the influence of alcohol don't need anything that will cause them to lose control. Because they will exaggerate the laughter, they'll make a joke more than what it actually is, and you'll lose control of them. So, when I'm speaking to them, my goal is to speak to them until they're sober!

Okay, so what do you do if you have to give a presentation to an audience that has been drinking? The first thing you do is not let the situation throw you. If you keep the thought in mind, "I'm there to empower and be of service to these people," and remember that part of being a pro means being like Gumby (flexible!), you won't have any problems. Some things you can do that will help increase your chances of success include keeping your content light, making your points extra-simple and easy to follow, and telling lots of stories. People on alcohol become more childlike, and children love stories.

Dealing with Hecklers or, "So That's Where the Egg Came from!"

If one person in the audience does get a little rowdy, don't get upset by it or let it throw you, simply join their world and play off it. A friend of mine who is one of the top magicians in the country was performing for an inebriated audience when an extremely embarrassing incident took place. He had just come out of the men's room before taking the stage to perform, and had forgotten to zip up his fly!

While he was making an egg appear for his first trick, the audience was too busy commenting to each other about his fly being down to care very much about the egg. Finally, someone yelled out, "Hey, your fly is down!" My friend, not missing a beat, calmly shot back, "I know that! Where do you think the egg came from!?" His quick and witty response brought the house down. If something off the wall ever happens during your presentation, roll with it. Remember, everybody loves a good sport.

Checking Out Your Room in Advance

Brown, like Joel Weldon and Patricia Fripp, feels that it is vital that you get to the room where you'll be speaking, early enough so you can nip any potential problems in the bud:

> I like to come in and get a feel for the energy in the place. Many times you'll discover some things that might have been disastrous for you, had you not come in to check those things out. It's very important that you test the microphone to see if it's a good mike. I think a hand-held mike, or a mike with a cord, is stronger than the average lavaliere. I don't like to use a lavaliere unless I've checked it out and know that it's particularly good.

> You might be speaking in a banquet room and there's a wedding going on next door with music blaring through the

walls. You want to be mindful of what the distractions are so you're not caught by surprise.

You might find that the distance between you and the audience is too far, and you want to make that distance shorter. One time I went to speak at a high school and, in checking out the auditorium beforehand, found there to be a twelve-foot-wide orchestra pit in front of me, beyond which the students sat.

I said to the principal, "Excuse me, would you help me improve my presentation? Could we extend the microphone to where the audience is? and I will stand down there to speak to them. I would rather be closer, because this orchestra pit puts too much distance between me and the audience. Otherwise, it's kind of impersonal and I prefer to be closer and more intimate. Would you help me do that?" Most people will cooperate with your request. But if you come in at the last minute and find that kind of setting, then you've got to deal with what you've got.

The importance of getting to your speaking engagements early so that you can deal with unexpected situations cannot be overstated.

The Value of Taping Yourself

Brown, like many of the other speakers in this book, feels that it's important that you tape-record your talks:

It's very important that you tape yourself. Why? Because you can't really hear and evaluate yourself while you're speaking. When you tape yourself, you can go home and listen to it and access yourself: "What worked? Did the audience buy into my message? Did I make the kind of impact that I wanted to make? Did I mispronounce any words or make any grammatical errors?"

You can listen to see whether or not your thoughts were organized. Did you cover all of the points you wanted to cover? Did you say all of the things you wanted to say? Sometimes you say something that's funny to the audience and you didn't even know that it was funny. Now you can use that story or quote or anecdote in another presentation.

So, you want to tape yourself so you can improve on that speech. Keep it and date it as a part of your "speaker improvement" library. You can compare it to other tapes to see how you're growing.

Another use for the tape-recording is as a potential product. If that audience loved the speech and gave you a standing ovation, there might be other people who would be willing to pay for that same speech.

▶ **SECRET #18: You want to tape-record your speeches not only as a way to give yourself feedback so you can grow and improve, but because when it gets good enough you can sell it as product to help others.**

Special Advice for the Beginning Speaker

When I asked Brown for some advice for the person just getting started in public speaking, he told me:

> I would encourage the person to speak often, and do it because you love it. Tape yourself so you can listen to the listening of the audience. I would encourage him or her to join organizations like Toastmaster or The National Speakers Association. These are organizations that are dedicated to helping you perfect yourself as a speaker. And never be satisfied with yourself. Realize that you haven't given your best speech yet and there's more within you. And learn from as many sources as you possibly can.

Special Advice for the Advanced Speaker

When I asked Brown for some special advice for the advanced speaker, he said:

I think it's very important that speakers set high standards for themselves. It's an honor to be able to speak to people, to touch people's lives. You have the opportunity to change lives and to influence people and their decisions about themselves, their future and their environment. Take that seriously and accept it as a blessing and commit yourself to giving them the best that you have.

Changing People's Lives Requires Energy

It's hard to motivate other people when you yourself are not feeling very energetic. Brown reminds us that we speakers must set the example by being in the best shape possible:

What are you like physically? People see you before they hear you. I think it's important that you have a program for yourself, that you eat properly and have a physical fitness program. Why? Because when you're speaking you're literally giving life; you're giving energy. Sometimes people come in feeling low and they want you to pick 'em up. So you've got to be a good vessel, you've got to be energetic, you've got to have some power. And in order to do that you've got to be in good shape.

When I travel, I go down to the gym or walk up and down the staircase. Or, if it's safe, I'll walk around in that community. Have a program of that nature for yourself.

Recharging Your Batteries

It's also important that we speakers have some time by ourselves to recharge our batteries. When we are presenting we are expending a lot of energy, so we must take the time to replenish ourselves. This includes giving our mind a rest. You can do this by meditating, listening to soothing music, or by simply quieting your mind for a few minutes. Says Brown:

> Like having energy, being centered is also extremely impor-
> tant to a speaker. Set aside twenty minutes a day, twice a day,
> for meditation or inner-reflection to calm yourself. You want
> to become an anchor; a lot of people are coming at you with a
> lot of ideas or their problems . . . you want to learn how to
> manage your own stress level. I play meditative music when
> I'm in the hotel room or at home, just to calm my own spirit.

For myself, I love listening to "new age" music, such as Yanni,
Enya, and John Tesh, as well as classical music to help calm my
spirit. In addition to listening to music that you really like, I
would also encourage you to pick up a good pair of headphones. I
recently purchased a pair of high-end Sony headphones (MDR-
V600) for about one hundred dollars, and I can't tell you how enjoyable, relaxing, and satisfying it is to be able to hear every note
of every instrument with perfect clarity. I now go back and listen
to old CDs, and the improved quality is so dramatic that it's like
hearing them for the first time. I think the saying really is true:
"Music soothes the savage beast!"

Protecting Your Instrument

Just as the quality of a musician's instrument affects the quality of
the music they are able to produce, so too does the quality of a
speaker's voice affect the impact of his or her message. Therefore,
we must do everything we can to protect our "instrument." If you
or I develop a sore throat or laryngitis right before a big speech,
we would be in a very unpleasant situation. That's why Brown
recommends that we take extra care to protect our voice:

> Protect your voice because that's your instrument. Sometimes
> our throats dry out; I think it's important that you drink a
> lot of water because it's good for your voice. If you find
> yourself hoarse, don't whisper, don't talk. Take the time to
> shut down, to relax, because vocal rest is very important.

> I've never missed a speech because of the fact that I couldn't
> speak well or that I was hoarse. I make special efforts to

protect myself. If I'm going in and out of different temperatures or environments, I cover myself and I make sure that I'm well protected. Do this so that when you get up to speak. you can use your voice, expressions, and the nuances and different shadings that you'd like to use without any problems or complications whatsoever.

The Million Dollar Callus

Brown has a callus on his left ear. When I asked him about it, he told me:

When I decided to get into speaking, I had no credentials, no reputation, no credibility, and no experience. So, I had to call a lot of people. I called over a hundred people a day, day-in and day-out, to ask for an opportunity to speak to their group. So this callus is worth several million dollars!

Brown's Greatest Challenge

When I interviewed Brown, he was going through the toughest challenge of his life. His beloved mother, Mamie Brown, had just passed away. Les spoke about how he relied on the strength of others to help him get through this most difficult time:

When my mother was dying of breast cancer, I had a lot of people who were praying with me, who talked with me during her suffering prior to her death, and that helped me to handle it. It was too much for me to bear by myself. Fortunately, I had people who cared about me and many who had gone through it who said, "Here's what you can do and here's how to deal with this." Wherever you want to go and whatever it is you want to do, you can't do it by yourself. And because of their support and because of them being there I was able to handle it, which was the greatest challenge I have ever faced in my life.

Brown's Number One Quality

Brown told me that he felt that his number one quality was:

I love people. And I enjoy making them happy.

You can always tell those speakers who genuinely care about people and enjoy helping them grow, versus those who do it because it's their job. The difference between the two, in terms of their impact on their audience, is like night and day.

The Essence of Brown's Message

As a speaker, it's important to be able to sum up the essence of your speaking topic in one or two sentences. Why? Because, when you meet people and they ask what you speak on, you want to be able to tell them in a concise and unambiguous manner. Here's what Brown told me when I asked what the essence of his message was:

Each of us can achieve far more than we can ever begin to imagine, and the secret is to work on yourself and never give up.

Brown's statement is succinct, powerful, and clear.

What Makes Brown Happiest

When I asked Brown what makes him happiest, he answered:

Bringing the speaker out in others. Also, when I know that I have put myself totally into my work. Giving each speech as if it were my last, knowing that if I died after I spoke, I wouldn't have any regrets.

Joy Onstage

I asked Brown where he got the infectious joy that he exudes onstage:

> It's because of my mother, who adopted me. She was a very happy person. In the midst of all the cynicism and the hopelessness, you really have to make a conscious, determined effort to be happy. I just resolved to do that. If you wake up in the morning in your right mind and if you have your health, that puts you one hundred percent ahead of the game. After that, all you have to do is use your time wisely and your imagination to create the kind of world you want.
>
> I think what people tap into most is that I'm so relaxed and that I'm enjoying myself. I laugh at my own jokes, I get tickled with myself, and I'm not intimidated by the audience. I love people. It comes through and they feel that; I want them to have a good experience with me and I make it my business to see that they do.

How Les Brown would like to be remembered:

"For a guy who was an average cornbread dude,
who loved life and lived it passionately to help others,
he made a difference."
LES BROWN

Les Brown's
Success Secrets Summary

SECRET #1: "When you open your mouth, you tell the whole world who you are."—Mr. Leroy Washington

SECRET #2: One good way to quickly improve your speaking is to ask your friends and family to let you know any time you mispronounce a word or speak in a way that's grammatically incorrect.

SECRET #3: Like Les did with his vocabulary and Arnold did with his calves, if you want to be successful you must be willing to objectively identify your weaknesses and then vigorously set about correcting them.

SECRET #4: When you have a big enough dream in your heart, you can overcome almost any obstacle.

SECRET #5: One of the best ways to win people over to your way of thinking is to be incredibly persistent, yet at the same time extremely polite. The two qualities are very hard to resist.

SECRET #6: Become a student of your profession and try to learn everything you can about it. The more you know, the more valuable you become and the more money you can charge for your time.

SECRET #7: "Someone's opinion of you does not have to become your reality."—Mr. Leroy Washington

SECRET #8: The best stories to tell are those that move you. Because if you were inspired by the story, and you convey that to your audience, they will be, too.

SECRET #9: Successful speakers know their audience! Do your homework and find out as much as you can about the group you will be addressing.

SECRET #10: Because the two groups may be coming from different places, make sure you get input from both management and the people you will be actually addressing.

SECRET #11: Use your opening to develop rapport with your audience, let them know you're in charge, and clearly state the problem (so they'll have a compelling reason to listen when you give them the solution).

SECRET #12: Use the middle of your presentation for your stories, examples, quotes and anecdotes.

SECRET #13: In your ending, you want to focus on solutions, review your main points, and leave them on a high.

SECRET #14: Take the time to craft a strong close. Remember, it's the very last experience your audience has of you. Make it a memorable one!

SECRET #15: Great speakers make each person in the audience feel as if they're talking directly to them.

SECRET #16: Claim the room as your own as soon as you get there. Say to yourself, "This is my room! I'm the one! No one else is supposed to be up here giving this presentation but me!" Everything about you should indicate this to your audience.

SECRET #17: Great speakers prepare for a presentation just like an actor prepares for a part; they work with the material until they've made it their own. This allows them to deliver it with confidence!

SECRET #18: You want to tape-record your speeches not only as a way to give yourself feedback so you can grow and improve, but because you can sell it as product to help others.

CHAPTER SIX

BORN: January 8, 1948
BIRTHPLACE: Waukeegan, Illinois

Mark Victor Hansen

"Great speakers bring their audience up to a new level of awareness during the brief few minutes they're together. They are so inwardly clear that this clarity of power communicates and gets the audience to go through a transformation; they come in, go through the cocoon stage, and leave the room a beautiful butterfly."

WHAT do the NBA, Disneyland, MTV, and Columbia Pictures all have in common? 1) They're all in the entertainment business, and 2) Their number one goal is to consistently provide their audiences with such an entertaining and fun experience that they'll want to come back for more. Their philosophy is, to paraphrase the movie *Field of Dreams,* "Entertain them, and they will come." Similarly, when giving a presentation to an audience, if a speaker fails to provide his or her customers (the audience) with an entertaining and fun experience, they'll go elsewhere for it.

One speaker who clearly understands the importance of keeping the audience entertained as he delivers his message is Mark Victor Hansen. When he gets up in front of a group, Hansen doesn't just give a speech, but rather a full-blown multi-sensory entertainment experience! One minute he's telling jokes (and gleefully laughing at his own punch lines), the next he's causing people's eyeballs to leak as he shares a heart-tugging story, and the next he's having the audience touch themselves at chest level and repeat back affirmations to him. Watching Hansen is a lot like watching a three-ring circus; there's so much stuff flying your way that your best bet is to fasten your seatbelt, hang on tight, and enjoy the ride.

Tom Peters' latest book is called *The Pursuit of Wow!* and that's what Hansen does; he "wows" his audience. From the moment he gets in front of them, like a keg of gun powder, Hansen is bursting with energy and completely blows the minds of the audience members before their seats are even warm. In other words, he's a dynamite speaker who knows how to have a good time with people, and one whom we can learn a lot from.

Travels 250,000 Miles per Year

Hansen's sense of humor, motivation, and unlimited belief in himself and his fellow human beings have put him in demand not just in the United States, but in Canada, England, Australia, and many other countries all over the world. (King of the frequent-flyer miles, Hansen racks up 250,000 miles per year traveling to his two-hundred-plus annual speeches.) Over the past twenty-one years, he has talked to over a million-and-a-half people through four thousand presentations in thirty-two countries. Although Hansen touches thousands of people a year from all walks of life with his inspiring message, one area in which he has made a big name for himself is the life insurance business. In fact, he is called "The Million Dollar Motivator" because he has motivated literally hundreds of life insurance agents to go out and successfully sell million-dollar policies.

Bestselling Author

Hansen's books include *Dare to Win, Future Diary, How to Achieve Total Prosperity, The Miracle of Tithing,* and the mega bestselling *Chicken Soup for the Soul* series, (which he co-wrote with Jack Canfield) and which has sold over five million copies! (Other books in this line include the *Chicken Soup for the Soul Cookbook* and *Chicken Soup for the Surviving Soul*). Hansen's one-hour TV special, *The Mark Victor Hansen Show,* aired on HBO, and he produced a pilot for PBS called *Build a Better You.* In addition, he has recorded numerous audio- and videotape programs, including *Unlimited Riches, Visualizing is Realizing,* and *Seven Magnificent Motivational Speakers.*

Hansen and his wife, Patty, live in Newport Beach, California, with their daughters, Elisabeth and Melanie.

A Big Man with a Big Heart and a Quick Wit

The first thing that hits you about Hansen is his size—he stands six feet, four inches tall. Secondly, he always seems to have a twinkle in his eye and a smile on his face—not unlike a little kid who just got his favorite toy for Christmas and can hardly contain himself. And thirdly, he talks extremely quickly. Once he gets going, few speakers can match his energy, enthusiasm, humor, and sheer *bon vivant* for life.

With Hansen, the one-liners and the motivational stories fly so fast that, to use a quote from Zig Ziglar, he resembles a cross-eyed javelin thrower: He may not set any records, but he keeps the crowd on their toes! His energy and presence are so strong that you sense that, for him, speaking isn't just a profession, it's a mission. Hansen is so enthusiastic, he makes Jack La Lane look downright lazy. (I've actually seen him dance a little jig after a presentation because he was so pumped up!)

Big Thoughts Produce Big Results

"You only get as far in the world as your desires are high."
MARK VICTOR HANSEN

Hansen likes to think big. Really big. While most speakers will tell you to set one or two goals, he encourages his audiences to set "too many goals . . . dozens, hundreds!" He says that in his own copy of *Future Diary,* he has 548 goals (now that's thinking big!). Hansen doesn't limit his penchant for thinking big only to goals. Quite often, his vision for people is larger than their own vision for themselves. This is one of the reasons why his audiences find him so inspiring. In a world full of people who are constantly telling you, "You can't, and here's why," Hansen's message is, "You definitely can, and here's why!" He's a big dreamer with a big heart who is truly dedicated to helping people stretch and grow and reach more of their unlimited and untapped potential.

The Power of Having a Large Vocabulary

Just as an artist uses colors to paint pictures on canvas, speakers use words to paint pictures in the mind of their audience. Therefore, it makes sense that the more words a speaker knows, just like the more colors an artist has to choose from, the more vivid and interesting the pictures they can create. One of the distinctive features of Hansen's speaking style is his energetic and creative use of the English language. Hansen loves words and is a master at using them to paint lasting and vivid word-pictures in people's minds. In fact, he often refers to himself as a "sesquipedalian," which means . . . well, I'll let him tell you what it means:

> I think of myself as a *sesquipedalian,* which means "word merchant." My definition of sesquipedalian, which I think is better than Webster's, is: the omni-efficacious use of words in the right place, at the right time, to get the right result with pictures in somebody's mind in the right way, right now!

(What a definition!) When I asked Hansen where he got the idea of painting word-pictures in people's minds, he said:

> Men like Dr. Norman Vincent Peale were masters at using words. He would launch you with an idea and then put in some verbiage, and lambaste you with three or four words in a row that just elevated you and escalated your thought form. So I said, "Boy, I'd like to do that." His student, Dr. Robert Schuller, is doing the same thing. Men like Cavett Robert can't even say good (one time); he's always got to say, "Good, good, good!" If you watch the speakers who can really make an imagination dance, all of them do what I call "impactive word clusters."

Impactive Word Clusters

Like his mentor, Cavett Robert, one way that Hansen uses the power of words to dramatically get his point across is by repeating a key word or phrase many times throughout a sentence or series of sentences. This serves to not only drive home his point, but to make it memorable, as well. When Hansen delivers his repetitive phrases or "word clusters," he does so in a very fast and rhythmic fashion, while at the same time emphasizing the key word each time he says it. For example, in sample number one in the following list of "Hansenisms," Mark emphasizes the word *right* each time he says it. The result is a memorable phrase that gets across the point in the mind of the audience that there is a "right" way to act that will bring positive rewards. Also notice Hansen's unique word construction in each of the following:

Sample "Hansenisms":

If you think right, talk right, and act right, you will meet all the right people for all the right reasons, and you will get all the right results right here and right now!

You ought to be rich in a good mental attitude, you ought to be rich in friendship, you ought to be rich in a good social life.

[The goal in being successful financially is that] you get to be, do, and have what you want because you want to do it, when you want to do it, how you want to do it.

I can win, you can win, we can win and we can all win together!

The house that I visualized and that I now live in is spacious, gracious, and palacious!

It's not what others think, do, or say about you that gets you, it's what you think about what others think, do, or say about you that gets you.

The Power of Repetition

One of the best known examples of the power of repetition comes from the late Dr. Martin Luther King, Jr. In his most famous speech, he repeated the phrase, "I have a dream . . ." eight times. Each time he said it, rather than becoming redundant, it dramatically increased the power of his message. By the end of the speech, the world understood that this man had a *serious* dream

in his heart. Do you think the speech would have been as impactful or memorable if he had used the phrase, "I have a dream
. . ." only once? No way!

A humorous use of this same technique was employed by Governor Ann Richards of Texas, during her speech at the 1988 Demo-
cratic National Convention. Her repeated use of the question,
"Where was George?" (referring, of course, to George Bush), after
listing another Republican miscue, brought the house down. Each
time she asked the question, it got a bigger laugh. In fact, after she
asked it the second time, the audience quickly caught on. Not only
couldn't they wait for her to say it again, but they would chant it
with her! (This is what's known as having the audience in the palm
of your hand.)

Had she only said it once, it wouldn't have been nearly as
funny or as powerful. But like a hammer hitting a nail, each time
she repeated the phrase, it drove her point home that much further. And, of course, take a wild guess which excerpt from her
speech aired on all the news broadcasts that night? You got it.

If you're looking for a fun and impactful way to punch up
your next talk, take a page out of Dr. King, Governor Richards,
and Mark Victor Hansen's book, and take advantage of the power
of repetition.

▶ **SECRET #1: By repeating a key word (or words) multiple times
within the same sentence (or speech), you dramatically increase
its impact on your audience and thus make the idea considerably
more memorable.**

Saying the Same Thing in Reverse

A sister to the repetition technique is something I call, "Saying the
same thing in reverse." I first spotted this technique in action
while watching a film on juvenile drunk drivers. A sixteen-year-old
boy, who had been arrested for D.U.I., was lamenting how much
money the nightmarish experience was costing him (in hopes that
it would dissuade other juveniles from making the same mistake).
He made the comment: "And then there are the lawyers; all
lawyers are expensive, no lawyers are cheap."

Because he used the words "expensive" *and* "not cheap" in the same sentence, it really drove home his point. You really understood that being arrested for "driving under the influence" is no fun, and that one of the many problems you will be faced with if you are arrested is having to hire a lawyer—and lawyers cost a lot of money, not a little. Had he just said, "Yeah, and you have to pay the lawyers too," it would not have had the same impact.

Here's another example of this technique: "The girl, far from being short, was extremely tall for her age." This makes it perfectly clear as to the stature of this person—this was one *tall* girl! To put this technique to work for you, the next time you have a presentation, simply go through your speech and highlight your key phrases. Then, go back and rewrite the key phrase (or word) in the "not this, but this" format used in my previous two examples. Don't put it off, do it now. (There, I just did it again!)

▶   **SECRET #2: By first saying what something is not, followed by what it is, you make that something dramatically more impactful, and thus more memorable to your audience.**

"Callback"

Another highly effective and fun technique that Hansen employs is the "callback" technique. This is when the audience shouts out or "calls back" a response to the speaker. It has its roots in the African American churches in the South, and is still quite popular today. Here's how it works: When the preacher gets his sermon rolling, the congregation, too fired up to just sit there quietly, shouts back throughout the service, "Amen!" "Hallelujah!" "Praise Jesus!" and other signs that they agree with the message being delivered to them. The effect is that the overall energy in the room is increased one thousand percent because the entire audience is fully engaged in the presentation—every speaker's dream-come-true!

In all of his speeches, Hansen will, at various times throughout the presentation, get his audience to repeat or "call back" affirmations to him. First, he'll set it up by saying, for example,

"One person can make a difference if they see themselves making a difference." Then he'll say, "Everybody repeat after me, 'I see myself making a difference.'" And the audience, in unison, repeats the affirmation back to him. Other times, Hansen will get the audience to "call back" simply by asking them a question. For example, he'll ask, "If you can be successful fast or slow, which way do you want to go?" and the audience will immediately shout back, "fast!"

The secret is to ask the question, or state the affirmation, with a lot of energy. Remember (I'll be reminding you of this throughout the book), the more you "get into" your presentation, the more your audience will. If you *ask* with gusto, they will *respond* with gusto. The next time you're giving a presentation, try the "call back" technique. I think you'll find it not only extremely effective, but a lot of fun.

▶ **SECRET #3: Having the audience "call back" to you key words and affirmations not only keeps them actively involved in your presentation, but it's a lot of fun!**

Great Speakers, Like Great Chess Players, Combine Techniques for Maximum Effectiveness

In chess, good players often use one chess principle in combination with another. For example, they will often bring out (develop) one of their chess pieces, while at the same time attacking one of their opponents. Since the "attacked player" is forced to move his piece (so it won't be captured), the first player is said to have developed a piece "with tempo." This means he gained some time—specifically one move (since his opponent had to spend a move to save his attacked piece)—while at the same time developing his own piece (rapid development is essential to winning in chess). Thus, our first player employed two principles at the same time to achieve maximum results.

In studying Hansen's video- and audiotapes for this book, I realized that he, like a good chess player, would often combine several different techniques at once for maximum effectiveness. For example, I noticed that he was combining the "call back" technique with another technique, *the power of touch*.

The Power of Touch

Hansen does this by having the audience touch themselves at chest level while repeating back to him an affirmation. Not only is this one more way to involve the audience (now they're not just saying something, but actually *doing* something as well), but the actual act of touching themselves helps to further stimulate their senses and thus increase retention of the material.

For example, Hansen opens many of his presentations by saying, "How many of you would like to be more successful than you've ever been in your whole life? Can I see your show of hands?" (The audience's hands shoot up.) Then he'll say, "Everyone touch yourself at chest level and say, 'I'm ready!' Hansen will then put his hand in the center of his chest and say, "I'm ready!" and, of course, the audience follows suit. Next he'll say even more enthusiastically, "Everybody say, 'I'm reeeeeeeeeally ready!'" And then, like a conductor leading his orchestra, he'll say, "Together . . . ," and both he and the audience will shout in unison, "I'm reeeeeeeeeally ready!"

This is usually followed by giggles and light banter as people genuinely get a kick out of participating as part of a large group. It's sort of like performing the wave at a sporting event; you enjoy doing it, but you're not exactly sure why—all you know is that everybody else is doing it and it's fun!

▶ **SECRET #4: Having your audience touch themselves at chest level while saying an affirmation not only increases their participation level, but it stimulates their senses, causing them to anchor your message at a deeper level.**

The Power of Humor

Of course, all affirmations don't have to be serious. Often times, Hansen does a humorous "call back" that goes like this:

Hansen: "In order to have all your dreams come true, you need to have *fun* all the time" (set up line). "What do you need to have all the time?"
Audience: "Fun!"
Hansen: "When we're at work, what do we want to have?"
Audience: "Fun!"
Hansen: "When we're at home with our family, what do we want to have?"
Audience: "Fun!"
Hansen: (punch line) "When you're getting audited by the IRS, what do you want to have?"
Audience: "Fun!" (And, of course, everyone breaks up laughing.)

I want to encourage you to come up with humorous material like this to include in your own presentations. How? By thinking about the opposite of what your audience would normally expect you to say. Since an IRS audit is about the last thing people think of when it comes to having fun, Hansen knew he would get a laugh by tagging it on to the end of his series of "straight lines."

Keep in mind that you might have to play around with your speech material for a while before you come up with a humorous line that works. The thought process goes something like this: "No, that's not funny . . . , maybe this . . . no, that isn't it either. Let's see, how about if I say . . . that's not quite it either, but we're getting closer. Maybe if I try it this way . . . ," and so on. Eventually you say something and realize, "That's it! That's what I was looking for!" The key is to not give up. Let's take a look at another one of Hansen's humorous "call backs."

Yes or Yes

This one is called "Yes or Yes!" The way it works is that Hansen will ask the audience a question and then tack on, "Yes or yes?"

at the end of it. For example, he'll say, "If you take these ideas and go out and use them, will they make a difference in your life, *yes* or *yes!?*" Since the audience was expecting him to say "yes or no," they are caught off guard and crack up over his gushing optimism.

While many speakers I talk to feel that their programs could use more humor, they don't do anything about it other than lament, "Oh, I guess I'm just not funny." Well, the reality is that humor doesn't just happen by itself—you must look for it! If you are constantly thinking, "What's funny about this?" or "What could I say in this situation that would be funny, offbeat, or unexpected?" and you don't censor your thoughts too quickly, your mind will eventually come up with *something*. And then you can build on that something until you come up with what it is you're looking for. Maybe something funny happened to you just recently that you can use to illustrate a point. Perhaps it was something even a little bit embarrassing. (Audience's love it when speakers tell stories of themselves.) Since I know you'd love to hear one about me, I won't disappoint you. . . .

An Embarrassing Incident

Whenever I want to make the point to my audience about the importance of being able to laugh at ourselves, I tell the following true story:

One day while stopped at a red light, I noticed an attractive woman stopped next to me in a red convertible. Suddenly, she whipped her head around and caught me staring right at her! I was so flustered that I reached up to my rearview mirror and pretended to be adjusting it. Unfortunately, I grabbed the mirror too hard, and the darn thing popped right off the windshield! So there I was, holding this mirror in my hand, trying to look cool, pretending like I *meant* to yank it off the window. Of course, I looked over and she was laughing her head off at me. When I realized how silly I must have looked, I had to laugh, too.

Another example of real-life humor happened to a friend of mine named Adam Christing. Adam is the president of a company called "Clean Comedians." Their motto is, "It doesn't have to be *filthy* to be funny!" When they were having their new stationary printed up, nobody bothered to proofread the copy before it went to press. The result? They were stuck with five thousand sheets of stationary that said, "At Clean Comedians our motto is, 'It doesn't have to be funny!'" To Adam's credit, he loves telling this story.

There are plenty of humorous things happening all around us which we can add to our presentations; all we have to do is keep our eyes open for them.

▶ **SECRET #5: Sharing a humorous story about yourself to illustrate a point not only makes your message more memorable, but it helps to establish a bond between you and your audience because it shows you can poke fun at yourself.**

Once you do find something that you think your audience will find humorous, don't be afraid to try it out on them. If it does get a laugh, great, you've got a new bit you can use. If it doesn't, you just might need to experiment with it a little to get it to work, or it just might not be a workable piece. Either way, don't be afraid to give it a shot. If it doesn't fly, just make a comment like, "Well, some jokes I do just for myself!" and quickly move on. Johnny Carson used to get his *biggest* laughs whenever a joke would bomb. Remember how he'd just stand there and stare in mock indignation at the audience, and then at the band, before finally throwing out a comeback that would invariably bring the house down? While his flawless timing played a major role as to why he was always able to get big laughs from "bad jokes," my point is that he never let a failed joke get him down or interrupt his flow.

▶ **SECRET #6: If a joke or other attempt at humor doesn't work for whatever reason, being the pro that you are, you quickly, confidently and smoothly move on to your next segment, without letting it throw you in the least.**

How to Take Command
of Your Audience

One of Hansen's many strengths is his ability to take command of an audience. When he asks them to repeat a phrase back to him or carry out a request, they enthusiastically do it. What is he *doing* that allows him to so effortlessly and confidently take complete command of his audience? And more importantly, what can we learn from him so as to maximize our own effectiveness when interacting with the audience?

I've isolated five things that Hansen does, and that you too can do, to effectively gain the audience's wholehearted cooperation. They are:

1. Ask with Confidence

First of all, whenever Hansen makes a request to the audience, he does so with complete and total confidence. Like any good leader, he issues his commands *fully* expecting that they will be complied with. This is extremely important. If you were to ask an audience to do an exercise, but you sounded tentative and unsure of yourself, they would think, "I'm not sure if I want to do this—this person doesn't sound too sure of herself." And while you might get compliance, it would be halfhearted at best.

Therefore, you always want to exude complete and total confidence to your audience (obviously, you want to do this *throughout* your speech, but especially while you're issuing directions). If you're attitude is, "I'm used to giving commands and having them followed; it's no big deal," your audience will sense this and go along with your request, simply because you've given them no reason not to.

By the way, one person who exudes an avalanche of confidence in everything he does, and thus is worthy of modeling, is Arnold Schwarzenegger. The man is the epitome of self-confidence. Take a look at any of his films or interviews; he always looks completely calm and in control. I've actually worked with Arnold on a project, and I can tell you that it's no act. Somewhere along the way he trained his mind to eliminate virtually all thoughts of doubt and fear. Watch him during an interview; if a reporter ever asks him something negative, he immediately turns it around into a positive, makes a joke out of it, or dismisses it as no big deal and acts as if the person is crazy for even asking the question. I'll never forget the time he was on *The Late Show* and David Letterman asked him how much money he made. Schwarzenegger cocked his chin back, gave him a "Terminator" look and said, "Vats it to you!?" It got a big laugh, because the audience knew that Arnold was not intimidated by the nosy talk show host.

▶ **SECRET #7: A request made in a confident tone of voice indicates to your audience that you are in command. If they sense that you are comfortable giving directions and that you expect them to be followed, you will have little trouble gaining their cooperation.**

2. Make Your Requests Easy to Do

The second reason why audiences follow Hansen's requests is because they're easy to do. Shaking their neighbors hands, repeating something back to him, or touching themselves at chest level while saying an affirmation—these are not difficult things to do. Remember: The simpler, the better.

▶ **SECRET #8: Whenever you ask the audience to do something, remember the acronym: K.I.S.S.: Keep It Simple Speaker!**

3. Make Your Requests Sound Fun

Whenever Hansen asks the audience to do something, he always does so in an energetic and enthusiastic manner. He makes whatever he wants his audience to do sound like fun, mainly because he is genuinely having fun telling them about it. And let's face it, who doesn't want to have fun?! If you are playful and enthusiastic, you can get people to do almost anything. Kids are experts at this. I remember when I was a kid, a friend said that he was going to start a secret spy club. I immediately wanting to be in it, not because I necessarily needed to be in a club— I'm not even sure I understood what a secret spy club was—but because he sounded so *enthusiastic* about it: "Yeah, we'll send away for fake bullet holes we can stick on windows, it'll be great. . . ." Looking back, I now realize what the appeal was to me; he made the club sound mysterious, a little dangerous, and most importantly, *fun*.

What we're talking about here is sales; the ability to successfully sell our audience on the idea that playing along with whatever we're asking of them is in their own best interest. By making your requests in an upbeat, enthusiastic, "you guys are going to love this" tone of voice, you are virtually guaranteed to get maximum participation.

▶ **SECRET #9: The more fun your requests of your audience sound, the more eager people will be to participate.**

4. Demonstrate What You Want Them to Do

When Hansen says to his audience, "Everyone touch yourself at chest level and say . . . ," guess what he's doing? That's right, he's touching himself at chest level. By taking the time to demonstrate what it is you want your audience to do, you alleviate confusion. Not only can they see exactly what it is you want them to do, but it also let's them know that you are not asking them to do anything you wouldn't do.

▶ **SECRET #10: Demonstrating to your audience exactly what you want them to do helps eliminate any confusion.**

5. Do It with Them

Whenever he asks the audience to do something, Hansen will do it too, right along with them. And when he asks them to say something back to him, he will also say it along with them. For example, when he says, "Everyone touch yourself at chest level and say "I'm reeeeeeeeeally ready for success!" he touches himself and says it along with them. Why is this significant? Because on studying a video of Hansen speaking, it was apparent that his energy level and vocal tone actually dictated how much enthusiasm the audience put into it. In other words, the more gusto he put into what he was saying, the more "oomph" the audience put into it. This is something that you'll want to keep in mind each time you get up to speak.

▶ **SECRET #11: The audience takes its cues from you; the more you get into whatever you're saying or doing, the more they will.**

So, to recap, the keys to getting maximum audience participation are: 1) give directions in a confident tone, 2) make sure the task is easy to do, 3) make it sound fun, 4) demonstrate exactly what you want done, and 5) do the exercise along with them (whenever possible).

The Speaker Who Inspired Hansen

Mark first thought of becoming a speaker when he was sixteen years old. He was driving down the highway in Wakeegan, Illinois, when suddenly he saw himself in his mind's eye speaking to 80,000 people! However, he soon forgot about his extraordinary vision until years later when, at the age of twenty-one, he saw a speaker that absolutely blew him away.

The speaker's name was Bill Sands, and he was addressing an auditorium of 1,500 high-school students. An ex-convict, Sands told the kids that he had been to hell and back. He told how when he was in prison his nose—which he pushed flat against his face—and his fingers—which he bent all the way back—had been broken by fellow inmates because he had resisted their attempts to rape him. His self-image shattered, he began to think of himself as the "losing-est" person who ever lived.

Then, one day, the warden gave Sands a copy of Napolean Hill's classic, *Think and Grow Rich*. After reading it and applying its principles, he made a firm decision to turn his life around. He started a program to help his fellow inmates upon release, and then went on to write a book about his prison experience. This eventually led to associations and organizations asking him to come tell his story to their group. The result was that "the losingest person who ever lived" ended up becoming enormously wealthy and successful. As Hansen sat there that day listening to Billy Sands touch the hearts of the 1,500 students in that high school auditorium, his own dream of becoming a speaker was rekindled. However, before he finally followed that dream, Mark made one last detour.

Hitting the Bottom: Bankruptcy and Depression

Hanson decided to get into the manufacturing and selling of geodesic domes in New York City. He actually might have made a good living off of Buckminster Fuller's dome-shaped living units if the year hadn't been 1974. That was the year that OPEC, the Arab oil cartel, decided to send petroleum prices crashing through the roof. Since Hansen's domes were made from a petrochemical product, he suddenly found himself going from making two million dollars to total bankruptcy within one year.

It's been said that adversity brings out a person's true colors. If that's true, Hansen's color was black, for he quickly sank into a deep, dark depression. On a scale of 1–10, Hansen recalls that he was a minus-twelve. He soon sought the sanctuary of his bed, where he stayed sleeping virtually around the clock. When he did go out, he drove a four-hundred-dollar, pitted-window, permanently air-conditioned Volkswagen (not unlike Anthony Robbins!), and wore the only suit the bankruptcy court had left him. One time, when he was walking out of the Pan Am building, the valet who brought him his car remarked, "Man, I'd have picked you for a Cadillac." "Me too," was all Hansen could dejectedly reply. Yes, twenty-six-year-old Mark Victor Hansen had hit bottom. The good news was that there was only one direction left for him to go.

Within Every Adversity Lies
a Seed of Opportunity

---

*"Life is a grindstone, and whether it grinds you down or
polishes you up is for you and you alone to decide."*
CAVETT ROBERT

Today, Hansen says that going bankrupt was the "best/worst"
thing that's ever happened to him. It forced him out of what he
shouldn't have been doing—selling domes—and into professional
speaking which, as the hundreds of letter he receives each week
only confirm, he should be doing.

It was while he was going through these tough times that
Hansen started listening to motivational tapes by Cavett Robert,
the founder of the National Speakers Association. Hansen realized that he had to change his thinking if he was ever going to
turn his life around. He approached Robert, a lawyer by trade,
and asked him if he would be his mentor. Cavett, who is as kind
as they come and genuinely enjoys helping people, was only too
happy to support the tall blonde Dane in his quest to become a
professional speaker.

How Hansen Got Started in
Professional Speaking

Although at first Hansen worried that he might be too young
to be taken seriously as a speaker, that all changed when he saw
a real estate speaker named Chip Collins. Collins, who was Hansen's age, was giving four talks a day to six or seven realtors at a
time, and charging $50.00 per person. Not only was he making a
comfortable living doing something he genuinely enjoyed, but he
was booked a full year in advance. This appealed to the enter-
prising Hansen.

Just as he had approached Robert, Hansen approached Collins
and asked him if he would teach him to speak and get the kind of

bookings that Collins did. (Obviously, Hansen practices what he preaches, which is: "You need to A-S-K to G-E-T!") Collins agreed to help on the condition that Hansen steer clear of the real estate market and focus, instead, on his own niche. Hansen concurred, setting his sights instead on church groups. This proved to be a good choice, as churches are always looking for speakers.

Finding His Life's Purpose

> *" . . . My passion is glowing and roaring like a fire,*
> *more now than it ever has."*
> MARK VICTOR HANSEN

Finally, Hansen was doing what he now believes he was put here to do:

> The minute I came into it, I felt I had found my calling, even though at the front end of the speaking business I was probably pitiful. But the audiences were nice. I was charging $25.00 a talk and doing four a day. I didn't know enough stuff to be of real service to them, but I had a burning desire and was passionate about the business. And my passion is glowing and roaring as a fire, more now than it ever has. I am just overwhelmed by the results my audiences are now getting because of me. I'm overwhelmed and astounded at what happens, and I'm the one who catalyzes it. I'm the gladfly for good!

Motivation by Any Other Name . . .

> *"It's always the individual who empowers a company,*
> *a family, a nation, or a church."*
> MARK VICTOR HANSEN

When I asked Hansen to define his overall message, he said:

> I'm a motivational speaker, although I've changed that title to use the current language, which is, "I'm a personal empowerment speaker." I try to stimulate everybody to be self-empowered, because if you're personally empowered, then you can empower others. It's always the individual who empowers a company, a family, a nation, or a church.

When I asked him why he chose "motivation" as his main topic, he replied:

> I chose this topic because that's who I am. I think a phenomenally impactful speaker comes from the well-spring of his or her own wisdom. I am an enthusiastic, encouraging, life-enhancing person who wants to walk around with a smile and get everybody to be in the consciousness. In spiritual language we call it "blissed-out consciousness," and in psychological language it's called "self-actualizing, fully-functioning behavior." That's the kind of level I'm personally subscribing and aspiring to, and I'm stimulating that in other people who are eager to be in what John Denver calls, "higher ground."

Sharing a Part of Who You Are

Hansen's first sentence, responding to why he chose motivation as he subject—"because that's who I am"—should be stamped on the forehead of every speaker. When you speak on a topic about which you feel passionately, and which comes from somewhere deep inside of you, you can't help but impact people with your message. (Of course, you must have confidence, good stories, snappy pacing, etc., but sharing *who you are* is the starting point for any effective presentation. True, while it is possible to just "download" information to your audience, they always seem to know (either consciously or subconsciously) when a speaker is genuinely sharing a part of him- or herself.)

Eliminating Inconsistencies
in Your Message

If your message isn't consistent with who you currently are, does that mean you must find a new topic? Not necessarily—but some changes will need to be made. For example, let's say that you want to speak on time management, but you have this little habit of running late all the time. Obviously, there's a conflict there. You can either A) get up and hypocritically speak on the subject anyway (something I, as well as all of the speakers in this book, find deplorable), B) speak on something else, or C) train yourself to start being on time! While solutions *A* and *B* speak for themselves, the beauty of *C* is that, once you do make punctuality a part of your lifestyle, you will be able to look out on the procrastinators of the world and say, "I was once where you are!" Not only will the power and conviction in your voice be a thousand times more convincing, but your credibility will also be greatly enhanced because *you* will have already made the changes (and are reaping the rewards) that you are asking your audience to make. Live testimonials are extremely powerful. This is the reason why speakers at Alcoholics Anonymous meetings almost always begin their talks by announcing how many days (i.e., "843 days!") they've been sober. This immediately let's the audience know, "Hey, I've been there."

▶   **SECRET #12: The more consistent your message is with who you really are as a person, the more effective you will be at delivering that message.**

Is Motivation Like Mashed
Potatoes: Too Fluffy?

Being a motivational speaker myself, I know that occasionally we are thought of as "all show and no go." In other words, we get people enthusiastic for the moment, but we don't give them the necessary tools for making long-term changes. While I personally feel that motivation is not "fluff," and that everybody needs some inspiration, I agree that the very best speakers both motivate *and* provide their audiences with solid information and practical "tools for transformation." When I asked Hansen if he ever receives criticism for being too "fluffy," he told me:

> I used to get that kind of criticism. . . . I don't hear it, personally, anymore. I have a lot of people sitting in my audiences before I start my talks who are cynical; they were brought there by their spouses. They sit there, as Cavett Robert would say, "like a tree full of owls in judgment."
>
> But then I hit 'em with a little bit of humor and some things like, "There can never be a recession or depression, as long as salespeople and entrepreneurs and marketers are out doing what it is they're supposed to do: keeping the philosophy of money high." And I say, "Look, you earn $25,000 because you don't have the awareness to earn $50,000. And you earn $50,000 because you don't have the awareness to earn $100,000!"
>
> All of sudden, these people start to wake up and they say, "Holy cow, this guy makes a difference." And then I tell them, "If you change your thinking you change your life. And if you change your perceptions and your assumptions you change your life." They start buying into it. I've got so many people who are saying, "I earn $10,000 more a month because of Mark."

Handling Criticism

Hansen knows in his heart that he is making a difference, so that gives him the confidence he needs to weather the "slings and arrows" that occasionally may come his way. Remember, the stronger you believe in your message, the more resistance you are going to get from those people who have a different belief system than you do.

Does this mean you should hold back when delivering your message so as not to offend anybody? Heavens, no! Sure, you always want to be flexible; if a better, more effective way comes along to make your point, you want to use it. But, since there's always going to be somebody who doesn't agree with what you have to say, you can't go changing your message every time somebody raises an objection.

As the saying goes, "If one person calls you a jackass, then *they* most likely have the problem. If ten people call you a jackass, you best start looking for a saddle to wear!" If one person doesn't like something about your presentation, don't worry about it too much. But if you're constantly hearing the same feedback, then you'll most likely want to make some changes. Obviously, if people are getting upset at what you're saying, then they aren't able to focus on your message and you've defeated your own purpose.

▶ **SECRET #13: The more committed you are to your message, the more resistance you will encounter from those individuals with a different belief system than yours. Knowing this going in means that you will be less surprised and better able to deal with their criticism when it arises.**

Controversy!

When was the last time you read something controversial in a book on public speaking? Well, you're about to. I debated quite a while before including the following story by Hansen, which he told me during the first of our two interview sessions. The reason? I didn't want to take away from the focus of the book by including a story on faith healing. However, since it did take place during one of his talks, and it does illustrate the tremendous healing power speakers can have on their audience, I've decided to include it. Here it is, in Hansen's own words:

> There was this lovely girl who was thirteen years old, and she had leukemia. Her doctor, who thought that she had nothing but a hope and a prayer, had heard me say to

share my tapes with everyone, especially the hungry, thirsty, and those who are desperate for this kind of insight and information.

He shared them with her. She then went to the Make-a-Wish Foundation to tell them that her final wish was to hear Mark Victor Hansen speak before she died. So she came to my talk with her family in Denver. I had her stand in front of this great audience and I had them all send her healing energy. I'm proud to say that she is now in remission.

Does that mean I'm a healer? No. It means that I set up the environment so there could be a lot of healing energy. And she was ready to get well; she had no real reason to light-beam off the planet!

You Are in the Healing
of Pain Business

While the idea of playing the role as a facilitator for healing, the way Hansen did, isn't for every speaker, we must understand that in, perhaps a less direct way, as speakers, we *are* in the healing business. Anytime you get up in front of an audience, you are there to heal a wound—to show people how to make pain go away, be it the pain of poor sales, the pain of low self-esteem, or the pain of not having enough money. How well you are able to provide solutions to alleviate this pain will determine how successful you are as a speaker. Let us not forget that what we say while up on that platform does indeed affect people's state-of-mind, and thus their lives. Therefore, we owe it to our audiences to focus on solutions and not problems. If *we* don't point out the positive in a situation and show people how to use their minds to heal and love instead of harm and tear down, who will?

▶ **SECRET #14: Look for the pain your audience is going through, find ways to alleviate that pain, and you will be enormously successful.**

How Hansen Comes Up
with His Material

---

*"There's too much information and
not enough insight and wisdom."*
MARK VICTOR HANSEN

When I asked Hansen how he comes up with his speech material,
he shared:

> Just like I'm doing with you right now. I spend a lot of time
> thinking out loud. God has blessed me with a really good
> mind. It's not linearly logical like a computer-oriented mind,
> but it's logical enough that I can do thought/feeling transfer-
> ence to the people who really get it. It gets them to have
> goose-bumpy flesh, like when I talked to ten thousand police-
> men in Los Angeles. They said, "We don't cry—we're like
> marines—but you sure did make our eyeballs leak!" I find
> out what galvanizes my emotive response, and then I go after
> doing that for somebody else.

This last sentence by Hansen is truly the secret to coming up
with good speech material for yourself. If you share with your
audience the stories and ideas that have touched or impacted you
in some significant way, they too will be moved. This is why taking another speaker's story is never as powerful as telling your
own story. You went through the experience yourself, so you can
give the story a richness and depth that no one else in the world
can give it.

▶ **SECRET #15: The best stories to tell your audience are those that
moved you. And the most powerful stories of all are those from
your own personal experience.**

Anytime you come across a story that moves you or an idea
that captures you're imagination, *write it down*. Remember, you

can't tell the story if you don't remember it, and if you don't write it down there's a good chance you'll forget it.

▶ **SECRET #16: Write down your stories, anecdotes, ideas and favorite quotes so you won't forget them.**

Of course, writing down your stories won't do you much good if you can't find them. That's why you'll want to keep a folder, journal, or computer file, of your stories, ideas, anecdotes, and favorite quotes. That way, when you need them, they'll all be in one place.

▶ **SECRET #17: Keep all of your stories, ideas, anecdotes, and favorite quotes in a folder, journal, or computer file so when you need them, they'll all be in one place.**

Humor Creates
Teachable Moments

While you might not have thought of humor as a tool, when speaking, it's a powerful way to keep the audience mentally engaged in what you have to say. If people are laughing and having a good time, they are going to be in a more open and receptive mood to hear your message. Here's Hansen on humor:

> One of the technologies that I use is heavy amounts of humor. Norman Cousins taught us that humor will enable people to live longer. I say it creates a teachable moment. People look for the humor and catch the message. I use more little one-liners than most other speakers. Sometimes, if an audience isn't "there," I keep doing that until I can get them.

It's true. Hansen tosses out one-liners like hand grenades throughout his presentation. Like little explosions, they serve to give people a mental jolt, to wake 'em up. Here is a sample of some of the one-liners that have tumbled out of the mouth of Mark "Henny Youngman" Hansen:

Teacher: "Johnny, what does *apathy* mean?"
Johnny: "I don't know and I don't care!"

One cannibal turned to the other and said, "I don't like my brother-in-law." And the second one replied, "Okay, than just eat the noodles!"

Lately, we've had so many earthquakes in Los Angeles that now when we say, "There goes the neighborhood," we mean it!

Hansen will sprinkle these one-liners throughout his presentation to keep his audience on their toes. Then, after he's used some humor to open them up, he'll follow up with a moving or serious story to make a point. Here's one such story he shared with me about how "what gets impressed (on the mind), gets expressed (in our reality)":

> One day, when my daughter was just three years old, the doorbell rang and it was the UPS guy who was bigger than Pavarotti. He said, "Hello," and my little daughter was frightened and ran around my leg at mach two with her hair on fire, almost knocking me into this guy. He said, "She's a shy girl, isn't she?" I said, "I'd appreciate it if you don't say that." And he said, "Why is that?" I said, "Every mental impression gets a later physical expression. It's what you say to yourself or what others say to you that you believe, think about, act upon, or acts upon you—this is what you become. And she will become shy if she buys into your affirmation."

> It's critical that you watch which affirmations you allow to go in. In computer language it's called, "Garbage in equals garbage out." Therefore, if we put successful affirmations in and successful word-pictures in, you get a successful life picture out of your mind!

Sum Up and Restate the Main Point of Your Story

Notice how, after Hansen told this story, he immediately restated its main point. In this example, it's that we must watch the affirmations we allow ourselves and others to put into our minds. Simple and straightforward. Exactly how you want your own summations to be. Incidentally, summing up and restating your main points is an excellent habit to get into. That way you can be sure the point that you wish to communicate to your audience is absolutely clear. While your listeners may have enjoyed your story, they might not have fully appreciated the point you were trying to make. (Remember, everyone interprets and filters incoming information based on *their* own unique past experiences, not yours; thus, inaccuracies can always creep into your message simply by the way the person processes the information.) By summing up, you impress upon your audience exactly what you want them to remember about the story.

Another reason for summing up is to simply reinforce the idea one more time. Since studies have shown that we are more likely to remember something the more times we are exposed to it, restating your idea helps your audience have a much better chance of remembering it. (Obviously, if your audience can't remember what you said, they can't use it.)

▶ **SECRET #18: By summing up and restating the main points of your stories, your audience will be more likely to remember them.**

"You've Got to Circulate to Percolate"

"You've got to ask everybody for the business. That's the difference between those of us who are booked and those of us who aren't."
MARK VICTOR HANSEN

Although he employs a full-time staff of five people to run his Newport Beach, California, office, Hansen is still actively involved in selling and promoting himself. Everywhere he goes, he is constantly asking other people for their business. Everywhere! Whether he's at the airport, a ball game, or just about anywhere where there are people, he is always introducing himself and making new friends and contacts. Hansen is a living example of what Cavett Robert means when he says, "You've got to circulate to percolate!"

While some speakers are selective about who they give out their cards to, Hansen gives out full-color-photo business cards to anyone and everyone! He knows they won't earn him any money sitting inside his wallet. And, of course, he is always asking people for their business card so that can he add them to his extensive mailing list and follow up with them later on. Here are a few of Hansen's thoughts on how he markets himself:

> I am still intensively solicitous on the telephone. I personally ask almost everybody I talk to—those who I think have the ability to hire me or to get me hired—for business. I suppose at the level that I'm at I don't need to be doing that, but I still stay active on the phone. The interesting thing is that if I put out that I want to get to a certain individual or group, even if my secretary can't get through, I'll still end up making contact somehow!

> I believe that a lot of speakers who are not employed would be fully employed if they got off of it and weren't afraid to ask for the business. I'm [constantly] saying things to myself like, "I'm getting more business and more money and bigger audiences than ever before."

> There's so much out there! If you start asking for the business, you'll pull away from the pack. If you're sitting on a plane, turn to the person next to you and say, "Do you do any meetings?" or "Do you know of any groups that do meetings?" They're going to start hiring you like you won't believe. You've got to ask everybody for the business. That's the difference between those of us who are booked and those of us who aren't.

▶ **SECRET #19: A sure-fire, no cost way to market yourself is to ask _everyone_ you meet for their business.**

The Eye of the Tiger

When I asked Hansen what one trait a speaker *must* have in order to be successful, he replied:

> You have to desire to speak more than anything else. Great speakers have a calling within them to communicate; and they communicate exceedingly well. They are absolutely passionate and intense. They have the eye of the tiger, the magnificent obsession.
>
> I can tell within thirty seconds of meeting someone whether they're on purpose toward some goal, because they start spilling over with effervescent enthusiasm about it. If they're not tuned-in and turned-on to their own greater good, I don't have time to waste on them. I would rather spend time with people going somewhere.

Hansen is absolutely right. As top-flight speakers, you and I should have a message to deliver to our audience that is burning inside of us. It should be our magnificent obsession, our quest; we should be so hungry to share this vision with others that we simply do not have the time to spend with people who aren't tuned-in to what's going on. Part of staying focused means knowing what to say "No!" to.

▶ **SECRET #20: Great speakers have a magnificent obsession; they have the eye of the tiger; they have a passion and an intensity to them that others can feel; they are going somewhere!**

The Three Stages of Speaking

Like every profession in life, Hansen feels there are certain stages that speakers tend to go through:

> You start out as a speaker who is "ego driven;" then you get out of that and want to serve the audience; then you want the audience to serve everybody else. Great speakers bring

their audience up to a new level of awareness during the brief few minutes that they're together. They get that person in the audience to go through a transformative process.

An enlightened speaker is one who is so inwardly clear that that clarity of power communicates and gets the people to go through the cocoon stage and leave the room a beautiful butterfly.

▶ **SECRET #21: As speakers, our job is to take our audience through a transformation of consciousness, from cocoon to butterfly.**

Know Where You're Going

You can only be a catalyst for transformation when you are crystal-clear on your outcome. When you have a mental picture clearly in your mind as to where you want your audience to be at the end of your speech, it will automatically drive your entire presentation. John F. Kennedy wanted his audience to feel the excitement of what it would mean to have a man on the moon by the end of the '60s. Lee Iacocca wanted the U.S. Congress to feel how patriotic and good for business it would be to bail out Chrysler. Did both men succeed? Yes! Why? Because they were both clear on their outcomes and knew exactly what they wanted their audience to think, do, and feel by the end of their speeches.

Take a few minutes right now to ask yourself, *"What do I want my audience to think, do, and feel at the conclusion of my presentation?"* Take as much time as you need to answer this one question—it's too important to the effectiveness of your presentation to just gloss over. Once you have your answer, you should make sure all your speech material supports this single goal. If *anything* in your speech detracts from your overall outcome, *throw it out!* It doesn't belong in your speech and will only dilute your impact on the audience. Remember, your speech (like a chain) is only as strong as its weakest idea (link).

▶ **SECRET #22: Before you begin your speech, you should always have a clear mental picture of what you want your audience to think, do, and feel at the conclusion of your presentation.**

What Goes Through Your Mind When You're Giving a Talk?

I wanted to know what Hansen thinks about as he is actually delivering his presentation. My thinking was that by knowing, specifically, what goes through a great speaker's mind, we could emulate those thought patterns, and our speaking would naturally improve. Hansen's answer is short, concise, and right on target:

> I think to myself, "Am I getting inside this person? Am I helping them so they can really make a difference with their life?"

Notice that Hansen's attention is not focused on himself, i.e., "I wonder how I'm coming off? I hope my hair still looks good, etc." Rather, it's focused on the audience and, specifically, whether he's reaching them or not. The question to ask yourself during your presentation is, "*Am I doing everything I possibly can with my body language, my tone of voice, my emotional energy, my delivery, and pacing to impact my audience?*" It's by asking yourself questions like these, while you are speaking, that will make you a powerful and effective speaker.

What to Do When You Blow It

Of course, it's easy to think positive thoughts when things are going well (as the Swedish saying goes, "*Everyone* is a good captain when the seas are calm"). But what do you tell yourself when things aren't going well and you know it? Because we speakers are human beings, there are going to be those occasions when we fall short of the mark, when we know that for whatever reason we could have been more effective. Here are Hansen's thoughts on not reaching an audience:

> The only time I ever feel bad is if I think my energy isn't communicating. On occasion I'll think, "Oh my God, I'm not doing it." Maybe I've been overintroduced, or the environment is too hot, or I'm just not reaching them.

I'm pretty far along, so I don't usually doubt whether I've got the talent to speak. But there are some situations where I doubt whether my energy is exactly right to hit an audience that day. Sometimes, when I've traveled for long periods and I'm tired, I doubt if I'm as clear as I'd like to be.

The Woman Who Was Going to End It All

A lot of the letters I get [from people who attended] talks where I blew it . . . there's that one guy who got it. And that was the guy who was cliff-hanging that day. That was the guy or gal who was going to snuff his or her life out that night. I just got one of those letters. The lady said that she was suicidal and that night she was going to end it, but my talk gave her hope. Out of one hundred talks I give, I'd say ninety-nine go exceedingly well, and I'm blessed and I'm thankful. The one that I blow usually causes me a lot of pain; however, one that I blew was one that had saved her.

You can't always read what's happening. You never know how "worse-off" somebody is in the audience. Maybe you can pierce the crack in their cosmic mental egg. The person may say, "He's right, I don't have to kill myself. There are people that live a lot worse than me. I'm an American; I've got a shot, I've got hope, and I have an opportunity."

▶ **SECRET #23: You never know who is sitting in your audience that needed to hear your message that day.**

Like Wayne Dyer and many other speakers, Hansen's message literally saved another human being's life. Keep this in mind the next time you begin to wonder whether or not what you have to say makes a difference. The truth is, you can't imagine how much your words may have meant to somebody who was sitting in your audience and who felt as if they couldn't go on. We speakers must realize that we do indeed make a difference in people's lives . . . sometimes more than we'll ever know.

A Lesson from Wayne Newton

Of course, sometimes the difference we make is not in the way we had planned. What makes the following story from Hansen so great is that it reminds us that even big-name speakers can occasionally make a bad decision in front of an audience—even when they know better:

> My wife and I had just seen Wayne Newton perform in Las Vegas. . . . It was the last show of the night, and people were throwing beer bottles at him! He just kept singing "Danke Schöen" and ducking beer bottles! I couldn't believe they were throwing beer bottles at a legend. He was wise enough to know that if you have a wise-guy audience, you just float with it and then get off the stage as quickly as you can.
>
> The next night I'm back in L.A., and I'm doing a talk for a bank. The chairman of the board is at the head table with his wife. My talk is going brilliantly well. I'm in the middle of telling my closing story, which is the "Bopsy story" from *Chicken Soup* Vol. 1 (page 61). The chairman's wife has had too much to drink and can't contain herself, so she starts talking. She is so loud and animated that everybody at the table starts listening to her instead of me. I stop talking and look at her and embarrass her out of her wit; I said, "Would you be so kind as to be quiet."
>
> Because she was inebriated, it was not the right thing for me to do. I should have finished, even though she was being totally rude and it was being videotaped by the company. I thought I was more important than she was and I missed what Wayne Newton had done the night before. The customer is always right. So, I not only mortified her, but she got up and said to her husband, "Harry, we're out of here!" Well, four hundred of the one thousand people in the audience got up and left with her! . . . That blew book sales, I'll tell you! (Chuckles.)

Like all great speakers, Hansen realized immediately what he had done wrong. It's not that great speakers never make mistakes, it's that they quickly learn from their mistakes and thus benefit and grow from the experience. The lesson here from Wayne and Mark is obvious: You're there for the audience, not the other way around.

▶ **SECRET #24: If your audience is ever rude, just remember the Wayne Newton story and "keep on singing." Above all, never, ever insult your audience; you're there to serve them!**

Dodging Dinner Rolls

Believe it or not, Hansen has actually had audiences throw dinner rolls at him during his presentation. It seems that all it takes is one inebriated executive to get the cute idea to chuck a bread roll at the speaker, and suddenly that opens up the floodgates for everybody to start bombing away. While this may seem funny to a drunk person, it is totally inappropriate behavior. Keep in mind that it wasn't because Hansen wasn't doing a good job; it was just that these people simply had too much to drink.

As a result of this experience, Hansen has inserted a clause in his contract which states that he won't speak after dinner if alcohol is served. While you might not want to go that far, any speaker who has been around for a while will tell you that if an audience has been drinking, their attention span is significantly reduced. This is something you'll definitely want to adjust to the next time you get up to speak and see wine bottles on the table (especially if they're next to big baskets of rolls!).

What to Do When Someone in Your Audience Dies!

I know, I know . . . why such a morbid topic? Because it *can* happen! Let's face it, people pass on every minute of every day and there *is* a chance that it could one day happen right in the middle of *your* presentation. If it did, would you know what to do?

Apparently Hansen did, but only because he did what you're doing right now—learning from what Cavett Robert calls O.P.E. (Other People's Experience).

Hansen had just attended a National Speakers Association meeting where a speaker named Roy Hatten told about how a lady had died in front of him and his audience during one of his presentations. Hatten shared with his fellow speakers how he had quieted the group and led them in prayer until the paramedics got there. I'll let Hansen take over the story from here:

> I was speaking at the Toastmasters International meeting in 1979, in Riverside, California. An eighty-nine-year-old lady had been given an award and then she had a heart attack in front of me (and the audience). The emcee said, "Mark will speak to us while we're waiting for the ambulance."
>
> Well, only because I had heard Roy Hatten a week before, I said, "Now we'll all pray and send her healing energy." The emergency guys got there and they tried to jump start her nineteen times in front of the audience—she was coming three feet off the stretcher! Her eyes were bugging out of her head—you can't do a talk after something like that! So, I called a fifteen-minute break and said that I would give a twenty-minute talk when we returned. And the audience ended up really loving me for it. I talked about how to be really alive while you live.

Hansen handled the situation most impressively. Not only did he follow Hatten's advice by leading the group in prayer, but he had the presence of mind to change his speech on the spot. And the title he came up with, "How to Be Really Alive While You Live," is really *the only* speech that could have been given after what that audience had just been through. Kudos to Hansen for a job well done at a most sensitive time.

(Of course, you could simply send the people home, but that only leaves everyone feeling down and disjointed. By doing what he did, Hansen was able to give some meaning to the woman who had passed on. He turned it into as positive an experience as he could by reminding the people in the audience to live each moment to it's fullest, because they never know when their number will be called. Being a Toastmaster and thus a speaker herself, I'm sure the woman would have appreciated Hansen's efforts. I know I would have.)

▶ **SECRET #25: If someone in your audience "passes on" during your program, the best thing to do while you're waiting for the paramedics is to lead the group in prayer and then, if appropriate, give a talk on "How to Be Really Alive While You Live." Above all, it's your duty to lead by example and help the audience remain as calm as possible while the situation is unfolding.**

(While I know of no other books on public speaking that cover this admittedly touchy area, I felt strongly that we should include it here. After all, it's better to get you thinking about it now, rather than when it's actually happening! The worse thing would be to suddenly find yourself in that type of a situation without a clue as to what to do. Now, if it ever does happen, you'll be better prepared.)

The Chicken Soup Phenomenon

With over five million books sold, Hansen and Jack Canfield's *Chicken Soup for the Soul* series has obviously touched a chord in people's hearts around the country. I asked Hansen what he thought the reason was for the "*Chicken Soup* phenomenon":

Americans have stopped talking. We think that people have stopped sitting out in rocking chairs, stopped sitting around the dinner table, and stopped sitting around the campfire and in front of the fireplace. What *Chicken Soup* does is get people communicating again, heart-to-heart, notion-to-notion. Teenagers, people with dyslexia, slow readers, non-readers, even prisoners have picked up our book and said, "This is the first book I've ever read."

Thirty Rejections!

Every author's dream is for the very first major publishing firm that sees his or her book to say, "Yes, this is exactly what we've been looking for! Sign here!" The reality is, however, that this is the exception and not the rule. In fact, *Chicken Soup* was turned down thirty times before it was finally picked up by a publisher. The irony is that after it came out, ten of the publishers who originally turned them down came back to them waving a million dollars at them (the biggest offer was 2.8 million dollars!) and said, "Ooops, we made a mistake. You guys were right and we were wrong. How about doing a book for us?"

This ought to give every writer reading this a boost of encouragement. The message is clear enough: *Don't give up*. Even if you have to go through thirty rejections, the next submission could be the one!

▶ **Secret #26: Remember that *Chicken Soup for the Soul* was rejected thirty times before it was finally picked up. It may take ten or twenty or fifty tries, but if you believe in your idea and don't give up, eventually you will succeed.**

The Biggest Mistake That Beginning Speakers Make

I asked Hansen to cite the biggest mistake that beginning speakers make:

What they miss is a principle I teach called, "pick the market and then write the speech." Find a market that has a problem, or, as Nido Qubein describes it, "something on their worry list." I know that the founder of Toastmasters, Mr. Smedley, says to write a great speech and then go out and find the market. But I say, find the market and then write the speech.

Hansen's Four Markets

The four basic markets on which Hansen focuses are: life insurance, chiropractics, multilevel marketing companies, and the big speaker rallies around the country. He interviewed the top sales superstars in the life insurance business (just as I interviewed the top professional speakers for this book) and then did a video- and audiotape program on them. From this, he put together a talk that's been enormously successful for him, called "How to Earn $100,000 a Year Working Four Hours or Less a Day Selling Baby Insurance Policies." Hansen found a market that no one else had tapped into and capitalized on it.

▶ **SECRET #27: Find a market that no one else has tapped into and design a talk that provides solutions to their pain and worries.**

Meditates Everyday

I asked Hansen how he comes up with his ideas:

> I work on it, I meditate on it every night. I get up at three o'clock just about every morning and meditate for at least an hour when nobody else is around. And then I write down all the stuff that I come up with. Like Og Mandino, who writes from eleven o'clock at night to six o'clock in the morning, I spend real quiet time saying, "How is it that I can communicate this burst of ideation so the words are literate and so omniattractive that they infiltrate somebody's mind and they hit at the quick of the consciousness to help that person transform?" (You're on your own as to what that last sentence means!)

Be Prepared, Because
When Your Ship Comes in . . .

*"My thoughts of prosperity always precede my
demonstration of prosperity."*
MARK VICTOR HANSEN

Hansen shared with me that as much as you try to prepare yourself for the success that you've spent years going after, when it
does finally happen, it can be overwhelming:

> A number of years ago, I wrote a book called *Future Diary,*
> which says that you ought to plan your whole future, be-
> cause when it hits, it hits all at once. I'm in the "all at once-
> ness" right now, as are many of the major speakers with
> whom I've spoken. Everything's hitting at once. And no
> matter how prepared many of us were, none of us were pre-
> pared enough.
>
> For example, when Jack (Canfield) and I wrote out what we
> wanted to have happen with *Chicken Soup for the Soul,* we
> said, "Wouldn't it be nice to have a movie, a weekly show,
> etc." Well, within a week's time we had two of those come to
> us all at once. We had the guy who created *The Merv Griffin
> Show* come to us, and we had a lady from King Features ap-
> proach us and set up a meeting with producer Vin De Bono.
> Howard Scripts has asked us to do a major film on *Chicken
> Soup for the Soul.* Oprah wants to do a show with us called,
> "Anecdotes from *Chicken Soup for the Soul,*" featuring
> many of the 101 storytellers in our book.
>
> So, it hit's all at once. What *Think and Grow Rich* says—
> which I used to read twenty-one years ago when I was bank-
> rupt—is that when riches begin to come, they come in such
> an avalanche and overflowing abundance, you wonder where
> they've been hiding during all the lean years.
>
> I know that Brian Tracy, Jim Rohn, Jack, myself, and every
> one of us is having exactly the same experience right now

because the media has just gone wild and the whole world wants self-help. America is the greatest country in the world for many reasons, but one is because we are the only country that has self-help books, tapes, videos, seminars, and that lifestyle. It doesn't exist in Japan. Our book is going to be in Japan and they expect it to be a number-one best-seller. We're currently number one in Canada and the United States, and we just signed contracts to get it in fifteen other countries.

Hansen's "Life Purpose" Question:

If I were provided with absolutely everything I want and need to release my full potential, to release my highest vision for myself and humanity, and I knew that all the resources of people, talent, time, tools, technology, and finances were there for me, what would I do for myself and for total humanity?

The Future of Professional Speaking

I think there are two things that speakers have to do. First, get more involved on the information super-highway, Second, do what Terry Brock did at the 1995 National Speakers Convention (in Irvine, California)—bring more media, more glitz, more entertainment value, more speed of change, more documentation, and more credibility (into your presentation). Where you can videotape somebody two minutes before you go on and put it on the screen and just wow the socks off the audience. I think this is relatively affordable to every speaker today.

▶ **SECRET #28: The future of speaking lies in multimedia, high-tech, high-value presentations.**

The Biggest Fear of All:
Uncertainty

I asked Hansen if there was anything that he is afraid of. His reply:

> One never gets rid of fear totally. Jack and I wrote a book called *The Aladdin Factor: How to Ask for and Get Anything You Want* (1995, Berkeley Books), which talks about the biggest fear of all: uncertainty.

> Uncertainty happens with everybody. You want to get to the next level so badly, and suddenly you're there, and now you get a whole different level of uncertainty. The uncertainty, as Dr. Harold Bloomfield calls it, is the stress of success. As I talked about before, when it hits all at once, everybody wants you and they all want you now. We have four book contracts and they all want us now.

Myth: When You Achieve Massive
Success, Stress Magically
Goes Away

After listening to Hansen's answer, I said, "So what I hear you saying is that no matter how big you get, there are always going to be some stresses and some challenges; they just get bigger."

> Yes, they get bigger. The assumption of the young speaker is, "Boy, when I'm making that kind of money and I'm getting that kind of fee, there won't be any problems." But the problems are more on a metaphysical level where you're asking yourself, "Can I get this done? Can I deliver everything that I've promised like I have done up until now?"

▶ **Secret #29: It is a myth to think that when you become enormously successful that all of a sudden stress and challenges simply go away.**

What Do You Know Now That You Didn't Know a Few Years Ago When We First Talked?

Since it had been a few years between our first and second interview, I asked Hansen the above question, to which he replied:

> That whatever you really hold in your mind's eye . . . the Bible says that as a man or woman thinketh in his or her heart, so is she or he. That demonstration ability is now viscerally mine. I now understand that I can play with it on a spiritual plane, bring it in the mental plane, and manifest it on the physical plane. And before, I had it as a theory. Now, thanks to *Chicken Soup* and a lot of miracles we've pulled off, I understand it at a deeper level.

> Right now, with all the floods, fires, and earthquakes we've been having, the universe needs us speakers to teach people how to have balance—to be centered, breathe deep, and live their life cogently and purposefully, out of mastership, and make their life a masterpiece.

How Mark Victor Hansen would like to be remembered:

"He motivated all those who wanted to be motivated, using all the tools that he had available."
MARK VICTOR HANSEN

Mark Victor Hansen's Success Secrets Summary

SECRET #1: By repeating a key word (or words) multiple times within the same sentence (or speech), you dramatically increase its impact on your audience and thus make the idea considerably more memorable.

SECRET#2: By first saying what something is not, followed by what it is, you make that something dramatically more impactful, and thus more memorable to your audience.

SECRET #3: Having the audience "call back" to you key words and affirmations not only keeps them actively involved in your presentation, but it's a lot of fun!

SECRET #4: Having your audience touch themselves at chest level while saying an affirmation not only increases their participation level, but it stimulates their senses, causing them to anchor your message at a deeper level.

SECRET #5: Sharing a humorous story about yourself to illustrate a point not only makes your message more memorable, but it helps to establish a bond between you and your audience because it shows you can poke fun at yourself.

SECRET #6: If a joke or other attempt at humor doesn't work for whatever reason, being the pro that you are, you quickly, confidently, and smoothly move on to your next segment, without letting it throw you in the least.

SECRET #7: A request made in a confident tone of voice indicates to your audience that you are in command. If they sense that you are comfortable giving directions and that you expect them to be followed, you will have little trouble gaining their cooperation.

SECRET #8: Whenever you ask the audience to do something, remember the acronym K.I.S.S.: Keep It Simple, Speaker!

SECRET #9: The more fun your requests of your audience sound, the more eager people will be to participate.

SECRET #10: Demonstrating to your audience exactly what you want them to do helps eliminate any confusion.

SECRET #11: The audience takes its cues from you; the more *you* get into whatever you're saying or doing, the more they will.

SECRET #12: The more consistent your message is with who you really are as a person, the more effective you will be at delivering that message.

SECRET #13: The more committed you are to your message, the more resistance you will encounter from those individuals with a different belief system than yours. Knowing this going in means that you will be less surprised and better able to deal with their criticism when it arises.

SECRET #14: Look for the pain your audience is going through, find ways to alleviate that pain, and you will be enormously successful.

SECRET #15: The best stories to tell your audience are those that moved you. And the most powerful stories of all are those from your own personal experience.

SECRET #16: Write down your stories, anecdotes, ideas and favorite quotes so you won't forget them.

SECRET #17: Keep all of your stories, ideas, anecdotes, and favorite quotes in a folder, journal, or computer file, so when you need them, they'll all be in one place.

SECRET #18: By summing up and restating the main points of your stories, your audience will be more likely to remember them.

SECRET #19: A sure-fire, no-cost way to market yourself is to ask *everyone* you meet for their business.

SECRET #20: Great speakers have a magnificent obsession; they have the eye of the tiger; they have a passion and an intensity to them that others can feel; they are going somewhere!

SECRET #21: As speakers, our job is to take our audience through a transformation of consciousness, from cocoon to butterfly.

SECRET #22: Before you begin your speech, you should always have a clear mental picture of what you want your audience to think, do, and feel at the conclusion of your presentation.

SECRET #23: You never know who is sitting in your audience that needed to hear your message on that day.

SECRET #24: If your audience is ever rude, just remember the Wayne Newton story and "keep on singing." Above all, never, ever insult your audience; you're there to serve them!

SECRET #25: If someone in your audience "passes on" during your program, the best thing to do while you're waiting for the paramedics is to lead the group in prayer and then, if appropriate, give a talk on "How to Be Really Alive While You Live." Above all, it's your duty to lead by example and help the audience remain as calm as possible as the situation is unfolding.

SECRET #26: Remember that *Chicken Soup for the Soul* was rejected 30 times before it was finally picked up. It may take 10 or 20 or 50 tries, but if you believe in your idea and don't give up, eventually you will succeed.

SECRET #27: Find a market that no one else has tapped into and design a talk that provides solutions to their pain and worries.

SECRET #28: The future of speaking lies in multimedia, high-tech, high-value presentations.

SECRET #29: It is a myth to think that when you become enormously successful that, all of a sudden, stress and challenges simply go away.

CHAPTER SEVEN

BORN: April 4, 1940
BIRTHPLACE: Croydon, England

Roger Dawson

*"A happy and successful person works diligently
to fulfill his dreams, rather than to spend a
lifetime dreaming of fulfillment."*

▼

BORN the son of a taxicab driver in London, England, Roger Dawson left high school at age sixteen to start his own business as a resort hotel photographer. However, being adventuresome by nature, he yearned to see more of the world. He procured a position aboard a ship as a photographer, where he traveled around the world not once, but four times! During his voyage, he heard about all the great opportunities America had to offer. Thus, in 1962 (with only $400 to his name), he purchased a one-way ticket to the United States and set out on the biggest adventure of his life.

Through hard work and perseverance, Dawson did indeed achieve the American dream. He became president of a large California real estate firm with twenty-eight offices, 540 sales reps, and sales of over 400 million dollars per year. His executive position allowed him a comfortable lifestyle that included luxury homes, expensive cars and all the perks that come with running a big company. However, amidst all this "success," Dawson went to work one day and suddenly realized that he no longer felt passionate about running a large company. He had made it to the top of the mountain and, like many people, found that the view didn't quite hold the thrill he imagined it would. While he enjoyed all the trappings his job afforded him, two of Dawson's core values are growth and freedom. Since his current position now left him feeling smothered and restricted, he knew it was time to move on.

It's Never Too Late to Do What You Love

The advice that many motivational speakers (including myself) give to people who are not happy in their present career comes down to two words: *Get out.*

We say this because we know that life is much too short to spend it doing something you truly don't enjoy. Dawson came to this realization himself at the age of forty-two, when working behind a desk ten to twelve hours a day no longer held the level of fun and adventure it used to:

> In 1982, I was in my early forties and president of one of the largest real estate companies in Southern California. However, I was going through a mid-life crisis and wondered whether I wanted to sit behind a desk for the rest of my life.
>
> I decided I didn't, and that's when I started thinking about professional speaking. Every Saturday morning we would have a different speaker come in and give a presentation at our sales breakfasts.

Dawson admits that becoming a speaker was, initially, the last thing on his mind. However, the more he thought about it the more he realized it would give him the freedom he so dearly wanted. Once he decided to "go for it," he turned to one of the legends in the motivational speaking business, the founder of the National Speakers Association, Mr. Cavett Robert:

> I got some excellent advice from Cavett who said, "The secret to picking a topic is to choose something specific enough that you can become known for it, and yet broad enough that everybody needs it."

▶ **SECRET #1: "The secret to picking a topic is to choose something specific enough that you can become known for it, and yet broad enough that everybody needs it."—Cavett Robert**

> You can have a topic that is super specific, but there is a very small market out there for it. Or, you can have a topic that everybody needs such as motivation, but which is not specific enough for you to become known for it.

While there are exceptions to what Roger is saying (clearly, Les Brown has been able to make a name for himself as a motivational speaker), his point is well taken. If you pick a topic that everybody is doing, unless you bring something original to it—such as Brown's dynamic energy and enthusiasm—you're simply not going to stand out from the crowd (and speakers who get lost in the crowd, no matter how good their message is, don't get many calls to speak).

On the other hand, if you pick something so specialized that the market is very small, then you're going to quickly run out of people to speak for. With this in mind, Dawson came up with his topic:

> There are some topics that fit both these bills, such as time management or stress management. But there were just too many speakers out there doing them; that's why I selected negotiation. It was probably the smartest thing I have done in my lifetime!

So, Roger chose negotiation because it fit within his criteria. However, it's important to note that because of his previous job, he had gained a lot of valuable experience as a negotiator, and thus had "earned the right" to talk on this most useful topic:

> In my real estate company we were doing a lot of negotiating. About 20% of all real estate transactions fall out after the contract is signed, but before the deal is closed. Something goes wrong such as the buyer and the seller have a disagreement or the buyer can't get the financing. That 20% fall-out rate meant that our company was losing something in the region of 100 million dollars a year. We were writing about 500 million dollars a year and only closing on 400 million.
>
> I determined that I would do what I could to stop that 100 million-dollar-a-year loss from falling through the cracks. When the sales agents couldn't handle the problems, and the office managers couldn't handle them, and the regional managers couldn't handle them, then I would get them.
>
> So, I was getting some experience with some tough negotiating problems. I discovered that with a few simple techniques a world of difference could be made. We ended up cutting that fall-out rate in half and picking up another 50 million dollars worth of business a year because of these techniques.

The Best Speakers Speak from Their Own Personal Experiences

It's this kind of hands-on experience, of having gone through "the school of hard knocks," that makes what Dawson has to teach so valuable. His ideas are not theory or something he's simply read in a book. Rather, the majority of his tips and techniques come from his own personal experiences.

What events and life experiences have you been through that might be of value to others? All of us have had things happen to us where we learned something quite useful, but unless we stop to write the experience down, we usually tend to forget it all too quickly due to our hectic lifestyle. That's why I strongly urge you to get into the habit of committing your more interesting life experiences to paper.

▶ **SECRET #2: If you have learned something from a life experience, chances are good that others will too. Thus, it's worth taking a few minutes to capture the experience on paper so as not to forget it.**

Some Things Are Simply Not Negotiable

The following is an example of how you can use your own life experiences as a farming ground for good speech stories. Whenever Dawson gives a presentation on negotiation, he always tells his audience that "almost everything" is negotiable. The reason he says "almost everything" is because of a phone call he received:

> A fellow by the name of Tim Rush once called me and said that he was driving down Hollywood Boulevard one night, listening to my cassette tapes, when he stopped off at a gas station to make a call. Well, when he got back to his car a guy stuck a gun in his ribs and said, "Okay buddy, give me your wallet!"

> Tim told me that because he had been listening to my tapes he said to the mugger, "Look, here's what I'm prepared to do. I'll give you the cash, but let me keep the wallet and the credit cards, fair enough?" And the guy said, "Buddy, you didn't hear me, I said give me the wallet!" And Tim had no choice but to comply. Sometimes you don't negotiate, but it's almost a hundred-percent rule.

Since Tim was not hurt, Roger is able to tell this intriguing yet somehow slightly amusing story during his presentation. However, occasionally he gets calls on much more serious situations, such as the time he received a phone call regarding a hostage situation. I'll let Roger take over from here:

> Several years ago I got a call from a fellow by the name of James from Sarasota, Florida, whose brother was a hostage in Iraq. James had been listening to my tapes and he was considering going to Iraq to see if he could get his brother out. He called me and said, "What do you think I should do, Roger? Can I negotiate him out of there? The state department is putting an awful lot of pressure on me not to go."
>
> Since he had been on the *Today Show*, my suggestion to him was that he go, but he take a journalist with him. That way he'd be a high-profile person going in and that would make him safer. Also, that would give his brother the best chance of getting out because he would then be a high-profile person coming out. The brother could then talk about the fact that he was released, which is what Saddam Hussain was looking for.
>
> Three weeks later I got a call from James saying that he was so excited because he had gone to Iraq and got his brother out. He said that if it hadn't been for me encouraging him, he never would have had the courage to do it.

It's stories like this one, knowing that he made a real difference in someone else's life, that reminds Roger just how important what he does is and how rewarding it can be.

Telling Other People's Stories

Of course, while the best stories to tell *are* those that you've personally been through yourself, this does not mean that if you come across a great story you should refrain from telling it because it didn't happen to you personally. The world is a very big place and you can't possibly experience everything that life has to offer. Therefore, if you hear of another human being's experience that you can truly relate to, and it ties in with your topic, you should absolutely consider using it in your presentation.

For example, a friend of mine once called me up and told me about an interesting thing that happened at a sales meeting she had attended that afternoon. It seems that one of the sales reps at her company got up and gave a fifteen-minute presentation to the group. However, she was so unprepared and nervous that her hands were visibly shaking. In fact, my friend told me, "Michael, she was shaking so much you could actually hear the papers in her hand rustle! While we all felt sorry for her, it was very embarrassing not to mention uncomfortable to have to sit through." Next my friend told me something that made a deep impression on me. She said, "As this was going on, I happened to overhear my boss, who was sitting next to me, lean over to his boss and whisper, 'And Sally wants to take on bigger accounts?! She can't even get up in front of our group without falling apart; how's she going to handle the pressure in front of a major buyer?'"

Wow, I thought, that certainly does illustrate the point of how poor communication skills can hurt you. But the story doesn't end there. My friend then went on to tell me about another sales rep at that same meeting who got up to speak right after Sally. Her name was Cindy, and because she was relaxed, prepared, and confident, she made a much different impression on the group. Said my friend, "It was amazing. Cindy was so confident in herself and her ideas, that she was able to convince everyone in the room that we should go ahead and bring out a new line of clothes, even though the initial marketing tests were less than spectacular. Her confidence and belief that we could do it sold us!"

As soon as my friend told me this story, I immediately asked her if I could use it in my presentations. She said that would be fine as long as I changed their names, which I agreed to do.

What made me think this story was worth retelling? Because, as I mentioned, it perfectly illustrated the importance of developing strong communication skills and how *not* having them can cost us dearly, both personally and professionally. In this case it clearly hurt Sally, as she literally talked herself right out of a promotion that she most assuredly wanted.

By telling this story, it helps me to make my point quicker and with far greater impact than if I simply stated that poor communications skills can hurt you, but didn't give a real-life illustration. True, this story didn't happen to me. But, because I understood the dynamics of the situation and could immediately identify with both Sally and Cindy, I knew I could tell the story and do it justice. And that's what you want to do. Like an actor deciding whether or not to play a part, if you can really relate to someone else's experience, and you can "grasp the emotional essence" of what they went through, then you should go ahead and tell the story. If the story moves you, it will move your audience. However, by the same token, no matter how good a story is, if you don't "feel it," you shouldn't tell it.

▶ **SECRET #3: You can effectively tell another person's story if you find that you can relate to it in some way and it moves you emotionally.**

By the way, when I say it's okay to tell another person's story, I'm not talking about telling another speaker's story. There are millions of stories out there and therefore no reason to take somebody else's. Be creative and come up with your own! That way, you don't have to worry if your audience has heard it—and besides, you'll sleep better.

Two Ways to Approach the Speaking Profession

The first time Roger and I met was over a lunch meeting, and it was at that time he told me that there were really only two basic approaches one could take to becoming a professional speaker:

> One is to have a topic that everybody wants to hear. Companies or associations select that topic and then they get you because you're an authority on that subject. The other approach is to try to convince people that you're the

world's greatest speaker and they should hire you, with your topic being secondary.

It's a hundred times easier to do it the way I did it. Emphasize the topic and then hopefully you become famous. Then one day you get hired because you are who you are, a headliner, and what you talk about is of secondary importance to them.

▶ **SECRET #4: There are two basic strategies for becoming a well-known speaker. One is to promote yourself, and the other is to promote your topic. Unless you're a celebrity, the latter is significantly easier.**

This is in fact exactly the way Dawson did it. He would basically say to companies, "Bring me in, and I'll show your people how to keep from leaving money on the table, which will immediately increase your profits." He knew that had he said, "Hi, I'm the charismatic, humorous Roger Dawson. Wouldn't you love to have me at your next meeting?!"—they would have responded, "Roger who? Sorry, never heard of you . . ." and speaking jobs would have been few and far between.

With his strategy of being topic-driven clearly in place, Dawson immediately went out and became a huge success in the speaking industry and within the first year was pulling down five-figure fees per appearance, right? Well, not exactly . . .

The Turning Point

Today Roger Dawson, with his charming British accent and his smooth and easy-going delivery is considered one of the elite speakers in the industry. However, when he was just starting out he had no idea as to whether or not he could make a living as a full-time speaker. In fact, he admits that for the first nine months, it looked doubtful. Then, something happened that would not only turn his career around, but would make him one of the best-known speakers on the subject of negotiation in the world.

Divine Intervention?

Oftentimes, you can look back over a successful person's life and point to one fortuitous event that almost single-handedly launched his or her career. When Elvis Presley went into Sun Records in 1953 to record a song for his mother, a secretary named Marion Keisker overheard him singing. Realizing his voice had the distinct sound that she knew her boss was looking for, she wrote down Presley's name and phone number. Several months later, Sam Phillips called Elvis and the rest is music history.

Dawson's "break through" happened in two phases. First, he recorded a set of tapes on negotiation:

> It was when I recorded the audio tapes . . . I always think of it as divine intervention—it had to be. I had done a talk for a real estate company and they wanted me to come back and do a three-hour seminar. I had sold seventy or eighty tickets to this seminar for $15 apiece. I thought to myself, "Wouldn't it be much better if I had a cassette program in the back that I could sell afterward to make some additional money." So, I sat down and over a period of three or four evenings, I recorded, "The Secrets of Power Negotiating."
>
> I have since re-recorded it four or five times and made it better. But the outline and the content of the program are basically the same as when I first outlined them. I've heard of authors who have done that. All of a sudden they get a concept for a book and they sit down and the whole book just flows out of them. And that's basically what happened to me with, "The Secrets of Power Negotiating."

You Never Know Until You Ask:
How Roger Got Nightingale-Conant
to Publish His Tapes

The second phase of the event that put Dawson's career over the top came about because of a chance conversation he had with his daughter on why some people are successful and others are not.

At the time, he had thought about going to the Chicago-based Nightingale-Conant, the world's largest distributor of personal growth cassettes, and asking them to publish his tapes. However, since they already had an album out on negotiation, he assumed they wouldn't be interested in another one:

> I was on vacation with my daughter—we spent five weeks traveling around Europe, and we were sitting out by a lake when she asked me, "Why is it that some people in America are super successful and other people, with all the same advantages, just don't seem to be able to make it?"
>
> I said, "Well Julie, I don't think many people are failing in America. I really think that the people who think they're failing are the people who never really went out and made the effort to get it done."
>
> As an example I said, "Take myself for instance. I speak on negotiation and I have a set of tapes on negotiating. Nightingale/Conant is the largest publisher of tapes in America, but I have never approached them because I'm convinced that they would not take a second program on negotiating. And I think a lot of people are like that. An opportunity is there but they talk themselves out of it. They convince themselves it wouldn't work and it would be a waste of time."

That evening, Dawson thought about what he had said to his daughter and realized the trap he had allowed himself to fall into. He had played psychic and assumed that Nightingale-Conant would not be interested in his program. Upon reflection, he realized that he really didn't know what their reaction to his tapes might be because he had never asked them. Sure, they might say no, in which case he would not have a Nightingale-Conant tape deal. However, since he currently didn't have one, what did he have to lose by giving it a shot? Nothing!

"You miss one hundred percent of the shots you don't take."
—WAYNE GRETSKY

So, he picked up the phone while he was still in Switzerland and called his office back in California. Says Roger:

> I said to the president of my company, "I want you to call Nightingale-Conant. I'm going to be speaking in Chicago next month and I want you to set up an appointment with them. I just want to walk in with my program and present it, and see if we can get anywhere with it." She set up the appointment, and they were very receptive. I walked in with the program and I asked them to listen to the first cassette on the album. They said, "You know, this is really a coincidence because our first negotiating program has been selling so well, we were looking for another negotiating program."
>
> It was just the right thing at the right time. It has become a huge best-seller for them. They've sold over ten million dollars worth of them!

Let's learn from Dawson's experience and never assume somebody isn't interested in what we have to offer unless they tell us otherwise.

▶   **SECRET #5: Assume everybody is interested in your product or service unless they tell you otherwise.**

Why Success Breeds More Success

One of the major benefits of overcoming your own self-doubt and taking action (such as Roger did with Nightingale-Conant) is that the next time you are in a similar situation, you will be much more likely to go for it. Why? Because you will now have a positive memory of a success from which to draw. In other words, the next time Roger faced a challenging goal all he had to do was think about how handsomely going to Nightingale-Conant had paid off and this will give him the confidence to take on new risks.

As author and management expert Michael LeBoeuf says, "That which gets rewarded gets repeated." So, each time you achieve success in your life, no matter how small, and you take a few moments to congratulate yourself, you are adding to your "success base."

However, I notice that people who are underachievers tend to discount their successes. They do this by saying, "Oh, it was nothing," or "I just got lucky." *No!* Take the credit—because you earned it. Even for the mini-successes: If this morning, you pulled into a tight parking space and were able to perfectly parallel-park your car, then take a moment to "bask in the glory" of a job well done!

Everything I've learned from interviewing and reading about successful people over the past decade has led me to conclude that *success is a habit*. And like any habit, the more you do it the better you get at it.

▶ **SECRET #6: Success is a habit—the more success you have, the easier achieving success becomes.**

How Dawson Turned Fear into Confidence in His Public Speaking

Like most speakers, Roger told me that when he was just starting out he was terrified of forgetting what he would say and looking foolish in front of his audience. However, with experience comes confidence. The more speeches he gave the more confident he became of his message, and the less his nerves bothered him. Eventually, like every good speaker, he got to the point where he could be speaking while simultaneously thinking about what he was going to say next:

> The words come very easily to me now. I can really think and speak separately. In other words, I can be thinking about something and still be confident that the right words are coming out when I'm in front of an audience.
>
> That used to give me a real panicky feeling because all of a sudden my mind would think, "I'm not concentrating on what I'm saying. . . . I don't know what I just said!" But

you do become comfortable with it so that you know you have said the right thing even though you may not have been conscious of saying it. It's a very interesting phenomenon.

The Zone

In sports, the term that is used to describe this phenomenon to which Dawson is referring, is called, "being in the zone." This is when an athlete is so in sync with the flow of a game that he or she can practically do no wrong. For example, when a basketball player is hitting everything in sight, the announcer will often say that the player has gone "unconscious," meaning that they no longer have to stop and think about every move. They're on automatic pilot. When asked, the player will say, "The basket looked as big as a lake. I felt as if whatever I threw up would go in."

As a speaker, you should strive to get into "the zone," whenever possible. You do this by becoming so connected with your audience, and so focused on your message, that your presence becomes riveting. People can't take their eyes off you because you're "in the flow." Your energy, passion and message have all come together to create an unforgettable experience. All systems are go. You're running on "all eight cylinders," and the result is pure magic.

▶   **SECRET #7: Great speakers are so in tune with themselves, their audience, and their message that they put themselves in a peak state known as "the zone."**

More Benefits of Speaking on a Topic That Is of Value to Many Different Industries

Another benefit of speaking on a topic such as negotiation (and as mentioned earlier, a major reason why Roger selected it) is because it can be of value to virtually any industry.

For example, right before our interview, Dawson had just come back from Hawaii where he had given a presentation to Jack-in-the-Box. He was teaching the corporate executives how to better negotiate salaries with their managers and assistant managers. In addition, he was showing them how to get better deals when acquiring land as well as how to negotiate more effectively with the construction companies who build their new restaurants.

And immediately following our interview, Roger was scheduled to speak for one of the largest manufacturers of pharmaceuticals in the country. Says Dawson:

> These are two completely different industries: fast food and drugs. I needed to learn a little bit about each of them and the problems they face in negotiating, so that I'm able to customize my talk to their particular industry.

Like Roger, my topics of motivation, self-esteem and maximizing one's potential are also non-industry specific. Thus, I customize each presentation for the particular group I'm addressing. In fact, I think this is one of the great things about being a professional speaker. You have the opportunity to learn about many different industries and professions—much more so than if you had a "normal" job.

Rusty Credit?

Embarrassing things can happen to you as a speaker that simply don't happen to those with "normal" jobs . . . like the time I got a call to give a presentation to an association of credit professionals at their monthly meeting. (If you have trouble making your credit card payments in a timely fashion, these are the people to whom you get referred.) The night of the event I walked to the back of the hotel where the meeting rooms were and found the one I was scheduled to speak in. As I entered, I couldn't help but notice that everyone in attendance was male (we speakers tend to notice these things). This struck me as odd, since the woman who had hired me never mentioned that the audience would consist of all men.

Not giving it any more thought, I walked up to what looked like the head table and announced in a friendly voice to nobody in particular, "Hi, I'm your speaker!" Instead of getting a warm greeting as is usually the case, everyone at the table just stared at me as if I was crazy! After laughing nervously, I did what any good speaker would have done. I quickly excused myself and made a dash for the restroom. As I entered, I found another gentleman already inside. I asked him if he was with the group out there. He said, "Why yes, I'm their speaker." "*You're* their speaker?!" I repeated, somewhat taken aback. "What topic are you speaking on?" "How to combat rust and other types of corrosion." "And what is the name of the group?" I inquired, still perplexed. "The American Pipe Fitters Association. Why?" I just mumbled, "Ah, no reason, just curious," and made a quick exit.

I then found the room I was *supposed* to be speaking in one door over! When I told the men *and* women at the credit professionals head table what had just happened, they laughed uproariously. I told them if they teased me too much, I would give them a talk on "how to combat rust and other types of corrosion." They behaved themselves.

▶ **SECRET #8: Great speakers take their jobs seriously, but never themselves.**

The Business of Speaking

While I have emphasized throughout this book how important it is to be passionate about your topic, to believe in yourself, etc., it's equally important that you run your office like a real business. I know, I know; you're one of the creative types and business is just not "your thing." What you want to do is spend all your time speaking and spreading the good word of your message. However, the reality is, unless your name is Steve Forbes and you can afford to fly around the country giving speeches while paying for everything out of your own pocket, you're going to have to make certain that you bring in enough income to both cover your expenses and make a profit.

How important are business skills to your success as a professional speaker? Well, according to Dawson, they're even *more* important than your speaking skills:

> I think one of the keys to success as a speaker is not how well you speak, but how good a business person you are. I see a lot of good speakers come into this industry and they just don't have any good business sense at all. They're talking to businesses and they're advising businesses so they should be good at it, but they don't really understand how to run a business profitably.
>
> I've been in business all my life, so I've always known the difference between gross income and net income and how widely spread apart they are. However, I must confess that until I got into the speaking business I simply didn't realize how much overhead speakers are faced with. The overhead in this business is phenomenal and unless you control it and watch it very carefully, you will go broke.

▶ **SECRET #9: One of the keys to success as a speaker is not how well you speak, but how good a business person you are.**

How Dawson Markets Himself

A friend and colleague of mine named Jim Zinger is always saying, "You've got to *smile* and *dial;* that's the name of the game." What he's referring to, of course, is marketing. You've got to let the good people of this world know about your goods and services. Here's how Dawson does it:

> We have a company that is constantly making calls to people and organizations. I think any speaker who is sitting back and waiting for the phone to ring is going to run into trouble. There are something like 9000 associations in America that have annual meetings and hire speakers. We have people who are constantly calling them—they use a book* of all the associations in the country.

*This mammoth directory (in both price and size) is called *The National Trade and Professional Associations of the United States,* and can be ordered from: Columbia Books, Inc., 1350 New York Avenue, Suite 207, Washington, D.C. 20005.

> We also use a book listing all the corporations in the country. We simply call them and explain what we do and see if there is any interest. If there is interest, we send a demonstration cassette tape out and follow up from there. So we are constantly promoting me.
>
> As you become better known, more and more of your business comes to you. About 40 percent of our business at this point is people calling us.

While successful speakers never stop marketing themselves, it is true that after you've been promoting yourself for a certain number of years, *and* you have developed a good reputation in the industry, agents and meeting planners start calling you. How do you develop a good reputation? By consistently doing a great job.

The way you always do a great job is by treating everyone with respect, and making sure that everything you do is done in a first-class manner. This includes everything from the way you answer the telephone to the type of content you pick for your programs to your letterhead. It all must be first-class. Remember, first-class doesn't just happen all by itself. It is up to *you* to make it happen. When this type of thinking becomes second-nature to you, you'll be well on your way to achieving the success you desire.

▶ **SECRET #10: As Jim Zinger says, when it comes to marketing yourself or your products, "You've got to smile and dial; that's the name of the game."**

How Much Should You Charge?

Trying to decide what to charge when you're first getting into the speaking business is something that all speakers must wrestle with. Actually though, the steps are pretty much straightforward and they're pretty much the same for every speaker. In the beginning, you speak wherever they'll have you. As you improve, you can start to charge a modest fee, maybe $50 or $100 for a thirty-to-forty-minute talk.

Assuming you stick with it, continue to hone your speaking skills and continue to market yourself on a consistent basis, eventually you'll get good enough to reach the next plateau. This is where you become a professional speaker and can charge several thousand dollars per presentation. I can't tell you exactly when this will happen for you, only that it *will* happen *if* you work very hard, learn from other successful people, pay your dues and don't give up. That may sound like a lot of effort, but that's what it takes to succeed. All I can tell you is that it's worth it. Here, in his own words, is how Roger did it:

> When you first get into the business, you're thrilled to get anything you can. I started off talking to service clubs, sometimes three a day, for nothing. I would do a breakfast meeting, a lunch meeting, and an evening meeting. If I sold a set of my tapes, I'd feel that I'd done well.

> When I first got a board of realtors to pay a $100 fee, we were thrilled to death. Then, as you get better known, you can raise your fees. And every year you re-evaluate your fee structure and say, "Do we feel we can take it up and make more money, or would we make less money because we would get less bookings." A lot of speakers, initially, while they are becoming well-known, overprice themselves. This hurts them and they have to come down.

> My objective is to keep increasing my gross income, while speaking less days per year. The first year I spoke professionally, I did 179 paid talks. Now, I do 100 paid talks in the ten months that I work—I take two months off—and I consider this a full schedule.

How Much Is Too Much?

Like all the speakers in this book, Dawson's fee is at the upper end of the spectrum in terms of what most speakers charge. I asked him if the size of his fee is ever a problem when companies are considering hiring him:

That's one of the things we address up front. We initially state my fee and if that amount is not within their range then we don't pursue them further. There are a lot of companies and organizations out there that simply do not pay our level of fee for speakers. Some of them have never paid a speaker; they're just accustomed to speakers coming in and speaking for free.

When we have a company approach us because they have heard my cassette tapes and they have said to themselves, "We have to get this guy," very seldom are my fee and travel expenses a problem.

"Hey, Getting Half My Fee Is Better than Getting None of It . . . Isn't It?"

Ask just about any speaker in front of a room full of other speakers and they will tell you with a perfectly straight face that they never, *ever* come down on their fee. Yeah, right. And cigarettes don't cause cancer. Since my goal is to make this book as "real world" as possible—meaning that it gives you real answers even if they're not always politically correct—I'm going to tell you flat out that just about every speaker in the business at one time or another has lowered his or her fee.

Let's face it, if you're just getting started in the business and you have your choice of making $500 on a Saturday night doing what you love, or staying home on a Saturday night doing whatever and *not* making $500, which option are you going to choose? Having said that, I must tell you that there does come a point when you reach a certain level in the speaking profession where maintaining price integrity does become extremely important. This usually happens when you start to become well-known and speaker bureaus begin using you. If word gets back to one that you charged them $5000 for a speech, but you agreed to do the same presentation for another bureau's client for $3,500, they might not be too happy with you.

Therefore, at some point, it is simply good business for you to publish your fee schedule and stick to it as closely as possible.

Besides, there are other ways to "reduce your fee" than just accepting less money. You can still get your full fee, but throw in a free set of tapes or a copy of your book to each attendee. Here are Dawson's thoughts on fee integrity:

> I think you're better off having a published fee schedule that lists what you will charge for a keynote, a half-day, and a full-day speech, and not deviating from it. However, since people do like to negotiate, we don't touch the fee, but we may do other things that would give them a win in the negotiation. For example, a keynote would normally be up to an hour. Perhaps I would do an hour-and-a-half talk and we would charge them the keynote rate, instead of the half-day rate. Or, we might include a few books or cassette programs in with the fee if we needed to.
>
> Again, we never touch the fee, because I think there's a credibility level there which has to be maintained. The moment a speaker suggests they would cut their fee, the meeting planner feels uncomfortable. They're not sure what they're getting. When a meeting planner has a whole meeting hinging on the success of a keynote speaker, they're usually less concerned with the amount of money they're paying than with the quality of the speaker they're getting.
>
> Once you've established yourself as a speaker, you want to be sure your fees are competitive (i.e., not too low). No meeting planner is going to risk his or her meeting on a speaker who he or she perceives is not charging a very high fee.

▶ **SECRET #11: Instead of lowering your speaking fee, the next time a client wants to negotiate, offer to throw in more time or a copy of your book or audiotapes for each attendee. And sometimes, you just have to walk away from a deal if they can't afford you.**

How Dawson Develops New Material

Here, Roger shares how he comes up with new material for his tapes, books and speeches:

I have a filing system where I read magazines on airplanes and so on, and anytime I read anything of interest, I tear it out and get it to my secretary and she files it. We have huge file drawers on just about any topic that you would want. For example, biographies of people; if I see one in a magazine I tear it out and we file it. We probably have biographies of two or three hundred people on file. So I have that resource behind me.

I carry a little pad of notebook paper with different categories at the tops of the pages. That way, I can jot down my ideas and rip it out and my secretary can just read the top of it and she knows what category to file it under.

By the way, I'm not a speaker who churns out a huge amount of books and tapes. Some people are very prolific. I only approach a topic when I have a deep personal interest in it.

While other speakers, such as Brian Tracy, can put out a wide variety of audiotape programs (he has out over a dozen), Dawson must have a personal interest in the material before he will invest the time in putting out a program on the subject. How about you? Are you a chameleon who can become passionate about any project once you make up your mind to "go for it," or do you have to genuinely feel enthusiastic toward it in order to "get into it?" Knowing which style is more "you" can make life much easier when it comes to creating new projects.

One audio album that Dawson was very excited about creating was called, *How to Make Your Life an Adventure*. However, Nightingale-Conant decided to change the title to *Secrets of Power Performance*. Dawson explains why:

I liked the original title, which sprang from the mid-life crisis that put me into the speaking business in the first place. Unfortunately, it didn't sell well under that title, so we changed it to "Power Performance—How to do the best you can and get the best out of other people," and it sold better under that title. The reason for this, we found out, was that a lot of people misunderstood the original title. They were saying, "Well, my life's a big enough adventure as it is!"

The thrust of the album is that life needs to be fun. That it starts one day and ends one day, and when you get to the end you're going to look back and say, "How much joy and satisfaction did I get from this thing?" not, "How successful did I become?" or "How much money did I accumulate?"

I've listened to this six-cassette album twice, and I can tell you two things about it: First, Roger had a good time making it. You can hear it in his voice and the many stories and anecdotes he tells throughout the program. He shows you a whole side to him that you never really get to see on his more serious negotiating and decision-making albums.

Secondly, I think its message is vitally important—that life should be a fun and exciting adventure, and not a serious and somber affair; and that it's not just whether or not you made it to the top of the mountain that counts (i.e., reached all your goals), but did you enjoy the journey along the way? Frankly, I don't think any of us can be reminded of this too often.

The Key to Success

When asked what he thinks is the real key to success, Dawson says:

> Persistence is the key to success in all things. There's a quote from Napoleon Hill's *Think and Grow Rich,* which says that "Every successful person finds that great success lies just beyond the point when they're convinced their idea is not going to work." And that's what separates the men from the boys or the women from the girls in this industry. When you reach the point where you think, "Wow, I've given it a good shot and it's just not going to work," if you can hang in just a little bit longer beyond that point, that's where success lies. And again from *Think and Grow Rich,* when success finally washes over you, it comes in such greater abundance than you ever imagined it would. It's like a huge tidal wave that just swamps you when it finally does happen.

▶ **SECRET #12: When you reach the point where you think, "Wow, I've given it a good shot and it's just not going to work," if you can hang on just a little bit longer beyond that point, that's where success lies.**

I think Winston Churchill summed it up best when he said to a group of kids graduating college, "Never, ever, ever, ever give up." And that really is the key to success.

How Roger Dawson would like to be remembered:

"He never gave up."
ROGER DAWSON

Roger Dawson's
Success Secrets Summary

SECRET #1: "The secret to picking a topic is to choose something specific enough that you can become known for it, and yet broad enough that everybody needs it."—Cavett Robert

SECRET #2: If you have learned something from a life experience, chances are good that others will too. Thus, it's worth taking a few minutes to capture the experience on paper so as not to forget it.

SECRET #3: You can effectively tell another person's story if you find that you can relate to it in some way and it moves you emotionally.

SECRET #4: There are two basic strategies for becoming a well-known speaker. One is to try to promote yourself, and the other is to promote your topic. Unless you're a celebrity, the latter is significantly easier.

SECRET #5: Assume everybody is interested in your product or service unless they tell you otherwise.

SECRET #6: Success is a habit—the more success you have the easier achieving success becomes.

SECRET #7: Great speakers are so in tune with themselves, their audience and their message that they put themselves in a peak state known as "the zone."

SECRET #8: Great speakers take their jobs seriously, but never themselves.

SECRET #9: One of the keys to success as a speaker is not how well you speak, but how good a business person you are.

SECRET #10: As Jim Zinger says, when it comes to marketing yourself or your products, "You've got to smile and dial; that's the name of the game."

SECRET #11: Instead of lowering your speaking fee, the next time a client wants to negotiate, offer to throw in more time or a copy or your book or audiotapes for each attendee. And sometimes, you just have to walk away from a deal if they can't afford you.

SECRET #12: When you reach the point where you think, "Wow, I've given it a good shot and it's just not going to work," if you can hang on just a little bit longer beyond that point, that's where success lies.

CHAPTER EIGHT

BORN: August 28, 1944
BIRTHPLACE: Burbank, California

Tom Hopkins

"You are not judged by the number of times you fail,
but by the number of times you succeed. And the
number of times you succeed is in direct proportion
to the number of times you can fail
and keep on trying."

▼

TODAY he is the epitome of the American success dream. He drives a Rolls-Royce, lives in a mansion in Paradise Valley, Arizona, with his wife, Debbie, and earns over a million dollars a year in speaking fees and several more million from product sales. Since 1974, when he began giving sales seminars, he has trained over three million people on how to become champions at the art of selling. His audio- and videotapes have sold in the millions and are considered to be essential tools for anyone considering a career in sales. He is also the author of seven books, including the classic, *How to Master the Art of Selling,* which has been translated into nine languages and sold over 1.2 million copies!

"... You'll Never Amount to Anything"

Believe it or not, with all this success, there was a time when Tom Hopkins considered himself a failure. When he was nineteen, he dropped out of California State University of Northridge after only ninety days and got a job carrying steel on construction sites. "Son, your mother and I will always love you, even though you'll never amount to anything," were the painful words he still remembers his father telling him. However, like all the speakers I interviewed, a sense of pride and self-worth burned deep down inside Hopkins. He knew he deserved more out of life—more money, more status, more satisfaction, and a greater sense of contributing to the world. So, he quit the construction job and got into real estate sales, where things quickly went from bad to worse. For the next six months he earned an average of just $42 a month and quickly sunk to an all-time low.

Like Mark Victor Hansen, the good news about hitting bottom for Hopkins was that there was only one direction he could go. He knew if he was going to have any chance at all of making it in sales, he desperately needed some training. With his last $150, he invested in a three-day sales training course that not only turned his life around, but set him on a course to eventually become one of the greatest sales trainers in the world.

> *"I had some real self-image challenges at certain points*
> *in my life—like being short of stature and*
> *being the smallest one on the football team."*
> TOM HOPKINS

J. Douglas Edwards

As we've seen throughout this book, often times there was one key individual who believed in these speakers when no one else would. For Les Brown, this person was his high school teacher, Mr. Washington. For Hopkins, it was J. Douglas Edwards, who was one of the top sales trainers in this country throughout much of the fifties, sixties, and seventies. Here's what Tom has to say about the man and the training that changed his life (from Dottie Walter's *The Greatest Speakers I Ever Heard* [1995, WRS Publishing]):

> At that J. Douglas Edwards' program, I was challenged, instructed, and inspired. Doug was a strict taskmaster. He expected us to work hard and excel in his course. After all, our livelihoods depended on our ability to sell. It was incredulous to him that any of the students in his course might not take the training seriously, or that they would do anything but their best.

> I believe he understood salespeople better than most trainers. He included competition in his course for salespeople. He had awards and trophies sitting there in the front of the room. He talked about them like they were made of solid gold. He created in me the burning desire to take home the first-place trophy for that class.

> My life changed in the field of selling because of that three-day Edwards' training session. Yes, I did win that trophy. I slept less than six hours during those three days. I refused to let myself disappoint this wonderful man who knew the greatness that was in me.

Because of Douglas's powerful communication skills and understanding of people, he was able to motivate Hopkins and others like him to tap into their God-given talents. While it's true that we all possess enormous abilities, sometimes they lie dormant inside of us for years until just the right person comes along and says just the right thing to get us to take action. This is the power that being a great communicator gives you—the ability to inspire others to reach for the stars *and* believe they can reach them.

► **SECRET #1: Good communicators inspire people to reach for the stars; great communcators make people believe they can reach them.**

Douglas made winning one of the gold trophies a tremendous honor reserved for only the very best, so, in the eyes of his students, they became highly sought-after prizes. Hopkins was willing to do whatever it took to win one, even if it meant going with a minimum of sleep for three nights straight. He did this, not because he desperately needed to fill an empty spot on his mantle, but because he so badly wanted to prove to himself that he could do it. During our interview, Tom revealed:

> The achiever has something to prove, either to his or her family, a spouse, a relative, or society. That seems to be the difference between the average and the great.

► **SECRET #2: Successful people often feel like they have something to prove to the world.**

When the end of the final day of the training came, and Mr. Edwards shook young Tom's hand and awarded him the trophy for best in the class, Hopkins was thrilled. For now, he had indeed proved that he *was* good at something. And, regardless of what his father thought, he was going to be successful in life.

I can relate to how great Hopkins felt when he won that trophy in Edward's class, because I had a similar experience. When I took the Dale Carnegie course, each week they would give out a pen for best speech. I remember how disappointed I was the night I thought I had given the best speech of the evening, yet was voted second-place by my classmates. However, all's well that ends well, as the very next week I did win the pen. Every time I look at it, I remember how hard I had to work for it, and the tremendous feeling of satisfaction I felt when I won it.

"In 1966, I was rewarded, at the age of 21, with the Sales and Marketing Executive Award in Los Angeles. No one had ever won it under age 25, and that's when I started thinking, 'Maybe I can be a success!'"
TOM HOPKINS

Edward's First Impressions of Hopkins

Interestingly enough, we are able to find out exactly what J. Douglas Edwards recalls about his first meeting with Hopkins, as he tells about it during his introduction of Tom on the audio album, *How to Master the Art of Selling Anything:*

> I remember a number of years ago, I was training a class. And there was a young man sitting in the front of that class, a 19-year-old kid. I couldn't help noticing him because he was trying to take the words down before I got them out of my mouth!
>
> I never saw a human being in my life take notes like he did. The comprehension just absolutely glistened in his eyes; he was understanding! Whenever I find someone like that, I always pay a little extra attention. I'm glad I did . . . because that young man became the greatest salesman that his field has ever seen . . . and he has gone on to take my place.

One of the things I like about this passage by Edwards is that it reveals some of the reasons why Hopkins became so successful. First, look where he sat: ". . . in the front of that class." Being a teacher myself, I'm always amazed how many students plunk themselves down in a chair in the back of the room. This makes no sense to me. If you're there to learn things that will enhance your life and help you become more successful, doesn't it make sense to sit right up front, close to where the action is? Of course, if you're not serious about learning anything, then I guess the back of the class is just fine.

You Can Pay Me Now, or You Can Pay Me Later

Douglas tells how Hopkins took notes ". . . before I got them out of my mouth." It was as if every word the great sales trainer had to say was worth $10, and Tom didn't want to let a single penny fall through the cracks.

The reason Hopkins was so adamant about soaking up Douglas's knowledge like a sponge, was because he had figured out that there's always going to be a price to pay to achieve anything worthwhile. That's just the way the universe works. He knew that by pushing himself to absorb everything that Edwards had to teach him, it would pay off down the line. However, those individuals who didn't want to have to go through the pain of pushing themselves during the class would eventually pay the price in lost sales and not knowing how to handle certain situations that were bound to come up. As the car mechanic in a well-known commercial once said, "You can pay me now, or you can pay me later"— implying that either way you're going to have to pay, and if you put it off until later, it's going to cost you even more.

▶ SECRET #3: Whatever you want in life has a price. Decide to pay that price quickly and energetically. That way, while others are still paying off their debt, you'll be busy reaping the rewards of your effort.

Just how much did J. Douglas Edwards' training help Hopkins? Well, in the following six months Tom went on to sell more than a million dollars' worth of $25,000 homes—a record that still stands to this day—and became the nation's number-one real estate salesperson. In 1976, he incorporated Tom Hopkins International, and for the past 20 years, he has presented 75–80 seminars a year throughout North America, Australia, Singapore, and Malaysia.

"Seeing the light of understanding dawn across the faces of my audience inspired me to become a full-time trainer."
TOM HOPKINS

Enthusiasm!

If asked to name the single most distinctive quality that Hopkins brings to his trainings, it would have to be his enthusiasm for the profession of selling. (In fact, if you didn't know better, you would think he was talking about one of his passionate hobbies, such as golf or tennis.) Things that most people normally think of as being unpleasant or arduous about sales, he has the nerve to actually make sound fun and exciting! For example, listen to how he makes the sales profession itself sound like the greatest ride to come along since Disneyland's Space Mountain:

> In selling, everyday is a challenge. Isn't that exciting!? It's the only business I know of in this country where you can be thrown to the heights of exhilaration, and in the same 48 hours, crashed to the depths of depression! Now that's exciting, isn't it? Say yes!

> In our profession, there's no one that limits your income but you! There are no income ceilings. You have the freedom to become as successful as you'd like to be!

The man is flat-out enthusiastic about selling, and if you listen to him long enough, you can't help but begin to get enthusiastic yourself. This is precisely what *you* want to do in your presentations. You should be so excited about your topic, that people walking by your room will stop and want to listen in—without even knowing what you're speaking on! Why? Because, like a powerful magnet, your enthusiasm compels them to want to stop and listen.

If you have a clear vision that you're genuinely excited about, people will be attracted to you, because unfortunately, most people don't have one. Although we live in a country with an abundance of wealth and opportunities—which are there for the taking *if* we are willing to invest a little effort and perseverance—most people can't get themselves to take consistent action. Thus, the vast majority of men and women, as Thoreau put it, "lead lives of quiet desperation." That's why when you, I, and every speaker in this book enthusiastically share our unique and powerful message, people are drawn to us like moths to a light.

▶   **SECRET #4: Your enthusiasm acts like a powerful magnet to draw people in and make them want to listen to your message. Like the American Express card, you should never give a presentation without it!**

Focuses on Teaching "How to" Techniques

"Twenty-six million people in America are professional salespeople and 50 million Americans use selling techniques in their professions."
TOM HOPKINS

While Hopkins' enthusiasm is one of the things he is known for, his own personal objective during his presentation is to give the people in his audiences the tools they need to succeed in sales:

> We've tried to stay focused and to have a reputation for teaching our students "how-to" communication skills that will make them more money. Motivation, enthusiasm, and goal-setting are very important to success and we do teach those skills; however, 85 percent of our training is focused on "how-to" techniques.

Hopkins told me the seven specific steps that he teaches during his seminars, from prospecting to getting qualified leads after you've made the sale:

The first step in professional selling that we cover is prospecting, both on the telephone and in person, as well as how to get an appointment with a decision-maker. We teach ten "non-referral techniques," which the salesperson uses to build their own business.

Secondly, we teach the proper way to make the initial contact with the prospect. This includes: eye contact, proper body language, hand shake, and all the little things that are so important when you first meet a person. People are judging you from the moment they meet you. In ten seconds, the average American says to him or herself, "Do I like this person? Do I trust this person?"

The third step in professional selling is the actual qualifying of the prospect. This means finding out if they have the financial ability to make the purchase, what their needs are, and how the benefits of the product can satisfy their needs. Most salespeople are selling what they want to sell, instead of questioning and qualifying to find out what the consumer wants to buy.

The fourth skill we teach is presentational tactics. This includes how to better show a prospect a product and demonstrate it with flair and excitement. This will help persuade the person who's listening to want to own the product and to know they will benefit from it.

The fifth technique is how to handle objections. We give a step-by-step methodology they can use to handle the most common objections to money, such as "It cost too much," "The payments are too high," "We just want to shop around," or "It's not in this year's budget." We also teach how to handle emotional objections such as, "I want to think it over," "We're going to discuss it with our attorney," or "We've been using the competitor's product and we would never change."

The sixth thing we teach is the actual steps of closing the sale. We show at our seminars, using large-screen video, the actual emotional and physical events that take place during the close. Finally, now that you've made the sale, we teach you how to get qualified, referred leads from your happy customer.

It's this emphasis on "how-to" techniques that Hopkins feels separates him from other sales training companies.

▶ **SECRET #5: Make sure that every speech you deliver contains at least three "how-to" action steps that people can take right away and see results.**

This is a direct influence from his early experience with J. Douglas Edwards, who made Hopkins' class memorize 60 closes, word for word! While today's customers are much more sophisticated and savvy than back in the 1960s, and reciting a canned close could backfire, Hopkins knows the value of drilling his students in the fundamentals of selling. In fact, it's because they don't take the time to learn the fundamentals that Tom believes so many people are afraid of selling:

> Most people are afraid of selling because they think you've got to be overpowering, or obnoxious, or over-aggressive. You don't! You need to know the fundamentals and basics, just like a professional golfer. There are small men who can hit a 275-foot drive, such as Greg Norman, just like the big men. The reason? They're doing the fundamentals: the proper grip, stance, and swing. It's the same in selling; you must approach it like a science. It's got to become something you're totally consumed with.

The Bottom Line: It Works!

In the end, the reason why Tom Hopkins has been so successful over the past twenty years, and the reason people keep coming to his seminars, reading his books, and listening to his tapes, is for one reason: It works! Says Hopkins:

> The bottom line is, people who use what we teach, make money. One man who attended a recent three-day seminar said, "There's only two words to describe why people keep coming to Tom's training: *It works!*" And as long as "*It works,*" we're going to continue to fill up rooms.

Do your customers say the same thing about your presentations? No matter how accomplished an orator you are, if the people in your audience can't immediately take what you teach them, implement it, and see results right away, than you're not doing your job. This is something that many top executives who speak at large meetings often forget. They give vacuous, flowery speeches that lack specific "how-to's." In other words, if you're a CEO or president of a company, don't just say to your employees, "Yeah, it's been a great year . . . you're great, I'm great, we're all great, blah, blah, blah."

People want guidance; they want to know, specifically, what they need to do to get more out of life—more satisfaction, more happiness, more money, etc. So, talk in tangibles: "Starting May 1, for every new customer that you get into the Ford dealership to test drive our hot, new Explorers, you will win ten points. At the end of the next six weeks, the salesperson with the most points can let us know how the weather is in beautiful, tropical Hawaii, because that's where they'll be vacationing for a week with their family, compliments of Ford!"

Okay! Now we're talking! This is tangible, this is something I can sink my teeth into and get excited about! If you're constantly thinking of ways to make things better for everyone around you, whether it's your fellow co-workers, family, friends, or customers, you can't help but become hugely successful. It's just a matter of time.

A Powerful Way to Boost Product Sales

One way that Hopkins makes things better for his customers is by offering a special package deal at his programs:

> I always offer my seminar attendees a "today only" package at a special investment. They have already invested in themselves to attend—I like to reward those who aspire to improve themselves by giving them more opportunities than our catalog shopper.

▶ **SECRET #6: If you constantly think of ways you can do more for your customer this week than you did last week, you will soon leave your competition in the dust.**

Ways Hopkins Stays Motivated

One of my favorite questions to ask motivational speakers is, "How do *you* stay motivated?" Hopkins does it by staying fit on the road, which can often be grueling, by sticking to an exercise program. In addition, he listens to inspirational tapes by other speakers, and reads uplifting books. Of course, the best source of motivation comes from the people at his seminars who tell him how much his training, tapes, and books have helped them. Here's more on Hopkins's own personal philosophy for life:

> My philosophy is balance in all areas of your life. You should strive to use your talents to have financial independence, so you're not dependent on family, or the government, when you get old. You should also strive to maintain your emotional stability. This means working on your self-image so that you can handle crisis and control stress. You should stay in shape by getting regular exercise, keeping your cholesterol down, and watching your weight. Most importantly, you should have a source of spiritual fulfillment, which means having a relationship with God.

Whether you agree 100 percent with Hopkins or not isn't really the issue. The crucial thing is that he is very clear on his own values and what's important to him in life. Are you as clear on your own values and philosophy for living life? If you're not (and most people aren't), set this book down right now and take a few minutes to write down in a journal your answers to the following two questions: 1) *What's important to me in life?* 2) *Do my day-to-day actions support what I say is important to me?*

▶ **SECRET #7: Is what you're doing on a daily basis getting you closer to the things that you say are important to you in life?**

For example, if you say health is important to you, but today you had two cokes and five donuts for lunch, clearly your actions aren't in line with your values! Obviously, one has to change. Either clean up your eating habits so you do in fact eat healthy, or continue to eat like a pig and, for the sake of congruency, scratch "healthy eating" off your list of values.

Uses Workbook During Trainings to Stay on Track

Since keynote speakers are generally speaking for an hour or less, they try to stay away from using notes. However, when you're giving an all-day training, as Hopkins usually does, then using an outline or workbook is a good idea:

> I use a workbook, which keeps me on target as to the material I need to cover. It also keeps me within the time period I must cover it in, so that I don't stray too far off of the subject matter.

▶ **SECRET #8: When doing presentations longer than an hour, it is a good idea to use an outline to make sure you don't leave anything important out.**

A lot of trainers use the same workbook that the participants use, except that theirs has notes scribbled all over it, reminding them to tell stories or give examples at certain points, etc.

Uses Returning Seminar Attendees to Gather Feedback

If you're not tapping your current customers for information, you're missing out on one of your most valuable sources for feedback. Hopkins uses his sales retreats as opportunities to find out from veteran "boot camp" alumni what's working and what's not:

My greatest gathering source is at my three-day seminars. I have what we call a debriefing period where I bring in people who are returning back to what we call "boot camp." We have about 20 percent who come back every year. They are the ones who share with us what's working, what's new, etc.

Because I'm the one who taught them, they're willing to share with me. This way, I'm keeping up with the trends, the economy, and with the sociological things happening with the people in our industry.

▶ **SECRET #9: Use your current customer base to obtain feedback, to collect stories (both success and horror) and other data that will help you design new programs and improve existing ones.**

The advantage of using Hopkins's "debriefing technique" is obvious. By going out and actually talking to your customers face-to-face, you're going to get a much better picture as to what's working and what's not, than if you just sent them out a dry, impersonal survey, asking them to check a bunch of boxes.

Why People Resist Change

When asked why he thinks some people who attend his seminars immediately go home and begin implementing his success techniques, while others go home and continue the status quo, Hopkins said:

First of all, nobody can change another human being until they're ready to change. A person who has reached adulthood has formulated values, work ethics, and discipline. They can't change until they are ready to go through the pain of change.

Many people who come to the seminar are in a comfort zone. They know what they have to make per month to pay their bills, and they know they can get by on this much work and keep their boss happy. They're not really ready to stretch and you can't make them.

However, some of the most successful men and women we trained were divorced and had children to raise; they had no choice, they had to make money! They went in with a desire that was overwhelming and they went through the process of change.

You can't change people, but you can affect change if they're ready or if you can make them believe they can do it.

▶ **SECRET #10: You can't change people (only they can change themselves), but you can affect change if they're ready or if you can make them believe they can do it.**

Tries to Always Remember What It Was Like to Be Hungry

Although Hopkins was raised without having a lot of money, by age twenty-seven, he was a millionaire. Yet, to his credit, he tries to stay as down-to-earth as possible. He does this by constantly reminding himself what it was like when he didn't have all the fancy cars and beautiful homes. In essence, he knows he's talking to an audience of people who are just like he was before he became successful. They're hungry and they have the desire to succeed, but not the skills. He knows his job is to provide them with those skills in an encouraging and supportive manner, sans ego:

I feel, when I get onto that stage, that I'm talking to a person who came to the seminar with a tremendous need. That's the person I want to help. I never talk over their heads and I never make them feel that I'm better than they are, because I'm not.

I think that's one of the reasons people like our training. I try to never forget what it was like to be broke. I never forgot what it was like to have doors slammed in my face because I was a teenager with no college education.

▶ **SECRET # 11: No matter how successful you become, never forget what it was like when you were just starting out, because those are the shoes most of your audience members will be in.**

The Greatest Reward

"I never dreamed all these wonderful things would happen to me—the accolades, the respect, and the admiration. I still pinch myself!"
TOM HOPKINS

While being paid a lot of money for our services is one way that society rewards us for a job well done, it is, of course, not the only way. Hopkins, like most of the speakers I interviewed, feels that the letters he gets from people telling him how he's helped make their lives better are the greatest reward of all:

> To me, the most rewarding part of what I do are the testimonies of people who have used our ideas and concepts to have a better life. We receive hundreds of letters from people who have taken what we have shown them and succeeded, even if at first they didn't think they could succeed.

> When you really love what you do and you've reached your financial goals, the real payment comes when the people you've taught come back to you with stories about how they've succeeded. You're almost living vicariously through them.

It's true. Once you've taken care of your financial worries, and you have your health, the biggest reward is having people come up to you (or write you a letter) and tell you how the things that you've said or written have profoundly changed their lives. It lets you know that all the hundreds (and in many cases, thousands) of hours you spent studying and reading and working on your speaking skills have all been worth it. You've made a positive difference in somebody else's life, and, after all, isn't that why we're here?

Why the Phoenix Is Hopkins' Company Logo

Like Brian Tracy, Hopkins sees the mythical bird, the Phoenix, as an analogy for his own journey, and uses it as his corporate logo:

> My life has been like that of the Phoenix. Legend tells of a magnificent bird rising from the ashes and ruin into a brilliant, multihued future of prosperity and tranquillity. I have triumphed over despair and failure and have dedicated my life to training and inspiring salespeople, who, like the Phoenix, can rise from wherever they are and strive to fulfill their highest potential.

How Tom Hopkins would like to be remembered:

"Tom Hopkins was blessed to have the talent to teach people how to get everything in life they wanted, if they made the commitment to serve their fellow man."
TOM HOPKINS

Tom Hopkins' Success Secrets Summary

SECRET #1: Good communicators inspire people to reach for the stars; great communicators make people believe they can reach them.

SECRET #2: Successful people often feel like they have something to prove to the world.

SECRET #3: Whatever you want in life has a price. Decide to pay that price quickly and energetically. That way, while others are still paying off their debt, you'll be busy reaping the rewards of your effort.

SECRET #4: Your enthusiasm acts like a powerful magnet to draw people in and make them want to listen to your message. Like the American Express card, you should never give a presentation without it!

SECRET #5: Make sure that every speech you deliver contains at least three "how-to" action steps that people can take right away and see results.

SECRET #6: If you constantly think of ways you can do more for your customer this week than you did last week, you will soon leave your competition in the dust.

SECRET #7: Is what you're doing on a daily basis getting you closer to the things that you say are important to you in life?

SECRET #8: When doing presentations longer than an hour, it is a good idea to use an outline to make sure you don't leave anything important out.

SECRET #9: Use your current customer base to obtain feedback, to collect stories (both success and horror) and other data that will help you design new programs and improve existing ones.

SECRET #10: You can't change people (only they can change themselves), but you can affect change if they're ready, or if you can make them believe they can do it.

SECRET #11: No matter how successful you become, never forget what it was like when you were just starting out, because those are the shoes most of your audience members will be in.

CHAPTER NINE

BORN: August 19, 1944
BIRTHPLACE: Fort Worth, Texas

Jack Canfield

"Self-esteem is based on one basic principle:
that you feel lovable and capable."

▼

ORIGINALLY a high school teacher from Chicago, today Jack Canfield is one of the hottest speakers on the planet. His mega best-selling book, *Chicken Soup for the Soul* (co-written with his partner in crime, Mark Victor Hansen), has spawned a series of spin-off books, including a *Chicken Soup* cookbook, as well as audio- and videotapes based on each book. As funny as it sounds, they have created a chicken soup empire!

Incredibly, thirty publishers turned down the original manuscript for *Chicken Soup for the Soul,* before Health Communications, Inc., out of Deerfield Beach, Florida, said, "Yes, we'll publish it." Ironically, many of the thirty publishers have since come back to Canfield and Hansen and said, "Oops, we made a mistake! Sure, we'd love to put out a book by you guys." That's what having a *New York Times* bestseller and over five million in sales will do for you.

Started Out As a High School Teacher

Back in the late 1960s, long before he became a best-selling author and world-class motivational speaker, Jack Canfield taught high school in Chicago. While he enjoyed teaching, he noticed—just like Leo Buscaglia had at USC—that many of his students had bigger issues than just not being able to read and write well. Jack began looking around for ways to motivate and inspire them:

> As I was working in this inner-city experience, I discovered that these kids I was teaching were very bright and very verbal, but they didn't believe in themselves; that's why they weren't succeeding.
>
> I began to look for solutions to that problem and I discovered W. Clement Stone, in Chicago, who had a program called, "The Achievement Motivation Program." Stone was the editor and founder of *Success Magazine,* and a big proponent of positive thinking, just like Napoleon Hill.
>
> I took Stone's seminar, and was so impressed by the classroom results I obtained afterward that I went to work for the

W. Clement & Jesse V. Stone Foundation and led those seminars! Stone's teaching still guides much of my work. Later I
studied psychotherapy and group work, which is the foundation for my in-depth seminars.

All of the things I was learning there about motivation and
self-esteem worked in the classroom. I started applying them
not only to education, but to my life and the lives of my
friends. Then I started doing workshops and sharing it
with everybody.

Gained Recognition in the Education Field

Having left the classroom, Canfield soon began to make a name
for himself in the education field by writing training manuals and
conducting seminars on how to teach self-esteem in schools:

> I spoke at a couple of conferences and I really got off on it. I
> liked the idea of making a contribution to the adults who
> were teaching the students.

Canfield was soon appointed by the California State Legislature to
the California Task Force to Promote Self-Esteem and Social Responsibility. He developed live and video-based self-esteem and
motivational trainings for several groups that were getting the
least amount of help in this area, but who needed it the most.
These included the Los Angeles County Jail, welfare recipients,
and inner-city youth-at-risk.

Eventually, Jack would go on to give seminars and trainings to
over 500,000 people worldwide. In addition, he would touch millions more via his many TV appearances, which include *The
Oprah Winfrey Show*, *The Today Show*, and *NBC Nightly News*.

Grew Up Shy

**"When I speak, people really know that I know what their
experience is, and that I'm not just speaking from books."**
JACK CANFIELD

While many people think that all motivational speakers are extroverts by nature, this is usually not true, especially in Canfield's case. He grew up feeling shy and as if he didn't quite fit in:

> I went to a private school as a scholarship student in the local town where I grew up. I felt inferior to those people who had more money. Then I went to Harvard on scholarship and I had classmates with names like Max Factor III and Larry Rockefeller and so forth. I felt as if I was in the group, but not quite of it. There was a sense of not feeling adequate.
>
> My self-esteem now is very, very high. But that's a result of years of workshops, trainings, self-reflection, meditation, and everything that I've done on myself.

While some people seem to have a natural flair for public speaking, such as Anthony Robbins, Canfield feels that this is not the case with him:

> I think some people have a gift for speaking, if you will. I don't think I had a gift; I think I had to work very hard to be the kind of speaker I am today.
>
> I had a message I wanted to share and my heart was in it, but there was a lot I had to learn about how to put together a speech and work with an audience. For me, it was probably five to six years before I was able to call myself a competent speaker, and it was only after ten to fifteen years of speaking before I was at the level that you might call world-class.

What's Your Secret?

Jack's speaking style is very down-to-earth and unpretentious. Thus, he comes across as very likable from the platform. However, I couldn't quite put my finger on just what it was that made him so effective with audiences. At the 1994 National Speakers Association Convention in Washington, D.C., I pulled him aside and said, "Jack, I've interviewed all these great speakers for my book, and I feel as if I have gotten a pretty good handle on where all of them are coming from . . . all except for you." Canfield didn't say a word, but just listened as I continued, "I can't quite figure it out; what is it that makes you such a powerful speaker? I mean, you don't radiate the raw power and charisma of Robbins, and you don't throw out hilarious one-liners every five minutes like Hansen. Yet, people really like you! What's your secret!?"

Jack knew I wasn't trying to insult him but was sincerely perplexed. And so, after giving me that boyish smile of his, he looked into my eyes and said, "It's because I have a good heart."

The sound you would have heard, had you been standing there, was that of my jaw hitting the floor. This was not the answer I was expecting. However, after letting his words wash over me for a few seconds, my whole face lit up because I suddenly realized what he was talking about. Whereas I had been looking at the obvious things that make up a good speaker, such as having a deep voice or massive charisma, Canfield reminded me not to underestimate the importance of having integrity and an honest character.

He went on to say, "What would you rather have, a friend who looks great but is flaky, or someone with a good heart who is always going to be there for you?" I replied, "The person with the good heart who I can depend on." "That's right," Canfield said warmly. Then, after giving me a big hug and a gentle pat on the back, he walked off, leaving me to bask in my newfound revelation. From that moment on, one of the first things I do anytime I see a new speaker is say to myself, "Okay, he sounds impressive . . . but does he have a good heart?"

▶ **SECRET #1: A speaker has a good heart if he or she puts the audience first, and cares more about helping them than looking good.**

Let me give you a personal example of what I'm talking about. Several months ago I got a phone call from *The Learning Annex* asking me if I could teach a class on how to create and market your own seminar. I said that I could. They said, "Great, could you teach it tonight!?" "Excuse me?" I said. "Our instructor is out with the flu and the class starts in four hours!" they explained. Reaching for my cape, I asked what hotel it was scheduled to be at.

After I arrived and set up, I greeted each of the students as they came in the room. After explaining that the scheduled instructor had the flu, I said: "Look, I know you paid for a three-hour workshop. However, I'm committed to you getting the material I've brought for you tonight. And that means that I'm going to stay here for as long as it takes, to make sure I get all your questions answered. If I have to stay until midnight, then that's what I'll do."

I must confess that these words probably would not have come out of my mouth ten years ago. That's because back then I didn't "get it." I didn't understand what it meant, as Danielle Kennedy said, to "give them every last drop of blood and energy [you've] got!" Having a great attitude and being willing to give your audience everything you've got, even on those days when you don't "feel like it," is what being a professional speaker is all about.

Clearness and Simplicity

Another quality that Canfield brings to his speaking is a remarkably clear and easy-to-follow style. He knows how to take a complicated subject, such as self-esteem, and break it down to a level that's easy to understand. For example, when Jack wants to illustrate to his audience why having high self-esteem is extremely important in life, he doesn't go into a bunch of Ph.D. theory; instead, he talks about poker! He tells each person in the audience to imagine that they are sitting across from him at a poker table, and that they have a huge stack of poker chips to play with, while he has only a few. Then he asks, "Who would have more fun playing, me or you?" The audience responds that they would. Canfield says, "Right, because if you lost some bets, it wouldn't affect you greatly, because you still have lots more chips to play with. But if I lost a few hands, it would wipe me out! Thus, I would have to play much more cautiously than you from the very beginning."

Jack goes on to say that that's what having high self-esteem allows you to do—take risks and have more fun in life. Those individuals with less poker chips (self-esteem) have to play it safe because they can't afford to lose what little they have. They also tend to be unhappy because they get down every time they lose a few chips (i.e., when something negative happens), because each chip is so precious to them. I really like this "poker chips and self-esteem" analogy, and I want to encourage you to come up with simple stories and analogies to illustrate the key points in your own speeches.

▶ **SECRET #2: Part of your job as a speaker is to take the complicated and make it simple and easy to understand for your audience. Good ways to do this are through stories, analogies, and examples.**

Love and Respect

Canfield's favorite quote is from Leo Buscaglia: "Love is life, and if you miss love, you've missed life." And like Buscaglia, Jack has found that the closer he comes to unconditionally loving and respecting all people, the better speaker he has become:

> My best trait, I would say, is that I totally and unconditionally love almost everybody. That comes from a lot of work, where I purposely worked on being more loving. I used to conduct a workshop called, "The Awakening Heart," and I really came to a state of fairly deep compassion for everybody.

> I think I can understand and accept people's experience so that when I speak, people really know that I know what their experience is, and that I'm not just speaking from books. They know that I really support them as to who they are. I support them in loving and accepting themselves fully and achieving and manifesting their own personal dreams and visions.

▶ **SECRET #3: Your effectiveness as a speaker increases dramatically when people know that you really understand their experience, not from having read books, but because you've been there.**

Dad, the Firecracker,
and a Little Boy's Pain

Just about everybody knows that the stories in Canfield and Hansen's *Chicken Soup for the Soul* books will "make your eyeballs sweat," as Hansen likes to put it. However, I was not prepared for the touching and heart-stirring story that Jack shared with me during our interview. I had asked him if people ever called him a wimp for being so open with his feelings during his seminars. It was then that he told me the following "eyeball sweater:"

People who call other people wimps, as I seem them, are individuals who are afraid of their own softer qualities. It's usually because, during childhood, they got in trouble for expressing those types of feelings.

I'll give you an example. I was doing a seminar in San Francisco and there was a guy there who was very tough, very macho. And he was getting more and more irritated as people would share their feelings, like when men were talking about their relationship with their dad, or they were crying, or whatever. At one point, this man stood up and went into this huge tirade about how these guys were wimps and sissies and so forth.

Later on, we did an activity we call "the significant failure to please" exercise. The assumption is that every person has had an experience where they were trying to please an important, significant other, like a parent or a teacher. Some how, that attempt backfired or failed, and so we no longer feel good about ourselves in that area of our life.

During that exercise, this man remembered being on Cape Cod during the Fourth of July when he was a boy. He and his brother were playing with a firecracker, an M-80, which he wasn't suppose to have. Their father, who was a football player, came out to check on them, and so the boy put the firecracker behind his back. His brother, who saw the fuse sticking out between his fingers, lit it with a lighter he had. The brother figured that he would see that the fuse was lit and throw it out toward the water.

Well, the boy didn't know what to do. He didn't know whether he should throw the firecracker, which would get him in trouble, or if he should hold on to it, which would get him in trouble. So, he froze, and it went off in his hand. His hand blew open and it was bleeding and charred and burned; he was scared and started to cry. His father reached out and smacked him on his face as hard as he could and said, "No son of mine cries because of a little pain!" And the boy forced himself to stop crying and kept it inside him.

The boy said to himself, "If I want to survive and receive my father's love, I have to not express my pain or sadness because, according to my dad, it's a sign of weakness." So when other people would cry, he sees them and says to himself, "they're weak." Because if he accepted their crying, he would then be angry at himself and his father because he would be thinking, "How come they get to cry and I don't?"

What he got at the seminar was that real men do cry, even though most have been shamed for having those kinds of feelings.

▶ **SECRET #4: Contrary to what we've been taught, real men do cry. You can have high self-esteem, be powerful, and yet still be sensitive and show your vulnerability.**

Conscious Versus Unconscious Speaking

When Canfield is onstage, he says that his mind works in one of two ways. Either, his subconscious takes over and he's basically channeling the speech—meaning that he's not thinking about it—everything is just flowing. Or, he's thinking about all kinds of things:

Sometimes, it's as if the speech is "doing me," as if it's coming through me. My conscious mind is out of the way and some deeper part of me comes forward. I can remember being sick and walking onstage, and it's almost like I'm totally healthy for three hours. Then, when I walk off the stage, about ten minutes later I feel sick again.

Then there are days when there are hundreds of things going through my mind. I'm watching the audience's reaction, I'm laughing at a joke, I'm looking to see if the audience is open and, if not, if there is something I can do to open them up. What about those people in the back who are here because their boss told them to be and they're reading the sports page; how do I get them involved?

(In the first part of Jack's answer, where the speech just seems to be coming through him, that's what I call "being in the zone." For more on this most fascinating phenomenon, check out Success Secret #7 in Roger Dawson's chapter.)

Different Strokes
for Different Folks

When it comes to the correct way to give a speech, the truth is that there is no correct way. What works for one speaker might not work for another. In fact, what works for one speaker on one occasion may not work for that same speaker on another occasion. That is why it's important for you to try out the ideas in this book for yourself and not to just take them at face value. While they might work fine for the speaker who recommended the idea, it might not be your "cup of tea."

Memorization Versus
Free-Form Speaking

While some speakers memorize their speech practically word for word, Canfield prefers to have a general outline of his main points, yet work in a more free-form style:

> I don't think I've ever given the same speech the same way twice. I know some speakers, like Nido Qubein, have these very clearly, wonderfully memorized speeches that are almost like a readout from a computer. I don't work that way. I have a general sense of what I want to say and then I start, and it goes where it goes and I end when I end.

I always cover my main points, but the examples are often different. If I'm working with a military audience, I might stress my own military school experience. If I'm working with a group of psychologists or a spiritually-oriented group, I might use a whole set of different examples. But I still make my same points.

▶ **SECRET #5: The decision as to whether to memorize your speech, or just the main points and use a more "free-form" approach depends on your own personal preference.**

The Lack of Self-Esteem in Our Country

"Here lies the cure to racism, greed, violence, and other social ills; people with high self-esteem contribute selflessly to the well-being of others. They are committed to action to a higher good for all."
JACK CANFIELD

I asked Jack what percentage of Americans he thinks suffer from low self-esteem:

In 1958, Robert Schuller, when he was writing his book, *Self-esteem, the New Reformation*, hired George Gallop, Jr., to go out and interview thousands of people across the country to determine whether or not people in America had high or low self-esteem, and what the percentages were.

Based on that survey, the Gallop organization concluded that two out of three Americans have low self-esteem. So it means there's a fairly large amount of people who need to work on that area of their life.

▶ **SECRET #6: The fact that two out of three Americans suffer from low self-esteem means that motivational speakers and self-help book authors will never be unemployed.**

Canfield Likes Having a "General Topic"

Like myself, Jack enjoys speaking on self-esteem, success, and personal growth, because it applies to everyone, regardless of their occupation:

> My talks aren't just on self-esteem, but what I like to think of as insight or wisdom for effective living. I feel very blessed to have a topic that appeals to so many people, unlike a lot of speakers who have a much narrower topic. For example, a topic like, "How to pass your family business on to your son," would be somewhat limited. Whereas my three topics—relationships, success, and feeling good about yourself—apply to just about everyone.

Jack's Role Models

It was the Reverend Jesse Jackson who first inspired Canfield to want to become a speaker:

> Reverend Jackson's oratorical skills moved me deeply, as they did everyone else in his congregation. In those days, Jesse would always end his sermon by having the audience repeat: "I am somebody! I may be black, but I am somebody! I may be poor, but I am somebody! I may be uneducated, but I am somebody!" I remember thinking I wanted to touch people deeply and move them in the same way.

I asked Canfield which other speakers have influenced him the most:

> I've learned a lot from Mark Victor Hansen, in terms of how to use humor, as well as how to be a master marketer and how to think really big. I've learned a lot from Wayne Dyer, in terms of personal self-disclosure. I've learned a lot from Leo Buscaglia, in terms of the importance of love and how to speak about love in a loving, powerful, humorous, touching way. I've learned a lot from Brian Tracy and Denis Waitley in terms of the whole arena of goals.

One Piece of Golden Advice

I asked Canfield what one piece of advice he would give someone to help them live their life better:

> The story that comes to mind as you ask that question is about an Indian guru who is guiding his disciples. One of his students says, "Master, you're so inconsistent; you just told that student to go left and you told the second student to go right. Which answer is right?" And the master replied, "Well, the first student was about to walk off the right side of the road and the second student was about to walk off the left side of the road. Therefore, I told them to go back toward the middle." Each person needs different inspiration and information in order to make their life work.
>
> However, if I had to reduce it to one basic thing, I would say: Just love and accept yourself, and express the truth of who you are in the moment. It's uncomfortable and it's scary, but you must simply express what you believe, what you feel, what you want, what you need, and what you don't like. You simply acknowledge what your feelings are, what your desires are, what your talents are. If you express these things, I find that people's lives work.

▶ **SECRET #7: The most important thing you can do to increase your own self-esteem is to love and accept yourself unconditionally.**

The Best Way Canfield Has Found to Market Himself

The key to marketing is visibility. Canfield finds that the more he is out speaking and the more books and tapes he puts out, the more people call him:

> The best way for me to market myself is to speak. I find that 80 percent of my work comes from people who have seen me speak somewhere else. The larger the conference or workshop, the more people who can go back to their company or association and say, "Gee, he was great; we ought to bring him in here."

I found that having tapes and videos out there helps, because it's like giving a speech. My advice to beginning speakers is to get out there and give talks. Give free talks to the Rotary Club or church—anywhere you can. Submit proposals to conferences. You give talks for two reasons: One, it's a way for you to hone your craft; and secondly, it's a way for people to see you.

If You Could Change One Thing

I asked Jack, "If you could go back and change one thing about your career, what would it be?":

I would have produced cassette tapes way before I did. I would have also written a book for the general public fifteen years ago—that was my biggest mistake.

I think the reason I didn't make tapes sooner was because I was afraid to think big. I didn't think I was good enough. When you give a speech it evaporates in the air as soon as you're done, but when you say it on tape it's there forever. I kept thinking, "I haven't organized my material enough," or "My voice isn't quite right," or "I haven't learned to enunciate correctly," or "I don't have that Earl Nightingale, radio announcer kind of voice."

So, I basically lived in fear about it. As soon as I did it, everyone loved my albums and said they changed their lives and helped them reinforce my speech material. Also, the tapes helped my income—they probably doubled it.

▶ **SECRET #8: Put out a set of audiocassette tapes A.S.A.P. Remember, Canfield waited several years, but when he finally did it, he doubled his income!**

Where Canfield Gets His Speech Material

The saying, "We speak about what we most need to hear ourselves," applies to just about every speaker I know. Jack selects his material based on one major criteria: Has it worked for me?:

Almost all the material I share with people is stuff that's worked and made a difference for me. I try everything that I teach, and I figure that if it doesn't work for me, it probably won't work for other people. That may be a mistake, but I don't feel ethical teaching stuff that I don't use in my own life.

The stories I share are things I've read or heard or experienced that have touched me. I'd say about one-third of the stories I tell come from other people. I hear them share them and I'm deeply moved and I think, "This deserves to be told." I figure if it touched me like that, then I hope it will touch others the same way.

▶ **SECRET #9: The best criteria for selecting speech material is to ask yourself: Does it work for me?**

Audience Participation Exercises

Canfield is a master at getting the audience involved in his seminars and speeches. Following are some of my favorite Canfield audience participation exercises. Keep in mind as you read through them that Jack practiced them over and over for many years. So, while he makes them look easy to do, they're not.

In order to successfully lead an audience through an exercise, you must: 1) Have complete command of the audience, 2) Be able to give directions clearly and concisely, 3) Be able to transition smoothly from one segment to another without any hitches, and 4) Be able to ad-lib or play off of any unexpected event that may occur. All of this takes lots of practice. The best advice I can give you is to take one exercise that you like and work with it over and over until you have that one down tight. Only then should you go on to learn a second one.

▶ **SECRET #10: The key to mastering audience participation exercises is to practice one over and over until you have it down. Once you've mastered one, then select another and repeat the process.**

Okay, let's see how the master does it . . .

Getting Out of Your Comfort Zone

In the following exercise, Canfield illustrates to his audience how anything new initally feels somewhat uncomfortable:

He starts off by asking the audience to clasp their hands together, like they were praying, and then says, "Notice which thumb is over which." Now comes a bit of Canfield humor: "If your left thumb is over your right, it means you're monogamous;" then, after a pause, he'll add, "and if your right is over your left, it means you're into sheep!" The audience laughs. (Note: If he thinks the line might be offensive to a particular audience, he'll simply make having your right thumb over your left mean something a little less provocative. Remember, part of being a pro means being flexible!)

Jack will then have them switch their thumbs (i.e., if their left was over their right, now the right is over their left). As the audience is voicing their discomfort, Jack will point out that it's because this "new way" is outside of their comfort zone. His point is that in order to grow in life, we have to get out of our comfort zone, and sometimes that can involve some discomfort, at least initially.

▶ **SECRET #11: Anytime you try something new, you are going outside of your comfort zone and thus may initially feel uncomfortable. This is good! It means you're growing!**

How to Make an Audience Member Want to Volunteer

I don't know about you, but every time I see a comedian or magician make fun of an audience volunteer, I cringe. I'm not talking about gentle teasing or the poking of innocent fun, but the, "I have the microphone and you don't and so we're all going to have a few laughs at your expense," kind of treatment.

What this entertainer doesn't realize is that by making the person feel uncomfortable onstage, they're never going to want to help out in a show again. Nor, for that matter, will anybody else in the audience who witnesses this tar-and-feathering of one of their own. Sure, the audience may laugh at Joe Jolly's put-downs, but it's more of a nervous laugh that's due to the person thinking, "Thank God that's not me up there," than any talent the performer might have.

How should you treat audience volunteers? With the same kind of respect you'd like to be treated. In fact, Canfield goes further in this direction than anybody I've ever seen. First, Jack sets it up by saying: "I need a volunteer—someone who is willing to receive a lot of warmth and energy and love and nurturing from the group."

Brilliant! After all, who doesn't want more of those things? Needless to say, Jack never has a problem getting people to volunteer at his seminars. What's more, he doesn't stop there. Once he selects a person to help out, he has the audience give the volunteer a 30-second standing ovation . . . for no reason! He does this because, as he points out, usually we have to *do* something to earn applause in our society. However, he just asks that the person sit back and let the warm applause wash over them. Then he'll ask the person how it felt. Either they'll say something like, "Great!" or, "I thought maybe it was for someone else," or whatever. The point is, he uses the moment to create a positive experience for his audience member. Next time you need a volunteer, why not take a few moments to make the person feel special?

▶ **SECRET #12: Always treat your audience volunteers with respect and make them glad they participated in your program.**

Lovely Parting Gifts

After he's done using the volunteer, does Canfield send the person back to their seat empty-handed? Not on your life! He gives them a cassette tape album, a book, or some other "lovely parting gift." Now, let me ask you a question: When Canfield needs a volunteer for a demonstration in a later segment, do you think he has any problem getting one? Hey, the gust of wind from all the hands shooting up practically knocks him over!

▶   **SECRET #13: Whenever possible, reward your volunteers for taking a risk and coming onstage by giving them a "lovely parting gift," such as one of your books or cassette albums.**

In addition to making people want to volunteer, another benefit of giving away product—which Canfield does, on average, four to five times throughout a typical presentation—is that it allows you to hold it up and tell the audience what it is. In essence, you get to do a five-second commercial for your product without it sounding like a hard-sell pitch. Another nice touch is that Canfield tells his audience that if they happen to buy his product during a break and then they win one, he'll buy the first one back from them so they don't feel as if they shouldn't have bought one.

Audience Ticklers

Keeping your audience interested and stimulated during your presentation is part of your job. Here are a couple of techniques Canfield uses to achieve this goal:

Stroke Them

One way to make your audience feel good, and thus pay more attention during your presentation, is to compliment them. Since everyone loves to be told how wonderful they are (although most people aren't told nearly enough), Canfield tells his audience that they are all winners. He's not doing it to manipulate them into liking him, but rather, because it's true. After all, as Canfield points out, they did win the biggest race of their life by beating out 50,000 other sperm to get here. Everyone in the room is a gold medalist! Since most people aren't used to receiving these types of "strokes," the audience just beams.

Let Them Stroke Themselves

Another way Canfield gets the audience to feel good is by having each person in the audience give the person sitting next to them a 60-second shoulder and neck massage. After having everybody stand, he'll say, "Take your palms and lightly pat up and down the persons back, down to their waist." Then, after a moment, he'll throw in, "Some of you have a strange definition of where the waist is!" And the audience laughs.

Next, he tells the audience to "Shake out your hands like they have dirty dish water on them (a great visual that makes his instructions crystal clear) . . . and you're going to give it back to the person—or get even!—depending on what happened to you." Again, since nobody in the audience was expecting the "get even" part, they laugh.

Tacking on a "Quickie Lesson"

Jack likes to tack on what I call a "quickie lesson"—a short bit of information given to the audience in-between activities—that reinforces the overall lesson plan. Thus, while he's in the middle of doing his audience massage exercise, he ties it in to his main topic by saying to the audience, "Based on all the research, what we know is that peak performers ask for what they want. So, if the person is doing it too hard, too soft, or missing the best spot by an inch (this also causes the audience to titter), ask for what you want!" And so the audience is reminded, in a fun way, about the importance of asking for what you want in life.

▶ **SECRET #14: Constantly look for fun ways to tack on "mini-lessons" to your exercises that reienforce your main topic.**

It's All in How You Set It up

Finally, Canfield concludes this massage exercise by giving the audience some directions that, if not handled properly, could offend some: "Now, I want you to slap on their butt, but do it respectfully! Wake up their seat—they're going to be sitting on it all day. Respectfully! (Again the audience laughs.) Okay . . . shake off your hands again."

Canfield points out that telling the audience to "do it respectfully" makes it okay for 95 percent of the audience to do it. This is because they've been instructed to do it by the trainer, and it's not being done disrespectfully. Says Canfield:

> It's fun, it wakes people up, it's titillating, and it breaks people's mental set and lets them know that they're going to be playful and having a good time.

Hug Three and a Half People?

Before having the audience sit down, Canfield gives them one more exercise:

> I'm going to ask you to do one more thing before you sit down. Some of you are going, "Oh boy!" and others are going, "Oh no, I can't believe it!" I want you to hug three and a half people and then have a seat!

Jack says that since most people's minds are thrown into a state of momentary confusion trying to figure out how to get half a hug, it ends up derailing any resistance they may have and they say to themselves, "Ah, the heck with it!" and just start hugging whoever happens to be closest.

Magicians have been using this technique for centuries; it's called "misdirection." In this case, Jack is using it to distract people's minds long enough to get them to participate in the exercise. While some might think of this as being manipulative, I disagree. Since nobody ever died from getting too many hugs, this is an excellent use of misdirection: to create a positive experience for people who may deep-down inside want to be able to give and receive hugs, but who might be too embarrassed. Canfield gives them permission, so they then give themselves permission to "go for it."

Again, the success of doing an exercise like this depends on the facilitator. The audience must trust you and know that you're not going to abuse or embarrass them. Once you've violated this trust, it's almost impossible to get it back. Finally, Canfield reminds us that you must use your judgment as to whether or not the audience you're speaking to is open to massaging and hugging:

As a speaker, you have to use your good judgment as to whether or not the group to whom you're speaking would appreciate the slapping-the-buttocks part and the three and a half hugs. A group of all-male stockbrokers might have a hard time getting into these last two exercises. Then again, you never know. . . .

Articulating the Resistance

One way that Jack helps to reduce people's anxiety about doing an exercise is to verbalize their resistance. In fact, this is exactly what he did just before he asked the audience to hug three and a half people when he said, "Some of you are going, 'Oh boy!' and others are going 'Oh no, I can't believe it!' " Says Canfield:

> By articulating the resistance that people may be experiencing, you give them permission to have it; and it also helps to evaporate it—simply by acknowledging it.

▶ **SECRET #15: By articulating resistance that people in your audience may be having to a process, you make it okay for them to have their feelings and you also help those feelings dissipate.**

A Powerful Exercise That Demonstrates Just How Much Our Thoughts Affect Our Performance

While Canfield didn't invent this most impressive demonstration, he does a masterful job of presenting it. The technique is from a science called *kinesiology,* which is more or less based on the premise that while we might be able to lie to others, we can't lie to our body. In other words, when we lie or think a negative thought, it causes our brain to become disoriented because it knows it's not being truthful and, therefore, is not in alignment with itself. This "incongruency" causes it to decrease the amount of energy available to our muscles. In kinesiology experiments, it can be demonstrated how this loss of energy makes us physically weaker.

After inviting someone up from the audience, Jack will ask them if they are right- or left-handed. If they are right-handed, he will use their left arm for the experiment (and vice-versa). First, he will have them hold their arm straight out, palm down. Then he will perform a preliminary test, which measures the person's natural arm strength. He'll say, "I'm going to push down on your arm; I want you to resist me as much as you can." After pushing the arm down a couple of inches, the person will tense up and Canfield usually won't be able to push any further (without getting into a pushing match, which isn't the point of the demonstration).

Next, he'll have the person say something true, like their first name. The person will say, "My name is Bill, my name is Bill . . ." Canfield will try to push his arm down, but again, it will hold strong. Then he'll say, "Okay, now I want you to tell a lie. Say that your name is Tom." And to the audience's astonishment, as soon as he says, "My name is Tom, my name is Tom . . . ," Jack will push down on his arm, using exactly the same amount of pressure, and down it will go!

Canfield will then ask the person to close their eyes and get in touch with their inner child. He'll ask them to repeat out loud, over and over, "I am a bad boy!" After they've said it a few times, Jack will again push down on his arm and, "Whoosh," down it will come. Then he will immediately ask the volunteer to repeat out loud, over and over, "I am a good boy." This time, when Jack pushes down, the arm remains strong and does not go down.

Canfield goes on to have the person think of a time when they failed at something, such as flunking a test in college or missing an important appointment. After waiting a few seconds for them to access this "negative" state, he presses on their arm and once again, down it goes like a lead balloon. So as to leave them feeling good, Jack asks the person to think of a "success"—a time when they succeeded at something they were proud of. And the arm stays up strong, stiff as a board.

If you've never seen this exercise done before, it can be a real mind-blower. Canfield knows that it seems incredible, and that most people are thinking that the reason the volunteer's arm is going up and down has nothing to do with positive or negative thoughts, but with the fact that he's simply pushing harder some of the times. That's why, if time permits, he will have the audience break up into pairs and try it on each other. Immediately the "oohs" and "aaahs," as well as the giggling, can be heard from different parts of the room as people discover for themselves that it does indeed really work. (And if you're a bit skeptical yourself, find a friend and give it a try. You'll be blown away.)

While I'm not advocating that you rush out and immediately put this demonstration into your next program, I did want to include it, because it's something that Canfield does in his programs, and it never fails to get a strong reaction.

The Back-to-the-Future Exercise

In this exercise, which I call "Back to the Future," Canfield will begin by having the audience break up into small groups. Then he will say, "Share with your group a success you had before you were eighteen years old." The reason he doesn't want them to use a current success is that someone who works at a 7-11, for example, may feel that their success is inferior to someone in the group who, for example, is a CEO. However, before the age of eighteen, Jack figures that most of us had relatively comparable successes while we were growing up.

After they've gone around the group, and each person has shared a success, Canfield will then ask everyone to close their eyes and think of a goal they really want to achieve. Then he instructs them to share this goal with their group, *as if it's now five years later, and they have already achieved it.* In other words, they are to use past-tense language for something that in reality hasn't yet happened. For example, if Julie currently earns $50,000 a year in sales, and her goal is to earn $225,000 a year within five years, then she would stand up and say, "Last year I earned $225,000, and it enabled me to take my family to Europe for the first time!"

Canfield requests that the rest of the group make sure that whoever is sharing their "future goal" is saying it with the same type of conviction and energy that you really would use if it had happened. In other words, it must be said without any doubt or hesitancy in the voice. The idea is to have them rattle it off with just as much certainty as if they were telling you what they ate for breakfast that morning!

The benefits to the participants for doing this exercise are many. They get group support; they hear other people get excited about achieving their goals and dreams, which gets them excited about achieving their own; they get to vividly experience (probably for the first time) what it's going to feel like when they do achieve it. And, they begin to develop a feeling that they really *can* achieve it.

If you decide to do this exercise with an audience, you'll notice people's faces come alive and light up with excitement. In fact, the whole energy in the room goes up. This is what happens when people get excited about their dreams—and it's really something wonderful to see, especially if you're the trainer who set the stage for making it happen.

The "Three Things I Like about You" Exercise

While I couldn't think of a snappy title for this exercise, nonetheless I really like it and wanted to include it. The basic idea is that each person in a group gets to receive positive feedback from everyone else in their group. Jack asks that each person in the group share with the individual whose turn it is, three things they like about him or her. So that the person can really enjoy the process and be free to "soak up the compliments," Canfield will request that someone else in the group jot down the three things on a piece of paper, so the person will have them to take home. As you can imagine, since most people rarely (if ever) have six to ten strangers telling them how special, attractive, smart, funny, etc., they are, the experience is very powerful and uplifting for each person.

Jack's Personal Mission Statement

Everyone should have a personal mission statement, as far as I'm concerned. In fact, we should be teaching our kids how to write one in elementary school. What is a personal mission statement

(PMS)? It's basically a declaration by you, stating your purpose in life, and how you intend to contribute and make a difference in the world while you're here. Here's Jack's PMS:

> I have dedicated my life to having everybody I teach, touch, or reach through my books and tapes leave with the feeling that they, too, are somebody. That they can make their deepest, most heartfelt dreams come true, if they only make the effort.
>
> I realize that the source of all love starts with self-love and self-acceptance. I believe peace between people and peace among nations starts with peace within one's self.

▶ **SECRET #16: If you don't already have one, spend an hour today writing out your own personal mission statement.**

And finally, we end with . . .

Jack's Philosophy for Life

I believe there is a God. I believe that we can each tune in to inner guidance from God, whether you call it tuning in to your higher self or praying to Jesus, or whatever your particular religious belief structure is. When you do this, your life is in a sense guided by the deepest part of yourself which is in tune with the external flow of the universe.

And then the question is, "Do you trust yourself to trust that voice and take action on it?" When people love and accept themselves fully, they do that. I believe that if everyone did what they truly in their heart believed, then the whole world would work.

But, I see so many people trying to be something they "should be," rather than being what they are. It's kind of like, if all the brain cells were trying to be liver cells, because they thought they were better! The body wouldn't work if this happened, because we need *all* the different cells. We need toe nails, and kneecaps, and colons. Some people start to think that brains are more important than hearts. But if the heart didn't beat, the brain wouldn't have oxygen . . . everyone has their part to play.

How Jack Canfield would like to be remembered:

"He loved and he made a difference."
JACK CANFIELD

Jack Canfield's Success Secrets Summary

SECRET #1: A speaker has a good heart if he or she puts the audience first, and cares more about helping them than in looking good.

SECRET #2: Part of your job as a speaker is to take the complicated and make it simple and easy to understand for your audience. Good ways to do this are through stories, analogies, and examples.

SECRET #3: Your effectiveness as a speaker increases dramatically when people know that you really understand their experience, not from having read books, but because you've been there.

SECRET #4: Contrary to what we've been taught, real men do cry. You can have high self-esteem, be powerful, and yet still be sensitive and show your vulnerability.

SECRET #5: The decision as to whether to memorize your speech, or just the main points and use a more "free-form" approach depends on your own personal preference.

SECRET #6: The fact that two out of three Americans suffer from low self-esteem means that motivational speakers and self-help authors will never be unemployed.

SECRET #7: The most important thing you can do to increase your own self-esteem is to love and accept yourself unconditionally.

SECRET #8: Put out a set of audio cassette tapes A.S.A.P. Remember, Canfield waited several years, but when he finally did it, he doubled his income!

SECRET #9: The best criteria for selecting speech material is to ask yourself: Does it work for me?

SECRET #10: The key to mastering audience participation exercises is to practice one over and over until you have it down. Once you've mastered one, then select a another and repeat the process.

SECRET #11: Anytime you try something new, you are going outside of your comfort zone and thus may initially feel uncomfortable. This is good! It means you're growing!

SECRET #12: Always treat your audience volunteers with respect and make them glad they participated in your program.

SECRET #13: Whenever possible, reward your volunteers for taking a risk and coming onstage by giving them a "lovely parting gift," such as one of your books or cassette albums.

SECRET #14: Constantly look for fun ways to tack on "mini-lessons" to your exercises that reinforce your main topic.

SECRET #15: By articulating resistance that people in your audience may be having to a process, you make it okay for them to have their feelings and you also help those feelings dissipate.

SECRET #16: If you don't already have one, spend an hour today writing out your own personal mission statement.

CHAPTER TEN

BORN: October 15, 1941
BIRTHPLACE: New York, New York

Joel Weldon

". . . the goal was always to get better. The better
I got at preparing, speaking, presenting, and
organizing, the greater the demand
for my services became."

▼

TO Joel Weldon, the only thing that matters in life are *results*. Don't bother to call him up and tell him how wonderful you thought his seminar was. What he's interested in is: What *action* did you take on the ideas that you learned from him?

Sound harsh? Maybe so, but it's this type of no-nonsense, bottom-line oriented presentational style that has made Weldon one of America's top seminar leaders. Companies such as IBM, Revlon, Warner-Lambert, Marriott, Nabisco, and Chart House bring him back year after year for one reason: He gets results. In fact, he guarantees it.

The Gutsiest Guarantee in the Business

While it's been said about life that "there are no guarantees," Joel Weldon has created one of the most unique guarantees of any speaker in the business. Quite literally, he puts his money where his mouth is—if his audiences don't like him, he doesn't get paid! Talk about pressure. To put this in perspective, it would be as if Joe Montana had given back a portion of his salary to the team owner *any* time his football fans weren't happy with his game day performance. Sounds preposterous, doesn't it? Believe it or not, this is exactly the kind of deal Joel Weldon makes with the companies that hire him. He *guarantees* them that he will receive at least a seven (on a scale of one to ten) on every evaluation form he passes out at the end of his program. For any card that averages below a seven, he deducts a portion of his fee!

Sample Weldon Evaluation Card

EVALUATION OF JOEL WELDON'S PRESENTATION
(please circle a number from 1 to 10)

A. How VALUABLE were the ideas and concepts to you?
10   9   8   7   6   5   4   3   2   1
highly   fairly   slightly   none

B. How EFFECTIVE was Joel's presentation of the material?
10   9   8   7   6   5   4   3   2   1
highly   fairly   slightly   not at all

C. COMPARED to other sessions on this subject area, how would you rate today's program?
10   9   8   7   6   5   4   3   2   1
better   equal   poorer   rotten

D. The idea I found most valuable was_____.

If Joel said or did anything that offended you or detracted from the value of this program, please write your comments on the back of this card. Thank you!

It's an indication of just how confident Weldon is in himself and his material, that he's able to make this gutsiest of guarantees. And you know what? He delivers! Audiences love him and consistently rate him high—his average rating for the past five years is 9.61! The reason for such high marks is the simple fact that seminar attendees recognize a first-class presentation when they see one. They realize and greatly appreciate all the time and energy that he puts into selecting, customizing, and delivering his material just for them.

The Time the Guarantee
Was Put to the Test

There was one time, however, when the credibility of Weldon's guarantee was put to the test. After giving a presentation for a large association, Weldon was shocked to receive one evaluation card rating him one, one, and two. Remember, the scale is one to ten, ten being *best*. What this person was saying was that Joel Weldon was without a doubt the worst speaker, with the worst material, he or she had ever heard! As you can imagine, Weldon was shocked.

(That's not to say that he's *never* gotten negative ratings before. As a matter of record, he's received 146 negative evaluations over the past five years. However, when you consider those 146 are out of 37,108 evaluations, or four-tenths of one percent, you realize just how impressive Weldon's track record is.)

However, true to his word, he deducted a portion of his fee from the invoice, and then sent it, along with *all* the cards, to the client. (The way Joel determines how much to deduct is by dividing his total fee by the number of attendees, thus determining how much each person "paid" to attend his program. Then he deducts that amount from the bill. For example, at the time of this meeting, Weldon's fee was $10,000 and there were 200 people in the audience. He divided $10,000 by 200, which came to $50 per head. So he deducted $50 from his fee on the invoice to the client.)

A few days later he got a phone call from the director of the association. The gentleman said, "Mary didn't think *this* card was coming!" When Joel inquired as to who Mary was, the director told him she was the wife of the president of the association. He went on to explain that when her husband had told her about Weldon's guarantee, she didn't believe it. She was sure that if he ever got any bad evaluations, he probably wouldn't turn them in. And so, she had filled out a card giving him two one's and a two, while remarking to her husband, "If this card doesn't come back, we'll know he's throwing away the bad cards and only sending in the good ones."

Of course, Weldon *did* turn it in, along with all the cards. When asked why, he replied, "Because it's the right thing to do." And he meant it. To him, it was far more important that he keep his word than try to make a few extra dollars. His honesty paid off: The association ended up booking him for *four* more meetings. Weldon reaffirmed what he already knew—that operating out of integrity not only helped him sleep better, but it's good for business!

▶ **SECRET #1: Integrity is good for business.**

The $18,000-per-Day-Plus-Expenses Speaker Who Never Intended to Become a Speaker!

While many speakers start out very early in life with a vision of themselves impacting vast numbers of people, this was not the case with Joel:

> I never intended to become a speaker! There was never a bolt of lightning hitting me that said, 'This is what you want to do for the rest of your life.' It was an evolutionary process. My career in selling had helped me to be comfortable with people one on one, but running a meeting or getting up in front of a group wasn't really anything I was comfortable with.

Competed in 1974 Toastmasters International Speech Contest

> I joined a Toastmasters Club in 1969 to overcome my fear of speaking in front of groups. As you get better at anything, you enjoy it more, and as I started to get better at speaking, I got more involved in Toastmasters. For five years I was heavily involved at the state level and in 1974, at the encouragement of my wife, Judy, I entered the Toastmasters International Speech Contest.

Weldon says that the secret when faced with competition is not to compete, but to create! An example of just how creative he is, is illustrated by the way he approached this speech contest. After winning at the district, division, and state level, he found himself in Kansas City, competing in the regionals. He knew he needed something powerful and unique to have a chance against the four other talented speakers who, like Joel, had all won at the state level.

What he came up with is nothing short of brilliant: When his name was announced to the audience, Weldon walked up to the lectern carrying a napkin. He wiped his brow and, without ever even looking up, said in a trembling voice, "Ladies and gentleman, after hearing the previous three speakers, I realize I'm not good enough to compete in a contest like this. I'm sorry if I've caused any problems, but I won't be able to give my speech." And he sat down!

The audience was shocked. This was, after all, the regional finals. Nobody knew what to do. Finally, the emcee walked to the lectern and with a shrug of his shoulders said, "Well, I guess, on with the show. Our next speaker . . ." And before he could say anymore, Weldon leaped out of his chair, grabbed the microphone out of the startled emcee's hand and commanded, "Sit down!" Then he turned to the stunned audience and said forcefully, "Ladies and gentleman, how many times do we see people who are ready to quit before they even start, just like that previous speaker who was ready to give up before he even attempted his speech!? How often does the fear of failure prevent all of us from doing things we really can do?"

Weldon destroyed the competition that day because his presentation was so unique and impactful. He won because he dared to try something novel; something nobody had ever seen before. He eventually went on to finish third at the international level, meaning that out of 60,000 speakers, Weldon was one of the top three! Weldon's novel opening to his speech that day was his way of saying to the audience, "Hey, I'm different! I'm *not* like every other speaker. Pay attention!" It's this drive to be different, to stand out from the crowd, that has helped form Weldon's personal credo, which is: "Find out what everybody else is doing and don't do it!"

▶   **SECRET #2: Find out what everybody else is doing and don't do it!**

Like Weldon, all great speakers go through the process of creating something about themselves or their product (message) that makes them unique.

QUESTION: In what way are you unique or different from your competition in the minds of your customers?

Identifying Your Unique Differentiating Factor

Joel Weldon's "guarantee" is one poweful way that he differentiates himself from all the other speakers on the market. Before Weldon came along, no speaker (as far as I know) had ever offered to actually guarantee their results. First-time customers find his offer extremely attractive as it takes away much of the risk in hiring him. It's important to keep in mind that this guarantee is an extension of Joel's personality, of who he is. Your Unique Differentiating Factor (UDF) should be a part of who you are. Here are some questions to ask yourself to help uncover what it is about you that's unique:

1. *What part of your personality seems to make the biggest impact on people?* Are you particularly funny? Confident? Intelligent? Any of these traits can be capitalized upon and turned into a UDF. For example, suppose you are an accountant who gives seminars on tax planning. Furthermore, suppose you happen to have an off-beat sense of humor. By weaving your humor throughout your presentation, you can become known for, and market yourself as, the "CPA who can help you laugh all the way to the bank!"

2. *Are you talented in a particular area?* Do you have a good singing voice? Can you play the piano? I know of several speakers who do both, and are remembered by their audiences because they incorporate these talents into their program.

3. *What are you most passionate about?* (Commenting on the zeal and enthusiasm southern preachers are known for exuding, one once remarked, "We set ourselves on fire and people come to watch us burn!") Having tremendous enthusiasm for your topic

can definitely help you stand out from the crowd. Tom Peters has taken his passion for excellence in the workplace and turned it into millions via his best-selling books, tapes, and seminars. What are some ways you can share your enthusiasm with your audience?

Important: Many people get discouraged if they feel they don't possess a particular personality trait or talent that stands out. There is no need for this. You can still develop a competitive edge by making the decision to become *excellent* in a particular area. You can work hard to provide your customers with solid, usable information. You can become known for being extremely dependable (this is Fed Ex's UDF). You can focus on doing such a superb job that people will want what you offer simply because you do it better than anyone else in your field! I want to encourage you to really take some time and come up with your own UDF. The time and effort you invest now will pay big dividends throughout the rest of your career.

▶ **SECRET #3: All great speakers have a unique differentiating factor. What is yours?**

Advertising Your Uniqueness

"Doing business without advertising is like winking at a girl in the dark: You know what you're doing but nobody else does."
ED HOWE

Of course, knowing that there is something unique about what you do is not enough. The audience must be made aware of this uniqueness and how it will benefit them. Joel emphasizes his unique "Weldon Guarantee" by inserting a copy of it into his information package. It explains the guarantee, how it works, and the benefit to the client (i.e., that if their people aren't happy, the client receives a refund). It's simple, straightforward, and irresistible.

▶ **SECRET #4: Emphasize your unique differentiating factor in all your promotional materials.**

Weldon has discovered that by developing and delivering a high-energy, high-impact program that really meets the client's needs, he can charge top dollar for his services and his clients will gladly pay it, year after year.

Used Speaking to Boost Audiotape Sales for Nightingale-Conant Corporation

As mentioned earlier, Weldon did not start out in life with the goal of one day becoming a professional speaker. Like Patricia Fripp, who started off giving free speeches to bring in more business for her hair-cutting business, Joel started off speaking in order to increase his audiotape sales:

> I was a distributor for the Nightingale-Conant Corporation, selling cassette training programs. When a company ordered cassette programs from me, I offered to do a sales meeting for them to get their people excited about using the tapes. However, I found that as companies started inviting me back to talk, it took away from my direct-selling activities. I had to charge them something, and that was $25.00 in the beginning.
>
> More and more companies started asking me to come back, so I raised my fee to $50.00 and a funny thing happened. I found I had more companies asking me to speak when I went to $50.00 than when I was at $25.00.
>
> So, I figured I could make it a $100.00 per talk. Over the next couple of years my fees gradually continued to increase until I made the real big step in 1977 of going to $200.00 for a local presentation. That year, 264 groups asked me to come and talk to them! Speaking, for me, really started out as sort of a service to my customers who had ordered these wonderful cassettes that Earl Nightingale had recorded.
>
> So, I never set out to be a professional speaker or to give a certain number of talks a year; that was never the goal. The goal was always to get better. It appeared that the better I got at preparing, speaking, presenting, and organizing, the greater the demand for my services became.

Offering a Super-High-Quality Program Makes Good Business Sense

It's interesting to note that in 1977, Weldon gave a whopping 264 speeches! Yet, ten years later, in 1987, he gave only 42 speeches; a reduction of 85 percent. However, his fees had increased by a staggering 1300 percent! Working less, but getting paid more makes good business sense to Joel. Even more importantly, each year, approximately 50 percent of Weldon's programs are for clients who have hired him before.

This is a real testament to just how effective Joel is; many of his clients hire him back year after year. And when they do use another speaker, often that speaker *hears* about Weldon. One well known speaker was once told by a client, "You better be good, we had Joel Weldon last year!"

One of the keys to Weldon's success is that he *consistently* exceeds the expectations of his clients and, therefore, his audiences. As Weldon himself says, "I promise a lot and then deliver even more."

▶ **SECRET #5: Promise a lot and then deliver even more.**

Remember, the key to this philosophy is that Weldon delivers on all his promises. He actually *does* what he tells the client he's going to do, and then some. In an era when hype, broken promises, and excuses are commonplace, Weldon's ethical way of doing business is as refreshing as it is an anomaly.

He credits the late Earl Nightingale for sharing with him the powerful concept that the money you earn is determined by three things: 1) the need for what you do, 2) your ability to do it, and 3) the difficulty in replacing you. Therefore:

The goal is to become so good at what you do that
when people think of your area of expertise,
they immediately think of you.

How do you become good in a particular area? By throwing yourself at it full force; by finding out everything you can about the subject; by studying the very best people in that industry and seeing what they're doing; by spending time *thinking* about ways to improve in that field; by attending seminars, listening to tapes, and reading books like this one. Remember, many people will read the same words that you're reading right now; but not all of the them will *act* on the ideas presented. If you are one of the few that take action, you *will* be successful.

"The only certain means of success is to render more and better service than is expected of you, no matter what your task may be."
OG MANDINO

Every day, ask yourself, "What can I do *today* to provide my customers with better service?" If you keep asking yourself this one question, and you vigorously follow up on the answers, you can't help but become excellent at your craft.

"We market ourselves in just one way: by doing great programs."
JOEL WELDON

Weldon decided early-on that if he did an outstanding program for his clients, not only would they want him back—thus creating repeat business—but they would also tell others. And that's exactly what's happened. While many speakers spend a lot of time and energy designing slick brochures and demo videos, Weldon's brochure and demo video is his seminar itself:

> We don't do any marketing, advertising, or promoting. We don't have demo audio- or videotapes. We don't do mailings or work through agents. We market ourselves in just one way: by doing great programs.

▶ **SECRET #6: Your best marketing tool is a great presentation.**

The Walt Disney Philosophy

Joel points out that one of the greatest promoters the world has ever known, Walt Disney, believed that doing something extremely well was the best way to attract new business:

> When you hire me for a program and you see the end result, two things will happen. You will want to hire me again and you will tell somebody else to hire me. This was something that Walt Disney taught his people in 1955 when he opened Disneyland. He said, "Do what you do so well that when other people see what it is you do, they'll want to see you do it again, and will bring others with them to show them what it is you do."

> Do the best job you can for your clients and the rest will take care of itself. That is our marketing philosophy. We've been doing this for over 20 and we still get more requests every year than we accept. All I have to do to maintain that is to keep improving!

Perhaps this quote says it all:

"Just make up your mind at the very outset that your work is going to stand for quality . . . that you are going to stamp a superior quality upon everything that goes out of your hands, that whatever you do shall bear the hall-mark of excellence."
ORISON SWETT MARDEN

The lesson from Joel is obvious: Before you worry about what colors to use in your brochure or how many copies of your video to make, your first priority should be to develop the very best presentation possible. After all, you can have the best-looking promotional packet in the world, but if your program is mediocre, you're not going to be asked back. Therefore, the key word is *value*.

*QUESTION: Am I giving my audience the maximum
amount of take home value possible in return for the time
and dollars they've invested in coming to my program?*

What is *take-home value?* It's solid, practical, *usable* information that a person in your audience can immediately put to use to improve their personal life, job performance/skills, or overall life experience.

Weldon is a fanatic about making sure that the ideas he delivers to his audiences can be used within twenty-four hours:

> One thing I spend a lot of time doing is making sure the ideas [that I present] are usable. They are not blue sky, they are not unrealistic, they are not long-range. They are things people can do in twenty-four hours; that's my criteria for organizing a program. If I can't present something they can do in twenty-four hours, I don't even talk about it.
>
> I don't presume to think that I'm going to change anybody's life, because I'm not there to give a life-changing experience. There are some speakers who do that. My goal is to offer one idea that they can use in twenty-four hours to help them be a little bit better tomorrow than they are today. If they do that, then I've been successful.

▶ **SECRET #7: Give your audience ideas they can put to use within twenty-four hours.**

Weldon's Style

One of the reasons why Weldon is one of the highest-paid seminar leaders in the country, and has been for many years, is because of his no-nonsense, intense, "Here's how it is" type of delivery. Weldon doesn't mince words. He knows he's done his homework, and once he's in front of a group he uses his naturally deep voice along with his tremendous enthusiasm to deliver his message. Here's a sample from a much talked about presentation he delivered to the National Speakers Association, called "Elephants Don't Bite":

How many of you would like an easy way [to be successful in the speaking business]? (Looks around audience) Forget it! There is no easy way! There is never an easy way to do anything that's going to be worthwhile. And if we ever figure out an easy way, there is very little opportunity to get paid for something that's easy! Why would they pay you if it's easy, if *anybody* could do it? If you went to a store and did whatever they needed you to do, they would pay you minimum wage. Why would somebody pay Zig (Ziglar) thousands to do what he does? Because it's so hard!

Let's keep that in mind that there are no free lunches—we have to earn it. Would you like to know the secret to how to get more bookings? It's probably the best-kept secret in America—six words, easy to remember, hard to do: *Promise a lot, deliver even more.* That's it!

When you get paid, they should write the check and feel that it's ridiculous and an insult to send it to you because it's so little for what you did! If they think it's too high, you probably promised a lot and gave them less.

Can you feel Joel's intensity as you read these words? The fact is, Weldon is an extremely focused, driven individual. He says he doesn't just focus, he *laser focuses* on his objectives. And not just in his business:

"I prepare the same way for a fishing trip as I do for a seminar—it's the same level of intensity and the same level of commitment."

JOEL WELDON

Without a doubt, the area that Weldon leaves the competition in the dust is in the amount of extensive preparation he does for each talk he delivers. He has taken the venerable slogan of the Boy Scouts of America, "Always be prepared," and made it his company's credo. In fact, he considers the amount of time and effort he puts into preparing a program his greatest asset:

My strength is in the amount of time that goes into understanding the audience's situation, the client's situation, the purpose of the meeting, and my role in the program. We drive our business by preparation; that's really the key.

"Thoroughness characterizes all successful men."
ELBERT HUBBARD

▶ **SECRET #8: Do you homework: Find out as much as possible about your audience.**

Weldon does a staggering fifty hours of preparation for every presentation he gives. And it makes no difference to him whether it's a one-hour or full-day presentation—he still puts in a full fifty hours worth of preparation for each and every program he delivers!

(It should be noted here that Weldon does not speak to the client until *after* the program is booked. Until then, his wife of over thirty years, Judy Weldon, runs his entire office. Only after the contracts have been signed does Joel get involved. The two of them feel that by having Judy handle the business end of things, this frees up Joel to focus all his time and energy on one thing: providing the client with the very best presentation possible.)

One of the reasons Weldon is so effective in exceeding his clients' expectations is because he takes nothing for granted. He wants to know, specifically, what is going on in that company, in that industry, and most importantly, in the minds of the people who will be attending his program.

Preparation: It's a Three-Step Process

Joel goes through a three-step process in preparing for his presentations. The first step is to decide which questions he will need to know the answers to. The second step is the actual asking of the questions of the right people (the gathering of the information), and the third step is the organizing of the information.

Step One: Asking the Right Questions

The first step for Weldon, as he prepares to research his client's company, is to find out the answers to some key questions. The purpose of these questions is to help give him a clearer picture of his client's world. Here are some of the questions to which Joel (and any good speaker) will want to know the answer to:

1. *What mindset will my audience be in when they attend my program?* (Upbeat? Down? Complacent?, etc.)

2. *What are some of the fears and challenges they're currently facing?* (Example: Because of layoffs and downsizing, they are afraid of losing their jobs. However, they're also resentful of management because they're doing twice the work they used to because their department is now understaffed. *Knowing this type of information ahead of time will make a big difference in how Joel prepares for the program.*)

3. *What are some of their joys?* (Example: Their company just merged with a leader in their industry and everybody is very excited about the future.)

4. *What's the purpose of the meeting at which I've been asked to speak?* (Example: The company just came off a record quarter in sales, management is thrilled, and they're bringing in Weldon as a reward.)

5. *What skills, goals or attitudes would management like to see the attendees leave my program with?* (Example: Become more effective leaders and managers, learn how to praise employees, and learn to lead more by example.)

It's asking these types of questions, above and beyond the standard, "How many people will be in attendance? What's the theme of the event, etc.?" that separates the great speakers from the average.

▶ **SECRET #9: Ask the right questions!**

"Luck is when preparation meets opportunity."

Step Two: Gathering
the Information

Weldon knows that there's a lot of truth to the saying, "A problem well-stated is half-solved." And so, like a doctor learning as much as he can about his patient before he operates, the first step for Weldon consists of speaking with numerous employees of the company that hired him. Because he truly wants to get a sense of where the company's at, he doesn't just talk to top executives, but front-line people as well. He knows that these people will have their own unique experiences and opinions about the company they work for that, in many cases, will be quite different from that of upper management.

The types of questions Weldon asks top executives when doing his preparation include:

- What is your objective in bringing me in to speak to your people?
- What do you want them to be able to do better, differently, or more effectively after leaving my program?
- What do you perceive as the biggest challenges facing your industry?
- Where do you see your company going in the next three to five years?

The types of questions he asks front-line workers include:

- What do you like most about your job?
- What areas give you the biggest headaches?
- What are you most proud of in your work?
- What areas do you think could be improved?

▶ **SECRET #10: Talk with as many people in the organization as possible.**

In addition, Joel collects as many stories and anecdotes as possible for use during his programs.

The Pesky Fly Story

A humorous example of how doing his homework really paid off for Weldon is illustrated by the following true story. Once, while doing his research on a particular company, he learned that for some reason they had a fly problem on the ninth floor of their building. It seems that no matter what they did, they couldn't get rid of some pesky flies that were hanging out on that particular floor.

Since he didn't see an immediate use for this information, he filed it away in his brain and forgot about it. Well, it just so happens that during his presentation for the group, a fly began buzzing back and forth right in front of his face. Without missing a beat, he swatted the fly away as he said into the microphone, "Get back to the ninth floor where you belong!" The audience went wild. They knew that Weldon had really done his homework to have known about their little fly problem and they really appreciated how he wove it into his talk.

By doing his homework, Weldon was able to take advantage of a situation that a less prepared speaker might not have been able to capitalize on. It's because of moments like this that Weldon knows that all his research is worth the effort and then some. What's more, it's these extra touches that his clients remember and keep them calling him back year after year.

By the way, in the course of his conversation with the company's executives or meeting planners, he will have them send him their company newsletter, financial and stock reports, and product brochures. In addition, he will round up related magazine and newspaper articles about that group's specific industry.

▶ **SECRET #11: Read everything you can get your hands on about the organization.**

Weldon's goal is to have the audience members say to themselves, "Wow, this guy really knows what he's talking about. I wonder how long he's been in our business?" Thus, when he researches a client, no stone goes unturned. Again, it's this willingness to go the extra mile, to prepare beyond the company's wildest expectations, that makes Weldon one of the most sought after seminar leaders in the country.

Step Three: Organizing
the Information

As Weldon reads through all the interviews, reports, and articles he's collected, he makes notes on a yellow legal pad. He'll make pages and pages of notes to himself about the company, their corporate philosophy, problems their industry is having, the direction in which the company is going, anecdotes the top executives and front-line people have shared with him, etc.

▶ **SECRET #12: Collect all your notes in one place.**

Once he's written out all his material, he then goes back over his notes and decides what his main points will be. This is where he really earns his pay. It's here that Weldon, through years of experience, is able to hone in on exactly what points will be most important to that particular audience he will be addressing.

Once he's carefully cultivated his list of main points, he then takes a stack of three-by-five index cards and writes down one main point per card. For example, he might write down, "The power of focus," and under this he will list the key stories and points he will use to illustrate the benefits of being highly focused on a specific project. Of course, he will be sure to tie it in to that particular group's product or service. When he's done with that card, he'll place it on the table in front of him, take a new card, and repeat the process all over again. The secret is that he writes down only one main point per card.

After he has his main points all laid out in front of him, he'll go back over each card, making sure all his stories and examples tie into, and relate to, the particular group he's addressing.

▶ **SECRET #13: Write down one main point, one story, and how it relates to that audience on each three-by-five card.**

Finally, Weldon completes his extensive preparation by providing his client with a detailed written outline of the entire contents of his program. All of this is done many weeks or months before he even steps foot on the platform!

Arrives at the Speaking Site Early

To Weldon, being professional doesn't stop with doing a lot of research. It permeates everything he does. For example, not only does he always arrive at the site of his seminar a day in advance, but his travel plans are arranged so as to avoid any possible problems:

> When I leave to do a seminar, I fly out on the first flight of the day, which allows me backup flights if there's a mechanical problem or a delay. If there's a weather situation, I'll leave an extra day early. We don't overbook seminars and we don't string them together.

Getting to the seminar site early allows Weldon to make sure everything is just right:

> I like setting up the meeting room, including moving chairs around and checking out the microphone. I enjoy going to any presentations that might be going on the day before my talk, as well as getting up very early the morning of my presentation to re-check the room.

▶ **SECRET #14: Arrive at the speaking site early.**

The tremendous benefit of Weldon's extensive preparation becomes apparent the moment he steps on the platform:

> By the time I'm introduced, all the preparation is done and there is no thought given to the material, the ideas, stories, examples, or the humor. My entire conscious focus is on the audience.
>
> I'm watching the audience, thinking what they're thinking, attempting to experience what they're experiencing. I'm looking for people who are buying in, signs of resistance, or things that might have passed over them that need to be restated in a simpler, clearer way. I'm thinking, "Do I need to slow down or speed things up? Do I need to move the break ahead?"
>
> Clients tell me that they're amazed that I am so tuned-in to their audience. Well, it's not amazing. There's nothing else for me to do. I have already done everything else!

▶ **SECRET #15: Thorough preparation allows you to focus 100 percent on your audience during your presentation.**

Doesn't Memorize Speech

It is interesting to note that Weldon does not commit any of his presentation to memory:

> I don't memorize anything. I think about the ideas and stories, and since most of them are personal stories, all I have to do is tell what happened and show how it applies to their situation. Since they are true stories and experiences, it's very easy to customize them for the audience I'm speaking too.

The Weldon Philosophy: As Good As You Are, You Can Be Even Better

Weldon doesn't believe that significant change happens overnight. Rather, he feels that if we are a little bit better today than we were yesterday, and we continue to improved day-in and day-out, eventually we'll get to where we want to be:

> My personal philosophy is to make very small improvements and never stop making them. It's not realistic to expect yourself to do tremendous things very quickly. I have not seen in my own personal life or in the lives of others that great things come easily. I think the more rewarding the end result is, the greater the effort expended to get there. There are very few overnight successes, yet I hear a lot of people talking about how you can do anything you want to do if you want to do it badly enough. I guess that's true, but my approach would be, "You can do a lot better than what you're doing now by doing a little better every day . . . and gradually, you will improve."

> Everything that is presented at our seminars is built around the idea that as good as you are now, you can be even better.

The ideas are presented in the three main areas that I have some experience in. Number one is sales, number two is management, and number three is personal development. And in those three categories we have about seventy hours of seminar material.

Our registered trademark and our company logo is an eight-ounce can that says: "Success Comes in Cans, Not in Cannots." We teach that your attitude plays the major role in whatever you're going to do; in sales, in management, and in your own personal life. You also need balance in all of these areas. All work and no play is not good, and family is very important.

My philosophy for life is the importance of the family and improvement. Judy and I have been married for thirty-two years and it's getting better every year. We've been in our home for over twenty-five years and we just finished our fifth major improvement. Our cars and boats have improved, as well as our physical health. We're in our fifties and we feel stronger and have more energy than we can ever remember having.

Our philosophy is that everything can get better. Our minds, our bodies, in fact everything in all areas of our life can get better! And we can do this by making little improvements; if we commit to steady, constant improvement, the end result will be overwhelmingly positive. That's because there's been such a solid foundation built.

▶ SECRET #16: Success starts with having a solid foundation.

When Joel graduated from high school in 1959, he spent seven years in construction as a carpenter. Something his boss once told him has proven to be a powerful metaphor in his life:

When I used to work in construction, my supervisor told me, "If we put our foundation in right, the rest of the building is easy." That philosophy has really guided us. If we pay our dues, take our time, do our homework, and do it right and with quality, whatever we put on top of this will have something to support it.

Imagine building a building with a poor foundation and then putting a beautiful edifice above. Eventually, through time, weather, and wind, the foundation will start to move. The building will weaken and crack, and eventually fall apart. You see that happen with a lot of people's careers. They go up quick and they go down just as quickly.

The Most Important Quality a Speaker Must Possess Is Credibility

When asked the most important quality for a speaker to possess, Weldon replied:

> I would say credibility. I think the one thing speakers underestimate is an audience's ability to read them and to know if what they're saying is really believed. If the ideas you present are what you believe in, you don't have to "turn it on" and "turn it off." It's not a stage performance or an act; what you see is what you get.
>
> One of the greatest compliments I've ever received was when a client picked me up from the airport, and on the way to the meeting site he told me about another speaker they had the month before. They told him that I was going to be their next month's speaker and they wanted to know what he thought of Joel Weldon. He said, "He is one guy who really believes his own stuff!"
>
> The fact is, I really do believe my own stuff! If you don't walk your talk, if you don't live your material and if you don't tell true stories, the audience picks up on it. Being credible is the most important thing! *Then* if you are enthusiastic, funny, dynamic, clear, focused, and you've customized the talk, now you've got something. Without that number one ingredient, credibility, nothing else really matters.

▶ **SECRET #17: The number one quality a speaker must possess is credibility.**

Learned from Watching
Poor Speakers

Oftentimes, a person can learn as much from a poor example as from a good one, by seeing what *not* to do. When Weldon was just starting out, he made a study of every speaker that he saw. Instead of sitting there passively watching their presentation, he would analyze what they were doing:

> I have learned more about speaking by watching people who were ineffective than by watching people who were effective. Every time I would go to a meeting, seminar, or presentation, I would study the reaction of the audience. In many cases, I would see speakers who used such small visuals that they couldn't be seen, or who didn't use them effectively.
>
> By seeing something presented ineffectively, I would think, "How could that be done more effectively, or how could I improve on that?" When I saw a speaker tell a joke that didn't go over, I thought about what he could have done to make the story or example more humorous. Some of the best techniques in my presentations have come from improving upon what other speakers have done poorly.

Weldon's Greatest Reward Is
When People Go Out
and Use His Ideas

In life, in the end, it's not what we think or say that counts, it's what we actually do. By now it should come as no surprise that an action-oriented person like Joel Weldon is not easily impressed. To put it bluntly, talk is cheap to Weldon. What makes him happiest, and what he calls "payday," is when people write him letters and tell him how they have *used* his ideas and concepts, how they have made a tangible difference in their lives.

For Weldon, "payday" comes not in the form of a check, but in a letter:

> Payday for me is after a seminar is over and the thank you notes start coming in. Comments like, "Here's what I've been

able to do with the ideas you've presented." Letters like that are by far the most exciting, stimulating, and rewarding part of this whole business. I'm action-oriented. Thought is important, belief is important, but to me what really counts is what people do.

I could say to you, "I really like you," but if my actions don't verify that, my words are meaningless. When an audience applauds or gives me a standing ovation, when people come up after the meeting and say, "This has changed my life," that has very little effect on me. It's nice, it's a good feeling, but it's not what keeps me in the business. What really excites me and keeps my commitment level so high is when I get the feedback of what people have done with the ideas.

Every letter we get is personally answered by me with a note thanking them for the feedback and encouraging them to keep using the ideas.

If You Don't Like Something, Find a Way to Improve It

One statement by Weldon that really captures the essence of why he is so successful is his response to the question: "What do you dislike most about being one of America's top speakers?" He replied:

I can't think of anything I dislike about what I do. I love the traveling, the clients, and the preparation work. And if there was anything, I would figure out a way to improve it!

This last sentence to his answer really gives us some insight into how Weldon's mind works. Not only does he love every aspect of the speaking profession (which is why he is so good at it), but if there *was* something he found distasteful, he would *immediately figure out some way to improve it*. What a great attitude!

▶ **SECRET #18: If you don't like something, find a way to improve it.**

It's obvious that Joel Weldon is a living example of what Washington Irving meant when he said:

> **"Little minds attain and are subdued by misfortunes; but great minds rise above them."**

How Joel Weldon would like to be remembered:

> **"He did what he said he was going to do, he did it well, and he believed in what he was doing."**
> JOEL WELDON

Joel Weldon's
Success Secrets Summary

SECRET #1: Integrity is good for business.

SECRET #2: Find out what everybody else is doing and don't do it!

SECRET #3: All great speakers have a unique differentiating factor. What is yours?

SECRET #4: Emphasize your unique differentiating factor in all your promotional materials.

SECRET #5: Promise a lot and then deliver even more.

SECRET #6: Your best marketing tool is a great presentation.

SECRET #7: Give your audience ideas they can put to use within twenty-four hours.

SECRET #8: Do your homework: Find out as much as possible about your audience.

SECRET #9: Ask the right questions!

SECRET #10: Talk with as many people in the organization as possible.

SECRET #11: Read everything you can get your hands on about the organization.

SECRET #12: Collect all your notes in one place.

SECRET #13: Write down one main point, one story, and how it relates to that audience, on each three-by-five card.

SECRET #14: Arrive at the speaking site early.

SECRET #15: Thorough preparation allows you to focus 100 percent on your audience during your presentation.

SECRET #16: Success starts with having a solid foundation.

SECRET #17: The number one quality a speaker must possess is credibility.

SECRET #18: If you don't like something, find a way to improve it.

CHAPTER ELEVEN

BORN: January 6, 1945
BIRTHPLACE: Chicago, Illinois

Danielle Kennedy

"I get a lot of satisfaction from working with the audience and helping them get 'ah-hahs' that will help them in their own lives. I feel very grateful and humble to have the opportunity to be a communicator."

▼

IN 1972, while raising five children all under the age of seven, Danielle Kennedy went into the real estate field. Amazingly, by her third year she was doing over 100 transactions annually and found herself in the top one percent in the nation in real estate sales. This earned her the title of real estate's "Six Million Dollar Woman," and she was soon being asked to speak at real estate board and association meetings.

Eventually, Prentice Hall came to her and asked her to write a book on how a woman with five children, no sales training, and every excuse in the world for giving up, made it to the top of the real estate field. The success of that book, *How to List and Sell Real Estate* (which has gone through six printings and sold 500,000 copies) has led her to write four more books, a monthly column for *Entrepreneur* magazine, and made her one of the most popular speakers in the industry.

One House, Many Rooms

As this chapter reveals, Kennedy has several sides to her. One is the confident and independent saleswoman, speaker, and writer who built up her own multi-million-dollar business and who knows her achievements can and do serve as a source of inspiration for others. Another is that of a sensitive, vulnerable, and, at times, insecure human being who is often plagued by self-doubt. And yet another is the doting mother who openly admits that her children are everything to her. Together, all these diverse parts make up the intriguing persona of Danielle Kennedy, whose career has become legendary in the real estate field.

A Natural-Born Speaker?

While it's often said that good speakers are made, not born, Kennedy comes close. From the very beginning, she was a talker. Says Danielle:

When I was nine months old, I talked in sentences. By the time I was eight, they were asking me to do public announcements over the loud speaker system at my Catholic school.

In high school, I was on the debate team and I was vice president of the drama club. In college, I was a speech and drama major. I did a lot of oral interpretation of literature and a lot of public speaking. I even had my own radio show on campus!

A People Person

While all this training in the area of communication would one day serve her well, probably the trait that is most responsible for her success is the fact that Danielle loves people. For as long as she can remember, she has always been a "people person":

I tell this story in my book about how when I was two years old I used to invite the whole neighborhood over to our house for coffee. In the old days in Chicago, where I was raised, the women had coffee socials and I would shout out the window, "Mrs. Salsbury, we got coffee, you bring the donuts!" I just always loved people.

How cute is that? Not only did little Danny want to invite people over, but she wasn't afraid to delegate!

Like Father, Like Daughter

Kennedy says that she got her warmth for people from her Irish father, who always made her feel important:

I think a lot of my caring for people came from my dad. He was the kind of guy who could walk into a room and people would say, "Don't I know you? God you look familiar." He was extremely well-loved.

He taught me something when I was very young—he said, "Always walk in like you own the place. That doesn't mean you're arrogant or conceited, but it lets people know that you understand that we're all alike."

Taking Down the Walls
That Separate Us

Kennedy feels that it's this letting down of our guard that, while it may be scary, is also what brings us closer to people:

> There really aren't these barriers and walls between people. We put them up; we self-impose these walls. For a long time I had some fear of being myself. But once I saw that what my dad said was right, that we're all alike and we all go through the same ups and downs and emotional roller coastering, and that universally we all want the same things . . . when I really got that, and connected with that internally, it made all the difference.
>
> People know when I come in, that I'm one of them—one of the gang. It doesn't matter if I go into an executive board room or if I'm speaking to a group of construction workers. My message applies to everybody. And it comes down to that basic philosophy: just walk in like you belong there!

▶ **SECRET #1: Always walk into a room like you own the place— not like you're conceited, but like you belong and you're glad to be there.**

Family Is Everything to Danielle

If you ask Kennedy what is the most important thing to her in life, she will tell you that it's not the money she makes, or even her career, but her children that mean the most to her. Here she shares, in a very personal way, why she feels so strongly about being a mother:

> I wanted to be a mother really badly. I had it in my mind that I wouldn't be able to have kids. My mom was told that she could never have kids—she and my father had been trying for ten years and had just about given up. Finally, she got pregnant and they said that it was a miracle! She and I almost died during my childbirth. It was a very difficult thing. I was put in an oxygen tent my first three days of life.

This intense experience left a deep impression on Danielle:

> I carried this whole thing inside me, that I had inherited this
> problem of not being able to have kids. Well, I got married
> very young, and I got pregnant on my honeymoon. It was
> exactly what I wanted to happen! It immediately took me
> out of these chains, these mental shackles that I had put
> myself in.

Like Kennedy, many of us have chains from our past that, like real
chains, hold us down. It's only when we acknowledge to ourselves
that these chains exist only in our mind, and that *we* are the ones
who hold the key, can we begin the process of freeing ourselves.
For Danielle, the process of healing began the moment she gave
birth:

> Then I just started having kids, one after another. And I got
> stronger and stronger after each one. I was just crazy about
> these kids and they were just crazy about me. I got the feel-
> ing that there wasn't anything I couldn't do. When I went
> through my divorce to my first husband and had to raise
> them myself, that was even more motivation.

A Big Breakthrough

For Kennedy, the period of her divorce, in the late seventies, was
one of the biggest challenges she has ever had to face. Being from
a Catholic family made it tough enough, but there were professional reasons that made it especially difficult:

> For me, a real breakthrough came when I went through my
> divorce in 1978 and 1979. I had been billed by Tom Hop-
> kin's company, who I worked for at the time, as this happily
> married wife and mother. He had no idea what my situation
> was, but it was pretty tough. I was scared to death to tell my
> audience that I was going through a divorce. I thought, "Oh
> my God, I'll lose all my credibility. The only reason they like
> me is because they think I'm happily married and success-
> ful." I went through the worst trip over it. . . .

It's amazing how we put ourselves through all kinds of stress because of our "image" and what we imagine people will think if
they found out who we *really* are. As you're about to see, the
truth is that people will accept us just as soon as we start to love
and accept ourselves. As with most self-judgments in life, we are
far more harsh on ourselves than other people are on us.

In a remarkably similar experience to the one Barbara De
Angelis went through, Danielle discovered that when she just "came
clean" with her audience, they didn't think less of her, but rather,
admired her for her honesty and willingness to be real with them.

▶ **SECRET #2: Audiences don't demand that you be perfect, but they
do demand that you be real and authentic with them.**

Says Kennedy:

> When I finally told my audience what I was going through,
> oh my God, the reaction was incredible. I told the story
> about my divorce, coupled with the loss of my best friend
> who had killed herself that year—there wasn't a dry eye in
> the house.

> There was so much love pouring to me, just healing energy. I
> think that freed me for the rest of my life, because I got over
> my fear. And I realized at that point that the only thing I ever
> had to be for the rest of my life, on that stage, was myself!

▶ **SECRET #3: The most important thing you can ever be onstage is
yourself.**

> I still get choked-up talking about it. Because when I got
> that, I just knew there was nothing I couldn't do. What my
> audience was saying to me was, "What we see, we want!" It
> was a major transformation, internally, for me. As my
> daughters would say, "It was soooooooo cool!"

Just like when Sally Fields said at the Oscars, "You like me, you
really like me!" when Kennedy saw that the audience liked her for
who she really was, it was a huge breakthrough for her.

One of the most important facts that beginning speakers fail
to grasp is that audiences truly want the speaker to succeed. They
want you to be good, if for no other reason than they don't want

to have to sit through a bad presentation! Knowing this can go a long way in helping to reduce your speaking fears.

The idea is to come from a place of, "I like my audience and they like me." When you develop this type of winning attitude, speaking can be a blast!

▶ **SECRET #4: When you see the audience as a group of new friends who are rooting for you to succeed, speaking becomes a lot less scary and a lot more fun.**

Goes into Real Estate

When Danielle first got married back in 1964, at the age of nineteen, motherhood and raising a large family were the main things on her mind. However, after having four children over the next seven years, she suddenly found herself having to go back to work while she was six months pregnant with her fifth child. It was then that she decided to go into the real estate field:

> I went into real estate sales because it seemed like something I could do right out of my house. Over a four-year period, I built up a 100 percent referral business with the intention of just supporting my family. And suddenly, the business started booming.

> I had no intention of having it turn into some kind of legendary career. It got to the point where I was asked to write a book and to share my success with others.

> That book, *How to List and Sell Real Estate,* which I co-wrote with Warren Jamison, has had a fifteen-year shelf life and has gone through six printings and sold 500,000 copies.

Gets Masters Degree

Like all high achievers, Kennedy strives to constantly hone her skills:

> When I saw the power of that book, and what it did for me, I went back to school. I spent $30,000 to go to USC to get a masters degree in writing. It took me five years.

> I went every Tuesday night—sometimes I had to fly a red-eye
> to get to the east coast to do the following day's presenta-
> tion. And it was the greatest thing I did. My writing skills
> went from a four to an eight, because I was forced to write
> plays, non-fiction, fiction, short stories, etc. When you write
> all that stuff and then you come back to non-fiction, your
> non-fiction is tight.

While many people Kennedy's age would have told themselves
they were too old or that it cost too much to go back to college,
she didn't let these excuses stop her. Her goal was to become a
better writer, and if that meant taking five years of her life and
spending thirty grand, then that's what it took.

As Kennedy points out below, regardless of our age we must
never stop learning and growing:

> Adult development is an ongoing process. Learning doesn't
> stop just because you're out of school. You continue to
> learn from mentors, the customers you serve, those you
> love, and those who betray you. Adult development contin-
> ues until death.

▶ **SECRET #5: Personal growth never stops! You want to constantly
develop and hone your skills in all aspects of life right up until the
day the good Lord calls your number!**

Success Attracts Luck

When Kennedy sold her first book, she attributed it to having
"lucked out" because she didn't even have a literary agent—Prentice Hall came to her!

While I would agree that it was certainly a bit of good fortune, the fact was that if she hadn't been out there making things
happen, working hard, and developing a reputation as a top pro-
ducer in her field, it would have never happened. I say this because it has been my experience that if you're out there every day
working hard and "putting out good stuff," the universe will respond accordingly. So, yes, while "the gods of good fortune"

may occasionally throw a bone your way, in most cases it's because somewhere down the line *you* planted the seeds for its occurrence.

The Phone Call That Got Kennedy a Six-Page Article in *Personal Selling Power* Magazine

"Never, at any point in your career, say, 'I don't make calls anymore.'"
DANIELLE KENNEDY

Like Mike Ferry, Kennedy thinks it's important that, no matter how big you get, you never stop being involved in the marketing aspect of your business. Here's an example of the good things that can happen when you are willing to pick up the phone and talk to people, especially if they have seen you speak:

> In 1994, I spoke to the Sales and Marketing Executive's International, in Norfolk, Virginia. Afterward, I got a list of everybody that was in that audience—200 names. I "warm called" those people within the next thirty days myself. The presentation went well, so as soon as I got on the phone and said, "Hi, this is Danielle Kennedy" they went, "Oh, gosh, we enjoyed your presentation so much, blah blah blah." Out of those calls I got ten jobs, with sponsors, in ten regions of the country.

> One of those names on that list was Gerhard Gschwandtner, the editor of *Personal Selling Power* magazine. He'd been in the audience. I started talking about my theatrical keynote. He said, "I'd like to do a six-page story on it." Nine months later it came out and I got more business. And it all came from my calling the man. Never, at any point in your career, say, "I don't make calls anymore."

The key, as Danielle points out, is that she jumped on the list of names while it was still hot, i.e., while she was still fresh in their minds:

> When you have a targeted audience who has heard you, and a copy of the list [of audience members], and you call them during that "impact range of time"—the next thirty to forty days—it's absolutely amazing what can come out of that.

▶ **SECRET #6: Whenever possible, get the list of names and phone numbers of the people in your audience and then call them within thirty to forty days of your presentation. Doing this can lead to good things that you never even imagined.**

Writes a Column for *Entrepreneur* Magazine

The old saying that once you make your first million, the second is easier, pertains to many things in life. Once Kennedy had written her first magazine article, others began to come her way:

> In 1994, I was asked by *Entrepreneur* magazine to write an article on my ten favorite books on sales and marketing for their August issue. I did it and they loved it. I got a call the next month and they wanted to make me a paid columnist! This forces me to write every month—to meet a deadline— and it keeps me sharp. Writing is like speaking—if you don't do it often, you start to loose the edge.

Speaks on Many Topics

Like all the speakers in this book, Kennedy has a variety of topics that she addresses:

> In addition to my speaking on management, marketing, productivity, and motivation, I do a program on fitness. I'm a former amateur figure skater, a runner, and am affiliated with the International Dance Exercise Association.

I talk about fitness for the business person, particularly for working parents, who have so much stress. They have to have a decent nutritional program and exercise plan.

I also have a spiritual side to my programs, because there's more to life than just the material things. There comes a time when you've made a lot of money or have had a great deal of success, and you say, "Hey, there's got to be more than this!" I try to show people that they need to tap into the spiritual, emotional, and the mental side of their lives.

Master One Garden Before Planting Others

It's important to remember that while Kennedy has made the crossover into other fields, such as insurance and banking, originally she specialized in speaking to only the real estate industry.

That's why she recommends to new speakers that they work hard to become well-known within one industry before trying to tackle other markets. She calls this "growing your garden with a single niche":

> Rosita Perez came from the social work industry; Patricia Fripp came from the beauty salon industry, Mary Wilson came from the insurance industry. First you perfect a single niche and get really good at it, and then you gain the credibility to talk to other industries.

This is what happened to Kennedy. Most people in the real estate field are networkers by nature, so when they would talk to their insurance agent or their loan agent, they would mention how great Kennedy was, etc. Eventually, they started calling her to speak at their meetings and conventions.

▶ **SECRET #7: By making a name for yourself in one industry, that will often give you the credibility necessary to get work in other industries.**

What Once Terrified Her Now Energizes Her

"I want to give them every last drop of blood and energy I've got! When I'm finished speaking, I'm completely spent."
DANIELLE KENNEDY

While it may seem hard to believe, especially after you've seen her speak, there was a time when Kennedy was terrified of public speaking. Yes, I know, she had no problem talking to people as a child or competing on the debate team in college. But remember, she has many sides to her, including a painfully shy one. While this may sound strange, it's actually more common than most people realize. For instance, when he wasn't performing, Johnny Carson was known to be painfully shy, especially at parties and other public functions. Likewise, when it came to standing up in front of a group of strangers and doling out advice on how to run a successful real estate business, Kennedy initially found it a very difficult thing for her to do:

> When I first started speaking, I was scared to death. I tell the story of how I used to go to the bathroom fifteen minutes before every speech, and as soon as I got off the stage I was back in the bathroom. Now I'm so at home and relaxed with my audiences that, when I'm up there, I feel kind of like Mother Earth; speaking gives me such a peaceful, happy, contented, energetic, and satisfying feeling.

> I could be absolutely exhausted before I start speaking, but during the speech, I'm energized by my audience. I want to tell them everything I know that's worked for me. I want to give them every last drop of blood and energy I've got! When I'm finished speaking, I'm completely spent. When the meeting planner tries to talk to me while driving me to the airport, I'll be out like a little kid, because I've given it 100 percent.

▶ **SECRET #8: Speaking can be a powerful experience when you realize it's a symbiotic relationship: You draw strength and energy from your audience just as they draw strength and energy from you.**

Being a Good Speaker Means Being Good at Living

In her typically outspoken and passionate way, Danielle explains why it's important to share with your audience something that's worthy of their time:

> I think the really good speakers are excellent at living. It has a lot to do with life experiences; they have allowed life to saturate them. Many people want to become a speaker, but what the hell have they got to say to an audience!?

> What gives me something to say is that I've immersed myself in life. Raising kids, struggling with a sales career, going through a divorce and re-marriage—these are the experiences that make a good speaker!

> When you mix life knowledge with passion, vulnerability, and a willingness to be authentic, you are going to be a dynamic speaker. It's not the "hocus-pocus, I make five million dollars a month, drive a Rolls-Royce" kind of bullshit!

> That kind of stuff doesn't fly with people. You look at a Wayne Dyer or a Leo Buscaglia, or even a Lee Iacocca, or a Cavett Robert. These guys are walking the tightrope with you—they put themselves on the line.

Like these great speakers, you too want to draw on your own life experiences—the good, the bad, and the ugly—to give your presentations richness and scope.

▶ **SECRET #9: The more varied and diverse life experiences you've had (the failures and setbacks as well as the successes), the more depth and wisdom you are able to bring to your presentations.**

"Who'd Have Thought You Would Have Achieved What You Have? You Were a Sick Little Scaredy-Cat!"

Not exactly the words of encouragement you'd expect a mother to tell her child. But Kennedy's mom (now we know where Danny got her outspokenness from) was simply telling it like it was. Says Kennedy:

> I was an only child and I hated it. I was very self-conscious and very, very shy as a little kid. My mother just said to me the other day, "Who'd have thought that you would have achieved what you have? You were a sick little scaredy-cat." And I was. I had pneumonia and I was sick constantly until I was twenty-one years old. Now I'm like a bull.

I included this excerpt from our interview because it demonstrates that people do change. Even if we didn't "have it all together" at one point in our life, it doesn't mean we can't turn things around and achieve success at a later point. I think this is something we all need to be reminded of from time to time.

Success and Self-Doubt: Can You Have Both?

While millions of Americans suffer from bouts of depression and self-doubt, Kennedy was the only speaker I interviewed that would openly admit to having to deal with this:

> This self-doubt has always been a part of me. As I get older, I'm able to cope with it and accept it a little better. Exercise helps me tremendously. If I wasn't running, if I wasn't exercising, I would have some real heavy-duty depression. But, because I run four times a week, I get those endorphins going and I get a natural high. That has helped me overcome my own personal insecurities and self-doubt, which have been

very much a part of me since I was a baby. Letting that play-ful, joyful side of me come out has also helped heal me.

How to Use Your Self-Doubt to Spur You on to Greatness

Rather than let her flaws and self-doubt hold her back, Kennedy thinks of them as pluses, and uses them to spur herself on:

> I think that the self-doubting is part of what makes me good at what I do. I say that because I think one of the things that I bring to my work, and which the audience gets, is a lot of humility and a real sense that I'm full of flaws; that I'm just my own silly self. A lot of that comes from the insecurity.

> I think that is also true of an actor. That insecurity is almost the driving force of what makes them good. If they didn't have that, they would not have that dimension that people love, that vulnerability.

Obviously, Kennedy isn't talking about dumping all your prob-lems on the audience—that would be a turnoff. Rather, she's talk-ing about letting them see you, "warts and all." This isn't always easy, as our first reaction is to only want to let people see our good qualities. However, done in an honest and unpretentious way, it can be quite effective.

I remember once seeing a woman get up to give a speech at a Toastmaster's meeting. She looked at the audience, smiled ner-vously, and said, "Gosh, I'm nervous!" We all laughed, and then she laughed, too. You could see that immediately she felt better for having "let the cat out of the bag," and she went on to give a fine speech.

▶ **SECRET #10: Instead of hiding your flaws, let your audience see them in an open and honest way. While this requires taking a risk, it makes you more human, and people will be able to relate to you at a much deeper level than if you only show them your "I'm so cool" side.**

Reporting Your Life Experience Can Help Others

In January of 1996, I called Kennedy's office to ask her if she had any additional thoughts about the speaking business she would like to add to her chapter in this book. She said, "Well, I'm speaking at the Los Angeles chapter of NSA on the ninth; why don't you come watch my presentation—I'm sure I'll have lots to say!" So, early that Saturday morning, I went to the Wyndham Garden Hotel in the City of Commerce, where the Greater Los Angeles chapter of the National Speaker's Association meets. Danielle was her usual high-energy and effervescent self, and in addition to telling us all about the high points of her career as well as all the bumps along the way, she closed her presentation by singing and dancing one of her original tunes from her one-woman show.

As I stood clapping along with the other ninety or so speakers, I thought about one thing in particular that she had said during her presentation that really made an impression on me: Our job as speakers is to report our life experience, our story, to our audience. That, along with a shot of encouragement, really is the best gift we can give. Here, in her own words, is a portion of what Kennedy said that morning to NSA:

> I really feel that my goal as a speaker and teacher is to report my story and to make it integrate into your history so that, together, we can lighten each other's load. Everybody speaks from their history. That's why if you try to speak from somebody else's history, you're a fraud, a phony!

▶ **SECRET #11: By sharing your story and unique life experiences with others, you help to lighten their load by showing how we're all not so different.**

When Bigger Isn't Always Better

Something that many entrepreneurs fail to realize is that running a big office, while it sounds exciting, can bring with it a host of problems. First, there's the large overhead, which eats substantially into your profits, and secondly, there's having to look after all your employees. As you're about to read, Kennedy discovered that it was when her company was at its biggest that she was having the least amount of fun running it:

> The time I was the unhappiest, in terms of my business, was when my company was grossing the most amount of money and I had the largest number of employees. Everybody in the speaking business at my level had a marketing team, so I thought I had to have a marketing team. One day I was driving down the freeway and I realized how miserable I was. I didn't enjoy coming home from being on the road and having to orchestrate ten other people's lives.
>
> I had become hard and angry. And those were the years we grossed the most! But here's the funny part: They weren't the years we netted the most.
>
> Now we have our operation down pretty clean and tight. There are just three of us: my husband and I, and my daughter. My son works part-time, and we take in temp help from time to time. We are netting more today than we were when we were grossing in the millions!

Money Allows You to Buy Time

> Now, I tell myself that I'm buying time. That's really the value of money. Time with the people we love, time doing the things we love. Every time a speaking assignment comes in, I have to look at what kind of time I will be buying.

▶ **SECRET #12: The real value of having money is that it allows you to buy time—time to do the things you love.**

Tom Hopkins: Mentor and Friend

Having someone who believes in you and can give you guidance and advice when you need it can be invaluable when you're just starting out on the road to success. Often, the journey is lonely and obstacle-filled, and having someone in your corner who has "been there" can make a world of difference. Kennedy has such a person in her corner, and he just happens to be one of the other speakers in this book:

> Tom Hopkins is my mentor. He's the one who originally heard me speak and got me going with the realtors. He said to me, "You've got to do this; the women and the men both need you. There's nobody filling the void in the business world. The women out there are growing in numbers and they need a spokesperson. You've got to be it!"

Obviously, Hopkins was successful in persuading Kennedy, and I'm sure both are glad that he was. If you don't have a mentor, you should seriously think about finding one. One way to accomplish this is by attending networking meetings in your industry. When you meet someone who is more experienced than you, get their business card and ask if you can call them. Assuming the chemistry is right, you can slowly build this initial phone call into a relationship. However, be respectful of their time. This person is most likely very busy and the last thing they need is somebody pestering them. The way to do it is to slowly, over time, stay in touch with them.

A fellow speaker and friend of mine named Terri Sjodin used this strategy to get the CEO of a major insurance company to be her mentor. Initially, she would just call him up every so often to let him know what she was doing. Pretty soon, he began calling her to see how her projects were going. This soon led to lunch meetings and now she has an open door to call him whenever she needs his advice.

▶ **SECRET #13: Having a mentor can often take years off your learning curve. Because they've "been there," they can give you invaluable advice and support.**

Going in with the Right Attitude

Danielle reminds us that if we go into every presentation knowing that we have a lot of "good stuff" to give our audience, and that they're going to love it, things will usually work out just fine:

I'm going to spend two days in Boston with a group of women who are fashion consultants—home-based businesses. I've done this program for Discovery Toys, and I've done it for Tupperware. It's going to be fabulous—I love these audiences! And I know, going in, that I have a lot to give. See, if you walk in feeling real doubtful, it may mean that you're questioning what the gift is you have to give them. For me, I know it's lots of stuff from the trenches.

▶ **SECRET #14: Go into every presentation with an attitude of positive expectency. You do this by being confident that what you have to give 'em is good stuff, that it can help them, and that they're going to love it!**

Have an Outline, but Be Flexible

Whenever you arrive somewhere to give a presentation, remember to stay open. What I mean by this is that although you have an outline of what you want to cover during your speech, you might pick up on some things just before you go on that could make your talk more relevant and interesting to your audience. Says Kennedy:

When I speak, I have an outline of what I want to speak on, but if I find after mingling with the people before my speech that they are in a completely different place than what the meeting planner told me, I will combine what I was going to speak on with what I found out when I got there.

Why Quality Should Permeate All of Your Marketing Materials

While it's true that we judge people by the clothes they wear, it's also true that in the speaking business, meeting planners and agents judge you by the quality of your marketing materials. That is why, as Kennedy reminds us, we should always put out the highest quality brochures and videos that we can afford:

We have very fancy packaging because you get to a point in your career where you really have to have the materials that are of equal magnitude to what you're putting out there. You have to have that beautiful video demo and the awesome audio packaging, because if you're really delivering quality work, you're pretty stupid if you don't have the packaging that goes along with it.

The Best Way to Market Yourself

It may not be very high-tech (although it *can* be if people use e-mail to do it!), but I couldn't agree more with Danielle when she says that word-of-mouth is still the very best form of marketing:

The all-time best way that's been proven to me to market yourself is word-of-mouth—where somebody hears you, they're touched by you, and they go out and tell somebody else. It's like a contagious, infectious, positive growth that just comes from excellent work. It's very subtle, almost an underground kind of thing, but it's very powerful.

Even great big companies use word-of-mouth. Yes, they have all that fancy-shmancy stuff, but it's just good, old-fashioned word-of-mouth that really brings 'em in. And it can make or break your career.

▶ SECRET #15: The very best form of marketing is word-of-mouth. It has the power to either make or break your career.

Questions New (and Seasoned) Speakers Should Ask Themselves

Whether you're just starting out in the speaking business, or have been speaking for twenty years, here are some questions that Kennedy recommends you ask yourself:

What am I passionate about?
What do I want to do?
What are the skills I possess?
What's the message that I have?
Who do I want to give it to?

Of course, the most important question you can ask yourself is, "Why do I want to be a speaker?" You see, there are right reasons and wrong reasons for wanting to be a speaker.

The Right Stuff

I can always tell when a speaker is speaking for "the right reasons." And that is when they're not doing it to gratify their ego or to foist their one-sided opinions on others, but rather, to genuinely help people. Maybe they went through a difficult time in their life and came out of it a better person and now they want to show others how to do the same. Or, maybe they figured out how to run a successful business and they want to share what they've learned with others.

Kennedy feels very strongly that it's important that you are clear on your reasons for wanting to be a speaker:

> There are healthy and unhealthy reasons for wanting to be a speaker. I feel having a calling to speak is a healthy reason, a desire to serve others. However, if we speak just to hear ourselves talk, it's exhibitionism. There are people who want to become speakers because they want to hear themselves talk. Speaking only for profit is another unhealthy reason, and so is because becoming a speaker looks easy.
>
> When gymnast Peter Vidmar does the Pommel horse, he makes it look easy. And skier Peekaboo Street makes it look pretty easy going down hill. When it looks easy, know that the past was filled with painful failure so that the future could be a success. Are you willing to pay the price?

In my mind there's really only one reason for wanting to be a speaker: to make a difference in the world while you're here. True, being well-paid for our time is certainly a great aspect of being a professional speaker (once you make it to a certain level), and as Mike Ferry pointed out in his chapter, we need to run a profitable business. However, if your main reason for being a speaker is to get rich, I think that over the long run you're not going to be very successful.

This leads us to our next point, which we should never forget:

Speaking Is a Privilege

Says Kennedy:

> What a wonderful privilege it is to stand up before an audience. We have to feel that gratitude before we step up onto the platform. Gratitude is the thing that when I feel it, I do my best work. And from gratitude comes abundance. No abundance or prosperity can come into our house without a grateful heart.
>
> Every time you get to a presentation, check out your gratitude level and do whatever it takes . . . a visualization process, thinking about people you are especially grateful for, or other speaking engagements that you've done in the past that have warmed the cockles of your heart. Really get into it before you get on the platform. It sure has helped me tremendously over the years.

▶ **SECRET #16: From gratitude comes abundance. No abundance or prosperity can come into our house without a grateful heart.**

The Core of Kennedy's Message

While Danielle speaks on a number of different topics, the core message of all her talks is, "If I can do it, so can you":

> My message is that I'm just like you and if I did it you can do it. I think that gives people hope. That's the whole point of what we speakers do. Giving people hope and a belief in themselves so they walk out feeling better about themselves.
>
> Not, "Oh god, she's awesome. I could never be like that." No, I don't go for that. See, I love it when they say to me, "I feel so good about myself after listening to you." To me, that's the greatest compliment in the world. I think people are badgered and beaten down every day of their life, and if they go someplace and they can reestablish and restore and rehabilitate some of their own self-worth . . . You can't put

a price tag on that! You can't pay a speaker enough money for something like that. It's the greatest gift we can give to society.

That's why I love parenting. See, in parenting, that's the greatest gift you can give your kids—their self-worth. If you raise a kid and the kid really ends up believing in themselves, and is self-motivated, you did something incredibly special.

▶ **SECRET #17: Making your audience feel good about themselves and about coming to your presentation can be just as important as the content you give them.**

Connecting in South Africa

I want to conclude Kennedy's chapter with this moving story about her experience in South Africa:

The teaching end of being a speaker is what I love the most. I get a lot of satisfaction from working with the audience and helping them get "ah-hahs" that will help them in their own lives. I feel very grateful and humble to have the opportunity to be a communicator.

One experience that really touched me was in 1984 in South Africa. I was on a speaking tour sponsored by *Cosmopolitan* magazine and I was pregnant with my sixth child at the time. The program was called "Women Who Win," and during my stay I spoke to thousands of women.

In addition, I spoke to about four hundred kids who had made it through high school. This is a very big deal over there, because most of the kids drop out of school by age eight. They live on the poverty belt and had to overcome tremendous challenges. For example, many had to share a bedroom with eight other children! These kids had just finished school, so I brought them all copies of my book, *Supernatural Selling,* which is basically about how to promote yourself.

Because I was this strange, white American woman coming to speak to them, at first, the children were extremely shy. Right before I began to speak, their teacher said to them, "Why don't you sing to Danielle." They began to sing and chant this beautiful song about the crucifixion of Christ. Even though it wasn't in English, it was so moving, it brought tears to my eyes.

After they finished that song, they went into this kind of rock-soul song. Well, I love to dance, so I started dancing. Suddenly, all these kids stood up and they started dancing! We all went into a sort of tribal bonding. They just went crazy when they saw this pregnant woman onstage dancing.

So, that's how I began my speech; not with words, but with movement! I went on to praise them for their accomplishments and then I taught them how to sell and promote themselves. They laughed so easily and were so alive—their eyes were popping out of their head! I realized God put me there, not for them, but for me.

Kennedy's Philosophy for Life

I really think we all come here with different kinds of gifts. I think our job while we're here is to find out what our gifts are, to develop them and then give them away.

How Danielle Kennedy would like to be remembered:

"She was peaceful, had a loving relationship with God, and left something of herself she was given to pass on."
DANIELLE KENNEDY

Danielle Kennedy's Success Secrets Summary

SECRET #1: Always walk into a room like you own the place—not like you're conceited, but like you belong and you're glad to be there.

SECRET #2: Audiences don't demand that you be perfect, but they do demand that you be real and authentic with them.

SECRET #3: The most important thing you can ever be onstage is yourself.

SECRET #4: When you see the audience as a group of new friends who are rooting for you to succeed, speaking becomes a lot less scary and a lot more fun.

SECRET #5: Personal growth never stops: You want to constantly develop and hone your skills in all aspects of life right up until the day the good Lord calls your number!

SECRET #6: Whenever possible, get the list of names and phone numbers of the people in your audience and then call them within thirty to forty-five days of your presentation. Doing this can lead to good things that you never even imagined.

SECRET #7: By making a name for yourself in one industry, that will often give you the credibility necessary to get work in other industries.

SECRET #8: Speaking can be a powerful experience when you realize it's a symbiotic relationship: You draw strength and energy from your audience just as they draw strength and energy from you.

SECRET #9: The more varied and diverse life experiences you've had (the failures and setbacks as well as the successes), the more depth and wisdom you are able to bring to your presentations.

SECRET #10: Instead of hiding your flaws, let your audience see them in an open and honest way. While this requires taking a risk, it makes you more human, and people will be able to relate to you at a much deeper level than if you only show them your "I'm so cool" side.

SECRET #11: By sharing your story and unique life experiences with others, you help to lighten their load by showing how we're all not so different.

SECRET #12: The real value of having money is that it allows you to buy time—time to do the things you love.

SECRET #13: Having a mentor can often take years off your learning curve. Because they've "been there," they can give you invaluable advice and support.

SECRET #14: Go into every presentation with an attitude of positive expectancy. You do this by being confident that what you have to give 'em is good stuff, that it can help them, and that they're going to love it!

SECRET #15: The very best form of marketing is word-of-mouth. It has the power to either make or break your career!

SECRET #16: From gratitude comes abundance. No abundance or prosperity can come into our house without a grateful heart.

SECRET #17: Making your audience feel good about themselves and about coming to your presentation can be just as important as the content you give them.

CHAPTER TWELVE

BORN: June 20, 1945
BIRTHPLACE: Orange County, California

Mike Ferry

*"I had a simple policy—I called twenty-five people,
five days a week for two years, and asked them
to hire me. That's how I started my business."*

▼

HE'S been called brash, arrogant, and cocky. Some say that at the very least he's too direct, while others call him down right abrasive. But love him or hate him, nobody is bigger in the real estate training industry than Mike Ferry, whose company, Mike Ferry Productions, does over ten million dollars a year in business. In addition, he holds the record for selling more product in one day than any other person in the seminar industry: $750,000 at one event!

Like John McEnroe in tennis, Ferry is one of the best in the world at what he does, and he's not afraid to tell you exactly the way he sees it. In an era when many speakers are more concerned with not offending their audience than with speaking the truth, Mike Ferry is a breath of fresh air:

> I'm told I'm too abrasive, that I'm controversial, that I pick on people too much. As a professional speaker, one of the things we have to do is find a way to move the people we're talking to. Move them to do something! I'm not very comfortable standing up there telling people that if we just love each other a lot we'll all be better people. I think Walt Disney said it best: "A burr underneath the saddle makes the horse run faster." I believe that very strongly.
>
> I do stimulate people. Either people walk away happy or mad after one of my programs. Usually, nobody walks away from one of my programs neutral. Personally, I don't think I'm very abrasive, although I'm very strong in my approach. I don't put up with a lot of incompetence, which I see every single day. And I'll confront the incompetence of an audience if I think they're not doing what they have to do.

Like Ferry, if you want to be an effective speaker, you absolutely have to care more about getting your audience to take action than with getting them to like you. Of course, for most us, this is not an easy thing to do. After all, we've been taught since childhood to avoid confrontation and to "not make waves." And thus, it's in our nature to want people to like us. However, as a professional speaker, you must remember that you have a job to do. You're not being paid to be liked, you're being paid to communicate a message to the best of your ability. Presumably, you were hired bcause you have something of value to say to the audience.

▶ **SECRET #1: As a professional speaker, you're not being paid to be liked, but to communicate a message.**

In Mike's case, he's figured out how to successfully list and sell real estate. Since many real estate offices have salespeople who are simply not producing what they should be for whatever reasons, they are happy to pay Ferry his fee. This is because they know that the information he will provide to their people will more than off-set his price.

However, Ferry is very smart. He knows a little bit about human behavior and he understands that if he were to just walk in and tell the people, "Here's what you need to do, blah, blah, blah," they would listen, nod their heads in agreement and then tomorrow go back to their same old mediocre ways. To help pre-vent this, he talks to his audience as if he expects them not only to listen and take notes, but to go out and *actually put his ideas into action*. In other words, while Ferry knows that his audience has certain expectations about him, he has certain expectations of his audiences:

> What happens is that we sometimes get real lax in our think-ing. Then, because of that, we get lax in our activities. I be-lieve that if I'm being paid by your company to come in and work with your staff, I think that there have to be expecta-tions—not only in what I do, what I talk about, and what I deliver, but in what they do, what they talk about, and what they deliver. Therefore, if we don't both have expectations we're not going to accomplish anything.

> Listen, if you're going to come to a program, pay attention, sit there, and do what you're suppose to do! Learn the mate-rial; if it's being taught to you, there's a reason for it. And then go execute it.

▶ **SECRET #2: Just as your audience has certain expectations about you, you should have certain expectations of your audience in terms of what you expect them to do with your material.**

Getting Your Audience
to Take Action

---

*"People live in a fantasy; I think that's the problem.
And a good speaker is there to jolt them out of the fantasy
and into the reality of what life's all about."*
MIKE FERRY

Even with your expectations, there are still going to be those in your audience who won't take action on your ideas, no matter how much they could help them. Because of this, Ferry tries to focus on those individuals in his audience who are really committed to producing results:

> The biggest thing is to try and find which people in the group are going to do something. If you take an audience of five hundred people, you know that only a small percentage of them will actually do anything really concrete or take any kind of action. The thing that goes through my mind while I'm speaking is that I have to make them do something. I'm constantly trying to figure out how to get the audience to take action.

▶ **SECRET #3: Ask yourself before every presentation, "How can I get this audience to take action?"**

> If we had an audience of one hundred people, we'd probably get twenty or thirty who would take some kind of action immediately. There would be another twenty or thirty who would fight me every step of the way. And then we would probably have another forty to fifty in the middle who wouldn't know what happened after they left!

> People live in a fantasy; I think that's the problem. And a good speaker is there to jolt them out of the fantasy and into the reality of what life's all about.

Why More People Don't
Take Action

When asked why it is that more people don't take action on his (or other speakers') ideas, Ferry says:

> I don't think that people really want to do well. I think people say they want to do well, but I don't think they really do. I think it's easy to sit back and watch somebody do something and think, "I'd like to do that too." But how badly do you want it? What price will you pay to get it? Will you fight for it? Will you go out and work for it? Most people won't.

It's true. Most people say they want to achieve certain things in life, but when it comes down to actually going out and doing it, they have "a good" excuse: I don't have enough time; I don't have enough money; I'm too fat; my skin is the wrong color; my father didn't love me enough; I don't have the education, etc.

Yet, for every excuse we have for not achieving our goals, there is somebody out there who has achieved what we want and they did so under far more difficult circumstances. Didn't anyone tell Heather Whitestone that deaf people don't become Miss Americas? Perhaps Colonel Sanders forgot that you simply don't go out and start your own chain of restaurants at age 65. And what could Oprah Winfrey possibly have been thinking when she became the most powerful (and richest) woman in the TV industry?

▶ **SECRET #4: For every excuse you have for not achieving your goals, someone else has done it under far more difficult circumstances.**

How Ferry Got Started in Speaking

In 1963, when Mike was eighteen years old, he attended a political rally at San Jose College. Although he didn't agree with the speaker's views, he was amazed by the man's ability to hold a crowd spellbound for two hours and work them into a lather. Says Ferry:

> Afterward, I went up to him and asked how he was able to speak for two hours without having any notes in his hands. He said, "If you believe in yourself and what you have to say, it's easy to talk."

After college, Mike got a job working for the Nightingale-Conant Corporation. While he liked the public speaking that his job required him to do, he found that he didn't enjoy giving motivational talks, which is what he was mostly giving at the time:

> I never felt comfortable with motivational type talks, although I was doing them every day, because I didn't feel that people could leave the program and have specific things to do. There wasn't any kind of action plan in the motivational talk. I felt that teaching people something was more important than telling them how to live their life right.

After four years at Nightingale-Conant, Mike became their national training director and was responsible for the sales activity of thirteen hundred people. Feeling that he wanted to go into business for himself, in 1973 Ferry left that job to go into real estate sales in Huntington Beach, California. There, he knocked on more than six thousand doors during one ninety-day period, listed as many as fourteen homes in a single month, and sold over 180 homes in eighteen months! Not surprisingly, he was named "top salesperson" three consecutive times.

Ferry Goes into the Real Estate Training Field

It was at this point that Mike decided it was time to start his own training company. After looking at five industries—stocks and bonds, insurance, direct sales, car sales, and real estate—it was obvious to him that his strength and expertise were in the real estate field. So, at age twenty-five, he started Mike Ferry Productions and quickly began to make a name for himself in the real estate training field.

The first thing he did was to go where the other successful speakers hung out, which was (and still is) the National Speakers Association. Although in those days it was nowhere near as big as it is today, he knew that if he wanted to be the best, he had to learn from the best. Says Mike:

> When I went to all the speakers meetings, I would go up and down the rows asking, "How do you sell yourself? How do you sell yourself? How do you sell yourself?" And they'd say things like, "I hand out brochures," or "I mail out flyers," or "I register with booking agencies." It was interesting to me that nobody had said, "I call people and ask them to hire me."!

Ferry's Twenty-Five-Calls-per-Day Marketing Plan

"Honest to God, you could be the worst telephone person in the world and if you make twenty-five calls a day, somebody is going to hire you!"
MIKE FERRY

Ferry realized that if he waited for someone to pick up the phone and call him to give a speech, as he puts it, "he could have waited for the rest of his natural life." So he developed a strategy which he says is responsible for getting his company off the ground:

> I had a simply policy—I called twenty-five people, five days a week for two years, and asked them to hire me. That's how I started my business.

> If you call twenty-five people every day to hire you, you will get jobs in spite of yourself! And I did it, so I proved it. It's all a numbers game—twenty-five calls a day, five days a week for the next couple of years. You might be thinking, "Well, I'm a little beyond that." Hey, I ain't; no way, if it means getting paid and building your business.

▶ **SECRET #5: If you call twenty-five people every day to hire you, you will get jobs in spite of yourself.**

Ferry was so committed to making his twenty-five calls per day that he even made them on days he gave a seminar:

> The days that I had a six-hour seminar, I made my calls before it in the morning, at noon at the break, and afterward. And when I was on the road I would do it from a phone booth just after getting off the plane. I would call and say, "I'm in Rochester doing a seminar today, and I was wondering if you wanted to hire me for next week?"

Is it any wonder that, with this type of dedication and commitment, Mike Ferry is the number one guy in the real estate training industry? Imagine what your business would be like if you developed this same level of commitment! Perhaps you could be tops in your industry.

In this chapter, Ferry provides you with many of the secrets that he uses to earn over ten million dollars a year! But he can't do it for you. Only *you* can apply these ideas and techniques and put them to work for you on a daily basis to create the kind of results that will make you proud. Ferry made his fortune, and you can make yours too. All you have to do is let go of all the excuses and just go do it.

"Losers blame their circumstances,
winners rise above them."
JOE GRIFFITH

Started Out with Only Two Talks

When Mike first got started, he had only two talks. One was called "How to List Real Estate Property," and the other was called, "How to Sell Real Estate Property." However, combined with his knowledge of sales and his willingness to make twenty-five calls per day, this was more than enough to get things rolling.

A Typical Ferry Sales Call

" . . . that's how you build your business.
You keep calling until your brain falls out."
MIKE FERRY

When he was just starting out, a typical cold call would begin by Ferry calling a real estate office and saying to the office manager, "Hi, my name is Mike Ferry. I'm a professional speaker. Have you been to my seminar before?" Of course, the person would almost always say no, since Ferry was just starting out and hadn't done very many! However, petty details aside, Ferry would continue: "The two topics that I speak on are 'How to List Properties' and 'How to Sell Properties.' With the staff that you have, which of those two topics is most important?" (Even Tom Hopkins would have to admire this alternate-choice question!)

The manager would respond, "Well, probably the one on 'How to List.'" Without missing a beat, Ferry would say, "In the 'How to List' seminar that I do, we cover three things: how to find a prospect, what to say to the prospect, and how to close them. Would that be of interest to your staff?" The slightly overwhelmed manager would respond, "Well, yes, of course." Now Ferry would go in for the close: "When you bring a speaker like me in, do you generally have the staff pay my fee or do you pay it yourself?"

Because this was back when Mike was just starting out and the training market was a lot less crowded than it is today, there was a good chance the manager had never hired a speaker before. So, often he would respond, "Well, I don't know." And wanting to be helpful, Mike would say, "Well, think about it. How many agents do you have?" "I have thirty-five agents." "Well, I charge five hundred dollars," explained Mike. If you divide that by thirty-five, the cost is fifteen dollars per head. Do you want to collect the money in advance or the day I get there?" And bingo, more times than not he'd book the seminar.

Of course, sometimes the manager would put off having to make an immediate decision by saying to Mike, "Could you send me some materials in the mail?" Ferry already had a response prepared:

> "As a matter of fact, I have a number of things I can send. I have an audiotape I can send; I have a brochure I can send; I have referrals I can send. What would you like me to send you? The audiotape. Great. Do you plan on listening to it? Yes. Good. When? The day after you get it. Great. So if I mailed it today, you'll have it by Tuesday. I'll call you Wednesday for an answer, fair enough?"

> And so you've got to call the guy back and keep on selling yourself and selling yourself and selling yourself. It's a pain in the neck, but that's how you build your business. You keep calling until your brain falls out.

Now, if it sounds like Ferry was being kind of pushy with the his prospect, you're right! However, he knew three things: First, that they needed his seminar. His experience in real estate had shown him that most agents don't know how to sell. This isn't a knock on them, it's just that they were never shown how. And Ferry knew that he could be the one to teach them.

Second, he understood that the manager is a human being and, like all human beings, when suddenly faced with making a decision that involves parting with money, they are going to be reluctant—even if it's in their own best interest to go for it. This is just human nature. So, Mike was willing to take the manager by the hand and, step-by-step, show him how he could afford to bring him in—either by paying for it himself or having his staff pay for it.

▶ **SECRET #6: Part of being a good salesperson is taking the prospect by the hand and showing them exactly how they can afford your service or product.**

Third and perhaps most importantly, Ferry knew that if he couldn't sell himself to the real estate companies, then he had no business trying to teach their agents how to be effective sales people.

When You're First Starting Out, You Should Be Your Number One Marketing Person

---

"If you are not already a good salesperson, you should become one. Because the best person to sell you is you."
MIKE FERRY

One of the questions that Ferry is frequently asked by beginning speakers is: "Should I hire somebody to do my marketing for me?" Ferry emphatically states:

> *No!* Because they don't know what you do well enough. So many speakers are waiting for someone to market them. My suggestion is: Sell yourself! You know you, you know your product, and you know your seminar. You're the one who should be the most excited about it—so call people!
>
> Spend all of your time selling yourself, because being a speaker is being a salesperson. If you can't sell an audience on doing what they're supposed to do, it probably means you haven't sold yourself.

▶ **SECRET #7: If you can't sell an audience on doing what they're supposed to do, it probably means you haven't sold yourself.**

> However, if you can sell yourself on sitting down and calling people to try and get them to hire you, making a good presentation to them, and asking them to buy you, then you can sell an audience on what they should be doing. I did this for about three or four years. Eventually, I had a database of about five hundred to six hundred people who would hire me.

Of course, once you have a achieved a certain level of success in the industry and people know who you are, then you can turn your marketing over to others. That way, you can spend your time creating new seminars and products. Says Ferry:

I have fourteen people marketing me and our various programs full-time. Cavett Robert made a great statement when he said, "A lot of people are great at marketing themselves, but they really have nothing to say, and yet they get hired. A lot of people have great things to say, but don't know how to market themselves so they can't get hired." I kind of took a combination of both of those things. I say, "Have great things to say, get great results, then market yourself like crazy."

A Near-Disaster in Rochester

When Mike was just getting started, he would carry a small box around with all his leads in it. One day he was sitting in a phone booth at the airport in Rochester, New York, making phone calls for an hour and a half. Suddenly, he heard his plane being called. He jumped up, grabbed his coat and his carry-on luggage, and ran to catch the plane. It was only when he was buckled in his seat and the plane was taking off that he suddenly realized, to his horror, that he had left his lead box—which contained the name, address and phone number of every prospect he had—in the phone booth! Luckily for Mike, he had put one of his business cards on the front of the box. A man found the box, saw his name and address on it, and mailed it back to him! Mike says the guy saved his life, and that whenever he finds someone's wallet or dayplanner, he pops it into an envelope and mails it back to the owner, because he knows exactly how much it will mean to them.

Ferry's Company Took Off When He Started Treating It Like a Real Business

"If you want to make money, give good service."
MIKE FERRY

Mike is a pragmatist. He is in the business of speaking not because he's trying to change the world, but because he wants to run a profitable business. And he knows that the best way to make a profit is to provide his customers with a quality product. I asked Mike: "If you could go back and change one thing about your career, what would it be?":

> That's a good question. If I had it to do over again, I would have probably developed the organization sooner. I've been doing this for twenty years, and the first four or five years I didn't have an organization of people to support me. It was pretty much myself and a secretary. When I made the decision to develop an organization and to follow strict business rules, my company took off.
>
> If I were to do it over again, instead of starting off being a speaker, I would have been a businessman in the speaking business. The first four years I was a speaker in the speaking business. When I made the switch to being a businessman who spoke, my business took off.

▶ **SECRET #8: You will become successful faster if you think of yourself not as a speaker, but as a business person who speaks.**

Applause or Profit?

One of the questions that Ferry asks beginning speakers is, "What is your purpose for doing a program? Is it to get applause or earn money from the job you do?" Ferry's point is that while getting applause may feel good, it's important that you always remember that you're running a business:

> Speaking is a business, and if you're in business you have to make a profit, and in order to make a profit you have to get paid! You can get all the applause you want, but if you don't get paid, you can't continue to go out and get more applause. You have to remember what your purpose is. My purpose is to run a business. My business is speaking. If I can't make the business profitable, I can't keep it—and I can't keep doing for people what I like to do.

▶ **SECRET #9: While making a difference in the lives of others is wonderful, keep in mind that if your speaking business is not profitable, you're not going to be around long enough to make a difference.**

You Must Be Clear on the Purpose for Your Business

One of the reasons Ferry feels so many speakers fail financially is because they don't have a clear purpose for their business:

> What is the purpose of your business? At my company, Mike Ferry Productions, we have a little tag line after our name that says, The Real Estate Resource Center. That's what we are. If you are a real estate agent, manager, broker, or owner, we can provide you with the seminars, workshops, products, and services necessary for you to succeed. That's what we do. That's our purpose. Saying that your purpose is that you "give talks" isn't good enough. You've got to be much more specific.

▶ **SECRET #10: Be sure you know and can clearly communicate to others the purpose of your business and the services it provides.**

Selling Product

Funny enough, Ferry recorded his first two products before he even began speaking. This was due to some advice he had received from Gunther Klaus and Mike Vance, two veteran speakers whom he greatly admired. They told him just as he was getting into the business that the future of speaking included selling lots of audiotapes, books, and films (video wasn't around yet). So, Ferry recorded two three-hour programs: one on how to sell houses, the other on how to list them. The programs sold for thirty dollars each, or both for fifty dollars.

Obviously, Ferry has come a long way since then. Today he carries twenty-four different products, ranging in price from seventy-five dollars to nine hundred and fifty dollars. Besides selling these items at his seminars, he employs twenty-two full-time sales people who sell his products over the phone, along with his workshops, seminars, and retreats. With a mammoth database that has over ninety-five thousand customers in it, his sales staff brings in an average of ten thousand dollars per day! Says Mike:

> We expect to have days like these because it's part of our business plan.

This is where many entrepreneurs fall short. They fail to build their dreams into their business plans (in fact, many don't even have a business plan), and thus they remain dreams forever. However, if you take the time to write a business plan that has a step-by-step method for how you're going to achieve your dreams, you increase your chances of making it come true a thousandfold.

▶ **SECRET #11: The way you turn the dream of having a $10,000 day in sales into a reality is by building the steps for its achivement right into your business plan.**

Some Things to Keep in Mind When Creating New Products

Ferry asks himself this question when deciding what his next product should be: *What do these people need (and want) to help themselves improve?* Says Mike:

> It's amazing; if you listen to your clients, they will help you create products.

▶ **SECRET #12: When deciding how to come up with new product, ask yourself, "What do my customers need (and want) to help themselves improve?"**

One of your goals as a speaker should be to develop as much quality product as possible. Ferry recommends, like Joel Weldon, that when you create these products you give them great information that they can use immediately as well as giving them specific "how-to" steps.

▶ **SECRET #13: Two things you can do to create product that will sell: 1) Give the buyer more than they asked for, and 2) Give them specific things to do to improve the quality of their life.**

One Hundred Tapes with Danielle Kennedy on Them!?

Many speakers procrastinate putting product out because they feel that it has to be just perfect. However, in the following funny story, Ferry reminds us that in many cases, as much as we hate to admit it, many of the people who buy our product will never listen to all of it anyway:

> When it comes to product, you're going to be your own worst critic. I've seen people record it over and over and over. And they go, "I hate, I hate it, I hate." Just go ahead and record it and sell it to them! Because you know what? Most of them aren't going to listen to it anyway!
>
> Back in 1985, Danielle Kennedy, who is a wonderful speaker, had the same cassette producer as I did. One time, they actually put her message on one hundred of my cassette tapes by mistake! Unbeknownst to me, I went out and sold them at a program. Then, one day, I got a phone call. The person said, "I'm having a problem with one of your cassettes." I said, "What's the problem?" They said, "The voice isn't right." So, they sent it back and after listening to it I realized it was Danny Kennedy!
>
> That's when I found out they had produced one hundred cassettes in my album with her voice. I sold all one hundred albums . . . and only one person called about it! I said, "Hmmm, I guess my great impact isn't as strong as I thought." That'll bring you back down to the ground.

▶ **SECRET #14: Don't use the excuse "it has to be perfect" to keep from putting out product. Once you get it out, you can always go back and improve it when it's time to duplicate (or print) more.**

How to Sell Product from the Platform

"How do you get people to buy your product?
You ask them!"
MIKE FERRY

I'll never forget the day that I finally figured out how to sell my products from the platform. After doing a one-hour presentation for approximately two hundred people, a crowd rushed up to my product table at the side of the room and bought everything I had. Then people literally began shoving checks at me asking me to mail them product.

I have to tell you it was a wonderful feeling, and the first time it happens to you, you'll never forget it. As I drove home, I tried to analyze what I had done differently at this speech versus others I had given. I realized that I had given my audience a tremendous amount of information that could be enormously helpful to them. What's more, I wasn't afraid to tell them so. In other words, for the first time, I stepped into the role of the "expert" for that sixty-minute period and said to my audience, "Look, if you want to get results, this is what you have to do." I didn't do this in a condescending way, but rather, I was extremely sure of myself and I knew that I knew what I was talking about. The audience could sense this, and since they could see the value of having more of this kind of information, they bought up all my product.

▶ **SECRET #15: Audiences will want to buy product from you if they believe that 1) You know what you're talking about, and 2) The information you're providing them with will help make their life better in some significant way.**

Here's a sample of how Ferry sells product from the platform:

"I've been speaking for an hour. How many think that the ideas I've shared with you, if applied, could help your business? Hold up your hand. (The audience raises their hands.) How many would like to have more ideas like this? (Hands go back up.)

> I have a little series here folks (holds up product). There are eighteen cassettes—about twenty hours—with 430 scripts of dialog on them. If you liked what I've been doing here today—I've given you all I can in the time allotted—if you'd like to have a lot more, you can buy the entire package for $145. I would recommend that you buy it; it will help your career dramatically. If you don't buy it, it's okay; but if you do, it will improve what you're doing."

This is Ferry's entire "product pitch" for one product, and it takes less than thirty seconds to deliver. The reason he doesn't have to "hard sell 'em" is because Mike knows that if he does a great job on the platform, they'll want to take more of him home for later.

▶   **SECRET #16: The secret to selling a lot of product is to be so good on the platform that the audience wants to take home more of you for later.**

Says Ferry:

> I did three seminars this week and we made forty thousand dollars in product sales. I like that. Last week we had 350 people and we did sixty-two thousand dollars in product sales. I like that. Why are they buying product? Because they look at what I am saying to them as something that can dramatically help them in their business. And they don't feel they can leave the room without it.
>
> If you do that, you don't have to worry about selling it to them because they'll want it. They don't buy because you make an elaborate presentation. They don't buy because you hammer them to buy. You have to create the kind of topic and the kind of program that is so important that they can't go without it.

Mike feels that too many speakers, even seasoned pros, sometimes spend too much time trying to sell their product from the platform. He recommends that, regardless of the length of your program, the most you should ever spend on selling your products from the platform is five minutes.

▶ **SECRET #17: Regardless of whether you're giving a one-hour, three-hour, or six-hour presentation, the most time you should spend selling your products from the platform is five minutes.**

One final product tip: Remember to set up your product in a nice display before your audience arrives. This means the table should have a tablecloth on it and the products should be nicely laid out and not just stacked in piles. If you make it look appealing to buyers, you'll sell more!

The Speaking Business Isn't for Everyone

Ferry often asks beginning speakers, "Is this really what you want to do with your life?" He points out that flying city to city and staying in a different hotel each week may sound glamorous, but it's a lot of work. You have to set up the room you'll be speaking in, get the lighting fixed because it's often not right, check the sound system, arrange the chairs, find out why half your product didn't arrive, have maintenance turn down the air-conditioning because the room is too cold, and finally, ask the banquet manager why she didn't tell you that they booked a five-hundred-person wedding reception with a live band next door to the room you're speaking in!

First Class, Coach, or Economy?

If saying all this hasn't scared the starry-eyed speaker off yet, then he tells them that if they are going to go into professional speaking, they had better decide which type of speaker they are: first class, coach, or economy. If you're a "first-class" speaker, according to Ferry, you get paid a reasonably high fee and you get hired back a lot because your content is very good. If you're a "coach" speaker, you charge a smaller fee, your content is just okay, and you don't get many dates. And finally, there's an "economy" speaker. That's the person who will speak any-where, anytime, for free. Obviously, the goal of this book is to get you to be a first-class speaker who runs a first-class or-ganization.

▶ **SECRET #18: Decide what kind of speaker/organization you want to run: first class, coach, or economy.**

Getting Control of Your Business

"If you're going to run a business for profit, you have got to get control of your business."
MIKE FERRY

To Ferry, it's all about making money, having fun, and getting con-trol of your business. Some questions he came up with to help you get better control of your business are:

- How often do you want to speak?
- Who do you want to speak to?
- What size audience do you want to speak in front of?
- Will they buy your products?
- What size fee do you want to be paid?
- What can you do to get hired back a second and third time?
- Are you willing to pay the price to get to where you want to be?

Says Ferry:

> Ninety-nine percent of the speakers in this country have no control over these answers. Most are just hoping that they get a speaking job and that it pays. And they'll go anywhere to do it. Now, when you're starting out, that's wonderful. But if you've been in this business ten to twelve years, that ain't so wonderful.

Topic Development

Mike has fifteen different topics he can speak on. Here's why:

> If you only have one topic and the company or association isn't interested in that topic, you're history. You have to have more than one topic. You say, "But I don't have that much more material." *Hey, that's your job!* Go find the material; that's what you're getting paid to do.

▶ **SECRET #19: Add two new topics to your speaking repertoire per year.**

It's also important that you make sure what you're telling your audience is the most current and up-to-date information available on the subject. In other words, if you're still giving the same talk you gave five or ten years ago, it's time to write a new speech! Says Ferry:

> Is what you're doing any good for your audience? Can they take your material and improve their life? If they can't, don't give it! Regardless of whether you're a humorist, a trainer, a motivational speaker, or a seminar leader, part of your job is to put information out that will help your audience do something with it.

Administration of Your Business

To run a profitable speaking business, Ferry recommends that you hire the following people to work for you:

• A Personal Assistant

The reason for hiring this person is so that you can do what you do best: go out and speak and create products and sell yourself. The more time you spend doing paperwork, the less you get paid. You can get a part-time college student for six dollars an hour to take care of your paperwork. Six bucks! Delegate.

- An accountant

This is someone to keep track of your money.
Of course, if you don't make any, it's not a problem.

- A good qualified marketing person

You need to have someone who thinks you walk on water.
There's the key. If the person believes that you have
changed their life, then they can work for you.
But if they're off the street and they have no idea
what you do, putting them in a marketing job to sell
you is like throwing your money right out the window.

How do you find this type of person? Usually they're from your audience. They may come up to you and go, "Oh my God, you are so fabulous." Now, when you've done it yourself like I did, then you can say to your marketing person, "Here's what's going to happen when you call on customers. Here's what you say. Here's what they're going to say."

But if you just turn over your business to somebody who doesn't know what to do, and you've never done it, you don't know what to say and they don't know what to say.

Creating Profit Centers

Ferry feels that the reason he's been so successful is because, from the very beginning, he didn't just think in terms of a speech and a book. Rather, he thought in terms of "profit centers":

Where are the profit centers in your business? For most speakers, it's giving a speech and selling a book. I determined quickly that *that* wasn't going to cut it. I had to have a lot of product to sell, to make the kind of money I wanted, to justify the kind of lifestyle I want.

I drive a Rolls Royce. I have a Porshe Carrera. I have a three-quarter-million-dollar home on a PGA golf course in Palm Desert. People say, "There he goes again bragging." No, I'm not bragging . . . that's what I have! I can afford to buy just about anything I want to, and that's a very good feeling. The reason I can do that is because I worked hard at making my business profitable.

Believe it or not, of all things we do in my business, my actual speaking fee brings in the least amount of profit. We have other sources of revenue, such as our Action Workshop. Then we have a three-day Superstar Sales Retreat, which we do for real estate people worldwide. We also have one for managers, called the Superstar Management Retreat. And we have a Spouses Retreat where we teach the spouses why the realtors act the way they do and how to deal with them all day long.

We created a membership organization—they get one cassette a month and a newsletter. We have video seminars, which are sold by my staff over the phone. And of course, we have our twelve-hundred-square-foot warehouse stocked floor to ceiling, and we have one guy full-time who just ships out product all day long.

The question you should ask yourself every day is: How can I make my speech more profitable? I spend more time thinking about this than anything else.

▶ **SECRET #20: Everyday ask yourself, "What is another profit center I can create for my business?"**

Ferry's Philosophy for Life

I friend of mine once said, "Show up, pay attention, tell the truth, and don't be attached to the outcome." I think that about sums it up.

How Mike Ferry would like to be remembered:

"Egotistically? He made a difference. Realistically?
He tried to make a difference."
MIKE FERRY

Mike Ferry's
Success Secrets Summary

SECRET #1: As a professional speaker, you're not being paid to be liked, but to communicate a message.

SECRET #2: Just as your audience has certain expectations about you, you should have certain expectations of your audience in terms of what you expect them to do with your material.

SECRET #3: Ask yourself before every presentation, "How can I get this audience to take action?"

SECRET #4: For every excuse you have for not achieving your goals, someone else has done it under far more difficult circumstances.

SECRET #5: If you call twenty-five people every day to hire you, you will get jobs in spite of yourself.

SECRET #6: Part of being a good salesperson is taking the prospect by the hand and showing them exactly how they can afford your service or product.

SECRET #7: If you can't sell an audience on doing what they're supposed to do, it probably means you haven't sold yourself.

SECRET #8: You will become successful faster if you think of yourself not as a speaker, but as a business person who speaks.

SECRET #9: While making a difference in the lives of others is wonderful, keep in mind that if your speaking business is not profitable, you're not going to be around long enough to make a difference.

SECRET #10: Be sure you know and can clearly communicate to others the purpose of your business and the services it provides.

SECRET #11: The way you turn the dream of having a $10,000 day in sales into a reality is by building the steps for its achievement right into your business plan.

SECRET #12: When deciding how to come up with new product, ask yourself, "What do my customers need (and want) to help themselves improve?"

SECRET #13: Two things you can do to create product that will sell: 1) Give the buyer more than they asked for, and 2) Give them specific things to do to improve the quality of their life.

SECRET #14: Don't use the excuse "it has to be perfect" to keep from putting out product. Once you get it out, you can always go back and improve it when its time to duplicate (or print) more.

SECRET #15: Audiences will want to buy product from you if they believe that 1) You know what you're talking about, and 2) The information you're providing them with will help make their life better in some significant way.

SECRET #16: The secret to selling a lot of product is to be so good on the platform that the audience wants to take home more of you for later.

SECRET #17: Regardless of whether you're giving a one-hour, three-hour, or six-hour presentation, the most time you should spend selling your products from the platform is five minutes.

SECRET #18: Decide what kind of speaker/organization you want to run: first-class, coach, or economy.

SECRET #19: Add two new topics to your speaking repertoire per year.

SECRET #20: Everyday ask yourself, "What is another profit center I can create for my business?"

CHAPTER THIRTEEN

BORN: July 17, 1912
BIRTHPLACE: Saskatchewan, Canada

Art Linkletter

*"If you want to become a great and successful
speaker, the one thing I can tell you is . . .
be famous! I can't tell you how that helps.
But, lacking that qualification, the thing you must do
is practice. You have to speak and speak. . . .
It's got to be polished and honed."*

▼

IN 1936, Dale Carnegie penned a breakthrough book on human relations called, *How to Win Friends and Influence People,* which has gone on to sell over fifteen million copies. In it, he states emphatically, "You can make more friends in two months by becoming interested in other people than you can in two years by trying to get other people interested in you." Imagine that. The secret to winning friends and influencing people lies in forgetting about ourselves and focusing on other people. Could developing this one skill really work the kind of magic Carnegie claims?

The answer is an unequivocal yes! In fact, one man who has made millions and achieved enormous fame by "becoming interested in other people" is Mr. Art Linkletter. One of the greatest interviewers of all time, Linkletter's career on radio and television spanned a remarkable forty-five years.

How good is he? When I happened to mention to an acquaintance that I was going to be interviewing Linkletter for this book, he told me, "I sat next to Art Linkletter on a plane ride once. After fifteen minutes with him, I would have done anything for that man!"

What had Linkletter done that had made this total stranger, after fifteen minutes, want to do anything for him? He simply put into action what Carnegie had talked about in his book. He showed *genuine* interest in the man by giving him his complete and undivided attention. In a word, he made the man feel *special*. As a result, the gentleman, according to his own words, "would have done anything" for Linkletter. How can you and I get people to respond to us the way Linkletter does? By forgetting about ourselves and giving people our complete and undivided attention. Because so few people really commit one hundred percent of their energy and attention to other people, when it is given, the effect can be most impressive.

On a personal note, I'll never forget the time I performed close-up magic for actor/director Henry Winkler. It was at a wrap party for a Billy Crystal movie that he had directed. I walked up to the Fonz and said, "Hi, Henry, would you like to see some magic?" I'll never forget what happened next. As he focused his attention on me, I felt this wave of energy hit me. I'm serious! His presence and eye contact were so powerful, that I felt as if he was seeing right inside my soul. I remember blushing slightly and thinking, "Wow, he's just given me his complete and undivided attention—I can feel it!" And in that moment I understood why women fall for him. It's very flattering to have a person look at you with caring eyes that say, "Yes, you have my complete attention, I'm all yours—nothing else exists in this moment but you and me."

Let's take a page out of Carnegie, Linkletter, and Winkler's (sounds like a law firm) book and start today to make a conscious effort to become sincerely interested in other people. Remember, the secret is to really be there, in the moment, with the person. While this may take some practice (as it is human nature to think of ourselves first), before you know it you will become so comfortable with focusing on the other person—and so pleased at the results—that you will begin to do it automatically. When this happens, you will have taken your interpersonal relationship skills to a whole new level.

▶ **SECRET #1: Being able to forget about yourself and become genuinely interested in other people is the key to success in sales, in speaking, and in life.**

Linkletter's Attitude: "I'm Just One of the People"

Another reason for Linkletter's tremendous success in dealing with people is that he doesn't have any airs about him. Many people, upon meeting him, come away saying, "He's so down to earth." Art explains it this way:

> As I travel, people talk to me, because I'm a guy who talks to people. When I traveled with big stars like Cary Grant or John Wayne, people would come up [to them] very respectfully and say, "I loved your pictures." With me, they'd give me a pat on the rear end and say, "Hey, Art! You know that time you . . ." And they'd just start talking to me as a friend. I'm not a star or a celebrity, I'm just one of the people.

What a great attitude! Yet, here's man who, if he wanted to, could feel pretty important about himself considering his life-long list of accomplishments. Don't believe me? Take a look for yourself:

For more than forty-five years, Art Linkletter was a major television and radio star. His show, *House Party,* ran on CBS day-time television and radio, five days a week, fifty-two weeks a year for twenty-five years! It not only won an Emmy Award, but was nominated four other times. His other hit show, *People Are Funny,* ran on NBC nighttime television and radio for nineteen years. It was nominated for three Emmys.

Linkletter has appeared in two movies, numerous TV specials, and has been awarded ten honorary doctorate degrees from colleges and universities.

All totaled, he has authored twenty-three books. His most well-known, *Kids Say the Darndest Things,* which was written in 1956, led all sellers for two years and is number fourteen on the list of all-time non-fiction best-sellers published in the United States! In 1986, thirty-two years later, *Old Age Is Not for Sissies* came out and it, too, became a best-seller.

He has been voted Grandfather of the Year (he has eight *great* grandchildren!), and in 1969 he was named Speaker of the Year by the International Platform Association. He served on the President's National Advisory Council for Drug Abuse Prevention and spent over ten years traveling around America speaking out against drug abuse.

Linkletter's business investments in oil, cattle, publishing, home building, land development, ranching, and manufacturing have made him a very wealthy man. In addition, he shares his business acumen with others by serving on no less than half a dozen boards of directors.

Credits Wife with Keeping Him Humble

Yet, through it all, he remains one of the nicest "big names" you'd ever want to meet. Art credits his wife, Lois, who he has been married to for fifty-nine years, with keeping his feet firmly planted on the ground. In fact, when they first got married, she said, "If the Lord will make you successful, I will keep you humble."

As the following story illustrates, she has made good on that promise: One night after receiving a big award, Art was driving home when he remarked to his wife, "Lois, you know, it's interesting what that man said tonight. There aren't really too many truly great men alive in the world today." To which she shot back, "I think there's one less than you *think* there is!"

Today, the Linkletters live on five acres of prime Bel Air real estate, dotted with 150 trees and a panoramic view that extends from downtown Los Angeles to the Pacific Ocean. The energetic couple loves to travel all over the world. In the summer they go to Hawaii, where the eighty-plus-year-old Art still likes to surf, and in the winter they can be found in Vale or Aspen swooshing down the slopes.

Took Up Skiing at the Suggestion of Lowell Thomas

It was over thirty years ago when his friend Lowell Thomas (who was seventy-five at the time) suggested to Art that he take up skiing. When he replied that fifty was too late an age to take up the sport, Thomas said, "No, it's the perfect time—everything's downhill from there on!"

(Thomas also told Linkletter that when he turned seventy-five, everything would remind him of something else. Says Art, "And it's true! You get a lot of us old duffers together and just say one word and we can go for hours: 'Oh yeah, I know that fella and . . .' ")

Born an Orphan in Canada

Like many of the speakers I interviewed, Linkletter came from inauspicious beginnings. He was born an orphan (like both Wayne Dyer and Les Brown) in Canada and was adopted by a Baptist minister named Fulton John Linkletter. The family moved to East San Diego when Art was still very young. It was there that he first attended grammar school.

First Speech on the Stage at
Woodrow Wilson Jr. High

On his way home from school one day, an eleven-year-old Art wandered onto the campus of Woodrow Wilson Jr. High School. There, he spotted a new school auditorium that was still under construction. The workers had all gone home for the day and, being curious, little Art decided to venture inside the huge, unfinished edifice.

Seeing the pristine wooden stage before him, he scrambled up its stairs and made his way to the center. As he looked out over the twelve hundred empty seats, his fertile imagination took over and he suddenly imagined the room filled to capacity. He thought to himself, "A large audience has come to hear me speak. I must not disappoint them." And taking on a posture of importance, he began to address the imaginary audience!

While he doesn't remember what he spoke about that day, Linkletter says with a chuckle that he went back on several occasions to give more "imaginary speeches." Obviously, at the time, he had no idea he would one day become a professional speaker. He was simply a young boy acting out his imagination on an empty school stage. Yet, it's clear that this strong desire to communicate with others was inside him from an early age.

Not surprisingly, when he did attend junior high school, Linkletter took an interest in debating. He also began giving talks to local service organizations, like the Rotary and Kiwanis Clubs. By the time he reached high school, his oratory skills were so good that they caught the attention of the school's speech teacher.

Mr. Hammond Takes an Interest
in Linkletter

Mr. Hammond, who wore a black patch due to an eye injury, was extremely popular with the kids. Why? Because he took a genuine interest in them. In order to teach the importance of being able to think on one's feet, he would have his students stand in front of the class and speak on myriad topics extemporaneously.

The very first time he got up in front of the class, Linkletter remembers Mr. Hammond saying, "Mr. Linkletter, why don't you speak on the subject of why coconuts have hair." And he had to immediately come up with an interesting opening, body, and conclusion, all on why coconuts have hair!

When Linkletter was finished, Mr. Hammond quickly threw out a new topic, and Art would repeat the process all over again. Mr. Hammond soon recognized that Linkletter had a flair for thinking on his feet, and, like any good educator, he sought to nurture and polish the youngster's natural comfortableness and poise in front of an audience. To this day, Linkletter credits Mr. Hammond with having a big influence on him.

Elwood T. Bailey Comes to Town

Just as Mark Victor Hansen had been inspired by Billy Sands, so too was Linkletter inspired by a powerful speaker. His name was Elwood T. Bailey, and he spoke one afternoon during a general assembly at Art's high school. Billed as "The World's Greatest Speaker," Linkletter had never seen anything like the sixty-five-year-old Bailey, whose manner and style were very bombastic and theatrical. A throwback from another era, Bailey had spent a good part of his life speaking on what was once known as the "Chautauqua Circuit."

The Chautauqua Circuit was a form of cultural entertainment back in the 1800s, before radio and TV were invented. Great speakers like Clarence Darrow, as well as vaudeville acts, would go around the country performing on this circuit. Since there were no microphones or loudspeakers back then, the speakers and entertainers had to project very loudly and dramatically. They used broad and exaggerated gestures in order to reach the people in the back of the large crowds.

Linkletter was completely captivated by Bailey and his stories that afternoon. He thought to himself, "Gosh, if only I had lived in those days, because that's the thing I would rather do more than anything in the world." Afterward, he went backstage to talk to Mr. Bailey. He asked him if it was still possible to speak on the Chautauqua Circuit. Bailey shook his head sadly and told the inquisitive teenager that it no longer existed. Although speakers spoke here and there, said Bailey, the days of traveling on the circuit were gone forever. Linkletter was disappointed, but, like Mr. Hammond, he never forgot the impression Elwood T. Bailey had on him.

Attends College with Thoughts of Becoming an English Teacher

During the 1930s, Linkletter attended college, where he studied English, drama, journalism, creative writing, and public speaking—all the things that are involved in communication. At the time, Linkletter thought he would eventually become an English teacher. But fate had other ideas. . . .

Gets Job at Radio Station

One day while he was making salads in the college cafeteria, Linkletter got a phone call from a local radio station. The station manager said, "This is Mr. Deller at KGB Radio Station; would you consider taking a job here?" Linkletter didn't have to think long: "Yes, of course." He didn't even ask what the job was, as this was during the Great Depression, and when you were offered a job you took it. Linkletter says that if the man had been a doctor and said, "Would you consider brain surgery?" he would have said, "Yes!" because things were so tough back then.

A Pioneer in the Art of Interviewing

Up until this time (1933), radio was used primarily to broadcast sports, drama, comedy, news, and weather. However, at age twenty-one, Linkletter changed all that by becoming one of the first broadcasters to interview people live on the air. Radio audiences found the spontaneous and unrehearsed nature of these live interviews to be both informative and entertaining. There was a sense that "anything could happen" on the air; the same feeling one gets when watching a tightrope walker without a net. This un-rehearsed and therefore totally unpredictable element helped make the live interviews a big hit.

Of course, it was Linkletter's warm personality and delightful sense of humor that turned casual listeners into devoted fans. He seemed to know just when and how to ask the right questions at the right time to get the biggest laughs. However, this was never done at the subject's expense. Rather, Art knew how to ask questions so that the person he was interviewing got the laugh, even if it was at Linkletter's own expense. Clearly, his time in front of Mr. Ham-mond's class had paid off as he proved himself adept at handling virtually anything that might come his way during the interviews.

By the way, Linkletter says that the best people to interview are children under ten and adults over seventy. Why? Because they say exactly what they think! So, the next time you're conducting interviews, instead of shying away from the elderly or the very young, go get 'em, because they could be the source of your very best material!

▶ **SECRET #2: The best people to interview are those over seventy and under ten, because they say exactly what they think!**

Having said the above, Linkletter's favorite people to interview are four- and five-year-olds. This is because they are guaranteed to say something totally honest and often priceless (hence the title of Art's biggest-selling book, *Kids Say the Darndest Things*). Linklet-ter says that stories about children appeal to just about everyone, for the simple reason that most people have children, or because each of us was once a child.

Out of the Mouths of Babes

Here are a few classics that have tumbled out of the mouths of children during interviews with "Mister Winkwetter" (as he has been called on occasion!):

One time he asked a child on his show what first-aid was. He was informed with a straight face, "It's your last chance to get well before the doctor gets there!"

When he asked a young boy what he wanted to be when he grew up, the tike replied, "I either want to be a doctor or a taxidermist." When Linkletter asked him why, he replied, "If I can't cure 'em, I'll stuff 'em!"

This gem happened when he asked a little boy what his favorite Bible story was: "Well, the Jews were being chased across the desert and they were pinned up against a big lake, and the Egyptian Army was going to kill all of 'em. And one of God's people said, 'We need a miracle,' and boy did they get one! The U.S. Airforce came in with their helicopters . . ." Linkletter interrupted, "They *didn't* teach you that in Sunday School." To which the boy confessed, "Well, no they didn't. But you'd never believe the junk they told us!"

One time, Art said to a little five-year-old girl, whose mother had her all dressed up for an appearance on his television show, "What a pretty little girl you are. What's the prettiest thing you have on?" And the little girl took her dress, held it over her head and said, "My pink panties with the red hearts!" Both Art and the audience fell out of their chairs laughing. When Linkletter tells this story, he tags on, "Now, I've tried that question with a hundred housewives . . . nothing!" And it gets a big laugh.

During one broadcast (remember, this was all live and spontaneous), Linkletter asked a little boy, "Did your mother give you any instructions before you came down to my show?" The little darling confessed, "Well, she told me not to tell you if you had bad breath." Knowing full well he was opening himself up to potential embarrassment, Art played along, "Do I?" And the boy replied, "I'd rather not say!"

Another time, Linkletter asked an eight-year-old boy why he thought his teacher had picked him to be on the show. The boy answered, "Because I'm the smartest kid in the class." "Did your teacher tell you that?" Art inquired. "No," said the boy earnestly, "I noticed it myself."

A Sign of Our Times

When asked if he thought kids would respond differently if he were doing his show today, Linkletter says:

> No; kid's from four to ten are still the same. They live in a world of their own. They're interested in having to eat spinach and having to go to bed too early and whether their mother loves them. It's after ten that the children have changed. After all, a steady diet of thousands and thousands of hours in front of the TV, watching tens of thousands of murders and mayhem and sex crimes has done a lot to hurt their response.

Linkletter is articulating what many people in this country feel: that there is way too much violence on TV. After all, if we assume children learn from watching shows like *Sesame Street,* why would we think they wouldn't learn from watching murders and brutality? Whether it's positive or negative, repeat it often enough and kids will begin to emulate it.

Linkletter points out just how much things have changed since he went off the air:

> My shows were about who had come the furthest to be in the audience, who was the oldest, interesting ways women had met their husbands, etc. Today, you see an unending parade of transvestites, kooks, sex maniacs, skin heads and all kinds of aberrations of the human race parading across the camera.

An accurate but sad commentary on our times.

The 1939 San Francisco World's Fair Debacle

Like all people, Linkletter has faced tragedy and disappointment during his lifetime. From a career standpoint, the disaster that befell him in 1939 was his most memorable. That year, the twenty-seven-year-old Linkletter was the radio director of the San Francisco World's Fair, which was held on Treasure Island. The fair's theme was "The Old West," and Art had put together the lavish opening ceremony. This was no small task, as it involved hundreds of actors, trains, and cattle, on a stage three hundred feet wide—this for the expected audience of four thousand people. Linkletter came to the project with considerable experience, as he had put together the opening for the World's Fair in Dallas, Texas, the year before, and in San Diego the year before that.

One day, a month before the fair was scheduled to start, the gentleman in charge of the entire event called Art into his office. Linkletter says that this man was "a tough old guy about sixty-five or seventy years old," who didn't like him because he was from San Diego. Back then, people from San Francisco had great contempt for anyone from Southern California.

The stern-faced man asked, with more than a hint of condescension in his voice, "Tell me, Linkletter, what are your plans for the opening of the fair?" Art began to outline some of the activities he had planned—which included the president of the United States, fireworks, a Marine band, and all the other activities—when he was suddenly interrupted. "That stinks! You have no imagination," barked the old man. Taken aback, Art said, "Suppose you tell me what you'd do?" His boss said, "Look over my shoulder and tell me what you see through the window?" Linkletter replied, "The Golden Gate Bridge." "Well, doesn't that bring any ideas to mind?" "Like what?" Art responded, still miffed.

"Well, the Golden Gate Bridge is the longest single span bridge in the world," said his boss, "and if you were an engineer, you'd know that every one of those cables that holds the bridge up has a different tension on it. As the wind blows across the Pacific and passes through those hundreds of cables, each one makes a different hum. I'd hook up a whole bunch of microphones from one end of the bridge to the other, patch them through a master control panel, and using that as a mixer, I would play *California Here We Come* off the Golden Gate Bridge to open the fair!"

Not believing what he had just heard, Linkletter couldn't contain himself. He blurted out, "Mr. Connick, you're crazy." And the old man replied, "Mr. Linkletter, you're fired!"

In Art's own words:

There I was, fired, just before the opening of the fair. I went home and my wife asked what I was doing home so early. I said, "Honey, you know how I've been telling you for the last two years that I've been underpaid, underappreciated, and overworked—that they don't realize who they have working for them . . ." She said, "You've been fired."

I said, "Yes, I've been fired. And I'm never again going to work for anybody in my life. I'm going to be me. If I make a mistake, I'll pay for it. If I do well, I'll get the money." And from that moment on, I have never worked for anybody. I originated my own shows, I sold them myself and I booked them myself. That way, nobody could ever touch my life with that kind of power again. I had been cut off at the knees by a man who was vindictive, short-sighted, and I think kind of crazy. And that changed my life. Within three months, after he fired me, I was making more money than he was. And I never took a backward step.

Just like Wayne Dyer and all the other speakers I interviewed, Linkletter has a fiercely independent spirit. From early on he realized that he wanted to be the one calling the shots. This is summed up by his statement, "If I make a mistake, I'll pay for it. If I do well, I'll get the money." Sink or swim, he was going to captain his own ship. And it all came about because of what at first appeared to be a major setback.

Not surprisingly, Linkletter's favorite quote is:

"Things turn out best for the people who make the best of the way things turn out."
JOHN WOODEN, EX-UCLA BASKETBALL COACH

▶ **SECRET #3: When you get burned in business, you can either sit around smoldering about it or you can do what all successful men and women do: Use the experience as a catalyst to fire you up to achieve something even greater.**

The Loss of His Daughter and How It Changed His Life

To a parent, there is no greater tragedy than the loss of a child. When the Linkletters lost their nineteen-year-old daughter, Diane, from an LSD overdose in 1967, they were completely devastated. However, a phone call from Dr. Norman Vincent Peale convinced Art that he should not let Diane's death be in vain. Peale told him to go out and talk to the families of America, and warn them of the dangers of drug abuse.

Although up until that time Linkletter's role in front of audiences had been solely to provide entertainment, he took Dr. Peale up on his suggestion. He began speaking out all across America for more than a decade about his tragic loss. In the process, he touched many thousands of hearts with his moving tribute to his daughter. Ironically, Art not only helped others, but this whole experience led him to a new profession—that of professional speaker.

Speaking Is More Rewarding than Being a TV Star

Just how important is public speaking to Linkletter? Some might be surprised to learn that he considers it more significant than even his prodigious and highly successful TV career:

> I found that I like speaking more than anything I've ever done, including being a TV star or making movies or working nightclubs.
>
> I had some forty-five years in show business on coast-to-coast TV and motion picture deals, which made me a so-called celebrity and famous . . . but I never really started living to my capacity and fulfilling my ability until I became a full-time speaker.
>
> It's been more rewarding to face audiences, and not just to entertain, but to motivate, to educate, to stimulate, to go away leaving behind something good in the hearts and minds

of those people. That has been more important to me than all of the TV and all of the radio honors that I have received.

People who don't know about the speaking business might think, "How can you get a kick out of getting up in front of three hundred people in an auditorium in Solana, Kansas, when for over thirty years, every time you walked onstage, you went on live TV to at least fifteen million people?"

What these people don't know is that the speaker doesn't feel the impact of the fifteen million people. He doesn't see them or hear them. You're aware that they're out there, and the money and everything reflects that you have that many, but a speaker in front of a live audience is getting the reaction directly and in the moment, from an audience he controls completely—if he's a good speaker.

The business of speaking, to me, is very exciting and very rewarding, more so than being a movie or TV star.

▶ **SECRET #4: You know speaking is your passion if the time you feel most alive is when you are in front of an audience, motivating, educating, stimulating, and leaving behind something good in people's hearts and minds.**

I hope the significance of Linkletter's words have made as much of an impression on you as they have on me. The fact that despite all his show-biz success, he "never really started living to his capacity and fulfilling his ability until he became a full-time speaker" tells you just how important public speaking is to him. And it's true—those of us who feel most alive when we are in front of an audience know exactly what Art is talking about.

As Speakers, We Are Role Models

Here are Linkletter's thoughts on what it means to be a professional speaker:

Speakers are a wonderful group of people who serve the nation in a time of turbulence, change, and crisis. All the headlines bemoan the fact that the world is going to hell in a handbag . . . yet, we lecturers are out there telling them in many ways—using different kinds of approaches and stories—to have self-esteem, to better themselves, to plan their lives, to have goals.

▶ **SECRET #5: As speakers, we serve as role models for society, teaching people how to set goals and have the confidence to believe in and go after their dreams.**

One of the first paid speeches Linkletter ever gave was with Cavett Robert, Norman Vincent Peale, Zig Ziglar, and Ty Boyd, at what has become known as "motivational speaker rallies." The five of them would go around the country during the 1970s, speaking in huge auditoriums to as many as fourteen thousand people at a time. Why would so many people come out to hear these great men speak? It's because they offered something that was (and still is) in short supply: a way of thinking and conducting one's life that, if applied consistently, will enable a person to achieve the success and happiness they so desperately seek.

In a time when politicians say one thing and do another, and sports, TV, movie, and rock stars are arrested on a regular basis, the public is clamoring for men and women to step forward and display real integrity, solid values, and positive leadership. The fact is that many people who are now currently holding leadership positions are suffering from a credibility crisis. This is a major problem because if we can't trust you, how can we trust what you're saying? And remember, once credibility is lost, it is awfully difficult to get back.

Therefore, as speakers, let's do everything we can to maintain our credibility. Let's set the example by showing people that we say what we mean and we mean what we say. By doing this, our audiences will respect us and, more importantly, we'll respect ourselves.

▶ **SECRET #6: Being a person of good character and integrity goes a long way in establishing your credibility; and credibility is vital to your success because audiences don't just listen to what's being said, but who is saying it.**

The One Thing You Must Do to Become a Successful Speaker

The question every speaker wants to know the answer to is: "What's the one thing I must do to become a successful speaker?" In the following, Linkletter addresses that issue with a quip, and then reminds us that, regardless of how much natural talent you possess, nobody succeeds without a whole lot of practice:

> If you want to become a great and successful speaker, the one thing I can tell you is . . . be famous! I can't tell you how that helps. But, lacking that qualification, the thing you must do is practice. You have to speak and speak. Record your speeches, play them over, listen to your speeches.

▶ **SECRET #7: Besides becoming famous, the most important step to becoming a successful speaker is to practice; you have to speak and speak.**

The fact of the matter is, no matter how good you are, or how much natural talent you have, it isn't good enough. It's got to be polished and shaped and honed. I don't think any speaker is really a great speaker who is not completely familiar with what he's talking about and, if possible, familiar with it from personal experience.

You can read all you want to about other people's adventures and success, but until *you've* had an experience . . . I became a good speaker because of the loss of Diane. I was talking about drugs across this country for ten or fifteen years in schools and every place else . . . I was an evangelist, I was making something in Diane's memory with what I was saying to those families.

In your case it might be something you've been through; a bankruptcy, which teaches you a lot of things, or a challenge that became successful . . . or not successful. Maybe you went down the Amazon in a canoe, talk about that. Whatever it is, you have to believe it. You have to think that what you're saying has some value and you can attest to it. There should be a core inside you about what you're talking about.

▶ **SECRET #8: The best speakers speak from personal experience. They believe in what they are saying and that it has value and can help others. They are evangelistic about their message.**

Enthusiasm [is also important]. It doesn't mean "Hooray!" It means an intense reflection of energy and an interest and a desire. That's why my current talks on growing old are so effective. Certainly nobody in their fifties can talk to seventy-five-year-old-people about growing old—you have to *be* old! And I'm old enough so that now when I say something about older people, they know I know!

What Thoughts Go Through a Great Speaker's Mind While He or She Is Speaking?

When you're up in front of an audience speaking, what kinds of thoughts are going through your mind? While most beginning speakers are focused on themselves, with thoughts like, "Gosh, I'm nervous," or "Wow, there sure are a lot of people out there," etc., great speakers are externally focused. They think thoughts such as, "Oh, I've given them three examples in a row; it's time for a funny story," or "I've been focusing on the people in front; I need to give some attention to those sitting in the back."

Here's what Linkletter thinks about while he's giving a speech:

Of course, the subject that I'm talking about is going through my mind. I never give exactly the same talk—I don't have a boilerplate talk. I've written twenty-three books, and so from these books along with my life experience, I'm improvising and recalling from my memory banks over fifteen hours of material. I use the stories and things in different ways. So when I'm speaking, I'm thinking, "Now let's see, I have a great story about this, and maybe I should tell this; no, I'll tell the other one . . ." I'm making up my talk as I go, so it's fresh and interesting to me.

Oftentimes people will come up to me before a talk and say, "Mr. Linkletter, I'm so looking forward to your talk tonight. I can hardly wait to hear what you have to say." And I say, "Me too!"

The Difference Between Speaking on TV Versus Speaking Live Before an Audience

The following bit of advice from Linkletter is like a gold nugget: Small, but priceless. He points out in just two sentences one of the major reasons why speaking on television is so much different than speaking before an audience:

> You have forty-million people listening, but they're in groups of two, three, and four. So your entire tone is different; you're not in front of a huge audience or at the back of a train.

Art is reminding us that whenever we are in front of a camera, we should talk in a natural and conversational tone of voice, as if we were talking to only a couple of people—because we are! We must resist the urge to raise the volume of our voice to "reach across the airwaves to the people," and instead concentrate on putting more warmth and intimacy in our voice.

This is great advice from a man whose sincerity and friendliness came across the airwaves for almost half a century.

▶ **SECRET #9: When you're speaking on television, keep in mind that you are only really addressing one to four people at a time. Thus, your tone of voice and gestures should be small and intimate, rather than large and grandiose.**

People Will Mirror Your Friendly, Accepting Attitude

It's worth noting that one of the reasons people find Art Linkletter so agreeable is because he finds *people* to be agreeable. He told

Dottie Walters, in her book, *The Greatest Speakers I Ever Heard,* "Dottie, people are the same everywhere I speak. They mirror my friendly, accepting attitude."

▶ **SECRET #10: By giving off a friendly, accepting attitude, you will find that people will tend to "mirror you," and respond in kind.**

How does Art give off a "friendly, accepting attitude" during his speeches? He explains:

> I try to make everyone in my audience feel as if I am speaking with them. Not at, or to them, but with them, so that as I speak and can see them nod in agreement I know we are making contact on an intimate level. I treat everyone as if each person were getting my total attention. It is why I never use notes or TelePrompTers, so as never to lose the eye contact so important to a speaker.

What you've just read is truly the secret to Art's warmth and caring about people—when he speaks, you feel he's talking *with,* and not at, you.

The Best Speakers Are Storytellers

Linkletter credits Dr. Norman Vincent Peale with impressing upon him that the best speakers are storytellers. He explains why:

> We're all kids at heart—we want to hear a story. And a story illustrates a point much more than a general broad statement of philosophy.

It's true; young or old, everyone loves to hear stories. In fact, this is one of the reasons the Bible is such an effective book—because it's made up of hundreds and hundreds of interesting and life-changing stories.

One of the stories that Linkletter likes to tell in his motivational talks is about the importance of letting our happiness shine through and touch the people we come in contact with:

Most of us don't realize that our attitudes are sometimes very off-putting to people. We should be watchful of how we are holding ourselves. I was shopping with my wife on Rodeo Drive a week ago, and I sat down while she looked through the jewels. I was sitting down because I always get weak and faint when she's looking at jewelry! And I noticed the manager of the store was a tall woman with gray hair, who was standing imperiously, as if the plumbing had broken somewhere! So I walked up to her and said, "Are you happy?" And she replied, "Of course I'm happy." And I said, "Why don't you notify your face?!"

Telling a story like that will make people remember my point more than repeating, "Smile, be happy, be friendly, exude warmth." And that's what I learned from Norman Vincent Peale. He's got a story for everything.

▶ **SECRET #11: Stories illustrate points much better and are more memorable than statements or dry facts.**

A Crusader for the Chronologically Challenged

Linkletter started out speaking on positive thinking, but now speaks on eight or nine different topics. These include humor, family, business, and one of his most popular presentations, *Old Age Is Not for Sissies,* based on his book with the same title.

Art feels very passionately about this program and considers himself a messenger for the positive aging of America. He says most emphatically, "It is not true that at a certain calendar date you should start having to apologize for taking up space on the planet!" However, this does not mean he has lost his sense of humor when it comes to growing old. He claims that, after seventy, if you wake up without any aches or pains . . . you're dead! He also says that there are three stages to getting old: middle age, old age, and "My, but you're looking good!" which is what he claims people say to you when you're *really* getting up there.

Linkletter says that after you're seventy-five or eighty, it is not necessary to say that you cannot have a sex life . . . *it's not possible,* but it's not necessary to say it! As he likes to add, "The one last winter was wonderful!" And of his friend George Jessel, Art boasts: "He has been married for forty-six years . . . and you couldn't find seven nicer ladies!"

The "Seventy-Eight-Year-Old Widow from Miami Beach" Story

A favorite story that Linkletter loves to tell, especially to senior citizens who can really appreciate it, is about the seventy-eight-year-old widow from Miami Beach. It seems that one morning she was looking out her kitchen window when she spotted a handsome, white-haired gentleman at the pool, whom she had never seen before. After giving her hair a spritz of "Xtacy," putting on a see-through blouse and a pair of gold lamé pants with red pumps, she eagerly shuffled on down to the pool.

Approaching the gentleman, she said, "Hello there. Who are you?" And the man said, "I'm a stranger." "That's nice," she cooed, "Where are you from?" "Up North," he replied tersely. Persisting, she inquired, "And what were you doing up North?" "Well, if you must know, I've been in prison for twenty-three years." "Oh," she said, "What happened?" He replied uncomfortably, "Well, if you must know, I killed my wife, cut her up into little pieces and put them down the garbage disposal." The woman's face lit up and she said, "Oh . . . then you're single!?"

Whenever Linkletter tells this story, he never fails to get a great reaction from the audience.

Humorous Openings

Humor has always been a big part of Linkletter's presentations, and he doesn't wait long to use it. Often, he'll say something funny immediately following his introduction.

When he was introduced at the National Speakers Association Convention in Orlando, Florida, in 1993, the emcee spent so much time going over his extraordinary list of lifelong accomplishments, that when Art finally took the stage, he quipped, "I expect some of you were looking for me to be wheeled out!" He then went right into a story about the time one of his great-grand-daughters introduced him at her school. Says Linkletter, "She took me by the hand, walked me out in front of her class and said, 'This is my great-grandpa. He's eighty-one and still alive!'" After the audience finished laughing, he turned the humorous little story into a powerful point by saying, "The important word there is *alive*. Not just physically, but alive . . . being curious and interested and challenged."

Notice that, when he initially came onstage, the first words out of Linkletter's mouth were 1) humorous (about being wheeled out and about still being alive) and 2) poking fun at himself. I've said it elsewhere in this book, but it bears repeating: Audiences love it when a speaker can poke fun at him or herself. The fact that Art isn't afraid to make fun of his getting older absolutely endears him to his audiences.

As speakers, we must connect with our audiences as quickly as possible. And since humor is a great "connector," it makes sense that we would want to include some right from the beginning of our presentation. I can honestly say in twenty-one years of doing presentations in front of audiences (both magic and speaking), I have *never* opened a program without doing some humor and/or a magic trick. I find that it takes a few minutes for audiences to "warm up" to you, and the humor/magic definitely helps to speed up the connection.

Find something about yourself that you can "poke fun at" in your opening remarks, and you, too, will win the audience over.

▶ **SECRET #12: Opening your speech by poking fun at yourself is one of the surest ways to win over an audience.**

A New Twist on an Old Bit

Linkletter has an original way of telling those old, "A funny thing happened to me on the way to the banquet . . ." jokes. He says to his audience, "I've been coming to banquets for years, and nothing funny has ever happened to me . . . *until tonight*." And then he tells the joke. A clever twist on an old stand-by.

▶ **SECRET #13: You can take an old gag or joke that you enjoy telling and make it fresh and new simply by changing the way you set it up.**

Linkletter's "Super-Speaker" Role Model

When I asked Linkletter if he had any role models in the speaking world, his answer was a bit unusual. He said that he had "combinations of role models," meaning that he took different attributes from different speakers. The more I thought about it, the more I liked his idea of taking the best attributes from all your favorite role models and putting them together to form a sort of "super-speaker." (In fact, why not pull the qualities that you like best from the fifteen speakers in this book and form your own "super-speaker" role model!) Here are Linkletter's thoughts on role models:

> I have combinations of role models, of different things that different people do. For instance, I loved the warmth of Norman Vincent Peale; he was like an uncle or a grandfather. I have a lot of that in me; I'm a warm, encompassing figure in front of an audience.
>
> Now on the other hand, I think Cavett Robert and Zig Ziglar have the sparks and the fireworks that were absent from Norman Vincent Peale, because they're more performers. I have some of that in me because of my show business background.
>
> Bob Richards, who was a minister and an Olympic champion pole vaulter, taught me the great value of using your own personal experiences. In fact, he would use not only his own stories, but also the stories of the athletes he had associated with, and how they became winners and champions. So, from Bob I learned how to use stories that reflect my own experiences successfully in the business, as well as stories about some of my great show business friends, such as Bob Hope, Lucille Ball, Cary Grant, and so on.

There are some speakers I admire and think are wonderful but they do things I wouldn't think of doing. I won't mention any names, but they use vaudeville tricks where they climb a ladder, or they have pails of water, or they'll pull a gun out of their pocket and fire it and use it to make a point.

Those things are interesting, but it would never occur to me to do anything like that. Also, I'm not the kind of speaker to go charging up and down the stage, loosing my tie, running my hand through my hair and haranguing the audience. That's another style, and while I like to see it and it's fun to watch and I think it's great for them, it's not for me.

My point is that while I pick and choose some qualities I like from a few other speakers, I really don't have any [one] role model. Everything I do really came out of my own experience. It goes back to when I was a youth; I learned by doing, not by watching and copying. I learned by being rebuffed or being encouraged, or by learning the skills that make a talk good.

▶ **SECRET #14: Instead of having just one speaker role model, pick the best traits from several of them to create a "super-speaker" who possesses all the qualities you like best!**

Success at an Early Age Allowed Him to Associate with the Rich and Famous

How does one get to spend one's life hanging around the powerful and the wealthy? Well, according to Linkletter, the best way is to become powerful and wealthy yourself!:

To begin with, I was successful very young. By the time I was twenty-seven, I was on the air coast-to-coast. That brought me in touch with a lot of people. Then I started making a lot of money and becoming a very successful businessman. When you are a successful businessman on boards of directors and running companies, you meet people who are doing the same things.

I've spent my life around very, very successful people who were big stars, CEOs, and heads of state. With the exception of Carter, I've known every president since Roosevelt, almost on a first-name basis. I've associated myself with great authors, presidents of universities, and business tycoons.

My close, intimate friends have included people like Henry Kaiser, Walt Disney, Richard Nixon, Ronald Reagan, and on and on. I just know these people, personally, on a first-name basis, and we sit around and we talk.

I belong to some very important clubs, like the Bohemian Club in San Francisco. Every summer we have a two and a half week encampment under the redwood trees in the Russian River area, north of San Francisco. For two and a half weeks I sit around intimate campfires with up to one or two thousand members who are the movers, shakers, and doers of the world.

I would sit there with a glass of beer or a lemonade and talk to Henry Kissinger or Herbert Hoover or Eddie Rickenbacker or Lowell Thomas and those kind of people. And you listen to these people as they talk about their personal lives, or their feelings or opinions. You gradually, from that great big mulch of experience, knowledge, and networking, establish a background of material that is a vast reservoir. Soon, it all mixes together to the point that it becomes your own. So, I've lived a very successful and rewarding life, surrounded by similar kinds of people.

▶ **SECRET #15: If you want to become rich and successful, develop relationships with rich and successful people!**

Always Had Confidence

Because Linkletter comes across to his audiences as being very confident and comfortable with himself, I asked him if there was ever a time when he doubted himself. He told me:

I never had any real doubts. I've always been confident, always thought things were going to work out, and many times they didn't! And when they didn't, I was totally surprised and frustrated, and thought, "That's interesting, we didn't do well." But it never occurred to me that next time I wouldn't do well. I was always a positive thinker, by nature, by inclination, and by practice. So while I've had some disasters, like everybody else, and I mean *everybody*, I say, "What are we going to do to make it better next time?" and next time it's better!

Humor, the United Nations, and a Delayed Reaction

As Linkletter was going around the country speaking about the drug epidemic, he was invited to speak in front of the United Nations by a young ambassador (at the time) named George Bush! Even while going before such an august group of dignitaries, Linkletter still found some humor in the situation. He says that when he spoke there, he didn't realize that his speech was being translated into 140 different languages, many of which took a different length of time to translate. All he knew was that when he would finish telling a humorous story, there wasn't a sound in the room. Then, a few seconds later, the Spanish would laugh, and then a moment later the French, then the Germans, then the Chinese and finally, as he likes to joke, the English!

The Time Linkletter Gave Advice to Richard M. Nixon

During Nixon's first bid for the presidency of the United States in 1960, Linkletter served as one of his advisors. As they were flying from San Francisco to Los Angeles, Linkletter turned to the future president and said, "Dick, whenever you can, do not make a speech . . . [instead] be at a microphone with no notes . . . so you're just chatting with them the way Roosevelt did."

(Linkletter had introduced Franklin Delano Roosevelt at one of his famous "fireside chats." Roosevelt was, according to Art, one of the first speakers who really understood how to use the microphone and how to draw the audience in by lowering his voice and creating a feeling of intimacy. He was also a master at going in and out of his written talk. He would ad-lib very cleverly and then, seamlessly, go right back into his written talk. Linkletter came away very impressed with Roosevelt's speaking skills.)

Here are Linkletter's observations about our thirty-seventh president:

> Dick Nixon was a made extrovert; he was not a born speaker. He learned the tricks, the devices . . . but it wasn't real because it wasn't him. He was the kind of a guy who could be funny and wonderful in a small group.

While Linkletter's thoughts on Nixon give us some insight into one of America's most colorful presidents, his relationship with another great American led directly to his becoming enormously wealthy due to one speaking engagement!

The Opening of Disneyland and How Linkletter Was Paid a Fortune

A personal friend of Walt Disney, Linkletter shared these memories about him at the 1993 National Speakers Association Convention in Orlando, Florida:

> Walt was an eternal child. He loved tinkering, dreaming up plots . . . he wasn't interested in cocktail parties, or who mattered, or where the power structure was. He was interested in making things.

> He and I became very dear friends and traveled in Europe. One time I saw him making notes in a notebook and I said, "What are you writing there, Walt?" And he said, "You notice all the lights are lit, millions of them, and none are out. And the benches are clean and freshly painted and there are lots of restrooms . . ." And I said, "That's fine, but why are you writing it down?" And he said, "Someday I'm going to

have a place like this for families, and I want it to be clean and comfortable, and so I'm just making notes."

Well, years passed and one day he said, "I'm going to build Disneyland." I saw it being built; I was out there many times. Walt said, "Art, would you like to emcee the opening of Disneyland?" He said, "Pick a couple of your buddies and the four of us will be spotted in different places around the park." Everything was live back then, there was no taping or prerecording. Nothing could be picked up or filled in; it had to happen as we threw it around.

So, I picked two friends of mine, Bob Cummings, the comedy star (he had his own TV show during the 1960s) who was a wonderful witty guy, and another fellow . . . ummm . . . oh, Ronald Reagan! (The audience laughed as Art feigned having trouble remembering Reagan's name.)

A Deal That Would Even Make Mickey Mouse Green with Envy

And then I negotiated the highest fee any speaker has ever gotten in the world for an appearance. The four of us did the grand opening and Walt said to me, "Well, you know Art, I've had a lot of cost overruns and I'm in no position to do a lot of hard negotiating with you because we are personal friends and you don't have an agent I can intimidate." Unlike most people in Hollywood, I didn't have an agent—I did my own selling. After all, I had the best opinion of myself that anybody could have—I didn't need an agent.

I said, "Walt, I sympathize with your problem and I'll do it for scale." That was $210 for two hours on coast-to-coast TV on ABC. He said, "You will? That's wonderful." And I said, "Yes, and you can be wonderful to me Walt." And he said, "In what way?" And I said, "Well, you have concessions for various things, and I'd like to have the concession for the sale of all films and all cameras at Disneyland for ten years." And he said, "You got it."

After the audience had "ooooohed" at the kind of money that deal must have been worth, even back then, Linkletter got a big laugh when he added ". . . that's one of the reasons I'm so relaxed when speaking dates don't come in!"

Linkletter's skill in negotiating this deal gives us some insight into his business acumen and vision. First of all, he knew Disney didn't have the money to pay him what he was worth. Secondly, he had enough foresight to realize that if Disneyland was going to be as big as Walt dreamed it would be, the sale of film and cameras would be worth far more in the long run than his fee anyway. So, he threw out a proposal that was a win-win for both sides: You can't pay me now, fine, I'll gamble on your theme park being a success, and if I'm right, I get paid my compensation plus interest. And the rest, as they say, is history.

▶ **SECRET #16: When negotiating your speaking fee, don't be afraid to be a little creative and a little bold and ask for the moon. As Art Linkletter's deal with Walt Disney showed, you just might get it!**

Success Is Doing What You Love

I thought it appropriate to end Linkletter's chapter with his thoughts on success. Coming from a man who has had a tremendous amount of it during his more than eight decades on earth, it's worth remembering:

> Success is doing what you like to do. Don't do anything because it's the way you're going to get rich, famous, or powerful. Do it because you love to do it. Because this life is not a rehearsal. This is it. And the trip through it is more important in many ways than just getting to the end of it and being a success at something you didn't like.

▶ **SECRET #17: Success comes from doing what you love. What good would it be if at the end of your life you have money and fame, but you achieved it doing something you didn't like for all those years?**

How Art Linkletter would like to be remembered:

---

*"Art Linkletter was a people person. He enjoyed people,
he studied people, he understood both young and
old people. He was a Canadian by birth, an American
by choice, a schoolteacher by training, a broadcaster
by vocation, a businessman by need, a Christian by
conviction, a sportsman by hobby, a lecturer
by demand and a humanitarian by heart."*
—ART LINKLETTER

Art Linkletter's Success Secrets Summary

SECRET #1: Being able to forget about yourself and become genuinely interested in other people is the key to success in sales, in speaking and in life.

SECRET #2: The best people to interview are those over seventy and under ten, because they say exactly what they think!

SECRET #3: When you get burned in business, you can either sit around smoldering about it or you can do what all successful men and women do: Use the experience as a catalyst to fire you up to achieve something even greater.

SECRET #4: You know speaking is your passion if the time you feel most alive is when you are in front of an audience, motivating, educating, stimulating, and leaving behind something good in people's hearts and minds.

SECRET #5: As speakers, we serve as role models for society, teaching people how to set goals and have the confidence to believe in and go after their dreams.

SECRET #6: Being a person of good character and integrity goes a long way to establishing your credibility; and credibility is vital to your success because audiences don't just listen to what's being said, but who is saying it.

SECRET #7: Besides becoming famous, the most important step to becoming a successful speaker is to practice; you have to speak and speak.

SECRET #8: The best speakers speak from personal experience. They believe in what they are saying and that it has value and can help others. They are evangelistic about their message.

SECRET #9: When you're speaking on television, keep in mind that you are only really addressing one to four people at a time. Thus, your tone of voice and gestures should be small and intimate, rather than large and grandiose.

SECRET #10: By giving off a friendly, accepting attitude, you will find that people will tend to "mirror you," and respond in kind.

SECRET #11: Stories illustrate points much better and are more memorable than statements or dry facts.

SECRET #12: Opening your speech by poking fun at yourself is one of the surest ways to win over an audience.

SECRET #13: You can take an old gag or joke that you enjoy telling and make if fresh and new simply by changing the way you set it up.

SECRET #14: Instead of having just one speaker role model, pick the best traits from several of them to create a "super-speaker" who possesses all the qualities you like best!

SECRET #15: If you want to become rich and successful, develop relationships with rich and successful people!

SECRET #16: When negotiating your speaking fee, don't be afraid to be a little creative and a little bold and ask for the moon. As Art Linkletter's deal with Walt Disney showed, you just might get it!

SECRET #17: Success comes from doing what you love. What good would it be if at the end of your life you have money and fame, but you achieved it doing something you didn't like for all those years?

CHAPTER FOURTEEN

BORN: April 18, 1945
BIRTHPLACE: Wimborne, England

Patricia Fripp

"To guarantee success, make sure your fee lags
behind your talent, rather than your talent
lagging behind your fee."

▼

ROBERT Mitchum once said, "No matter what you do, do your best at it. If you're going to be a bum, be the best bum there is." And Uta Hagen said, "We must overcome the notion that we must be regular. It robs us of the chance to be extraordinary." One speaker who is always pushing herself to be her best, and who is an extraordinary example of what we can become if we are determined enough, is the inimitable Patricia Fripp. Known for her distinctive English accent, beautiful outfits, flamboyant hats, and dynamic presentations, "Frippy" (as her friends affectionately call her), has a drive to succeed that is as tenacious as it is inspiring.

Her secret? Fellow speaker Emery Austin pegged it when she said to an audience while introducing Patricia, "She never stops trying to figure out how to do it better." It is this quality of never being completely satisfied, with constantly striving to make tomorrow's speech better than yesterday's, that has made Fripp one of the most successful speakers in the business. The first thing that she can teach us is that if we want to get better at speaking (or anything else for that matter), we must ask ourselves every day: "How can I do this better?"

▶ **SECRET #1: If you aspire to be one of the best in your field, ask yourself everyday, "How can I do this better?"**

It's by asking questions such as this, and then taking action on your answers, that will soon take you out of the ranks of the ordinary, and elevate you to the extraordinary. The secret is that you must do it on a daily basis. ("Did he just say we should ask ourselves how we can be better *everyday?*" Yes, *everyday!*). You must ask that question *fully expecting* an answer. See, you're not wishing things were better; instead, you're saying you *know* they can be better and you want your mind to tell you what you have to do to bring this into reality.

Once you develop the habit of constantly thinking, "How can I do this better?" (It's what Anthony Robbins, in his chapter, called CANI: "Constant and Never-Ending Improvement"), your brain will automatically begin to come up with new ways you can be more effective, without your having to prompt it. When this happens, you will begin to achieve breakthroughs and have insights that you would have never before thought possible—all because you demanded more from yourself. Try it for the next thirty days and see for yourself how much more you get accomplished. It's a fantastic feeling.

The Business of Speaking

One of the things Fripp understood very early on about becoming a professional speaker (and which many speakers fail to grasp), is that speaking is 1) a business, and 2) like any business, you have to be good if you are going to last. Here's Fripp:

> Don't think that this business (the speaking profession) is that different from any other business. To make it in the hairstyling business, [first of all] I had some innate talent. I got better because I had incredible teachers. I practiced more than anybody I ever worked with. I learned the value of developing relationships with customers. I learned to be highly visible in my community.
>
> It doesn't matter how good you are; you always need to keep in touch with the people who have done business with you in the past. And always try to get in touch with people who don't do business with you now, but who could in the future; the same as in any other business.

▶ **SECRET #2: The most important element in building your business is keeping in touch with your customer.**

Your Presentation Is Your Product

Fripp also understood that her presentation was "her product," and so it had to be very good to go up against the other "products" (presentations) on the market. This is why, in 1988, she decided to work harder on her presentation skills than she ever had before. Now, keep in mind this is *after* she had already been named "One of the Ten Most Electrifying Speakers in North

America" by *Meetings and Conventions* magazine, after she had served as the first woman president of the four thousand–member National Speakers Association, and after she had spoken in front of audiences as big as nine thousand! To Patricia, being good simply wasn't good enough—she wanted to be the best she could be.

Her first step was to take a comedy workshop. This was immediately followed by an acting workshop for speakers. When she felt she still wasn't getting the kind of results she was looking for, she hired the acting instructor for a private consultation. For five hours, at one hundred dollars an hour, he went over her promotional video with her, looking for ways they could strengthen the impact of her stories.

Two hours into the coaching session, Fripp was dismayed to find they were still working on her first story. By the end of the five hours, she walked out of the session completely exhausted and overwhelmed. She felt that she had so much to fix that she couldn't possibly give her upcoming speech, much less charge the client her $2,500 fee (at the time).

Of course, she did end up giving the speech and it went just fine. However, just the fact that she thought about not giving the speech when she realized how much more she still had to learn shows how seriously she takes her job and how committed she is to giving her clients only the very best.

Now, here's the point: If Patricia Fripp, at her level, is willing to invest not only time and money in improving herself, but also willing to open herself up to the sting of criticism in order to improve at her craft, then so can you and I! This means that we not only audio- and videotape our presentations, but we seek out a coach (someone with more experience than us) who can give us their honest feedback on our performance, as well as ways we can make it better. (Praise feels good, but you will grow ten times more from constructive criticism.)

Growth from Pain

Fripp says that out of that painful coaching session she grew tremendously. She knew once she mastered her weaknesses, it would raise her program to an even higher level. And indeed, at the 1996 National Speakers Association convention she was given the "Cavett" trophy—NSA's most prestigious award, and the speaking profession's equivalent of the Oscar.

▶ **SECRET #3: Serious speakers are willing to open themselves up to constructive criticism so they can objectively identify and then correct their weaknesses.**

In order to fully appreciate just how far Fripp has come, we need to go back and see where she came from.

Born in England

Born in the small English town of Wimborne, Fripp became a hair stylist at age fifteen. When she was twenty, she moved to San Francisco without a job, place to live, or contacts. However, she did have three things: 1) a great deal of ambition, 2) an open mind, and most important of all, 3) an assumption that if she worked hard enough she would succeed.

In 1969, she began to attract media attention by becoming one of the first women to style men's hair here in the United States. In 1975, she started traveling nationwide for a hair-care product company doing seminars for hair stylists. I'll let Patricia take over from here:

> I was teaching them how to cut hair, but I had enough sense to realize that if someone is listening to you for four hours, just talking about hair isn't going to keep their attention. So I would tell little funny stories, promotion ideas, and things I had done right and wrong in my business.
>
> Well, the talking part of what I was doing was so successful, the company expanded the seminars to a second day. I would do hair on one day and a seminar the second day. One of my clients in my salon said, "If you're speaking, come give a speech to the Golden Gate Breakfast Club." This was a group of businessmen who had been meeting for eighty years and every week they wanted a free speaker!

Being the star of my Dale Carnegie class, from day one I never stood behind a lectern, never used notes—the notes were in my head—and I would always wander through the crowd and ruffle the men's hair! I would utilize my personality.

Hold the phone! Fripp's last sentence, "I would utilize my personality," is a huge tip. Getting as much of your personality into your presentation is what is going to make you stand out from Joe and Jane Average. Audiences don't just want to know dry facts and statistics (they can get those from a book), they want to know why *you* think what you're saying is important. One way you do this is by putting your own unique "spin" on the information as you deliver it. For Fripp, this meant getting right down into the audience and running her fingers through men's hair. Who knows, maybe they had even heard her point before, *but the way she did it* may have been just what was needed to make her point memorable.

Obviously, in order to put more of your personality into your presentation, you must know what your personality is. The saying, "know thyself," really applies here. For example, if you tend to see the funny side of life, then the last thing you want to do is make a serious presentation. Instead, let your natural sense of humor come out during your talk. I guarantee that if you do this, both you and your audience will have more fun.

▶ **SECRET #4: Getting as much of your own personality into your presentation is one of the best ways to not only make your material more memorable, but to make yourself more memorable to your audience.**

Let's get back to Fripp's story:

[The Golden Gate Breakfast Club] recommended me to a second group and then to a third group, and then I realized after my third talk that people who came to hear me speak came into my salon. At this point I still didn't think about ever being a speaker; this was just to promote my business. We then began saying to our clients, "If you can get together twenty of your employees, I'll come give you a free talk on how to work together as a team." All I asked was they let me tell everybody where my salon was.

Up to this point, Patricia was using speaking solely as a way to bring in more customers to her salon. However, as you're about to see, attending her first National Speakers Association convention in 1977 changed all that. Still, notice that she didn't just rush right out and quit her day job. Seeing the big picture, Fripp realized that if she was going to build up a successful speaking business, it was going to take time, just like it had taken time to build up her hair styling business:

> I first decided I wanted to be a speaker in 1977 when I attended my first National Speakers Association convention. I realized that speaking was what I wanted to do when I grew up! I went into the hair business at age fifteen. At thirty I had signed a ten-year lease. At thirty-two I went to NSA. I realized, unlike some people who go to NSA, that becoming a speaker is definitely a long-term goal; it's not something where you get all excited and go home and quit your job.
>
> I had also invested fifty thousand dollars into my hairstyling salon, so I needed to make that successful and profitable. I put a goal of eight years, when my lease was up and when I'd turn forty, as to how long I would give the speaking career. I'd hoped that by then I would be doing well enough that I would be able to keep the salon if I wanted to, but not because I needed the money. Quite frankly, at that time, I had no idea how big and successful I'd get.
>
> Back then I also had a product distribution company and, as my speaking grew, I sold my product distribution company to my sales manager. I actually retired from the hairstyling business one year before my goal, at age thirty-nine. That same year I became president of NSA.

Again, the point here is that Fripp did not become a great speaker overnight. Rather, she took her time, set a goal for herself and, like the tortoise, made sure and steady progress until one day she had gone further than even she could have imagined.

Uncertainty During Her First Year
As a Full-Time Speaker

It would be misleading to imply that everything went smoothly during Fripp's transition from hairstylist/speaker to full-time speaker. The fact that at first, quite naturally, she didn't have as much work as she would have liked did cause her some concern:

> During my first full-time year as a professional speaker, when I wasn't as busy as I am now, there were some tight financial months, and you begin to think, "Oh God, am I really doing the right thing?" Happiness and success are the same thing to me: never sweating cash flow.

Success means different things to different people. To Fripp, she is happiest when the money is coming in. So, when things initially weren't moving as quickly as she would have liked, rather than get down on herself, she simply rolled up her sleeves and worked harder.

Why didn't she just throw in the towel and say, "Well, I tried. I guess it wasn't meant to be." There are many individuals who do exactly that every year. They dabble in speaking for a while, find they can't make a living at it, and get out lamenting, "It's just too competitive."

Believing in Yourself

The reason has to do with Fripp's belief system. She believed in herself and had enough self-confidence that she knew she would somehow make a go of the speaking profession, just like she had with her hair salon.

Remember what Barbara De Angelis said about confidence?: "Confidence isn't knowing how to do everything. Confidence is having enough faith (belief) in yourself that you can go out find the answers that you need." Fripp didn't know exactly how she was going to make her speaking business work; all she knew was that she would find a way. And of course, she did!

You may be reading this thinking, "Okay, great. Fripp believed in herself. But how do *I* develop this kind of self-confidence?" You do it by first having small successes and then building on them.

Confidence Comes from Success

For example, there was a time in your life when you were very little, and you were just learning how to tie your shoes. You probably don't remember how frustrated you got the first dozen or so times you tried it. However, did you give up? No! You kept on trying to tie your shoes until one day—success!—you did it. That gave you the confidence you needed to be able to put on any pair of lace-up shoes.

The next time mom took you to the shoe store, you took one look at all the shoes on the shelf that were your size and thought, "I know how to wear all of you!" There was no doubt or fear in your mind, just a wonderful feeling of confidence. Because of your previous success with your first pair of shoes, it gave you the confidence that you could handle any pair of lace-up shoes.

▶ 	**SECRET #5: You develop the confidence to face a new goal by re-membering previous successes you've had in the past and saying to yourself, "Since I've done these other things, there's no reason why I can't be successful at this new goal."**

Because Fripp had achieved success cutting hair, and she knew she was good at it, it gave her the confidence that she could suc-ceed at other things, such as public speaking:

> There was a time when I was cutting hair and I was new in the men's hairstyling industry. Then, one day, I suddenly real-ized that when I say to someone, "This is what you should do with your hair," I knew beyond a shadow of a doubt that I was absolutely right.
>
> I was famous in the hairstyling business for doing things with men who didn't have a lot of hair—I made them look like they had a lot more hair. You know how many men would sweep their hair around to the front? Well, what I did was cut it all off! When I would talk to stylists about

doing this, they would ask, "How do you talk people into letting you do this?" Well, I never had any problem with this because I was so confident and I knew . . . and I knew that I knew!

Eventually You Get to the Point Where You Know That You Are Good

It gets this way in speaking, where you just know that you're good without getting cocky. At first, there is a time when, if the audience doesn't respond, you take it personally. Then, there comes a point where, as Bill Gove says, "You are responsible to your audience, not for your audience." In other words, I am going to be prepared, researched, sober, and well-dressed, but I can't guarantee the audience will be!

For example, I was booked to speak on the sixth day of a six-day conference. It was to take place in a convention hall with 2,200 seats, of which they told me that probably 1,700 would be filled. Well, 250 turned up! And because they had these big screens they were projecting me on, nobody sat in front—they could see the screens better from the back. Now, it's hard to have a lot of energy when you're in this enormous place. I absolutely did the best I could; however, I did not have a good time. I don't just speak for the money; I want to make a contribution, have a good time, *and* make my money!

There are going to be those times every once in a while when things aren't going to go as well as you would have liked. Fine. As this story illustrates, it happens to the best of 'em. Learn from it and move on. Sometimes things are going to happen that are outside of your control. Clearly, there was nothing Fripp could have done about the fact that only 250 showed up when she was expecting 1,700. All she could do was make the best of it.

Note, however, that she did not get down on herself or beat herself up about it. That's where knowing that you are good really comes in handy. You aren't afraid to say, "Hey, I've done this enough times to know that it's good; however, I can't do it all by myself!" If the audience has been drinking (remember Mark Victor Hansen's story?) or they simply don't show up, as in this case, you learn what you can from the experience and move on to your next speech.

▶ **SECRET #6: Your job as a speaker is to give the audience the best that you have; however, you cannot control their response. As Bill Gove says, "You are responsible *to* your audience, not *for* your audience."**

Your Confidence Will Grow As You Do

Keep in mind that your confidence will grow over time, as you grow. The more experiences you go through, the more successes you get under your belt, the more confident you will become. In fact, when I asked Fripp if she was always as confident as she appears today, she replied:

> No, not to this same extent. It just comes from years and years and years of doing it and doing it and doing it! Confidence comes from success. And in the beginning when you don't have the successes yet, you don't have quite the confidence.

Being Driven Is Not Necessarily Bad

While many people would consider Fripp to be extremely driven, she reminds us that being driven, contrary to popular belief, is not necessarily a bad thing. It's only bad if you feel frustrated and stressed out about your work:

> When I do anything, whether it's taking gourmet cooking lessons or giving dinner parties, which I use to do before I got so involved in business, I do it one hundred percent.
>
> People talk about being a "type-A personality," but the latest statistics show that type-A personalities only have heart attacks if they're experiencing a lot of frustration and they

don't feel in control of their life. I have always loved what I do for a living so much that I have never felt as if my work has deprived me of anything.

Those of us who feel passionately about speaking rarely feel stressed out for very long. Sure, everybody has their moments, but on the whole, most of the successful speakers I know genuinely love their work and couldn't imagine doing anything else.

The Difference Between Being Pushy and Pushing for Excellence

Those of us who do have a passion for excellence often have to deal with people who seem to have a passion for mediocrity. Consider the following scenario:

Mary has been hired by an association to give a presentation at a hotel when, upon arriving, she notices that the lighting where she will be speaking is extremely dim. Upon further inspection she sees that a number of the light bulbs in the ceiling, as well as in three of the four spotlights, are burnt out.

After spending fifteen minutes trying to find someone who can help her, she finally locates the hotel electrician and explains the problem. After shaking his head from side to side, he starts to mumble about having to get a ladder, and how he doesn't have the right bulbs anyway, etc. Finally, not wanting to make a big deal out of it, Mary just nods her head and slowly walks back to the conference room. She has resigned herself to the fact that the audience isn't going to be able to see her very well and that it's going to be a very long night.

The fact that Mary, in our example, didn't want to "make a big deal out of it" is understandable—she didn't want word getting back to the meeting planner that she was difficult to work with. However, as Fripp reminds us on the next page, we are there to perform a job which the client has paid us good money to do (the amount is immaterial). Therefore, whenever possible, we should always strive to create an optimal speaking environment for our audience:

When I speak, I get to the hotel early and I check out the set-up of the room. If it's not right, I'll say to the hotel people, "Look, you need to bring the back rows forward, you need to narrow this aisle." I'll say to the photographer, "Yes, you can take my photograph, but please do not take it during the first half-hour because that's when I will be building rapport with the people. If you leap up and try to take pictures during the beginning of my talk, it will totally distract the audience."

I figure that a meeting planner is not only hiring me to give a speech, but they are hiring my twenty years experience attending meetings. My job is to help tell them how I can earn the money they pay me! If I say, "I need the lights brighter," and they reply, "Oh well, it's fine." I say, "Believe me: I *need* the lights brighter!"

I know what works for my performance. If the audience can't see me well, or there are distractions, such as photographers running around, that's going to affect the overall impression that the audience has of me. So again, my job is to tell them how to make me successful.

▶ **SECRET #7: When setting up for your speech, if conditions aren't right, don't be afraid to ask firmly for what you want. Remember, if something is worth doing, it's worth doing right.**

You say, "God, isn't she pushy." No, that comes from the confidence of knowing what works and wanting to make the program a success for them. Now, I try to do it in the nicest possible way. For example, if they want to put me on after a half-hour of award presentations, I'll say, "The modern way of meeting planning is to have your speaker on first. That way, after I'm finished, you can give out all these wonderful awards and then, when it's over, all their friends can race up and congratulate them. But if they have to wait forty-five minutes before they can congratulate them, it kills the excitement." If they still insist on having me go on last I say, "Fine, whatever you like."

So there you have it—first Fripp asks for what she wants. If she doesn't get it, she politely, but firmly, explains why she is asking for things to be done this way (because it's in the client's best interest!). If her request is still denied, she doesn't argue or cause a scene. She knows that they are paying her fee and so, in the end, they have the last word. In that case she simply goes out and does her best under the given conditions.

A Pro Gives His or Her Best, No Matter What the Conditions

Yes, there are going to be those times when you try your best to have a new microphone brought in or the seating changed, and it seems that no one wants to cooperate (even when it would be in their own best interest to do so). Then, like Patricia says, you simply go with it.

Remember, anyone can give a great speech when everything is perfect. It's when things aren't perfect, when you are forced to work under less than optimal conditions, that separates the pros from the amateurs. While an amateur might think, "This isn't fair, I can't work under these conditions," a pro says to him or herself, "Fine, if this is what they want, I'll do the best I can with it. As long I can get my message out to the audience, that's all that matters." And they mean it.

I will tell you now about a time early on in my career when I didn't understand this. I was speaking at the Long Beach Naval Station in Long Beach, California, one sunny June day. When I arrived, I inquired about using their overhead projector for my presentation. I was told that it was checked out. Then, a few minutes later, I was told one had been found. Well, what they had found was the old, broken-down projector that the new one (which was checked out) had obviously replaced. It was so old, I had to use Scotch tape to hold the mirror in place. Unfortunately, the tape kept slipping and, right in the middle of my presentation, my overhead would jump from the screen to the ceiling! Each time, with the audience staring at me, I tried to quickly fix it, but the tape would always let go and—Whoop!—suddenly my overhead would be projected on the ceiling. Finally, I got so annoyed I blurted out, "Of course, it helps if you have good equipment to work with."

Well, the guy who had found the overhead projector for me was not amused with my comment. How did I know this? Because he glared at me from the back of the room for the entire rest of my speech with an expression that said, "I go and find this machine for you, and you put it down?" You know what? He was right. This is what I had to work with and my attitude should have been, "While this machine isn't the best, I'm lucky to at least have something to work with." Or, I should have not used it at all. (Actually, what I *should* have done is brought mine from home.) However, complaining about it out loud only made me look bad. I learned a lot from that experience, and I hope my sharing it with you will prevent you from making the same mistake I did.

▶ **SECRET #8: Never complain about anything in front of the audience; it only makes *you* look bad.**

First I say that you should accept nothing less than the most optimal conditions when it comes to your speaking environment; then I advise you not to complain if what you have to work with is second-rate. Am I contradicting myself? No. What I'm saying is that you should fight like crazy to make the conditions as good for your audience as possible, but if there are things that are simply out of your control, then you should make the best of the situation. Being strong, but flexible, is the hallmark of every great speaker.

The Key to Fripp's Presentations: Understanding the Needs of Her Customers

To get a better understanding of exactly what she does, I asked Fripp to tell me about a typical presentation:

Yesterday I did my third program for GTE, which has been so outrageously successful that everyone there thinks I walk on water. First of all, I asked very specific questions about what they wanted and then I delivered it. What they wanted was to make sure that all these people that work on the telephone understand what customer service is and how they make a difference in the company.

They introduced me by saying, "We couldn't bring all our customers here, but we have brought in Patricia Fripp, who represents our customers. She will talk about what customers want." GTE had been telling their people to sell, then they came back and told them customer service was what counted. Basically, they had confused them. My message to them was that giving good customer service is very good for sales. I gave them some real-life examples from my own life as to why that was true.

Let's look at it from a meeting planner's standpoint. First, I deliver what I say I'm going to. If they ask me to do something I can't do, I tell them. The way I say it is, "I'm so busy and so in demand that I'm not going to accept an engagement that I can't guarantee I'll be good at."

Secondly, I'm very easy to deal with; I'm not a prima donna. I always call the meeting planners the night before the speech and let them know I arrived safely. You wouldn't believe how many speakers don't do that. It's peace of mind for the meeting planners.

My office provides them with wonderful information to help them make their decision to hire me. We also provide every group with a handout, which outlines my key points.

Now, the audience likes me because I'm entertaining, but I also give a real message. I'm kind of funny and cute, and in the right circumstance, which fortunately is more often than not, I'm quite charismatic. I'm a great storyteller; people don't remember what you say, they remember the pictures that you create in their mind. Make a point and then tell a story. I hang around and schmooze with the people before I go on. I often work as my own warm-up act. I come into the audience and, as I said, ruffle one fellow's hair. I guess after doing this for twenty years I got quite good!

Companies Buy Much More Than Just a Speech

As you can see, there's quite a bit involved when Fripp decides to take on a speaking engagement. This brings out a good point: While many people cannot believe the amount of money many of the top speakers earn per speech ($3,500–$5,000 is average, while the celebrity types earn $25,000 and up), what they don't realize is how much effort goes into every presentation. As you can see, the time involved is much more than the sixty minutes (or whatever it is) actually spent in front of the audience.

The companies for which Patricia works pay for her hours of preparation, as well as time spent traveling to, coming from, and "hanging out" at the event. And, as she mentioned, they are also paying for her twenty years of experience. What this means is that they are virtually guaranteed of getting a great program. This is the reason top speakers are so well paid: They can deliver!

▶ SECRET #9: When a company hires you, they are paying for much more than just a speech. They are also paying you for all the time and energy you put into preparing your presentation, traveling to, "hanging out" at, and coming from the event, as well as all your years of experience.

Marketing: The Name of the Game is *Visibility*

To the professional speaker, having a great message is only half the ball game. The other half is letting people know about it— that's where marketing comes in. Patricia markets to speakers bureaus because companies and associations call them every day looking for speakers for their upcoming conventions, meetings, rallies, etc. Because she is constantly sending new things about herself to the bureaus, they are more inclined to book her because 1) she's good and 2) she's easy to work with. Here, specifically, is how she does it:

I market to agents. I send them a monthly memo, a monthly calendar, full-color brochures without my address and phone number (so the bureaus can put their own numbers on them), reprints of news articles, as well as video- and audio-tapes without my phone number on them. And I'm not chintzy. I order my videos two hundred at a time, so if you want me to send you ten, I'll send you ten.

I belong to five convention and visitor's bureaus in the San Francisco Chamber of Commerce. I try to be visible at these events. If I can't attend a meeting, I'll donate tapes and books and things as door prizes so at least my name is mentioned when I'm not there.

I belong to a group called "Speakers Roundtable," and we have a group newsletter that we send out to everyone on our mailing list a few times a year. We also share leads at the end of every month that are non-agent jobs. If we think that some of the leads would be good prospects for me, I send them a letter, a brochure, and a response card.

I also have a master mailing list which contains the names of everyone who has ever used me or inquired about me or bought product from me. We mail to them about twice a year. I run ads here and there, and I also go through phases when I do radio show interviews.

I have times when I spend more energy on public relations and other times when I don't. I also have articles that I've written and columns that I will give to anyone to print anywhere. I'm not concerned about making money; I just want my name out there. So, it's a combination of things; I think it just all works together.

If your name is all over the place for a long enough time, people will start thinking you're famous. Let's face it, non-celebrity speakers are famous people no one ever heard of!

Fripp's Hats:
a Clever Marketing Tool?

Singer Johnny Cash is known for always wearing black. Elizabeth Taylor is known for, among other things, wearing expensive jewelry. And Patricia Fripp is known for wearing beautiful and distinctive chapeaus:

> When I'm at NSA meetings and out and about, I always wear hats. And it absolutely amazes me that people honestly think I'm stupid enough to wear hats when I speak. That would be a stupid thing for me to do! I wear hats because part of my overall marketing strategy is to be well-known. When you walk into a room somewhat outrageously dressed . . . I go to events with five hundred people in attendance, and I'm the only one in a hat. People come up and say, "Oh, I knew that was you, Patricia, I saw the hat."

It's true. I've attended a number of NSA events with Patricia, and her hats do indeed attract a lot of attention.

One Major Difference Between a Beginning and a Professional Speaker

"Always have more to say than you have time to talk."
DRU SCOTT

The above quote is one of the differences between a beginning speaker and a professional. That is, while the pros only impart to the audience a portion of what they know about their topic, the beginner often tells everything they know. This can be a real problem if you're asked to speak for longer than you had expected.

The Time Fripp Had to Cover
Onstage for Zig Ziglar

When Fripp first started out in the speaking business, her dream was to someday share the platform with Zig Ziglar. While she has since done this on numerous occasions, the very first time she unexpectedly had to go onstage and fill in for him until he arrived from the airport:

> The first time I [spoke on the same bill as Zig Ziglar] was at a big rally in northern California, in a big auditorium. I did my one hour polished and rehearsed presentation—a fabulous speech—and then [we took a] break.
>
> The promoter of the event was not there, but his staff was all huddled in a corner and they looked very worried. They said, "Zig's plane has not even landed!" I said, "Well, you can give them a break until he gets here, but some people won't even wait an hour for Zig. Or, someone better get onstage and entertain them. I'm assuming none of you want to do it; it better be me."
>
> Fortunately, in my early days, I used to give time management seminars. So, after I had already given my polished, rehearsed speech, I stood up and said, "Zig isn't here yet, but we're going to talk about time management until he gets here."
>
> At least I had something to say, that I had said before, which was at least a halfway decent filler. One of my friends waved, Zig walked in, I finished my sentence and said, "Here's the man you've been waiting for, Zig Ziglar."

What would you have done if you had been in Fripp's shoes? Would you have had enough material (and poise) to hold the audience until Zig arrived? If so, what would you have talked about? It's worth thinking about now; that way, if it ever does happen, you'll be prepared.

▶ **SECRET #10: "Always have more to say than you have time to talk."—Dru Scott**

How to Make Your Stories Significantly More Effective

While the stories you want to use in your presentation may be clear to you (because you've lived them), you can't always assume they'll be crystal clear to your audience. Thus, it helps to tell them to a friend or two, so you can get some feedback about areas of the story that may be a bit muddled. Says Fripp:

> We know what happened because we see it in our mind, but it isn't always as clear to the audience. By running the story by someone else, they will ask you questions that will help make the story clearer to your audience.
>
> I have a friend I work with who asks me questions like, "Well, Patricia, where were you standing when you said that?" or, "How come they didn't hear you?" And so you talk the story, then have it transcribed, and then you work it over until you come up with your vignette.

Going over your stories with a friend is an excellent idea. Of course, in Fripp's example, where she was standing in her story may not be critical to the point she's trying to make; however, it's often adding small details like this that can help an audience better visualize the scene.

I want to encourage you not to be afraid to tear your stories apart with a friend. It's only by asking tough questions that you will be able to really make improvements. After investing just a couple of hours vigorously going over a story, you'll be amazed at how much better the two of you can make it. Your reward will be that from then on whenever you get up in front of an audience to tell it, you can do so with confidence because you know the story is a winner.

▶ **SECRET #11: You can dramatically strengthen your speech stories by spending a few hours going over them with a friend and eliminating any superfluous parts and/or adding any relevant details.**

Fripp's Creative Corkboard Center

Although most speakers' system for organizing their seminar material is usually pretty unexciting, I must say that Fripp's system is both creative and unique. I use a two-foot by three-foot corkboard to post notes and ideas to myself, but an entire "corkwall?" What a great idea!:

> I gather notes, articles, quotes, and thoughts, and I put them in a file. Then, I go down to my creative thinking center that I have downstairs, which has an entire wall corkboarded. I will pin the material up on the wall in the order that I think it belongs. Some of the material will be things I've never done before and some will be old things I've revised.

The reason this is such a good idea is because, like most speakers, you probably have a folder for speech ideas, either in a drawer or filing cabinet, which is crammed full of scraps of paper containing quotes, stories, facts, articles, etc. However, when you go to sort through the hodge-podge to put a new speech together, the whole operation quickly turns into a nightmare.

Fripp has come up with a simple yet powerful solution to avoid having to go through this traumatic experience. Instead of keeping the scraps in a folder, put them up on a huge cork-covered wall where you can not only see them, but have enough space to freely move them around to your heart's content. This eliminates the old "making piles on your desk" method that is so cumbersome. Give this "cork method" a try and your speech *will* eventually come together. (Of course, whether the speech is good or not will depend on how good the information is on the scraps of paper; but at least you'll be organized!)

▶ **SECRET #12: To easily and effortlessly organize your speech material, try using a cork-covered wall!**

To Be a Speaker, You Must Speak!

"The purpose of speaking is to order, clarify, and intensify the experience for the audience."
PATRICIA FRIPP

Here's what Fripp told an audience of speakers at the 1988 NSA Convention in Phoenix, Arizona, regarding the most important step to becoming a speaker:

> From the very beginning you have to speak. Bill Gove eloquently told us that Ken McFarland said, "If you want to speak, then speak." He did not say speak for five hundred dollars, speak when everything fits in with your requirements, or when you can sell products. Just speak!

Like Art Linkletter, Patricia's advice is that if you want to be a good speaker, you must do a lot of speaking. Having four-color stationary and a blazing computer is all very nice, but it doesn't do for you what being in front of a live audience three or four times a week will do.

Even reading this book isn't enough—you must get out there and actually do it. This is because you need the confidence that can only come from going in front of an audience, messing up, figuring out how you could have done it better, and then trying again. Eventually, things will start to fall in place for you and you'll begin to understand many of the ideas in this book at a deeper level, (i.e., rather than just reading about connecting with the audience by using humor, strong eye-contact, etc., you will have actually done it).

Finding Audiences to Address

Okay, so how *do* you go about finding audiences to address when you're just starting out? Says Fripp:

> You start [by contacting] everybody on your Christmas card list, everybody you know and do business with, and everybody who owes you a favor.
>
> In the beginning, develop a good thirty-minute speech that you can give in the Rotary and Kiwanis Clubs, because that's how we all start. Activity begets activity; if you don't have a brochure, the way you get work is by speaking at least three times a week.
>
> I started speaking to promote my hairstyling business. I would tell every single client that I wanted to give a talk.

> I would ask them, "Will you get ten employees together? I'll
> give a free talk." If you tell everyone you know that you have
> a speech, I promise you, you will get a few audiences.

If you put the word out to enough people that you have a speech,
and assuming it's on a topic that is of interest to people, you will get
speaking invitations. As Patricia mentioned, Kiwanis, Lyons, and
Rotary Clubs, as well as chambers of commerce, are always looking
for free speakers. You can call directory assistance to get the phone
numbers of your local clubs and chambers. When you call, ask to
speak to the club's program chair. In most cases, you'll be able to
arrange a speaking date on the spot.

After you've given a number of free speeches, eventually the
thought will cross your mind, "Hmmm, I wonder how I can get
paid for giving my talks?"

How to Know When You Are Ready to Start Charging a Fee

So, how *do* you know if you're ready to start collecting a paycheck for your speaking services? The always blunt but honest
Fripp says:

> Frankly, when you're still practicing in the early days, you
> are not ready to get the really good, thousand-plus dollar
> jobs. You're not ready yet.
>
> When you are speaking for nothing and somebody comes up
> to you and asks how much you would charge to say that to
> their group, then you can start charging! If your response is,
> "I have given thirty-five talks and no one has ever asked me
> that question," well, then you can fill in the blanks!

In other words, your audience will let you know when you're
ready to start charging. If, when you're finished speaking, people
rush up to you and ask for your business card, and then over the
next few weeks your phone rings with invitations to speak at
their events, that's a clear sign you're ready to start charging for
your services. If that's not the case, then continue to hone your

speaking skills. If you work hard, take your speaking seriously enough, and don't give up, eventually you will be good enough to start charging a fee.

How Much Should You Charge?

The answer to how much you should charge to speak at an event depends on a number of variables. How in demand is your topic? How well-known are you? (Obviously, NBA coach Pat Riley, who charges forty thousand dollars per speech, can get this hefty fee because he falls in the category of celebrity speaker. Companies aren't just paying for the information, they're paying for the fact that it's Pat Riley who's delivering it!) And of course, how good you are will also play a role in determining your fee.

In the end, though, it's the marketplace that determines exactly what you can charge. If you ask one hundred dollars for a speech and you have no takers, then obviously you're not ready to charge that much. On the other hand, if you're charging $2,500 per talk and your calendar is full, then maybe it's time to start charging $3,500. Your own experience combined with talking to other speakers, as well as speaker's bureaus, will help you determine what someone with your level of experience and expertise can expect to be paid.

I'd like to conclude this section on fees with a quote by Fripp that really says it all when it comes to deciding how much you should charge:

"To guarantee success, make sure your fee lags behind your talent, rather than your talent lagging behind your fee."
PATRICIA FRIPP

Working with Speakers' Bureaus

Generally speaking, speaker's bureaus are like banks: When you need them, they're not interested in you—it's only after you're successful that they want your business. This isn't because bureaus are mean, it's just that they're in business to make a profit. And the way they make that profit is by taking twenty-five to thirty percent of your fee. If you're not good, they can't charge a lot of money for you, and if they can't charge a lot of money for you they don't make any money. Therefore, they can only afford to work with speakers who have proven that they can "deliver the goods," so to speak. Remember, if they get their client a speaker that lays an egg, that client isn't going to be thrilled with that bureau, and they might just decide to look elsewhere for their future speakers. Like the speaking business itself, the bureau business is very competitive.

Note: In the following paragraphs, when Patricia says "agent," she's referring to someone who runs a speaker's bureau (which uses many different speakers). She is not referring to what you'd traditionally think of as an agent, such as a sports agent or acting agent, who typically only represents a few clients. Okay, here's Fripp on "speaker agents":

> At the beginning of your career, you speak; you do not worry about agents. When you are ready, the agents will find you. As you get more visible in the speaking business, their clients go to them and say, "Can you find that tall speaker with the southern accent that used to be Miss America?" (Jeanne Robertson)
>
> An agent's job is to find the perfect speaker for their client, the meeting planner. If you're visible in NSA speaking, they will find you. Many of the agents with whom I now work, I met at NSA.

Why Not Paying Agents Their Commissions Can Cost You Big-Time Down the Road

One of the deals you agree to whenever you work for a speaker's bureau is to pay it a commission on any future job that arises from the event at which it originally booked you. Some bureaus ask that you do this for the immediate thirty-six months following your presentation, and others say it's forever. It just depends on the bureau. Fripp explains why it's to your advantage to be forthright about any bookings you get through a bureau:

> Every time you have an inquiry, you have to say, "How did you hear about me?" in case it was from an audience where an agent booked you. Then, you call the agent up and tell them the good news: "*We* just made some money today because someone heard me at the speech you booked last year!" That's how you maintain, develop, and nurture a relationship.

Besides being the right thing to do ethically, letting an agent know about subsequent bookings that stem from their event is also good for business. After all, suppose you were an agent and you had your choice of recommending to a client two speakers, both of whom charge the same and are equally qualified to make that presentation. If one is very good about paying commissions, and the other has been known to have "amnesia," which one would *you* recommend?

▶ **SECRET #13: Paying agents a commission on referrals from a speech you did for them is not only the right thing to do, it's good for business, as they will be highly motivated to want to use you again.**

Meeting Planners

Meeting planners are those individuals within an organization or association whose job it is to set up the company's meetings. This includes everything from choosing the site, to booking the hotel, to hiring the speakers. It's a huge undertaking and until you've actually done it, you have no idea the amount of work involved. That's why Fripp reminds us to always be polite, professional, and courteous when working with meeting planners:

> When dealing with meeting planners, be gracious. It amazes me how many meeting planners I have spoken to who have said, "When I tell speakers they did not get the job, they

hang up or they're rude." Do you realize you might not have been chosen this year, but they might choose you next year? We always write a note saying, "Thank you for considering us. Please keep our materials in your file; we would love to be considered for another year."

[When they tell you they've selected another speaker] always say, "You have made a wonderful choice, we know you'll have a terrific convention."

Good advice. Here's more:

The Difference One Phone Call Can Make

When a meeting planner does use you, be sure to give them a call when you arrive at the hotel site. This not only shows that you're a pro, but, as Patricia points out, it relieves them of worrying about whether or not their speaker is going to show:

> Although it only takes a minute, calling a meeting planner and letting them know that you've arrived at the hotel helps alleviate a major concern: Will the speaker show up on time? Do you realize that meeting planners worry?! [For example, recently] I got in at nine o'clock on a Tuesday night. I was going to speak at eight o'clock the next morning, the third keynote speaker for a three-day conference.

> I called the meeting planner and said, "I just want you to know I arrived, I'm going to go bed early, and I will meet you at seven o'clock in the morning." She said, "Thank you so much; you are the first speaker this week that had the courtesy to call and let me know that they'd arrived. . . . I was very nervous."

▶ **SECRET #14: Always call the meeting planner as soon as you arrive at the hotel site. This will alleviate any worries they may have about their speaker showing up on time.**

Your Job Is to Make the Meeting Planner Look Like a Genius

Because meeting planners are under a tremendous amount of pressure to put on a successful event, anything and everything you can do to make their job easier will be greatly appreciated by them. And it goes without saying (but I'll say it anyway) that the better the job you do and the easier you are to work with, the greater your chances of being invited back to speak again.

In fact, Patricia says that after you do a presentation, you want the meeting planner to say two things: "Not only were you worth more than we paid you, but you were the easiest speaker we have ever done business with."

Here's one example of how Fripp makes it easy on meeting planners:

> When they say to me, "How long is your speech?" I say, "Exactly what time do you want me to get off and I will finish within two minutes either way."

With an attitude like that, is it any wonder Fripp is asked back by meeting planners to speak again and again?

▶ **SECRET #15: After your presentation, you want the meeting planner to say two things: "Not only were you worth more than we paid you, but you were the easiest speaker we have ever done business with."**

Always Confirm, Never Assume

Patricia's motto is, "Confirm, don't assume," when it comes to working with meeting planners. She understands how busy they are, and so she tries to make it easy on them in every way possible, including sending out confirmation letters that use a bullet-point format. That way, everything is clear and unambiguous:

Sample of a Bullet-Point Confirmation Letter:

- Thank you for having us speak at your event.
- Date of your event is:
- Speech starting time:
- Speech ending time:
- Location:
- Fee:
- You will: (make hotel reservations for speaker, duplicate speaker's handouts, etc.)
- We will: (ship product to the hotel, arrive the evening before and have dinner with your CEO, etc.)

While this is by no means a complete confirmation letter, you can readily see how clear and concise it is, which means fewer mistakes are made on both ends. Fripp has found that meeting planners definitely prefer this bullet-point format over lots of "wordy paragraphs."

It's also a good idea to include a self-addressed envelope (stamped is even better) with your confirmation letter. This way, the meeting planner can quickly sign their copy, enclose a deposit (if one is required), and pop it in the mail to you without having to stop and address an envelope. While this may seem like a small thing, remember, it's doing a lot of these "small things" that will quickly move you past the crowd and into the ranks of the successful professional.

Bring an Extra Copy of Your Handout

Experience has taught Fripp that bringing an extra handout to her speech is a good idea. This is because, occasionally, the copies that were supposed to be waiting for her at the event never got made. Rather than panicking, if you have brought one with you, you can have the hotel run off copies and life is good. However, if you don't bring a backup copy, and your handouts weren't duplicated (or they were, but they're back in the client's office), you're not going to be a happy camper.

Don't Assume Your "Room Setup" Instructions Will Always Be Carried Out

Even though she sends "room set-up" instructions to the meeting planner, Patricia doesn't assume they will get passed along to the hotel. This is why Fripp recommends getting to your speaking site early:

> The difference between a beginning speaker and an established speaker is that the established speaker controls the environment. They go early enough to make sure there is still time to reset anything that doesn't work.

And even if you have inspected the room you'll be speaking in the night before, a lot can happen in eight hours, as the following story illustrates.

A Meeting Planner's Worst Nightmare

Here Fripp tells about a meeting planner who thought she had everything under control, but soon found her worst nightmare had become a reality:

> A couple of years ago I gave a speech in Berkeley. This was a very important conference for the person who hired me. He had spent millions of dollars buying a conference center and millions more renovating it. On this day he had invited 150 meeting planners to an all-day seminar for a very classy

event. They had panels, me as a guest speaker, a gourmet lunch . . . they spent thousands more on four-color glossy brochures.

The woman in charge of pulling this event off was very organized. She went the day before and laid out the four-color glossy brochures on all the tables, along with all the pamphlets and information from the sponsoring organizations in the community. She then put up a big sheet with a sign on it that said, "*Do Not Remove! For Tomorrow's Meeting.*" She went home and slept well. You do, when you're well-prepared.

She got up in the morning and put on her white silk suit. She felt like a movie star. She went in at eight o'clock in the morning, an hour early, just to putter around and have coffee. When she opened the doors to the conference room, she screamed! The janitor did not speak or read English. He thought these were the leftovers from yesterday's conference and had thrown out all the brochures!

As fate would have it, she heard the garbage truck drive by. She ran down the stairs screaming, "Help. Help! Do you have brochures?" She explained her situation and asked, "Can I look and see if you have my brochures?" "Okay lady, if you want to get in" came the response. Can you imagine rummaging through the rubbish? To make matters worse, the hotel next door had had a Hungarian banquet the night before!

She did retrieve her brochures, but lost one shoe and tore her hose. At the luncheon she sat on the panel; she couldn't stand up because she had lost her shoe. Slightly reeking of goulash, she smiled as she answered the questions in her white silk suit.

Horror of horrors. While this meeting planner did everything she could think of to prepare a beautiful meeting, she didn't count on a non-English-speaking janitor almost ruining her whole event. The moral: No matter how organized you are, you must be prepared for *anything!* It was only because she went down to the room early, an hour before the event started, that she was able to save herself from total disaster.

▶ **SECRET #16: The difference between a beginning speaker and an established speaker is that the established speaker controls the environment. They get to their event early enough to make sure there is still time to reset anything that doesn't work.**

Brochures

One of the biggest questions when you're just getting into the speaking business is, "At what point should I invest in a brochure?" Fripp recommends that you don't rush out and get a brochure until you're certain you know what it is you are going to be speaking on:

> Don't race to have a brochure. They cost a lot of money and there are a lot of people who are very successful who will tell you they have wasted thousands of dollars creating the perfect brochure. Then they came to NSA and realized it was all wrong and it didn't work, or they were so embarrassed and they never sent it out again.

> So wait. Don't invest a fortune in a brochure until you know what you are going to talk about.

If Money Were No Object

The criteria that Fripp uses when she is ready to invest in a brochure and other marketing materials is an interesting one. She asks herself, *"If the world were perfect and money were no object, what would I do?"* In other words, when Fripp does decide to do something, it's first-class all the way.

While she held off spending the big bucks on her promotional material until 1987, when she did make the investment it was a hefty one: four-color press kits, four-color cassette packs, four-color video covers, a new demo video, new stationary, and—get this—forty-thousand postcards with her picture on it.

How Do You Get Famous?
Try Sending Out 40,000 Postcards!

Here's Fripp on the strategy behind the postcards:

> If you talk to any meeting planner, they are bombarded with mail. They get so much it's a wonder they even remember [any of it]. I decided to send them something without an envelope, something they didn't have to open which, hopefully, would get their attention.
>
> I bought 40,000 oversized four-color postcards, with my name and face on it. How do you get famous? You send out 40,000 postcards with *Fripp* on them! On the back was a message that said: "To help make your next meeting a success, Patricia Fripp, speaker for all reasons." There was also an 800 number if they wanted my video.
>
> The frustrating thing is that you don't know when it's appropriate to start doing this, and I can't tell you. All I know is that 1987 was exactly the right time for me.

One rule of thumb I *can* give you is that it's time to throw away your old promotional literature and get new materials printed when *you* become *better* than your brochure. Says Patricia:

> I have thrown away a lot of brochures and cassette covers because many of my friends have said, "Patricia, your packaging is not as good as you."

▶ **SECRET #17: It's time to throw away your old promotional literature and get new materials printed when *you* become better than your brochure.**

Audio- and Videotapes

Following this line of thinking, Fripp recommends that you have an audio tape, but that you not make too many because, as she quite rightly puts it, "You get better, and your tapes do not!"

In regard to whether or not you require a videotape, Patricia has discovered that they are in fact necessary once you get over a certain fee:

> For those charging two thousand dollars and up, you need a demo video to compete. Meeting planners tell me that if five speakers are competing for one job, and they have two videos, they will look at those first. If they find the speaker they like, you probably won't be considered if you only have an audiotape. This is not my opinion; meeting planners have told me this.

▶ **SECRET #18: When your fee reaches the $2,000-and-above range, videotapes become a necessary marketing tool, as meeting planners almost always need to see one before they'll hire you.**

If You Have to Apologize for It, Don't Send It Out

"Please ignore the feedback on side two of my audiotape, as the hotel's sound system was acting up." "Here's my old brochure; the new one is at the printers." While it seems to be human nature to want to apologize for our promotional materials—*don't do it!* The truth is, your clients don't really care. They have their own worries. What they want is the best material you can give them with no excuses. The following true story by Fripp is a case in point:

> [The owner of a company] looked in the NSA directory and found twenty speakers who sounded like they could present a program for his company. He wrote each of them and said, "I am interested in three speeches and we would like you to attend an industry convention; please send your materials."

> We did, and the feedback I got from him was, "Patricia, you were the first person to respond. The quality of your materials were by far the most superb, *and you were the only person who did not apologize for at least one thing you had sent!*"

Amazingly, some speakers didn't even respond to the client's request at all. Not so amazingly, Fripp got the job.

▶ **SECRET #19: If you have to apologize for a piece of promotional material, you shouldn't be sending it out.**

Why You Should Consider Hiring Someone to Answer Your Phone

Imagine picking up the telephone to call IBM during normal business hours and, after four rings, you hear a click and a "whirrrrr," followed by: "Hi. This is Ted. Sorry no one is in right now. If you're having a computer problem, please leave your name and telephone number and we'll get back to you. By the way, we're having a special on Pentiums this month. See ya!" Beeeeeeeeeep.

Obviously, there's no way a big company like IBM is going to have an answering machine taking people's calls. And one of the reasons is because it says "small time" to the caller. Fripp feels very strongly that if we are going to be in the business of speaking, we should do everything we can to project a first-class professional image to our clients. And that includes hiring someone to answer our phones:

> I do not believe that, when you get serious about this business, you can survive without a real person answering the telephone. I cannot tell you how many times in one month people say, "Can you Federal Express a packet now? We are making the decision tomorrow morning."

> If you have a machine and you call in that night, you cannot even be considered. Now, you don't have to be that

smart to know that if you are not even considered, you are certainly not going to get the job!

If an agent calls you to see if you are available on a date to submit for consideration, and they have no idea when you're going to return the call, do you honestly think they're going to wait three days? No, of course not. How you work it out, I don't know. But you have to be aware of it if you get serious. You have to run your business like a real business.

Helping Yourself While Helping the Physically Challenged

My guess is that while you probably agree with Fripp's points, you may feel that hiring someone to answer your phone is just too expensive. However, a very good solution, and one that Patricia got from fellow past NSA President Tom Winninger, is to hire someone who is physically challenged.

There are many people all over the country who are wheelchair bound and cannot leave their home, who would be a fine addition to your business. All they would need is a phone and your calendar in front of them. If you found someone who was dependable and hardworking, you would not only be helping yourself, but another human being as well. What's more, you could probably work out a very reasonable salary/commission arrangement with them. All it would take is a phone call to your state department of rehabilitation. Who knows? Maybe by this time next week you could have a person instead of a machine answering your phones. It's worth considering.

Fripp's Business Philosophy

When I asked Patricia what her overall philosophy is when it comes to business, she told me it was what her father had taught her:

> Don't concentrate on making a lot of money, but rather, con-
> centrate on becoming the type of person that people want to
> do business with. If you do that, you most likely will make a
> lot of money.

Like Art Linkletter, as well as many of the other speakers I interviewed, Fripp's advice is to not focus on the money. She points
out that if you become the kind of person people enjoy doing
business with, quite naturally, you're going to have a lot of people wanting to do business with you. And then, of course, the
money will follow.

▶   **SECRET #20: Rather than focusing on money, work on becoming
the kind of person people like to do business with, and the money
will follow.**

Fripp On Integrity

In typical "tell it like it is fashion," Fripp has some very strong
feelings about people speaking on a topic that they really have not
earned the right to talk about:

> I really have a problem with people standing up talking
> about success when they're making about thirteen thousand
> dollars a year. I'm sorry, I don't think it reeks of integrity.

It's true. To have any credibility with an audience (not to mention
integrity with yourself), you must have done what it is you are
asking them to do. For example, how many exercise videos would
Jane Fonda have sold during the 1980s if she weighed three hundred pounds? Answer: zero. It was because she looked terrific and
everyone wanted to be in the kind of shape she was in that her
workout tapes sold like crazy. People could see by looking at her
that she had earned the right to speak on exercising.

Make certain that before you choose to speak on a particular
topic, you ask yourself: "Have I earned the right to speak on this
topic?" If the answer is no, then you must figure out a way to get

the experience you are lacking (e.g., if you want to do sales training but have never sold anything, then getting a job in sales should be your first goal). The alternative is to find a new topic—one that you are qualified to speak on.

The Private Fripp

What is one thing that people don't know about Patricia Fripp? Probably that in private she's a lot more reserved than when she's at a public gathering or speaking in front of a group. She reveals:

> The public Fripp is very much like the private Fripp, except the private Fripp is a bit quieter. When people see you on-stage being outgoing, they find it hard to believe that when you're sitting on airplanes you never talk to anyone. I do like my quiet time. I like to read. I like to be peaceful. It doesn't bother me to be alone in a hotel room. I like being alone. . . . it's a luxury!

Contrary to what most people think, those who are in the public spotlight value their private time tremendously and are not always "on." After all, they, too, need time to recharge their batteries.

Admires People Who Have Achieved Their Life's Ambition

While Patricia doesn't have any role models per se, she does admire people who have created the kind of life for themselves that they truly wanted:

> I don't model myself after anybody, but I do have a lot of people I admire for different reasons. Some of my heroes are people like Oprah Winfrey and Dolly Parton; people who made themselves who they wanted to be.
>
> I have created the Patricia Fripp I wanted to be, I have created the life I wanted. In my introduction it says, "Patricia

has created her own version of *The Lifestyles of the Rich and Famous.*" And I admire those people who have done that with their life, who literally have turned themselves into who they wanted to be.

In the speaking business, I admire people like Jeanne Robertson because she's so funny and original. I admire Layne Longfellow because he does things that I couldn't do; he can sing at his programs. He has real credentials and a great education, which I don't have. So I admire that.

Giant-Sized Publicity:
The Hastings Contest and the
Ten Billboards

To give you an idea of how Fripp's mind is always looking for new ways to promote herself, consider the Hastings's Woman of the Year contest. In order to raise money for the Leukemia Society, Hastings said that whoever raised the most money in one month would get a giant-sized picture of themselves splashed across ten huge billboards in the San Francisco area. As soon as Fripp heard about the contest, she went to work contacting businesses and friends until she had raised over thirty thousand dollars. Needless to say, she won the contest. Capitalizing on the event, she took a publicity photo of herself standing next to one of her billboards and used it to generate even more media exposure via newspaper and magazine articles, and radio and TV interviews. How many other thousands of people saw the ad for the contest and didn't give it a second thought? Yet, Fripp's instincts told her that this would be an unbelievable marketing coup. She then made up her mind to go out and make it happen.

Tapping into the
Awesome Power Within You

I include this story not because I think everybody should run out and get their picture up on a billboard, but because it demonstrates the kind of drive Fripp has to succeed. And you know what? If Fripp can do it, so can you. She has simply tapped into a belief in herself that she can do anything she sets her mind to. Once you understand that the same God that created her created you, and that you have the same power and potential inside of you as she does, your life will never again be the same.

▶ **SECRET #21: There's nothing that Fripp or any of the other speakers in this book have done that you couldn't do too. Always remember that the same God that created them created you.**

Don't Compare Yourself to Other Speakers

I would like to end Fripp's chapter with her important reminder that we should never compare ourselves to other speakers, especially those who are not the norm:

> Bob Murphy has never had a brochure. He is an exception! You hear that Zig Ziglar and Art Linkletter make over ten thousand dollars a speech. They are the exception. You hear that Tom Peters will never have lunch, meet with the meeting planner, or go to a dinner because he saves himself for the main event. He is an exception.

Patricia is right. A big trap that many speakers fall into is constantly comparing themselves to other speakers. Forget about what anybody else is doing. All that matters is what you're doing. And your job is to be the best *you* you can be. Remember, you've got your own set of unique skills and a perspective on this world that is all your own. If you work hard and develop your own style, you'll be on your way to becoming the success you always knew you could be!

How Patricia Fripp would like to be remembered:

"That with Patricia Fripp,
what you saw was what you got!"
PATRICIA FRIPP

Patricia Fripp's
Success Secrets Summary

SECRET #1: If you aspire to be one of the best in your field, ask yourself everyday, "How can I do this better?"

SECRET #2: The most important element in building your business is keeping in touch with your customers.

SECRET #3: Serious speakers are willing to open themselves up to constructive criticism so they can objectively identify and then correct their weaknesses.

SECRET #4: Getting as much of your own personality into your presentation is one of the best ways to not only make your material more memorable, but to make yourself more memorable to your audience.

SECRET #5: You develop the confidence to face a new goal by remembering previous successes you've had in the past and saying to yourself, "Since I've done these other things, there's no reason why I can't be successful at this new goal."

SECRET #6: Your job as a speaker is to give the audience the best that you have; however, you cannot control their response. As Bill Gove says, "You are responsible *to* your audience, not *for* your audience."

SECRET #7: When setting up for your speech, if conditions aren't right, don't be afraid to ask firmly for what you want. Remember, if something is worth doing, it's worth doing right.

SECRET #8: Never complain about anything in front of the audience; it only makes *you* look bad.

SECRET #9: When a company hires you, they are paying for much more than just a speech. They are also paying you for all the time and energy you put into preparing your presentation; traveling to, "hanging out" at, and coming from the event, as well as all your years of experience.

SECRET #10: "Always have more to say than you have time to talk."— Dru Scott

SECRET #11: You can dramatically strengthen your speech stories by spending a few hours going over them with a friend and eliminating any superfluous parts and/or adding any relevant details.

SECRET #12: To easily and effortlessly organize your speech material, try using a cork-covered wall!

SECRET #13: Paying agents a commission on referrals from a speech you did for them is not only the right thing to do, it's good for business, as they will be highly motivated to want to use you again.

SECRET #14: Always call the meeting planner as soon as you arrive at the hotel site. This will alleviate any worries they may have about their speaker showing up on time.

SECRET #15: After your presentation, you want the meeting planner to say two things: "Not only were you worth more than we paid you, but your were the easiest speaker we have ever done business with."

SECRET #16: The difference between a beginning speaker and an established speaker is that the established speaker controls the environment. They get to their event early enough to make sure there is still time to reset anything that doesn't work.

SECRET #17: It's time to throw away your old promotional literature and get new materials printed when *you* become better than your brochure.

SECRET #18: When your fee reaches the $2000-and-above range, videotapes become a necessary marketing tool, since meeting planners almost always need to see one before they'll hire you.

SECRET #19: If you have to apologize for a piece of promotional material, you shouldn't be sending it out.

SECRET #20: Rather than focusing on money, work on becoming the kind of person people like to do business with, and the money will follow.

SECRET #21: There's nothing that Fripp or any of the other speakers in this book have done that you couldn't do too. Always remember that the same God that created them created you.

CHAPTER FIFTEEN

BORN: March 31, 1924
BIRTHPLACE: East Los Angeles, California

Leo Buscaglia

"I think a great deal of the fear and anxiety people
feel in public speaking comes from the fact
that they haven't done enough research and
rehearsal. Every lecture I've ever given,
all the PBS and tape lectures have been
worked on for months . . . and then I
can give the illusion of spontaneity."

▼

TRULY one of the giants in the self-help field, Dr. Leo Buscaglia's thirteen books have sold over eighteen million copies, gone through twenty-four editions, and been translated into nineteen languages. What's more, *Loving Each Other* was the nineteenth best-selling hardback in the entire decade of the 1980s. Leo's warmth, sincerity, and ebullience for life draw sellout crowds—which have numbered as many as ten thousand—to his lectures. And his PBS specials are always some of the most-watched events of the year by public TV viewers.

Dr. Hug

Buscaglia (pronounced Boo-*scal*-ya) is affectionately known as "the hug doctor" by his millions of adoring fans. This is because he'll often stay three to six hours after a speech to give each member of the audience a hug, an autograph, or an opportunity to take their photo with him. While the idea of total strangers hugging might sound a bit weird to some, it's what happens when people get around Leo. His very presence just seems to bring out the softer, more loving side in people. One year, when he attended the American Booksellers Convention in Anaheim, California, he actually had hardcore New York editors and publishers hugging each other!

A Life-Changing Event

While Buscaglia has always been passionate about life and people, a tragic event occurred in 1969 while he was teaching linguistics at the University of Southern California that affected him deeply. One sunny afternoon, a bright and beautiful twenty-two-year-old student from one of his classes drove her car to the cliffs in Pacific Palisades, got out, and with the car motor still running, leapt to her death. Upon hearing of her suicide, Buscaglia was deeply saddened. He realized that it didn't do any good to teach children the three Rs if we didn't first teach them how to love themselves.

Love 1A

He went to the school administration and proposed that he teach a course on love. They said, "What a great idea!" and immediately gave him their blessings . . . *not!* Says Buscaglia:

> They were horrified at the idea. And my colleagues thought I must have meant a course on human sexuality. Everyone thought I was crazy. The only way I could get it approved was to offer to teach it with no salary and no fees.

At the first meeting of the class, which was simply called "Love 1A," they expected fifty people to attend. Six hundred showed up. It caused such a sensation that the *National Enquirer* sent a reporter to do a story on the class. When the university caught wind of this, they went into a panic. The very idea of a "trash tabloid"—whose usual fare consisted of mothers who gave birth to Martian babies and three-headed talking goats—doing a story about one of their courses would forever tarnish their reputation as a respectable institute of higher education.

Their fears, however, turned out to be misplaced as the writer not only wrote a respectable/favorable story, but was so impressed with what she saw that she signed up for the class! In fact, that's how most people reacted when they heard about this "radical new class," which was the only one of its kind in the country being offered on a university campus. Either they thought it was a great idea and wanted to immediately enroll, or they thought it was the dumbest thing they had ever heard and it just confirmed their suspicions about people from Southern California.

Despite all the jokes and sexual innuendoes about what kind of homework was required and how it gave the term "social intercourse" a whole new meaning, the class continued to gain in popularity. Again, this was due to Buscaglia's tremendous ability to instantly connect with people and make them feel good about themselves. Listening to him speak, you knew that he was not only a master communicator and storyteller, but that he genuinely loved people, regardless of their race, creed, or nationality.

Within a few short years, he gained national prominence and was invited to speak at universities and conferences all around the world to spread his enthusiastic message of love, joy, and hope. To understand where this message first came from, we must go back to Buscaglia's roots.

Little Leo

Buscaglia grew up in a multiethnic neighborhood of East Los Angeles, where Germans, Jews, and Italians all lived together. His next-door neighbor was a rabbi and his best friend was Japanese. Because his family was poor, Leo and his brothers and sisters had to go without expensive toys, such as bicycles and roller-skates, which many of the other kids had. In addition, because his family was Italian, he had to endure teasing from other kids. For example, at school, while most of the kids dined on peanut butter and jelly and bologna sandwiches, Leo would pull out polenta or calamari. When the children would ask him what he was eating, he would tell them, only to be taunted with screams of, "Euweeeeee! Buscaglia eats squid! Gross!"

Celebrating Your Uniqueness

"You're an apple! Be the best apple in the world!"
ROSA BUSCAGLIA

To his credit, Buscaglia didn't let the teasing get to him. This was due to the wise life philosophy his mother had instilled in him:

> My mother used to tell me and my brothers and sisters and cousins and aunts and uncles—all of us were living in the same house—that we were different from everyone else. That we ourselves were unique, and that we had something to give. And that we shouldn't compare ourselves to somebody else, because it's like comparing an apple with an orange.
>
> "You're an apple! Be the best apple in the world!"—that was her way of putting it. And it kind of gave you a sense of

dignity. You didn't feel like you were competing with people. For instance, I didn't think my sister was a lot smarter than me, but rather, that she had different skills than I did, and both of us had something to contribute.

Growing up in that type of atmosphere was really essential, and it's something I've carried into my teaching. When I taught elementary school, I didn't demand that those thirty-two second-graders all be exactly a like. I celebrated their differences, their uniqueness, and I let them know that they were unique and different and that they had certain things they should be proud of.

▶ **SECRET #1: Never compare yourself to anyone else. You are unique! And what you have to contribute is special and different than what somebody else has to contribute.**

By the way, Rosa Buscaglia wanted her son to grow up to become a barber. She rationalized that people would always need their haircut and that way he would never go hungry. Coming from the world she lived in, this made complete sense. However, luckily for us, Leo followed his heart and became a teacher to the world.

Papa Buscaglia

"The worse sin in the world is going to bed as ignorant as you had awakened in the morning."
TULIO BUSCAGLIA

Although Tulio, Leo's father, never made a lot of money during his lifetime, he had a great passion for learning, which he passed on to his children. At night, he would ask each of them what they had learned that day. Leo remembers running to the encyclopedia on more than a few occasions so he would have something to tell his father when he asked, "What did you learn today, Felicia?" (pronounced Fee-LEE-Chay—it's Leo's middle name and means *happiness* in Italian). Says Buscaglia:

We always had something to tell him that we had learned, because we made a point to learn it.

A Thirst for Knowledge

"The only purpose in having knowledge is to share it."
LEO BUSCAGLIA

No doubt because of his father's influence, Leo developed a love for books at an early age. So much so that one day he set an ambitious goal for himself: He decided he was going to read every book in the Malabar Street Branch Library! He implemented his plan by checking out the first six books that began with the letter *A,* and was fully prepared to work his way through the thousands of books until he got to *Z.* Fortunately, a caring librarian figured out what Leo was up to. She patiently explained to him that if he continued his plan, he would read a lot of bad books that were in the beginning of the alphabet, which would prevent him—for quite a long time, anyway—from reading some really great ones that happened to be at the end of the alphabet. Young Leo saw the logic in her thinking and gratefully took home an armload of the classics to read, such as *Moby Dick.* Says Buscaglia:

> I wanted to know everything! I wanted to experience everything! I wanted to know everyone! I was never satisfied with just being placated by knowing the person next door or by reading one book. I wanted to read hundreds of books!

Teachers

"Being a teacher is being a communicator."
LEO BUSCAGLIA

One of the reasons Buscaglia became a teacher was no doubt due to the fact that he had so many good role models around him who both encouraged and inspired him:

That librarian taught me about the joy of literature. I also had a drama teacher who taught me about the wonderful dynamics of how to communicate with an audience. And there was an English teacher who once sat me outside a bungalow in high school and said, "Did you know that you have a very lovely writing style that's very simple and conversational and easy to understand? You can use this as a resource." I had never known that; no one had told me that I could write. It made a difference.

All these people instilled a sense of security and dignity in me. They helped me to grow.

Be Anything but Boring!

One of the reasons Buscaglia is such a great teacher/speaker is because he was forced to sit through his share of boring speakers in graduate school, and he vowed never to be one:

Having gotten my doctorate degree, I had to sit through some pretty dreadful speakers. And I always thought to myself that I would not want to be that way. I just cannot understand how people can allow themselves to get before an audience and bore them to death. Even if they do have something to say, it seems to me they could find some wonderful, original, exciting way to say it!

▶ SECRET #2: As a speaker, your job isn't just to have something exciting and interesting to say, but also to say it in an exciting and interesting way!

The Smorgasbord Method of Teaching/Speaking

"Learning is a leading out, not a forcing in."
FRENCH PHILOSOPHER

Buscaglia's style of teaching/speaking is to give his audience a plethora of ideas, stories, and anecdotes, all laced with words of wisdom, and then let them pick and choose what they want:

> You're a very foolish person if you think you teach people by telling them. My concept of teaching has always been to set up a gourmet table and invite people to eat, recognizing that if you have a diversity of food, everybody will find something that he or she likes.

> But if you have only a few little dishes, you're going to find people who dislike them. When you bring people to the table, you say, "Help yourself to whatever you want. Why not try the artichoke, because you might like it. If you don't, discard it and don't have anymore artichoke; try something else next time."

> All we need [in order] to be the perfect "us" is already in us. What the teacher does is help us get in touch with those things, and encourages us to bring them out. And when we do, [the teacher] reinforces them and celebrates them, and then says, "Now go in again and find something else."

▶ **SECRET #3: Rather than simply give their students the answers, good teachers draw answers out of their students and then encourage them to look for more.**

What Death Has to Teach Us

Making peace with death seems to go against the very nature of our essence, which is to survive at any cost. Yet, Buscaglia reminds us that until we do [make peace with death], we can never be truly free to live life to its fullest:

> The greatest teacher of all is death. Death is an enormously magnificent, dynamic teacher. It's democratic; it comes to everyone. And when you make your peace, truly—not just talking it—with the fact that you are mortal, and that you are not going to live forever, all at once things really become passionate. I cannot tell you how many people who,

when they found out they had a terminal illness, all at once become great lovers of life.

Death says to us, "Don't wait!"—because it can come at anytime. You don't have to be ninety years old to die. Little children die. So it can come at anytime in your life. Knowing that, step aside from it and live! Life is the gift you're given while you're waiting for death. And it doesn't matter who you are, or how famous you are, or how many people you've influenced—you're going to go!

If you can look at death as a positive experience, suggesting that you live life, then anything else is insignificant and pales.

Whether you are rich or poor, big or little, black or white, death is coming! And so, rather than fret about it, you're much better off using it as the ultimate reminder to pay attention to the people and experiences that make up your life.

▶ SECRET #4: You can either fear death, or you can use it as a positive reminder that each day of life you are given is a precious gift.

Paying Attention

"The moon is there, but we don't know it, because we never bother to look at it."
LEO BUSCAGLIA

Another reason Leo is such a great speaker, is because he is a great observer of people and the world in general. The better you become at paying attention to the world you live in, the better job you can do of reporting to your audience the interesting experiences and people from your life. Obviously, this is not something that is going to happen all by itself—you must consciously make an effort to really see the people and things around you. Says Buscaglia:

We know so little about the people we love. Our children's faces . . . they're there, but we don't look at them. We don't even look at the face of the person that we love. And that's one of the great tragedies.

Do you know about your mother's first date? Do you know about the first man that kissed her? Do you know about her greatest moment of despair?

When I would ask the students in my Love class the color of their mother's eyes, only thirty percent of any class I asked was able to tell me! Most of the time we don't have time nor interest to know about it. And these people die, and then we wonder why we have nothing to hold on to.

▶ **SECRET #5: Learning to really pay attention to the people and events in your life will make you a better communicator.**

Love

"When you've missed love, you've missed the essence of life."
LEO BUSCAGLIA

Wherever Buscaglia goes to speak, the topic is always a variation on one theme: love. That's because he feels that the majority of the problems in this world stem from the fact that most people have never learned *how* to love. Hence, they aren't able to truly love themselves or others, and are missing out on what he considers the essence of life.

While most people think that knowing how to love is something you're just born with, Leo says that in reality it's a skill. And like any skill, you must work on it everyday if you want to get good at it:

Everybody assumes that he or she is a lover. Love is a learned phenomenon. And if you want to learn it, like everything else, you have to put in the effort to do so.

Of course, Buscaglia is used to being called naive and unrealistic, and it doesn't bother him in the least:

> In order to be a lover in a world where it isn't reinforced, you have to be willing to stick your neck out. But, you do run the risk of people thinking you're empty-headed, or naive, or a phony.
>
> I open my arms to everything. To all experiences, to all people. To do that you must be very vulnerable. Some people see this as foolishness. I see it as the most essential trait for changing and growing and becoming.

He points out that in our country, with all the crime, stress, and concern over making money going on everyday, most people don't give the subject of love much thought anymore; after all, "Who has time?":

> Usually, the more simple cultures are the ones where love is most prevalent. I went to Bali, and there they live love! If you travel through small villages in Mexico, they invite you into their homes to eat and talk. In little towns in Italy, the people embrace you. Love is harder to express in a "civilized" society where people are besieged with worry about their cars, their jobs, and their money. And love gets pushed to the background.

A sad but true commentary on modern society. So, how do you become a better lover of life? The first step is to decide to:

> Love is a decision you make. You have to decide that you're not going to join the negative people. You're going to be a positive person.

The next step is not to sit around waiting, but to go out into the world and create the kind of positive, loving experiences you want:

> If you want love, don't sit in your living room and wait for it. Love doesn't come to people who wait! It's an active thing; it's a verb. If you want excitement in your life, you've

got to make it. If you want beauty in your life, you've got to create it. Don't wait for it!

▶ **SECRET #6: Be a proactive force of love and creativity, rather than a passive blob of inactivity and uncertainty.**

Learning to Express Love

"Love is very simple; it is we who are complex."
LEO BUSCAGLIA

Many people have a hard time expressing their love. One thing that can make it easier is if we remember that love is not only expressed by what we say, but also in our actions. Here, Leo reminds us that it's often the little things we do, as well as the way we do them, that can make somebody feel loved:

> Affection has to do with writing a little note and putting it in the refrigerator that says, "Honey, I don't know what I'd do without you." Or, when she comes home and she's dented the car and you say, "It's okay, it's only a car, are you all right?"

No Strings Attached

"If you're going to love, you're going to have to learn how to compromise."
LEO BUSCAGLIA

One of the hallmarks of a good lover is that they are able to give away their love, as well as physical gifts, with no strings attached:

A gift is only a gift, by definition, if it is given freely, in joy, with no strings attached. And that's true of love.

▶ **SECRET #7: For something to truly be a gift, it must, by definition, be given with no strings attached.**

Buscaglia On What
Makes a Great Speaker

No doubt the biggest reason for Buscaglia's success as a speaker is his love and passion for life. In fact, when asked why he thinks he's such an effective speaker, he replied:

I think it's because I feel very strongly about what I talk about, and I believe very strongly in what I'm talking about.

Indeed, Buscaglia goes on to say that a great speaker is like a zealot, in that they are so excited about their ideas that they can't wait to share them with others:

A great speaker is a great communicator. It's somebody who has something really special that he or she wants to offer, and then finds the best means to share that with others. They feel like a zealot, that they must give it to someone else, because of their enthusiasm. You've got to feel it and you've got to want to share it desperately with someone else.

When I have an idea about which I feel strongly, and I succeed in communicating that to an audience, I am really, really thrilled.

Airing Stuffy Rooms

I asked Buscaglia what he thinks about while he is speaking to an audience:

I am thinking, "Am I actually reaching the people? Am I finding the best ways of opening doors that have, perhaps, been closed in the past? Am I airing rooms that have become stuffy? Am I doing this in a very gentle way?" I don't want to throw custard pies in people's faces, but I do want to at least send some sparks out that will enliven their lives and enlighten them.

Being a Speaker Gives You Power

> *"Words can either create or destroy;*
> *they can enrich or diminish."*
> LEO BUSCAGLIA

Being a speaker carries with it a big responsibility. Because you are up in front of the room and are the focus of attention, what you say does affect people. That's why Buscaglia feels it's important that speakers encourage their audience to look to themselves for answers, and not to see the speaker as the source for their power:

> To me, the art of communication is one of the most exquisite arts. If you can affect somebody's life by something you have to share and that you believe in strongly, that's an awesome power. This is why you have to be very careful not to imprison the people who feel strongly about what you're talking about. Because you do have power. If you are a strong motivational speaker, you have to be sure that what you're giving your audiences liberates them, not ties them to you.

The way you avoid taking people's power is by speaking from a place of humility and love, rather than ego and control.

The Magic of Words

> *"I love to see words bounced around magically*
> *by great orators."*
> LEO BUSCAGLIA

Like an artist uses colors to paint a picture on canvas, a speaker uses words to paint a picture in people's minds. Here's Buscaglia on why we should be constantly increasing our vocabulary:

> The linguist says that we are our words. We think with language, and if we have a limited language, we have a limited thought process. Those people who have facility with language can expand their worlds! That's why we should never stop reading and talking and listening and learning because the brain has no limitation. *We* are the ones who set the limitation.

A Frightening Word

In his interview with Tony Robbins on *PowerTalk,* Buscaglia shared how a certain word sends chills up his spine:

> A word that frightens me and limits ninety percent of our population is *no.* "No" sends chills up my spine when I hear somebody say it. And they say no to life and no to love and no to beauty and no to art and nature and God! And they just no, no, no their way through life!
>
> It's terrifying because life is yes, and love is yes, and beauty is yes, and joy is yes. And even pain is yes; not no to pain. The greatest lessons I've ever learned in my life I've learn through pain. Now, I'd prefer learning through joy, that would be the best way, but sometimes life isn't like that. There are no bad experiences. The only bad experiences are the ones we don't learn from.

▶ **SECRET #8: The only bad experiences are the ones you don't learn from.**

The Biggest Mistake Speakers Make

When I asked Leo what he thought was the biggest mistake speakers make, he didn't hesitate for a moment:

Walking out onstage and being unprepared—thinking, "I can do it. I can wing it. This is just another one of those things." You have a tremendous responsibility to your audience and you have no right to waste their time. I object to those speakers who, because of their reputation or whatever, think they don't have to continue to grow and find new ways of communicating.

I feel very strongly about this: *Never wing it!* Regardless of the circumstances, you prepare. Even when I was teaching my undergraduate classes at USC, I would orchestrate every lecture. I would never go into any class with a bunch of notes and feel I could just talk off the top of my head. I would decide what it was that I was trying to teach or share with my students on that particular day. What is the best way I can get this material across? What interesting and exciting and motivating ways can I use?

Every lecture I've ever given, all the PBS and tape lectures have been worked on for months and months. Then I can give the illusion of spontaneity. It's the same in any art form. Nureyev doesn't just go on the stage and dance "Swan Lake." He rehearses for eight hours a day, seven days a week, for months! And then he walks onstage and he looks as if he's creating the choreography as he's going along.

The same thing is true if you are a communicator; you cannot be lazy. If you want to communicate, you've got to sit down and work on it. Make sure that everything you do and say is deeply felt and understood by you. When you do that and rehearse it enough, it alleviates a great deal of the fear and anxiety.

I think a great deal of the fear and anxiety people feel in public speaking comes from the fact that they haven't done enough research and rehearsal. So when the time comes for them to speak, they get completely tongue-tied.

▶ **SECRET #9: The biggest mistake speakers make is not preparing properly for their presentation.**

Give Up Trying to Be Perfect

*"Some of the biggest problems arise
when we begin to believe that we are perfect,
or that the world should be perfect."*
LEO BUSCAGLIA

Those of us who are perfectionists know exactly what Buscaglia is talking about in this quote. Sometimes, we forget that we are human beings and get discouraged when we fall short of our goal or feel we should have done more. Equally as unrealistic, we forget that the people we deal with everyday of our lives are human beings, too. And so when they make a mistake we throw our hands up in the air and curse at the never-ending "gross incompetence that runs amok in the world."

However, leave it to Buscaglia to get us back on the right track and remind us that, "first and foremost," we are human beings, and human beings are far from perfect. Once we not only understand this, but joyfully accept it, life just seems to run a lot smoother:

> If you see yourself first and foremost as a human being, then, when you're trying to communicate with another human being, you can't fail. It's when you have the idea that you have the answers or that you're perfect that you tend to fall on your face.

▶ **SECRET #10: Once you not only understand, but also joyfully accept the fact that human beings (and that includes yourself!) are not perfect, life just seems to run a lot smoother.**

Only Uses Self-Effacing Humor

*"If you learn to laugh at yourself,
you'll never run out of things to laugh at."*
LEO BUSCAGLIA

As you might expect, Buscaglia never uses humor to put down others. Instead, he tells funny stories about himself, his childhood, and his Italian family:

> Whatever humor or stories I use, they're always personal. I don't use humor at the sake of somebody else. They're always crazy things about myself.

> To so many people life is a very serious business. First of all, it is not a business! And it's not serious. And unless you have a sense of humor in this crazy world, you'll surely go mad.

Why Success Hasn't Gone to Buscaglia's Head

Given all the success he's had, I asked Leo how he's managed to stay so humble:

> I think egos, as far as I'm concerned, are laughable. The one thing I've never lost touch of is that I'm a human being. I've never demanded perfection of myself and therefore I've never demanded it of anyone else. I know that I don't know everything. In fact, I know almost nothing. I know that I'm constantly changing. So, I'm not embarrassed about making mistakes and being vulnerable and learning from others.

> I think, too often, that a speaker who becomes in great demand thinks they know it all. That they don't need to continue to grow and learn and change. So they keep saying the same thing, again and again and again. I think that's just too bad.

From Being Poor to Being Rich

"The best reason to make a million dollars
is so you can give it away."
LEO BUSCAGLIA

Although Buscaglia grew up poor, and now he's a multi-million-aire, I noticed he never talks about money in any of his interviews. When asked why, he responded:

> Because it's the most insignificant aspect of anything anybody does. The funny thing about money is, the more you think about it, the more it goes out the window. You do what is right for you, you live in dignity, you give everything that you can, and if the money comes, that's wonderful. But if it doesn't, that's wonderful too.
>
> In my book, *The Way of the Bull*, I wrote about how I traveled through Asia for three years and lived in all kinds of conditions. I studied with some Buddhist teachers, and I realized that we need very, very little to survive in this world. And if you truly believe that, then money is something that is there for convenience.
>
> It's nice to have it; it adds comfort to your life. But, basically we can all survive with one decent meal, a tiny little area to sleep in, and our own dignity.
>
> I don't eat that much; I don't travel that much anymore. The pine trees are free; the sun is free; the air is free; the beaches are free. I have wonderful friends who don't charge me for their friendship! So what do I need a lot of money for? I find by giving it away that you can help others to grow in their dreams. And that really is the most satisfying thing that money can do.
>
> During the 1980s, you were measured by how much money you had, which is crazy. I was living on thirty-five cents a day when I was traveling through Asia! If I lost everything tomorrow, I could go back to doing a thousand things and be very happy to live on subsistence wages. I never have placed much emphasis on money, maybe because I spent most of my life without it. When the money did come, I realized it could be used for good things and so I spent most of my time giving it away.

I have to tell you that every time I read Buscaglia's philosophy on money, I can't help but think of Mike Ferry's views on the same subject and it makes me chuckle. To me, this is what makes this book so much fun; that you can have two very successful individuals with differing points of view. I see my job as one of presenting all the speakers and their various thoughts and ideas to the best of my ability, and I leave it for you, my dear reader, to decide which ones are right for you. As Buscaglia says, "Take the stuff you like and discard the rest!"

Walking Your Talk

By the way, Leo does "walk his talk" in regard to giving away money. He founded the Felicia Foundation, which gives money to educational projects that teach people the joy of giving.

Making sure that what he projects on the platform is the same as who he is off of it, is extremely important to Buscaglia:

> One thing that I've been most pleased about is that when people meet me, after having heard me speak or read my books, they say, "Goodness, you're just like what you talk about." I always figure that's the greatest compliment they can pay me. I don't "turn on" when I go before a microphone; I'm still me, just the way I am talking with you right now.

> This is one thing I'm most proud of—that I am the person I project. That means a lot, because I've met so many people who in their work, project all kinds of sincerity and eagerness, and then when you meet them, it's just not there.

> The most important thing and the thing which we will each be held accountable for is that we live in honesty and dignity and that we be what we truly are.

> If we are going to project ourselves as something that people might want to model themselves after, then we must be very cautious never to disillusion anyone. And if we find that we can't maintain that kind of dignity and reality and truth and honesty, then we should go do something else, where we are not affecting people's lives.

If there's one thing this world needs more than ever right now, it's people who operate from integrity and "walk their talk."

Differences in Style:
Buscaglia Versus Tony Robbins

"My style is like what you'd find around an Italian dinner table after three glasses of wine."
LEO BUSCAGLIA

When asked if he had any role models in the speaking world, Leo said:

> No. Though I admire what some people do, their style is very different than mine, and I think that's good. Take Tony Robbins; he's very dynamic, but his style of speaking is not mine. I'm more of a homebody, you might say. I draw on very simple things, using easily recognizable metaphors and similes. I appeal to the humanness in everybody; not that Tony doesn't, but he has a more powerful, stronger approach to speaking. My style is like what you'd find around an Italian dinner table after three glasses of wine.

Charisma

It's Buscaglia's contention that we all have the ability to be charismatic, but that it takes a certain level of caring, honesty, and commitment to your message:

> Charisma, I think, is basically a presence. It's being able to stand up before an audience and be yourself. The most charismatic people that I know are people who are not afraid to reveal who they are. They are still growing and changing, but they're wanting so desperately to share. Even in conversation, there are moments when people become very charismatic. They feel so deeply about what they're talking about.

> People who come before an audience and are able to get their rapt attention are people who usually care very deeply about the audience. They have deep respect for them and recognize that they're there to learn and to grow.

There are many types of charismatic speakers; some are bombastic and overwhelming and others are very soft spoken. But the essence of both is that they are sincere and caring. They love their audience and they have a deep respect for them; and they love themselves and have a deep respect for themselves—so they're not going to sell themselves cheap.

▶ **SECRET #11: Charisma comes from caring very deeply about your subject, your audience, and yourself.**

Creativity

"The purpose of art is to educate."
LEO BUSCAGLIA

Buscaglia has tremendous admiration and respect for artists and other creative people in our world. This is because he knows they help us see new and wonderful things that we are not able to see in our own mind. It's only after a Rodin comes along and carves a statue of a man sitting on a stump with his hand under his chin that we say to ourselves, "Ah, yes. Of course, he's thinking. . . . What a brilliantly simplistic and yet inspiring piece of art."

Buscaglia believes that everyone could be creative if they simply stopped thinking of themselves as not being creative:

All of us could be creative and would be if we believed that we could be. But because somebody defined for us in the second grade that we were not artists, or we were not dancers, or we were not great baseball players. . . . we believed them. Therefore, we didn't become great dancers and great artists!

▶ **SECRET #12: The first step to being creative is believing that you are creative.**

Respect

"When you gain respect for all 'personkind,'
you free them and you free yourself."
LEO BUSCAGLIA

Leo attributes much of his success with people to the fact that he has enormous respect for their feelings:

> If anything has made it possible for me to survive almost anything and everything, it's a tremendous respect for the dignity of every human person. There is no one I've ever met who, when I got below the superficial veneer, didn't have something rich and wonderful to give me.

▶ **SECRET #13: You know you've achieved a certain level of growth when you can genuinely respect other people and their feelings, even if they differ from your own.**

It's Never Too Late to Learn
How to Love Yourself

"There's a lifetime of learning still ahead of me."
LEO BUSCAGLIA

One of Buscaglia's core beliefs is that, regardless of your age or what you've been through, it's never too late to learn how to love yourself:

> The essence of my philosophy is that self-esteem and even love are learned. And that anything that can be learned, can be learned at anytime, if you put in the effort. I firmly believe we make our own joy and happiness and love, and our own lives.

No Pity Parties!

As Leo goes on to say, we must let go of feeling sorry for our-selves if we truly want to have high self-esteem. Sadly, many peo-ple would rather spend their energy hanging on to the past and being miserable, than letting go of it and living in the present and being happy:

> Don't waste the effort by sitting around crying about what you didn't get! You realize that you didn't get it; it's too bad that you didn't get it, but you don't spend your life bemoan-ing the fact and accusing people and saying I can't do those things because I never got whatever.

> You get off that merry-go-round that doesn't lead you any-where and you begin to recognize that you are still in con-trol. You're a grown-up now and you can start creating your new picture yourself. You get your brush and colors, and you paint a new picture and then in you go!

Buscaglia acknowledges that everybody gets a little, as he puts it, "kooky" from time to time, but the key is to stop yourself when you realize what you're doing:

> I think that every kooky form of human behavior has to be experienced by all of us. All of us go through a period where we do that, but then there are those who will continue to do that and live in frustration, and there are those who will say, "Why am I doing this?" And then they'll stop! The process is a very unique one and it's in our hands.

But Leo, Don't You Ever Get Disappointed?

I asked Buscaglia if he *ever* gets disappointed in life:

> I don't think I've ever had a disappointment. I mean that in all honesty. No matter what has happened to me in my life, I've always been able to switch it around to something

positive—something that I can grow and learn from. So as far as I'm concerned, there are no failures, only challenges for me to change and to grow, to understand and to learn.

Like every human being, I've had ups and downs. But the downs, especially now, are far less down and more like ups.

Everyone thinks that maybe my life is all joy and all magic and all wonder. I don't live in a separate world. I live in the same world that everybody lives in. I have to deal with the same traffic, the same income taxes, with the same bigoted people. The difference is the way in which I approach these things. I don't see that there are really any bad experiences. I think every experience has value. The sad part of an experience is when you don't learn from it.

Learning something from each experience you go through is really what life's all about.

Hope

*"If you don't believe in miracles, then you're
not being realistic."*
DR. BERNIE SEGAL

One thing that Buscaglia believes everybody needs is hope; that it is essential to life and to achieving your dreams:

Hope says that there are no impossibilities. Anything you can dream, you can realize. Anything that you set out to do, you can do. Hope is essential for love, and hope is essential for life.

I hope (no pun intended) you've enjoyed reading Buscaglia's chapter as much as I've enjoyed writing it. Finally, I leave you with . . .

Leo's Philosophy for Life

I see life as a tremendous gift. Every morning you wake up to fantastic possibilities. I would like to spend the rest of my life realizing those possibilities. I want to learn and to grow. I want to experience; I want to understand; I want to love, care, and share. I want to do all the marvelous things that are available to a human person. Whatever happens after that, I leave in greater hands than myself.

How Leo Buscaglia would like to be remembered:

"Here lies Leo, who died living."
LEO BUSCAGLIA

Leo Buscaglia's
Success Secrets Summary

SECRET #1: Never compare yourself to anyone else. You are unique! And what you have to contribute is special and different than what somebody else has to contribute.

SECRET #2: As a speaker, your job isn't just to have something exciting and interesting to say, but also to say it in an exciting and interesting way!

SECRET #3: Rather than simply give their students the answers, good teachers draw answers out of their students and then encourage them to look for more.

SECRET #4: You can either fear death, or you can use it as a positive reminder that each day of life you are given is a precious gift.

SECRET #5: Learning to really pay attention to the people and events in your life will make you a better communicator.

SECRET #6: Be a proactive force of love and creativity, rather than a passive blob of inactivity and uncertainty.

SECRET #7: For something to truly be a gift, it must, by definition, be given with no strings attached.

SECRET #8: The only bad experiences are the ones you don't learn from.

SECRET #9: The biggest mistake speakers make is not preparing properly for their presentations.

SECRET #10: Once you not only understand, but also joyfully accept the fact that human beings (and that includes yourself!) are not perfect, life just seems to run a lot smoother.

SECRET #11: Charisma comes from caring very deeply about your subject, your audience, and yourself.

SECRET #12: The first step to being creative is believing that you are creative.

SECRET #13: You know you've achieved a certain level of growth when you can genuinely respect other people and their feelings, even if they differ from your own.

Author's
Concluding Thoughts

▼

WELL, there you have it, 267 Success Secrets by fifteen of the greatest speakers in America. Now it's up to you to take these powerful and proven bits of information, ideas, and tips, and begin to immediately put them into action. Remember, these ideas work. Each speaker is living proof of this. So, if you try something and it doesn't work for you, don't give up on it. Just tweak it a little bit until it does work.

One last thing. My purpose in writing this book was not to provide you with an ABC list of how to become a great speaker. Rather, my idea was to let you in on how great speakers think. Because if you truly understand their thinking processes, their level of commitment, and their overall confidence and positive attitude toward life, you will be able to go out and succeed at anything you put your mind to.

Remember to enjoy the journey, and *never give up!*

Michael Jeffreys is the author of 9 books. He has two stories in *Chicken Soup for the Soul Vol. 3,* and has articles published in *The Whole Person, Reader's Digest, Success,* and *Entrepreneur Magazines.* Currently he is a spiritual teacher in Los Angeles who assists people in awakening to their true nature, which is prior to all thoughts, beliefs and conditioning and has never come or gone. His *Awakening Blog* can be found at: www.mjeffreys.com and the Michael Jeffreys' Awakening Community can be found on Facebook at: www.facebook.com/ groups/415496431893041/

"If a beautiful sunset is seen, how much more beautiful is WHAT is seeing it?"—MICHAEL JEFFREYS

CPSIA information can be obtained at www.ICGtesting.com
Printed in the USA
BVOW06s0851141015

422400BV00007B/98/P